State Territory and International Law

This book proposes a re-interpretation of Article 2(4) of the Charter of the United Nations to read, or at least include, respect for the inviolability of State territory.

While States purport to obey the prohibition of the Use of Force, they frequently engage in activities that could undermine international peace and security. In this book the author argues that State practice, *opinio juris*, as well as contentious and advisory opinions of the International Court of Justice, have promoted the first limb of Article 2(4). Although wars between States have decreased, the maintenance of international peace and security remains a mirage, as shown by the increase in intra- and inter-State conflicts across the world. The author seeks to initiate a rethinking of the provision of Article 2(4), which the International Court of Justice has described as the cornerstone of the United Nations. The author argues that the time is ripe for States to embrace an evolutive interpretation of Article 2(4) to mean respect, as opposed to the traditional view of the threat, or the use, of force. He also evaluates the discourse regarding territorial jurisdiction in cyberspace and argues that the efforts made by the international community to apply Article 2(4) to cyberspace suggest that the article is a flexible and live instrument that should be adjusted to address the circumstances that endanger international peace and security.

This book will engineer a serious debate regarding the scope of Article 2(4), which before now has always been limited to the threat or use of force. As a result, it will be of interest to academics and students of public international law, as well as diplomats and policymakers.

Fr Josephat C. Ezenwajiaku, a Catholic priest of the Congregation of Fathers of Jesus the Saviour, completed his PhD at Brunel University, London. He also holds *Iuris canonici Licentiatus* from the Katholieke Universiteit Leuven, Belgium. He was the Director of Works for four years at Madonna University, Okija, Nigeria. He has also held the position of the director of Pilgrim Newspapers, a subsidiary organ of Our Saviour Press, Nigeria, and now Madonna University Press, Nigeria, for two years.

Routledge Research in International Law

Available:

The Future of International Courts
Regional, Institutional and Procedural Challenges
Edited by Avidan Kent, Nikos Skoutaris and Jamie Trinidad

The Far-Right in International and European Law
Natalie Alkiviadou

International Law and Revolution
Owen Taylor

The Responsibility to Protect in International Law
Philosophical Investigations
Natalie Oman

The Responsibility to Protect in Libya and Syria
Mass Atrocities, Human Protection, and International Law
Yasmine Nahlawi

Public Private Partnership Contracts
The Middle East and North Africa
Mohamed A.M. Ismail

WTO Jurisprudence
Governments, Private Rights and International Trade
Wenwei Guan

State Territory and International Law
Josephat Ezenwajiaku

For a full list of titles in this series, visit www.routledge.com/Routledge-Research-in-International-Law/book-series/INTNLLAW

State Territory and International Law

Josephat C. Ezenwajiaku

LONDON AND NEW YORK

First published 2021
by Routledge
2 Park Square, Milton Park, Abingdon, Oxon OX14 4RN

and by Routledge
52 Vanderbilt Avenue, New York, NY 10017

Routledge is an imprint of the Taylor & Francis Group, an informa business

© 2021 Josephat C. Ezenwajiaku

The right of Josephat C. Ezenwajiaku to be identified as author of this work has been asserted by him in accordance with sections 77 and 78 of the Copyright, Designs and Patents Act 1988.

All rights reserved. No part of this book may be reprinted or reproduced or utilised in any form or by any electronic, mechanical, or other means, now known or hereafter invented, including photocopying and recording, or in any information storage or retrieval system, without permission in writing from the publishers.

Trademark notice: Product or corporate names may be trademarks or registered trademarks, and are used only for identification and explanation without intent to infringe.

British Library Cataloguing-in-Publication Data
A catalogue record for this book is available from the British Library

Library of Congress Cataloging-in-Publication Data
Names: Ezenwajiaku, Josephat Chukwuemeka, author.
Title: State territory and international law / Josephat Ezenwajiaku.
Description: Abingdon, Oxon ; New York, NY : Routledge, 2020. |
Series: Routledge research in international law | Based on author's thesis
(doctoral – Brunel University London, 2017) issued under title: Respect for the
inviolability of state territory. | Includes bibliographical references and index.
Identifiers: LCCN 2020005624 (print) | LCCN 2020005625 (ebook) |
ISBN 9780367353988 (hardback) | ISBN 9780429341526 (ebook)
Subjects: LCSH: Territory, National. | International law. |
United Nations. Charter. Article 2(4)
Classification: LCC KZ3675 .E94 2020 (print) |
LCC KZ3675 (ebook) |
DDC 341.4/2--dc23
LC record available at https://lccn.loc.gov/2020005624
LC ebook record available at https://lccn.loc.gov/2020005625

ISBN: 978-0-367-35398-8 (hbk)
ISBN: 978-0-429-34152-6 (ebk)

Typeset in Galliard
by Taylor & Francis Books

Contents

Foreword	vii
Acknowledgements	ix
Table of cases	xi
Table of treaties	xv
List of abbreviations	xx

1	General introduction	1
2	Setting out the theoretical framework	7
3	Inviolability of State territory and Article 2(4) of the UN Charter	48
4	Expanding the frontiers of Article 2(4) to cyberspace	91
5	Breaches of State territory	123
6	Non-State actors, Article 2(4) and the sanctity of State territory	157
7	An attempt to formulate a theory of respect for the inviolability of State territory	182

Bibliography	213
Index	239

Foreword

Since its adoption in 1945, the UN Charter has been the subject of endless scrutiny. International tribunals, regional tribunals and domestic courts have referenced it persistently, enamelling its significance for human aspirations to achieve international peace and security, human development, and prosperity for all. Commentators of all persuasion have found its provisions and their own interpretations of them a useful starting or concluding point for their positions across many disciplines. In its deliberations and resolutions, the UN General Assembly persistently references it. Perhaps the most invoked, applied and therefore widely interpreted provision of the UN Charter is Article 2(4).

The purposes of the UN Charter are articulated in Article 1, amplifying the opening statement to the Charter. The preamble refers in this regard to the determination to save succeeding generations from the scourge of war. But how? Article 2(4) sets out the substantive norm for achieving that. It is not surprising that it appears to have received the lion's share of scholarly scrutiny as to its proper meaning. Perhaps because its meaning has been lost, my own teacher, Thomas Michael Franck wondered in his seminal work: "Who killed Article 2(4) …?" If Article 2(4) is dead, then the UN is dead, one might assume as this is the provision that sets out the *modus operandi* for the pursuit and maintenance of the UN mission.

For all these decades since its adoption, commentary on Article 2(4) appears to have been skewed towards the prohibition of the threat or use of force and made it the focal point. But Article 2(4) is a very compound sentence that requires careful reading. Perhaps this book awakens us to that fact. Could the meaning be better understood by breaking down the sentence into the prohibitive statement, and the example of it? If the prefix statement of Article 2(4) is a mere example of the sort of behaviours that the suffix and main substantive statement prohibits, then the focus by commentators on the example rather than on the main provision, namely, the declaration of the inviolability, sanctity and unequivocal protection of State territory under international law, assumes a greater importance.

In this monograph, Fr. Josephat has attempted a re-evaluation of the interpretations of the UN Charter's foremost provision. The International Court of Justice has repeatedly referenced Article 2(4) as the cornerstone of modern international law. Fr. Josephat tests many of the assumptions hitherto unquestioned in the overwhelming history of interpreting Article 2(4) of the UN Charter. His style, depth and manner will enthuse practitioner and scholar alike. A worthwhile contribution on the theory and interpretation of Article 2(4) that deserves attention.

Benedict Abrahamson Tendayi Chigara
Professor of Public Law
College of Law, Qatar University
2020

Acknowledgements

I am grateful to God for His love upon me.

I thank the Founder of my Religious Congregation, Very Rev. Prof. Emmanuel M.P. Edeh CSSp for sponsoring my further studies and his moral support. I equally thank the superior general of my Congregation, Very Rev. Fr. Jude Okenyi *FJS* and indeed all the Saviourites for your prayers.

I thank Professor Ben Chigara for his encouragement and assistance in the course of this research. Professor Chigara supervised my doctoral thesis at Brunel University London and graciously wrote the Foreword for me. I am equally grateful to Reverend Dr William Richardson of the Archdiocese of Dublin who supervised my thesis at Katholieke Universiteit Leuven, leading to the award of *Iuris Canonici Licentiatus* degree. Comments, observations and recommendations of anonymous reviewers enriched me profoundly and for this I am grateful.

Many people have played several roles at various stages in my academic life, and I am deeply grateful to them. I salute authors I quoted in this work or from whose ideas I borrowed. I isolate for special acknowledgement, the contributions made by Professor Abimbola Olowofoyeku, Professor Nicholas Tsagourias, Professor Manisuli Ssenyonjo, Dr Olufemi Amao, Fr. Josephat Ezeanolue CSSP and Dr Charles Olubokun. I thank my mum Maria Ezenwajiaku and other family members for standing by me in solidarity and love. God bless all of you.

Josephat C. Ezenwajiaku

Table of cases

Abyei Arbitration (Government of Sudan v Sudan People's Liberation Movement/ Army) Final Award (2009) 30 RIAA 145–416.

Application of the Convention on the Prevention and Punishment of the Crime of Genocide (Bosnia and Herzegovina v Serbia and Montenegro) Judgment ICJ Reports (2007) p. 43.

Arbitral Tribunal Constituted Pursuant to Article 287, and in accordance with Annex VII, of the United Nations Convention on the Law of the Sea in the Matter of an Arbitration Between Guyana and Suriname (Permanent Court of Arbitration, The Hague 17 September 2007) 30 RIAA 1–144.

Armed Activities on the Territory of the Congo (Democratic Republic of the Congo v Uganda) Judgment ICJ Reports (2005) p. 168.

Award between the United States and the United Kingdom relating to the Rights of Jurisdiction of United States in the Bering's Sea and the Preservation of Fur Seals (United Kingdom v United States) Award (1893) 28 RIAA 263–276.

Award in the Arbitration Regarding the Delimitation of the Maritime Boundaries between Guyana v Suriname (Award of 17 September 2007) 30 RIAA 1–144.

Barcelona Traction, Light and Power Co. Ltd (Belgium v Spain) Judgment ICJ Reports (1970) p. 3.

Case Concerning a Boundary Dispute Between Argentina and Chile Concerning the Delimitation of the Frontier Line Between Boundary Post 62 and Mount Fitzroy (Argentina v Chile) 22 RIAA 3–149.

Case Concerning Delimitation of the Maritime Boundary in the Gulf of Maine Area (Canada v United States of America) Judgment ICJ Reports (1984) p. 305.

Case Concerning East Timor (Portugal v Australia) Judgment ICJ Reports (1995) p. 90.

Case Concerning Military and Paramilitary Activities In and Against Nicaragua (Nicaragua v United States of America) Judgment ICJ Reports (1986) p. 14.

Case Concerning Oil Platforms (Iran v United States of America) Judgment ICJ Reports (2003) p. 161.

Case Concerning the Aerial Incident of July 27th, 1955 (Israel v Bulgaria) Preliminary Objections Judgment ICJ Reports (1959) p. 127.

xii *Table of cases*

Case Concerning the Land, Island and Maritime Frontier Dispute (El Salvador v Honduras: Nicaragua intervening) Judgment ICJ Reports (1992) p. 351.

Case No. 2013–19 In the Matter of the South China Sea Arbitration between the Republic of the Philippines and the Peoples Republic of China, Award PCA (12 July 2016).

Case of Issa and Others v Turkey (Application No. 31821/96) Judgment ECtHR (2004).

Case of Roman Zakharov v Russia (Application No. 47143/06) Grand Chamber, Judgment ECtHR (2015).

Case of S.S "Lotus" (France v Turkey) Collection of Judgments, PCIJ Series A, No. 10 (1927) 19.

Case Relating to the Territorial Jurisdiction of the International Commission of the River Order, Judgment PCIJ Series A, No. 23 (1929) 26–27.

Certain Activities carried out by Nicaragua in the Border Area (Costa Rica v Nicaragua) Judgment ICJ Reports (2009) p. 1.

Continental Shelf (Tunisia/Libyan Arab Jamahiriya) (Memorial of Libyan Arab Jamahiriya) Pleading ICJ Reports (1980) p. 455.

Continental Shelf (Tunisia/Libyan Arab Jamahiriya) (Reply of the Libyan Arab Jamahiriya) Pleading ICJ Reports (1981) p. 103.

Corfu Channel (United Kingdom v Albania) (Merits) Judgment ICJ Reports (1949) p. 4.

Denunciation of the Treaty of November 2nd, 1865 between China and Belgium (Belgium v China) Orders of 8 January, 15 February and 18 June 1927 PCIJ Series A, No. 8 (1927) p. 5.

Fisheries Jurisdiction (Spain v Canada) (Jurisdiction of the Court) Judgment ICJ Reports (1998) p. 432.

Frontier Dispute (Burkina Faso/Republic of Mali) Judgment ICJ Reports (1986) p. 554.

Guyana v Suriname, Award PCA (2007) 30 *RIAA* 1–144.

In the Matter of the Bay of Bengal Maritime Boundary Arbitration between the People's Republic of Bangladesh and the Republic of India, Award PCA (The Hague, 7 July 2014).

Investigation of Certain Incidents Affecting the British Trawler Red Crusader (1962) 29 RIAA 521–539.

Island of Palmas case (The Netherlands v USA) (The Hague, 1928) II RIAA 829–871.

Jurisdictional Immunities of the State (Germany v Italy: Greece Intervening) Judgment ICJ Reports (2012) p. 99.

LaGrand (Germany v US) ICJ Reports (2001) p. 466.

Land and Maritime Boundary between Cameroon and Nigeria (Cameroon v Nigeria: Equatorial Guinea Intervening) Judgment ICJ Reports (2002) p. 303.

Land, Island and Maritime Frontier Dispute (El Salvador/Honduras: Nicaragua Intervening) Judgment ICJ Reports (1992) p. 350.

Table of cases xiii

Legal Consequences for States of the Continued Presence of South Africa in Namibia (South West Africa) Notwithstanding Security Council Resolution 276 (1970), Advisory Opinion ICJ Reports (1971) p. 16.

Legal Consequences of the Construction of a Wall in the Occupied Palestinian Territory, Advisory Opinion ICJ Reports (2004) p. 136.

Legal Status of Eastern Greenland (Denmark v Norway) Judgment PCIJ Series A/B, No. 53 (1933) p. 21.

Legality of the Threat or Use of Nuclear Weapons, Advisory Opinion ICJ Reports (1996) p. 226.

M/V "SAIGA" (No. 2) (Saint Vincent and the Grenadines v Guinea) Judgment ITLOS Reports (1999) p. 10.

M/V "Virginia G" (Panama v Guinea-Bissau) Judgment ITLOS Reports (2014) p. 4.

Nationality Decree Issued in Tunis and Morocco, Advisory Opinion, PCIJ Series B, No. 4 (1923) p. 7.

North Sea Continental Shelf cases (Federal Republic of Germany/Denmark; Federal Republic of Germany/Netherlands) Judgment ICJ Reports (1969) p. 3.

Nuclear Tests (New Zealand v France) Judgment ICJ Reports (1974) p. 457.

Prosecutor v Akayesu (Case No. ICTR-96-4-T) Trial Chamber I ICTR (1998).

Prosecutor v Alfred Musema (Case No. ICTR-96-13-A) Trial Chamber I ICTR (2000).

Prosecutor v Kunarac et al. (Case No. IT-96-23-T) Trial Chamber, Judgment ICTY (2001).

Prosecutor v Duško Tadić, International Tribunal for the Former Yugoslavia, Case No. IT-94-1-A (1999) 38(6) *ILM* 1518–1623.

Questions of Interpretation and Application of the 1971 Montreal Convention Arising from the Aerial Incident at Lockerbie (Libyan Arab Jamahiriya v United States of America) Order of 14 April 1992 ICJ Reports (1992) p. 114.

Question of Jaworzina (Polish-Czechoslovakian Frontier) Advisory Opinion PCIJ Series B, No. 8 (1923) p. 5.

Republic of Somalia v Woodhouse Drake & Carey (Suisse) S.A. and Others [1993] 1 QB 54.

Republic of the Philippines v People's Republic of China (Memorial of the Philippines, Volume 1, 30 March 2014).

Responsibilities and Obligations of States with Respect to Activities in the Area, Advisory Opinion, ITLOS Reports (2011).

S.S. "I'm Alone" (Canada v the United States) (1935) 3 RIAA 1609–1618.

S v Petane [1988] 3 SALR 51.

Second Stage of the Proceedings Between Eritrea and Yemen (Maritime Delimitation) (17 December 1999) 22 RIAA 335–410.

Sovereignty over Pedra Branca/Pulau Batu Puteh, Middle Rocks and South Ledge (Malaysia v Singapore) Judgment ICJ Reports (2008) p. 12.

Territorial Dispute (Libyan Arab Jamahiriya/Chad) Judgment ICJ Reports (1994) p. 6.

xiv   *Table of cases*

Territorial Sovereignty and Scope of the Dispute (Eritrea v Yemen) (1998) 22 RIAA 209–332.

The Case of S.S. Lotus (France v Turkey) Judgment PCIJ Series A, No. 10 (1927) p. 3.

The Kingdom of the Netherlands v the Russia Federation, Award on the Merits, PCA (14 August 2015).

The Prosecutor v Akayesu (Case No. ICTR-96–4-T) Trial Chamber I ICTR (1998).

The Prosecutor v Alfred Musema (Case No. ICTR-96–13-A) Trial Chamber I ICTR (2000).

The Prosecutor v Du [Ko Tadi] (Case No. IT-94–1-T) Judgment Trial Chamber ICTY (1997).

The Prosecutor v Duško Tadić a/k/a "Dule" (Case No. IT 94–1-AR72) (Decision on the Defence Motion for Interlocutory Appeal on Jurisdiction) ICTY (2 October 1995).

The Prosecutor v Omar Hassan Ahmad Al Bashir (ICC-02/05–01/09) (4 March 2009).

The Prosecutor v Radislav Krstic (Case No. IT-98–33-T) Judgment ICTY (2 August 2001).

The Prosecutor v Tadić (Duško) (Case No. IT-94–1-A, ICL 93) Appeal Judgment ICTY (1999).

Tunisia v Libya Continental Shelf case, Judgment ICJ Reports (1982) p. 18.

United States Diplomatic and Consular Staff in Tehran (United States of America v Iran) Judgment ICJ Reports (1980) p. 3.

Western Sahara, Advisory Opinion ICJ Reports (1975) p. 12.

Table of treaties

Accord on the Creation of the Commonwealth of Independent States (1996) 20 *Harvard Ukrainian Studies* 297–301.

Charter of the Commonwealth of Independent States (with Declaration and Decisions) (Adopted at Minsk on 22 January 1993, entered into force on 24 January 1994) 1819 UNTS 58.

Charter of the Organisation of African Unity (Done at Addis Ababa on 25 May 1963, entered into force on 13 September 1963) 479 UNTS 39.

Charter of the Organization of American States (Signed at Bogotá on 30 April 1948, entered into force on 13 December 1951) 119 UNTS 3.

Conference on Security and Co-operation in Europe Final Act (Signed at Helsinki on 1 August 1975) (1975) 73(1888) *Department of State Bulletin* 323–350.

Convention (IV) Relating to the Protection of Civilian Persons in Time of War (Done at Geneva on 12 August 1949, entered into force on 21 October 1950) 75 UNTS 287.

Convention and Statute on Freedom of Transit (Concluded at Barcelona on 20 April 1921, entered into force on 31 October 1922) 7 LNTS 11.

Convention for the Protection of Cultural Property in the Event of Armed Conflict (Done at The Hague on 14 May 1954, entered into force on 7 August 1956) 249 UNTS 240.

Convention for the Suppression of Unlawful Acts Against the Safety of Civil Aviation (Signed at Montreal on 23 September 1971, entered into force on 26 January 1973) 974 UNTS 177.

Convention for the Suppression of Unlawful Acts Against the Safety of Maritime Navigation (Done at Rome on 10 March 1988, entered into force on 1 March 1992) 1678 UNTS 221.

Convention for the Suppression of Unlawful Seizure of Aircraft (Signed at The Hague on 16 December 1970, entered into force on 14 October 1971) 860 UNTS 105.

Convention on International Civil Aviation (Done at Chicago on 7 December 1944, entered into force on 4 April 1947) 15 UNTS 295.

Convention on Offences and Certain Other Acts Committed on Board Aircraft (Signed at Tokyo on 14 September 1963, entered into force on 4 December 1969) 704 UNTS 220.

xvi *Table of treaties*

Convention on Rights and Duties of States adopted by the Seventh International Conference of American States (Signed at Montevideo on 16 December 1933, entered into force on 26 December 1934) 165 LNTS 19.

Convention on the High Seas (Concluded at Geneva on 29 April 1958, entered into force on 30 September 1962) 450 UNTS 11.

Convention on the Physical Protection of Nuclear Material (Signed at New York and Vienna on 3 March 1980, entered into force on 8 February 1987) 1456 UNTS 124.

Convention on the Prevention and Punishment of Crimes Against Internationally Protected Persons (Opened for signature at New York on 14 December 1973, entered into force on 20 February 1977) 1035 UNTS 167.

Convention on the Prevention and Punishment of the Crime of Genocide (Concluded at Paris on 9 December 1948, entered into force on 12 January 1951) 78 UNTS 277.

Convention on the Territorial Sea and the Contiguous Zone (Concluded at Geneva on 29 April 1958, entered into force on 10 September 1964) 516 UNTS 206.

Convention Relating to the Regulation of Aerial Navigation (Signed at Paris on 13 October 1919, entered into force on 29 March 1922) 11 UNTS 173.

Convention Relating to the Status of Refugees (Signed at Geneva on 28 July 1951, entered into force on 22 April 1954) 189 UNTS 150.

Convention (IV) Respecting the Laws and Customs of War on Land and its Annex: Regulations Concerning the Laws and Customs of War on Land (The Hague, 18 October 1907), available at <http://avalon.law.yale.edu/20th_century/hague04.asp> accessed 11 November 2019.

Council of Europe, *Additional Protocol to the Convention on Cybercrime, Concerning the Criminalisation of Acts of a Racist and Xenophobic Nature Committed Through Computer Systems* (Concluded at Strasbourg on 28 January 2003, entered into force on 1 March 2006) 2466 UNTS 205.

Council of Europe, *Convention on Cybercrime* (Concluded at Budapest on 23 November 2001, entered into force on 1 July 2004) 2296 UNTS 167.

Declaration Recognizing as Compulsory the Jurisdiction of the Court, in Conformity with Article 36, Paragraph 2, of the Statute of the International Court of Justice (Washington D.C., 14 August 1946) 1 UNTS 11.

General Treaty for Renunciation of War as Instrument of National Policy (Signed at Paris on 27 August 1928, entered into force on 25 July 1929) 94 UNTS 57.

Geneva Convention for the Amelioration of the Condition of the Wounded and Sick in Armed Forces in the Field (Done at Geneva on 12 August 1949, entered into force on 21 October 1950) 75 UNTS 31.

Geneva Convention Relative to the Protection of Civilian Persons in Time of War (Done at Geneva on 12 August 1949, entered into force on 21 October 1950) 75 UNTS 287.

Geneva Convention Relative to the Treatment of Prisoners of War (Done at Geneva on 12 August 1949, entered into force on 21 October 1950) 75 UNTS 135.

Hague Convention IV – Laws and Customs of War on Land (Signed at The Hague on 18 October 1907, entered into force on 26 January 1910) 36 Stat. 2277.

Table of treaties   xvii

Inter-American Conference on War and Peace, "Act of Chapultepec" (Concluded at Mexico on 3 March 1945) (1945) 12(297) *Department of State Bulletin* 339–340.

International Convention Against the Taking of Hostages (Signed at New York on 18 December 1979, entered into force on 3 June 1983) 1316 UNTS 205.

International Convention for the Suppression of the Financing of Terrorism (Concluded in New York on 9 December 1999, entered into force on 10 April 2002) 2178 UNTS 197.

International Convention on Civil and Political Rights (Concluded at New York on 16 December 1966, entered into force on 23 March 1976) 999 UNTS 171.

International Convention on Economic, Social and Cultural Rights (Concluded at New York on 16 December 1966, entered into force on 3 January 1976) 993 UNTS 3.

International Convention Relating to Intervention on the High Seas in Cases of Oil Pollution Casualties (Concluded at Brussels on 29 November 1969) 970 UNTS 211.

League of Arab States, *Charter of Arab League* (Done at Cairo on 22 March 1945, entered into force on 10 May 1945) 70 UNTS 248.

Organisation of African Unity, *Constitutive Act of the African Union* (Adopted on 11 July 2000, entered into force on 26 May 2001) 2158 UNTS 3.

Project of an International Declaration Concerning the Laws and Customs of War (Done at Brussels on 27 August 1874).

Protocol Additional to the Geneva Conventions of 12 August 1949, and Relating to the Protection of Victims of International Armed Conflicts (Protocol I) (Concluded at Geneva on 8 June 1977, entered into force on 7 December 1978) 1125 UNTS 3.

Protocol Additional to the Geneva Convention of 12 August 1949, and Relating to the Protection of Victims of International Armed Conflicts (Protocol II) (Concluded at Geneva on 8 June 1977, entered into force on 7 December 1978) 1125 UNTS 609.

Protocol for the Suppression of Unlawful Acts of Violence at Airports Serving International Civil Aviation, Supplementary to the Convention for the Suppression of Unlawful Acts Against the Safety of Civil Aviation (Signed at Montreal on 24 February 1988, entered into force on 9 August 1989) 1589 UNTS 474.

Protocol for the Suppression of Unlawful Acts Against the Safety of Fixed Platforms Located on the Continental Shelf (Signed at Rome on 10 March 1988, entered into force on 1 March 1992) 1678 UNTS 304.

Protocol of Signature Relating to the Statute of the Permanent Court of International Justice Provided for by Article 14 of the Covenant of the League of Nations (Done at Geneva on 16 December 1920) 6 LNTS 380.

Protocol on Non-Aggression (Concluded at Lagos on 22 April 1978, entered into force provisionally on 13 May 1982) 1690 UNTS 39.

Protocol Relating to an Amendment to the Convention on International Civil Aviation (Signed at Montreal on 10 May 1984, entered into force on 1 October 1998) 2122 UNTS 337.

Protocol [II] on Prohibitions or Restrictions on the Use of Mines, Booby Traps and Other Devices as Amended on 3 May 1996 (Protocol II as Amended on 3 May 1996) Annexed to the Convention on Prohibitions or Restrictions on the Use of

xviii   *Table of treaties*

Certain Conventional Weapons which may be Deemed to be Excessively Injurious or to have Indiscriminate Effects (Done at Geneva on 3 May 1996, entered into force on 3 December 1998) 2048 UNTS 93.

Rome Statute of the International Criminal Court (Done at Rome on 17 July 1998, entered into force on 1 July 2002) 2187 UNTS 90.

Statute for the Permanent Court of International Justice (Done at Geneva on 16 December 1920, entered into force on 8 October 1921) 6 LNTS 390.

Statute of the International Court of Justice (Adopted at San Francisco on 26 June 1945, entered into force on 24 October 1945) (1945) 39(3) *American Journal of International Law Supplement* 215–229.

The Alma-Ata Declaration (Done on 21 December 1991) (1992) 31(1) *International Legal Materials* 147–154.

The Covenant of the League of Nations (Adopted at Paris on 29 April 1919, entered into force on 10 January 1920) (1919) 13(2) *American Journal of International Law Supplement* 128–139.

The Treaty of Peace with Germany (Signed at Versailles on 28 June 1919, entered into force on 10 January 1920) (1919) 13(3) *American Journal of International Law Supplement* 151.

Treaty Banning Nuclear Weapon Tests in the Atmosphere, in Outer Space and Under Water (Concluded at Moscow on 5 August 1963, entered into force on 10 October 1963) 480 UNTS 43.

Treaty Between the Ukrainian Soviet Socialist Republic and the Russian Soviet Federative Socialist Republic (1996) 20 *Harvard Ukrainian Studies* 291–296.

Treaty of Mutual Guarantee Between Germany, Belgium, France, Great Britain and Italy (Done at Locarno on 16 October 1925, entered into force on 14 September 1926) 54 LNTS 289.

Treaty on Friendship, Cooperation and Partnership between Ukraine and the Russian Federation (1996) 20 *Harvard Ukrainian Studies* 319–329.

Treaty on the Limitation of Anti-Ballistic Missile Systems (Signed at Moscow on 26 May 1972, entered into force on 3 October 1972) 944 UNTS 13.

Treaty on the Non-Proliferation of Nuclear Weapons (Adopted at London on 1 July 1968, entered into force on 5 March 1970) 729 UNTS 161.

Treaty on Principles Governing the Activities of States in the Exploration and Use of Outer Space, including the Moon and Other Celestial Bodies (Concluded at Washington, Moscow and London on 27 January 1967, entered into Force on 10 October 1967) 610 UNTS 206.

United Nations Agreement for the Implementation of the Provisions of the United Nations Convention on the Law of the Sea of 10 December 1982 Relating to the Conservation and Management of Straddling Fish Stocks and Highly Migratory Fish Stocks, 2167 UNTS 3.

United Nations, *Charter of the United Nations* (Signed at San Francisco on 26 June 1945, entered into force on 24 October 1945) 1 UNTS XVI.

United Nations, *Convention on the Law of the Sea* (Concluded at Montego Bay on 10 December 1982, entered into force on 16 November 1994) 1833 UNTS 397.

Table of treaties xix

United Nations, *Convention on the Protection and Use of Transboundary Water-courses and International Lakes* (Done at Helsinki on 17 March 1992, entered into force on 6 October 1996) 1936 UNTS 269.

United Nations, *Vienna Convention on the Law of Treaties* (Concluded at Vienna on 23 May 1969, entered into force on 27 January 1980) 1155 UNTS 331.

U.S.S.R. – Estonia: Treaty of Non-Aggression and Peaceful Settlement of Dispute (Signed at Moscow on 4 May 1932; ratifications exchanged on 18 August 1932) (1933) 27(4) *American Journal of International Law Supplement* 167–169.

U.S.S.R. – Poland: Treaty of Non-Aggression (Signed at Moscow on 25 July 1932; ratifications exchanged on 23 December 1932) (1933) 27(4) *American Journal of International Law Supplement* 188–190.

Vienna Convention on Consular Relations (Done at Vienna on 24 April 1963, entered into force on 19 March 1967) 596 UNTS 261.

Vienna Convention on Diplomatic Relations (Done at Vienna on 18 April 1961, entered into force on 24 April 1964) 500 UNTS 95.

Vienna Convention on Succession of States in Respect of Treaties (Done at Vienna on 23 August 1978, entered into force on 6 November 1996) 1946 UNTS 3.

Abbreviations

EC	European Community
EEZ	Exclusive Economic Zone
FRY	Former Socialist Federal Republic of Yugoslavia
ICAO	International Civil Aviation Organisation
ICC	International Criminal Court
ICJ	International Court of Justice
ICT	Information and Communications Technology
ILC	International Law Commission
ITLOS	International Tribunal for the Law of the Sea
NATO	North Atlantic Treaty Organisation
OAS	Organisation of American States
PCA	Permanent Court of Arbitration
PCIJ	Permanent Court of International Justice
SC	Security Council
UN	United Nations
UNCIO	United Nations Conference on International Organization
UNCLOS	United Nations Convention on the Law of the Sea
US	United States of America
VCLT	Vienna Convention on the Law of the Sea

1 General introduction

1.0 Introduction

The birth of the United Nations brought significant changes to the conduct of international relations. For the first time, the world powers successfully formed a supranational organisation to promote global peace, security and cooperation among States. Thus, Article 2 paragraph 4 of the Charter of the United Nations[1] has been described by the International Court of Justice (ICJ) as "a cornerstone of the United Nations Charter."[2] Consequently, the world has witnessed a tremendous decline in inter-States wars since the United Nations Charter went into force. However, time has passed, and the situation of warfare has changed significantly. For instance, cyberspace and unmanned aerial vehicles have unleashed unconventional modes of warfare in a manner that has watered down the potency of Article 2(4). In fact, there are reports that Article 2(4) is already dead.

This book, which substantially modifies my doctoral thesis, deconstructs Article 2 (4) and observes two things. First is that Article 2(4) has two limbs to it for ensuring international peace and security. Second is that State practice and scholarship have overexploited the first limb and neglected or excluded the second limb. In the short term, the highly prized world peace has remained a mirage because of States' proxy interference and intervention in the internal affairs of other States. As shall be seen, internationalised armed conflicts are on the increase while inter-States armed conflicts decrease.

This book argues that the first limb refers to the prohibition of the threat or use of force against a State by another State. Scholarship has focused exclusively on this limb. However, what constitutes a State has become increasingly tenuous with non-States actors dominating international political space. The second and mutely referred to is what this book focuses on. Its neglect might even be the reason why

---

1 United Nations, *Charter of the United Nations* (Signed at San Francisco on 26 June 1945, entered into force on 24 October 1945) 1 UNTS XVI, art. 2(4) [hereinafter *UN Charter*].
2 *Armed Activities on the Territory of the Congo* (Democratic Republic of the Congo v Uganda) Judgment ICJ Reports (2005) p. 168, para. 148 [hereinafter *DRC v Uganda*].

2 General introduction

international peace and security have been remote since the Second World War. It is the requirement to respect the inviolability of State territory.

This book argues that the second limb is the dominant norm or at least complements the prohibition of the threat or use of force. It seems that compliance with the doctrine of respect carries with it the prohibition of the threat or use of force. This interpretive approach to Article 2(4) has some advantages. First, it gives the required maximum protection to States' territory, which now includes cyberspace. Second, it minimises the levity with which States treat Article 2(4) when they breach other States' territory while claiming not to have violated international law. Third, it stands the chance of enhancing the maintenance of international peace and security.

By emphasising the primary substantive norm, respect for the inviolability of State territory becomes the focal point. How to achieve that in a complexly ever-evolving world dynamic of inter-State relations becomes the issue. This objective is not defeated from the outset since it is in the interest of States that others respect their borders. Besides, a careful analysis of the *travaux préparatoires* of the United Nations, particularly, States submissions, interventions and debates that went on in various Committees that drafted Article 2 (4) leads to the finding that States want other States to respect their territory. Besides, it falls within the confines of the purposes and principles enunciated in the UN Charter.

The approach adopted in this book departs from the traditional view that restricts the meaning of Article 2(4) to the threat or use of force.[3] While the black-letter law should be applied, an interpretive approach allows purposes, principles, circumstances and context in which the law was enacted to be taken on board. Seventy-five years after the United Nations Charter went into force, it is pertinent to re-evaluate how Article 2(4) has fostered international peace and security which is *primus inter pares* among the other purposes of the United Nations. Strict compliance with its tenets cannot be circumvented lest the international community slides back to another war through unorthodox means.

While Louis Henkin applauds States for being law-abiding,[4] Thomas Franck laments the demise of Article 2(4).[5] This book argues that the intention of the founders of the United Nations to build a peaceful international community has been distorted partly due to over-dependence of the member States on the first limb of Article 2(4). Hence, scholarship dissipates its scarce energy debating about breaches that qualify as *de minimis* incursions or an armed attack[6] to the detriment of a

---

3 *Case Concerning Military and Paramilitary Activities in and Against Nicaragua* (Nicaragua v United States of America) Judgment ICJ Reports (1986) p. 14, paras 98–101, 190–191, 227 [hereinafter *Nicaragua* case].

4 Louis Henkin, *How Nations Behave: Law and Foreign Policy*, Second Edition (New York, Columbia University Press, 1968) 49.

5 Thomas M. Franck, "Who Killed Article 2(4) or: Changing Norms Governing the Use of Force by States" (1970) 64(4) *American Journal of International Law* 809–837.

6 Olivier Corten, *The Law Against War: The Prohibition on the Use of Force in Contemporary International Law* (Oxford and Portland, Hart Publishing, 2010) 77.

General introduction 3

complete prohibition.[7] It suffices to say that this kind of debate emboldens States to engage in mere frontier incidents or support nefarious activities of non-State actors. They do so while claiming that they comply with their obligations under Article 2(4), notwithstanding that incremental breaches sow the seeds of mistrust which germinate to conflict and a precipice to world's anarchy.

Other factors exacerbate the situation. First, the *Case Concerning Military and Paramilitary Activities In and Against Nicaragua* provides that a State shall be a victim of an armed attack to avail itself of the right to self-defence. Second, an armed attack should have been committed by or attributed to a State if committed by non-State actors. Third, a State that alleges that another State sponsored an armed attack against it must prove that the perpetrators are agent or organ of the accused State. Fourth, the burden of proof is on the State that alleges, and it must show that non-State actors are dependent on the accused State or are under their effective control.

Additionally, the recognition of cyberspace as part of States' territory calls for a review of the scope of State territory as traditionally held. A reappraisal is vital for two reasons. First, the fluid nature of cyberspace, because of the free-flow of economic activities, information and cybercrime, has changed the dynamics on how States exercise their sovereign functions. One feature of cyberspace is that States exercise overlapping sovereignty in it. Moreover, globalisation has eroded exclusivity traditionally associated with States' sovereignty. In other words, it is difficult for States to take full control of cyberspace activities without the cooperation of other States. Although States have assumed territorial jurisdiction in cyberspace through legislation, a unilateral enforcement of cyberlaws is difficult without the cooperation of other States. It is even harder when cyber-related offences are sponsored by States or carried out by their agents because of the problematic threshold of attribution. Although the cyberspace-related crimes are non-kinetic, they may cause physical harm to a State that is a victim of cyberspace attacks.

In some cases, the effects of cyberspace attacks may be equivalent to those caused by conventional war. Yet it cannot be regarded as a physical force as understood in 1945. Therefore, cyberspace has changed the meanings attributable to conventional war, and new adaptations of Article 2(4) are imperative. The same rationale applies to other unconventional means of waging war such as intercontinental ballistic missiles and unmanned aerial vehicles. These changes disengage Article 2(4), which according to the ICJ requires "sending armed forces" of a State into the territory of another State.[8] The idea that war is fought by human beings is becoming outmoded because of the risks involved.

This book examines how Article 2(4) might be expanded to include respect for the inviolability of State territory. This approach is not a wild guess but relies on States' written submissions, interventions and debates that went on when the

---

7 Tom Ruys, "The Meaning of 'Force' and the Boundaries of the *Jus ad bellum*: Are Minimal Uses of Force Excluded from UN Charter 2(4)?" (2014) 108(2) *American Journal of International Law* 159–210.
8 *Nicaragua* case (n 3), para. 195; *DRC v Uganda* (n 2), para. 97.

4 *General introduction*

Charter and other instruments which prohibit States from interfering in the internal affairs of other States were drafted. The issues involved shall be discussed in six chapters after this brief introduction.

Chapter 2 is a theoretical framework upon which subsequent chapters build. Its approach and methodology are not strictly legal but bi-disciplinary in that it incorporates political philosophy as far as reasonably practicable while threshing out the origins, meanings and theories upon which the notion of State territory anchors. Also, it examines how concepts such as sovereignty, jurisdiction and control relate to State territory. It analyses the scope of State territory as traditionally designated and evaluates the evolution of State territory from ancient times. The last section of Chapter 2 explores how the search for peaceful coexistence culminates in the Peace of Westphalia. Despite reasonable objections to the Westphalian origins of territorial sovereignty, Chapter 2 argues that the Peace of Westphalia consolidates the idea of territorial sovereignty.

Chapter 3 is entitled inviolability of State territory and Article 2(4) of the UN Charter. It offers a detailed analysis of Article 2(4) of the United Nations Charter. The purpose of Chapter 3 is to draw readers' attention to the deliberations that went on during the drafting of Article 2(4). It argues that since some States propose that Article 2(4) should be extended to include economic coercion and others recommend the insertion of the word "inviolability," it suggests that some member States intend a broad meaning. This position is supported by the peremptory character of Article 2(4). Besides, the debate regarding the nature of Article 2(4) was revisited before the United Nations General Assembly adopted Resolution 2625 (XXV) in 1970. Such developments point to the second limb of Article 2(4). Otherwise, the General Assembly Resolution 2625, which is aimed at the "progressive development and codification of the principles of international law"[9] would have been a failed project if it repeats the existing norm. Therefore, Chapter 3 argues that "respect" and "inviolability" could be implied into Article 2 (4) because both concepts have been codified in bilateral and multilateral treaties that pre-existed or are contemporaneous with the UN Charter. Therefore, legal antecedent abounds. Besides, legal instruments that came much later, after the UN Charter went into force, also codified them.

Chapter 4 subjects narrow meaning of Article 2(4) to cyberspace's test and discovers some shortfalls for the following reasons. First, cyberspace offences are non-kinetic. Often and in terms of the *jus ad bellum*, such attacks are ancillary art of war. Even when their effects are grave or cause physical damage, it is difficult to equate that with an armed attack. While this book considers it utterly inadmissible to violate a State's territory under any guise, claims that non-kinetic attack is equal to physical attack is preposterous. On this count, the direct application of international law to cyberspace is reasonably practicable if the broader meaning of Article 2(4) is taken on board. Second, the UN member States have exercised executive, legislative and judiciary functions in cyberspace. Technically, States' territorial sovereignty now includes cyberspace. It is much easier to argue for an

9 UNGA Res. A/RES/2533 (XXIV) (8 December 1969), preamble para. 5.

General introduction 5

all-inclusive prohibition under Article 2(4) than the current efforts to adapt international law to cyberspace. However, Chapter 4 welcomes efforts to expand territorial sovereignty to cyberspace because of the dangers which unregulated cyberspace poses to national security but cautions that narrow application of Article 2(4) is not the way to go.

Chapter 5 evaluates the negative impacts which restricting Article 2(4) to the threat or use of force have on the United Nations' peace agenda. It examines breaches of States territory on land, air and at sea, focusing attention on those breaches often classified as *de minimis* or mere frontier incidents. It argues that the narrow construction of Article 2(4) has short-changed international peace and security. This is not because States have not been observing the precept of Article 2(4) but because the narrow interpretation has inadvertently encouraged small-scale violation of States' territory. This has resulted in distrust and mistrust among States. For instance, it is surprising that espionage is not illegal. Insofar as that remains the case, the flame of suspicion will be kept alive in the heart of States. Consequently, peace and security become scarce and unaffordable commodities. This chapter underscores that breaches, especially those short of the threat or use of force, are factual and sources of internationalised armed conflicts. Chapter 5 seeks to debunk the claim often made that such breaches fall beyond the whip of Article 2(4) or that international peace and security are safeguarded if States comply with the narrow scope of Article 2(4).

Chapter 6 evaluates statutory exceptions to the prohibited act under Article 2(4) in the context of conducts or otherwise of non-State actors. It questions whether a State could enforce self-defence against non-State actors occupying part of the territory belonging to another State without the consent of that State or if not authorised by the Security Council. The purpose is to show that minimalistic compliance with the norm of the first limb of Article 2(4) may not enhance international peace and security because of the effects of covert and overt support which States give to non-State actors. Regrettably, States are the addressees of the UN Charter such that self-defence is unavailable to or remotely accessible against non-State actors. Consequently, the legality of the United States of America's war on terror without the consent of the host States after the 9/11 terrorist attacks is still debated. The jurisprudence of the court does not seem to allow self-defence against non-State actors if such groups are not agent or organ of the State or the said conduct is not attributed to the State. But discussions underway post-9/11 appear to use more inclusive language. Chapter 6 interrogates legal issues involved in supporting non-State actors or fighting such groups without the consent of host State or if not authorised by the Security Council. It argues that State practice has not shown a significant departure from old tradition.

Chapter 7 attempts to formulate a theory of respect for the inviolability of State territory. It tries to provide a theoretical and conceptual analysis of some basic terminologies – respect and inviolability. It starts by examining what respect means, different kinds of respect and why respect is vital for peaceful coexistence. It situates respect in the context of the principle of sovereignty equality of States as derived from the philosophical anthropology based on the notion of the

6 *General introduction*

fundamental equality of all human beings. As subjects of international law, States have a similar footing. Therefore, the abolition of the doctrine of might is right (conquest) could not have been more reasonable if not based on the fundamental assumption of equality of States. In a world riddled by inequalities, international peace and security could remain a political gimmick unless altruism ascends the throne of the world political empire. States, as a subject of international law, provide the necessary platform for this to happen. Otherwise, parochial national interest will continue to subvert the overall common good.

1.1 Clarification of key concepts

This book is titled *State Territory and International Law*. It seeks to construct an argument to support the thesis that Article 2(4) should be broadened to include respect for the inviolability of State territory. We acknowledge that "inviolability" often refers to the dismemberment of a State territory by force. But here, "inviolability" and "respect" are used either as synonyms or together to mean any conduct that belittles territorial sovereignty of a State. Although each has a distinct legal connotation, we prefer to use both words to refer to the same thing, whether used separately or together. Therefore, respect and inviolability are used interchangeably to mean the same thing. Article 2(4) is used here as an abridged form of Article 2, paragraph 4 of the United Nations Charter.

1.2 End in view

This book intends to stimulate academic discussions in a way that might lead to changing the international community's interpretation of Article 2(4). There is a need, and indeed an urgent one, to re-focus the discourse on Article 2(4) to respect for the inviolability of State territory because it stands a better chance of enhancing international peace and security. Inasmuch as lip service is paid to a lesser form of violations of State territory, international peace and security may not be realised. A case in point is the diplomatic row between the United States and Russia over the latter's alleged meddling in the former's electoral process.

2 Setting out the theoretical framework

2.0 Introduction

The idea of territory triggers a mental construct of a delimited portion of the earth's surface in which States exercise authority to the exclusion of others. Its content relates to other concepts such as power, jurisdiction, sovereignty, independence and authority. Political scientists believe that territory pre-exists Statehood and confers legitimacy upon State. Therefore, an enquiry into the modern territorial States should first examine the primordial political structures. Territory is relatively recent and perhaps evolved out of the ancient city-State and designates "a world divided up in political, territorially delimited units."[1] While globalisation unifies, territory delimits international boundaries and insulates States from the forces of globalisation. As Wolfgang Friedmann said, international law regulates conflicts of power and interests.[2] This chapter examines the origins of territory from political and legal perspectives.

2.1 Clarification of context

First and foremost, we need to situate this book within the context of the United Nations project. The United Nations was established in 1945 when the Charter was adopted. One of the aims is "to save succeeding generations from the scourge of war …" so that nations shall "… live together in peace with one another as good neighbours."[3] *Prima facie*, the United Nations is established to "maintain international peace and security"[4] among States. To that end, Article 2(4) prohibits the UN Member States "from the threat or use of force against the territorial

---

1 Martin Kuijer and Wouter Werner, "The Paradoxical Place of Territory in International Law" in Martin Kuijer and Wouter Werner (eds), *Netherlands Yearbook of International Law 2016: The Changing Nature of Territoriality in International Law* (The Hague, Asser Press 2017) 4.
2 Wolfgang Friedman, *The Changing Structure of International Law* (London, Stevens & Sons 1964) 53–54.
3 United Nations, *Charter of the United Nations* (Signed on 26 June 1945, entered into force on 24 October 1945) 1 UNTS XVI, preamble paras 1 and 5 [hereinafter *UN Charter*].
4 ibid., art. 1(1).

8 *Setting out the theoretical framework*

integrity or political independence of any state ...”[5] The Founders envisioned a world order where respect for State territory should be the hallmark of international relations. The former UN Secretary-General, Boutros Boutros-Ghali, reiterates this fact in his report on *An Agenda for Peace*.[6]

Shortly after the Second World War, the UN prevailed on Russia to withdraw its troops from Iranian territory and facilitated the peaceful withdrawal of French and British soldiers from the Syrian and Lebanese territories respectively. The UN promptly responded in the Korean war in a way that yielded a positive outcome[7] and the International Court of Justice (ICJ) condemned Uganda’s refusal to withdraw its troops from the territory of the Democratic Republic of the Congo.[8] Presently, the UN engages in peacekeeping mission across the Middle East and Africa.[9]

This book argues that the UN peace agenda has not been entirely successful partly because of the way peace has been construed as the absence of war. Peace must be pursued holistically through the principle of territoriality.[10] Therefore, Article 2(4) of the UN Charter needs an evolutive interpretation to read as follows: respect for the inviolability of State territory. This call should not be taken lightly despite Elden’s characterisation of territory as “a violent act of exclusion and inclusion.”[11] Agnew’s description of territory as a “trap”[12] has been addressed by Elden.[13]

2.2.1 *Working definition of territory*

How territory is defined depends on the discipline. For some political theorists, it could be a delimited boundary within which States exercise power and control. Jonsson *et al.* defined it as “a cohesive section of the earth’s surface that is

---

5 ibid., art. 2(4).

6 Boutros Boutros-Ghali, *An Agenda for Peace: Preventive Diplomacy, Peacemaking and Peace-Keeping* (New York, United Nations, 1992) 10.

7 Eddy Asirvatham, “The United Nations and World Peace” (1958) 19 *Indian Journal of Political Science* 45, 46.

8 *Armed Activities on the Territory of the Congo* (Democratic Republic of the Congo v Uganda) Judgment ICJ Reports (2005) p. 168, paras 28–166; *Military and Paramilitary Activities In and Against Nicaragua* (Nicaragua v United States of America) (Merit) ICJ Reports (1986) p. 14, para. 206 [hereinafter *Nicaragua* case].

9 Assefaw Bariagaber, “United Nations Peace Mission in Africa: Transformation and Determinants” (2008) 38 *Journal of Black Studies* 830–849.

10 People like Cox argue that territory cannot be discussed in isolation of territoriality. The latter concept “refers to actions designed to exercise control over some area: the territory.” See Kevin Cox, *Political Geography: Territory, State and Society* (Oxford, Blackwell, 2002) 29.

11 Stuart Elden, *Terror and Territory: The Spatial Extent of Sovereignty* (Minneapolis, University of Minnesota Press, 2009) xxx.

12 John Agnew, “The Territorial Trap: The Geographical Assumptions of International Relations Theory” (1994) 1 *Review of International Political Economy* 53, 54.

13 Stuart Elden, *The Birth of Territory* (Chicago and London, The University of Chicago Press, 2013) 3; Stuart Elden, “Thinking Territory Historically” (2010) 15 *Geopolitics* 757.

Setting out the theoretical framework 9

distinguished from its surroundings by a boundary."[14] Cohesion appears not the most appropriate word to use because most States are rift apart by peoples fighting for secession. A similar difficulty one encounters while defining a State[15] because "the formation of a new State is ... a matter of fact, and not of law."[16] Even the International Law Commission (ILC) has not come up with a universally accepted definition.[17] Based on Hugo Grotius' understanding of a State as "a complete association of free men, joined together for the enjoyment of rights and for their common interest,"[18] territoriality is "a basis of power."[19]

Oppenheim defines territory as "that definite portion of the surface of the globe which is subjected to the sovereignty of the State."[20] As Max Huber held in *Island of Palmas*[21] case, territory allows a State the right to exercise its functions to the exclusion of others. The notion of exclusivity seems to be changing with the evolving idea of cyber-territory, although there are States without delimited boundaries.[22] As held by the International Court of Justice (ICJ) in *North Sea Continental Shelf* cases, it is not an article of faith that all "the land frontiers of a State must be fully delimited and defined."[23] Nonetheless, a delimited territory is vital since jurisdiction is territorial.[24]

2.2 Political theories of territory

A two-day "Workshop on 'Theories of Territory beyond Westphalia',"[25] which was held at the Goethe University of Frankfurt intensified the political discourse

14 Christer Jonsson, Sven Tagil and Gunnar Tornqvist, *Organizing European Space* (London, Sage, 2000) 3.
15 Thomas D. Grant, "Defining Statehood: The Montevideo Convention and its Discontents" (1999) 37(2) *Columbia Journal of Transnational Law* 403–458, 408.
16 James Crawford, *The Creation of States in International Law*, Second Edition (New York, Oxford University Press, 2006) 4.
17 ibid., 31.
18 ibid., 6.
19 Elden 2013 (n 13), 4.
20 L. Oppenheim, *International Law: A Treatise*, Third Edition (London, Longmans, 1920) 305; Robert Jennings and Arthur Watts (eds), *Oppenheim's International Law*, Ninth Edition, Volume 1: Peace, Parts 2–4 (London and New York, Longman, 1996) 563 .
21 *Island of Palmas* case (The Netherlands v USA) (The Hague, 1928) II RIAA 829–871, 838 [hereinafter *Island of Palmas* case].
22 Jure Vidmar, "Territorial Integrity and the Law of Statehood" (2013) 44(4) *The George Washington International Law Review* 697–747, 702; Abdul Aziz Jaafar, "The Majority of Potential Maritime Boundaries Worldwide and the South China Sea Remain Undelimited: Does it Matter?" (2013) 4(1) *The Journal of Defence and Security* 1–10.
23 *North Sea Continental Shelf* cases (Federal Republic of Germany/Denmark; Federal Republic of Germany/Netherlands) Judgment ICJ Reports (1969) p. 3, para. 46 [hereinafter *North Sea Continental Shelf* cases]; *Territorial Dispute* (Libyan Arab Jamahiriya/Chad) Judgment ICJ Reports (1994) p. 6, paras 44, 52.
24 *The Case of the S.S. "Lotus"* (France v Turkey) Judgment PCIJ Series A, No. 10 (1927) 18 [hereinafter the *Lotus* case].
25 For details, visit Justitia Amplificata Centre for Advanced Studies, "Workshop on 'Theories of Territory beyond Westphalia'," available at <www.justitia-amplificata.de/

10 *Setting out the theoretical framework*

on the origins and theories of State territory. The convenors claim that "[t]erritory is one of the most under-theorized concepts that we rely on both in political theory and international relations."[26] It received much-needed attention from the late 1990s onwards when political theorists like David Miller, Cara Nine, Hillel Steiner, Anna Stilz and Avery Kolers invested in it.[27] Over the same period, political analysts were investigating "whether the territorial, sovereign nation-state is or is not in decline"[28] due to the influence of multinational organisations and the effect of globalisation on States' internal politics.

For Miller, territorial rights are derivative and consist of "a piece of land, second, a group of people who live on that land and, third, the political institutions that govern those people in that place."[29] Three features are involved – land, people and a government. Under this model, territory belongs to the people before the State expropriated them. It calls to mind Hugo Grotius' idea that States are formed when free people come together to form a government.[30] Invariably, we are back to Hobbes' Social Contract Theory.[31] However, a group theory does not explain how conquest became a valid mode of acquisition[32] and why a State's territories extend beyond habitable land.

Simmons defines territory as "that portion of the earth's surface acknowledged to belong to the state by the world community or by an appropriate international agency."[33] But suppose that all manner of land grabbing is eliminated, why should "State A" exercise right over a specific portion of the earth to the exclusion of others? Simmons argues that *ab initio* "territoriality *is not* a necessary feature of organised, law-governed human associations."[34]

en/events/events-archive/workshop-on-theories-of-territory-beyond-westphalia.htm l> accessed 8 May 2019.

26 Ayelet Banai and Margaret Moore, "Introduction: Theories of Territory Beyond Westphalia" (2014) 6(1) *International Theory* 98, 99.

27 ibid., 99; see also, Avery Kolers, *Land, Conflict, and Justice* (Cambridge, Cambridge University Press, 2009) 66–99; Anna Stilz, "Nations, States, and Territory" (2011) 121(3) *Ethics* 572–601; David Miller, "Territorial Rights: Concept and Justification" (2012) 60(2) *Political Studies* 252–268.

28 Banai and Moore (n 26), 99; John Agnew, "Sovereignty Regimes: Territoriality and State Authority in Contemporary World Politics" (2005) 95(2) *Annals of the Association of American Geographers* 437–461; Stephen D. Krasner, "Rethinking the Sovereign State Model" (2001) 27(5) *Review of International Studies* 17–42; Michael Mann, "Has Globalization Ended the Rise and Rise of the Nation-State?" (1997) 4(3) *Review of International Political Economy* 472–496.

29 Miller 2012 (n 27), 253.

30 Crawford 2006 (n 16), 6.

31 Thomas Hobbes, *Leviathan*, edited by R. Tuck (Cambridge, Cambridge University Press, 1991) 121.

32 James Crawford, *Brownlie's Principles of Public International Law*, Eighth Edition (Oxford, Oxford University Press, 2012) 220.

33 A. John Simmons, "On the Territorial Rights of States" (2001) 11 *Philosophical Issues* 300–326, 303.

34 ibid., 303 (emphasis not in the original).

Setting out the theoretical framework 11

Territory can be classified into two broad categories: *res communis* and *res particularis*. Territory in the latter sense is traceable to John Locke's political philosophy which provides that human beings through consent form "*one body politick.*"[35] Individuals, Locke argues, can acquire *terra nullius* by adding value to it.[36] Ultimately, States inherit territory from individuals who consented to form *one body politick*. However, Simmons' analysis dwells more on the capacity of an already established political entity to exercise lawful control over a people or a circumscribed portion of the earth surface to the exclusion of all others. The five ways it could be done are:

> (a) rights to exercise jurisdiction (either full or partial) over those within the territory… (b) rights to reasonably full control over land and resources within the territory that are not privately owned; (c) rights to tax and regulate uses of that which is privately owned within the state's claimed territory; (d) rights to control or prohibit movement across the borders of the territory … and (e) rights to limit or prohibit dismemberment of the state's territory …[37]

The ground for States to exercise these rights could be "primary" or "derivative;" primary if the *potestas* derives from "free consent" of their citizens or derivative if it applies to aliens.[38] Ultimately, a "state's territorial rights are derived as well from its rights over subjects. For a state's rightful territory is to be understood as that geographical area exclusively and legitimately owned, occupied, or used by the State's subjects."[39] This presupposes social contract but does not explain how a State's territory extends to *terra nullius* or territorial seas. The implied social contract neither adumbrates the correlative duties nor clarifies whether the masses can revoke a power of attorney conferred upon a State. If territory were required for the dispensation of justice, proper control and equitable management of resources, at what point can a State be deemed to have abrogated its rights?

2.2.1 Individualist theory of territory

Individualist theory of territory is traceable to the right of natural persons to acquire or own a property. It promotes the idea of justice as "a rule vesting each person with a right to equal freedom."[40] According to John Locke, natural law permits all human beings the inalienable rights to avail themselves of every means of their preservation.[41]

---

35 John Locke, *Two Treatises of Government*, edited by P. Laslett (Cambridge, Cambridge University Press, 1988) § 95, p. 331.
36 ibid., § 37, pp. 294–295.
37 Simmons 2001 (n 33), 306.
38 ibid., 307.
39 ibid.
40 Hillel Steiner, *An Essay on Rights* (Oxford, Blackwell, 1994) 216.
41 Locke 1988 (n 35), §§ 25–33, pp. 285–291.

12 Setting out the theoretical framework

According to Kant, consent could be express or implicit; the latter applies when people acquiesce to a political arrangement that brings about civic order. By consent, individuals cede their right of ownership to the State in exchange for adequate protection. Miller's differentiation of the right of "individuals over portions of the earth's surface" from the "territorial rights" of States[42] typifies the puzzle of primordiality between the chicken and the egg. John Locke and Immanuel Kant disagreed on this very issue. While Locke favours the primordiality of an individual's proprietary rights, Kant endorses territorial rights of States.[43]

Since individuals may acquire proprietary rights illegally, Steiner maintains that "a group's legitimate territorial claims can extend no further than the legitimate territorial holdings of its members or their agents."[44] This position agrees with a Lockean thesis that individuals in pre-civic society have transferable rights which can be activated by consent.[45] For Kant, what existed in pre-civic society was "*common possession* of the land of the entire earth (*communio fundi originaria*) and each has by nature the will to use it (*lex iusti*)."[46]

The conflicting opinions coming from this school could harm the credibility of its doctrine. If land, *ab initio* was *terra nullius*, then individuals' right to acquire and transfer has merit. Based on the Kantian model, land, *ab initio*, was common possession. This creates some difficulty in understanding how States acquire rights over land. For Kant, "since the earth's surface is not unlimited but closed, the concepts of the Right of a state and of a Right of nations lead inevitably to the Idea of a *Right for all nations* (*ius gentium*) or *cosmopolitan Right* (*ius cosmopoliticum*)."[47]

It seems that States have exclusive right over their territories. In England, the monarch has absolute ownership of land, which in the past was acquired by individuals through the right of inheritance.[48] Beneath this individualist theory is perhaps "the Platonic myth of the *gêgenis*, the idea that people were born (*gen*) of the earth (*gê*); and the autochthonous Athenian or Theban myths – from *autokhthôn*, born from the earth (*khthôn*) itself (*autos*) of one's homeland."[49]

Miller wanted to reconcile the divergent views[50] but later rescinded his position.[51] The summary of his view on territorial claims consists of three things: "the right of jurisdiction, that is the right to make and enforce law throughout the territory in question …" "the right to control and use the resources that are

---

42 David Miller, "Property and Territory: Locke, Kant, and Steiner" (2011) 19(1) *The Journal of Political Philosophy* 90–109, 90.

43 ibid., 91.

44 Hillel Steiner, "Territorial Justice" in Percy B. Lehning (ed.), *Theories of Secession* (London, Routledge, 1998) 61–70, 65.

45 Locke 1988 (n 35), § 95, p. 331.

46 Immanuel Kant, *The Metaphysics of Morals*, translated by M. Gregor (Cambridge, Cambridge University Press, 1991) § 16, p. 87.

47 ibid., § 43, p. 123.

48 John Hudson, *Land, Law and Lordship in Anglo-Norman England* (Oxford, Clarendon Press, 1997) 65.

49 Elden 2013 (n 13), 22.

50 Miller 2011 (n 42), 94–98.

51 Miller 2012 (n 27), 254.

Setting out the theoretical framework 13

available in the territory…" and "the right to control the movement of goods and people across the borders of the territory."[52]

2.2.2 Nationalist theory of territory

The nationalist theory teaches that territory evolves from the amalgamation of territories occupied by nations, people or groups. An example is the formation of the United States of America,[53] although students of public international law may classify the process leading to those amalgamations as annexation or cession or conquest. Yet nationalist sentiment (as a result of spiritual, material and cultural attachment of indigenous peoples to land) may lead to disintegration of a State's territory.[54] Territorial disputes between States and peoples are often based on the latter's claim that the former forcefully confiscate territories belonging to them[55] or that States expropriate resources in their land without adequate compensation or in a manner harmful to their environment.[56]

The ability to control a territory largely determines how nations behave.[57] Nations here refer to a people with a unique cultural, ethnic, tribal or religious affinity. At the heart of a collective mindset is a shared identity which distinguishes them from other classes, cultures or ethnic groups that make up a civic State. A shared sense of oneness is fostered by a strong spiritual and material attachment to their territory. As Grosby observes,

> [t]he existence of the nation, whether Israel or the modern nation-state, is predicated upon the existence of a collective consciousness constituted by a belief that there exists a territory which belongs to one people, and that there are a people which belongs to only one territory.[58]

The nationalist theory could be an ideology which holds that "the state derives its territorial rights from the prior collective right of a *nation* to that territory."[59] The conditions to acquire territory from a *nation* are: "(a) the nation it represents has a prior right to the land in these areas and (b) the state is properly

---

52 Miller 2011 (n 42), 92–93.
53 Stilz 2011 (n 27), 572.
54 Erica-Irene A. Daes, "Some Considerations on the Right of Indigenous Peoples to Self-Determination" (1993) 3(1) *Transnational Law and Contemporary Problems* 1–11, 4–6.
55 Robert A. Williams, "Encounters on the Frontiers of International Human Rights Law: Redefining the Terms of Indigenous Peoples' Survival in the World" (1990) 39 (4) *Duke Law Journal* 660–704, 682.
56 Amnesty International, "Oil and Injustice in Nigeria: Ken Saro-Wiwa" (2005) 32 (106) *Review of African Political Economy* 636–637, 636.
57 John Etherington, "Nationalism, Nation and Territory: Jacint Verdaguer and the Catalan Renaixenca" (2010) 33(10) *Ethic and Racial Studies* 1814–1832, 1815.
58 Steven Grosby, *Biblical Ideas of Nationality: Ancient and Modern* (Winona Lake, Eisenbranus, 2002) 27.
59 Stilz 2011 (n 27), 574.

14 *Setting out the theoretical framework*

authorized by that nation."[60] Many nations might come together to form a state on a condition that each nation is entitled to secede if it so chooses. A case in point is Article 72 of the 1977 *Constitution (Fundamental Law) of the Union of Soviet Socialist Republics* that grants Union Republics the right "to secede from the USSR."[61] An argument based on nationalist theory supports the origin of the State's territory but it does not account for how States acquire rights over territories uninhabited by humans. Besides, the delimitation of internal boundaries for administrative convenience does not always reflect the boundaries of "nations" and often constitutes a source of conflicts and crashes between nations within a State.

The nationalist theory is not formidable in explaining territorial rights. First, it assumes that a nation enjoys cohesiveness among its members because they share one cultural or spiritual identity, or because they claim to be the first settlers. An argument based on settlement is mostly measured by the value added to the land by settlers. Stilz contends that such an approach is "a purely functionalist account of state authority"[62] and does not explain why a value added to land by emigrants abroad does not cede the legal title to their countries of origin. If nations occupying territories add value to the land, how does that translate to jurisdiction over the entire area under the State's control? Besides, the Social Contract Theory obliges a State to add value to the territories of its citizens and not vice versa. The nationalist theory of territory has its shortfalls but is credible because the UN Charter[63] and the Bill of Rights[64] recognise that peoples (nations) have such a right.

2.2.3 Statist theory of territory

The statist theory has been described in various ways by various authors. Stilz talks about "the legitimate state theory"[65] while Miller describes it as the "statist theories of territory."[66] Simmons talks about "conventional rules,"[67] although his approach

---

60 ibid.
61 *Constitution (Fundamental Law) of the Union of Soviet Socialist Republics* (adopted at the Seventh (Special) Session of the Supreme Soviet of the USSR, Ninth Convocation, 7 October 1977) (Moscow, Novosti Press Agency Publishing House, 1988), art. 72. For how nationalist sentiment affects territory, see Marlene Laruelle, "The Paradigm of Nationalism in Kyrgyzstan. Evolving Narrative, the Sovereignty Issue, and Political Agenda" (2012) 45 *Communist and Post-Communist Studies* 39–49.
62 Stilz 2011 (n 27), 576.
63 *UN Charter* (n 3), arts 1 and 55 protect "the principle of equal rights and self-determination of peoples." Technically, "peoples" refer to "nations."
64 United Nations, *International Covenant on Civil and Political Rights* (adopted on 16 December 1996, entered into force on 23 March 1976) 999 UNTS 171, art. 1; United Nations, *International Covenant on Economic, Social and Cultural Rights* (adopted on 16 December 1966, entered into force on 3 January 1976) 993 UNTS 3, art. 1.
65 Stilz 2011 (n 27), 578.
66 Miller 2012 (n 27), 254.
67 Simmons (n 33), 309.

Setting out the theoretical framework 15

is a bit legal because it envisages an international framework that makes such acquisition possible. For instance, Simmons discusses "the extent to which states' particular claims conform to the ideal or conventional rules governing such claims."[68] The statist theory does not investigate the pre-political era. It has some flaws because "[t]he actual international conventions governing the titles to and boundaries of state territories are sufficiently vague and controversial as to be virtually useless in any attempts at justification."[69]

For political theorists such as Sidgwick, States can expropriate land from individuals and groups for two reasons: first, to maximise production for the benefit of all, and second, for "the prevention of mutual mischief among human beings."[70] Conceptually, the statist theory operates a utilitarian principle if as Barry says "the greater aggregate gain should be preferred to the less …"[71] is the determinant. The necessity of international boundaries should all States promote the interests of the masses residing within their territories is rarely discussed. Again, Sidgwick's argument that territory is an antidote to individuals' mischief appears paternalistic. In history, States, loosely speaking, have committed genocide against their people. Besides, not all States' national interests accommodate the individual interest of their citizens. To that end, the statist theory stands if and only if the objectives it sets out to achieve are deliverable to all[72] or compatible with the interests of its populace. This is a high threshold which is difficult to attain. Therefore, there is a need to balance the interests of States with those of the "nations" and "individuals."[73] In summary, none of the theories examined above can fully justify the origins of a State's territory – whether individually or cumulatively. Each contributes to explaining the origin of States' territory, but none is sufficient to account for what the modern international law recognises as valid modes of acquisition.[74]

2.3 A conceptual derivation of State territory

The principle of territoriality[75] became a benchmark for the maintenance of peace and order when, for an author like Teschke, the "exclusive territoriality" became

---

68 ibid.
69 ibid.
70 Henry Sidgwick, *The Elements of Politics*, Second Edition (London, Macmillan, 1897) 252.
71 Brian Barry, "Self-Government Revisited" in Ronald Beiner (ed.), *Theorizing Nationalism* (Albany, State University of New York Press, 1999) 251.
72 Miller 2012 (n 27), 255. *Cf* Frank Dietrich, "Territorial Rights and Demographic Change" (2014) 6(1) *International Theory* 174–190, 176 (arguing that a State's territorial rights are derivative).
73 Sidgwick (n 70), 225–229; 310–328.
74 Malcolm N. Shaw, *International Law*, Fifth Edition (Cambridge, Cambridge University Press, 2003) 420–429.
75 "Territoriality" designates the "basic principle of jurisdiction." For how the principle has evolved in continental Europe, see Cedric Ryngaert, *Jurisdiction in International Law*, Second Edition (Oxford, Oxford University Press, 2015) 49; the *Lotus* case (n 24), 18;

16 *Setting out the theoretical framework*

synonymous with "the modern state-system"[76] in the nineteenth century. Elden is sceptical about designating "territoriality" as "territory" because of what he considers "an unhealthy degree of conceptual imprecision regarding the terms *territory* and *territoriality*."[77] Besides, schools of thought abound on when exclusivity over a certain portion of the earth's surface became a norm.[78]

These preliminary objections notwithstanding, we use both concepts as a synonym and proceed to examine territory from the viewpoint of the Peace of Westphalia. But before we proceed, we shall examine the world of the ancient period when personality prevailed over State territory; particularly in Ancient Greece and Roman antiquity. This is to verify Kassan's claim that "the principle of territorial law and sovereignty was unknown in the ancient world. It was even vague in the Middle Ages. In fact, kingdoms during the medieval period had vague and uncertain boundaries."[79] Equally, it has been suggested that "sovereignty was not associated with dominion over a territory."[80]

2.3.1 Ancient Greece

States' territories in Ancient Greece were not delimited as we have it today. This fact can be deduced from the works of Plato and Aristotle on the origin of State. Plato's works, the *Republic*[81] and the *Laws*[82] provide some insights into the political demography of the time and the views of Aristotle are expressed in his work on *Politics* and the *Nicomachean Ethics*. Comments on these works are sketchy but Elden's analysis is a bit detailed.[83] The four keywords that relate to territory from Elden's viewpoint are *"polis, topos, Khora*, and *ge."*[84] We shall focus on the *polis*.

In Plato's work on the *Laws*, there are passages where the Athenian uses *"Kleinias"* to describe where to site a new *polis* and how to divide the land. According to Gottmann, the debate on delimitation arose because of the growth in population and the need to resettle people in a new "empty territory."[85] However, Elden cautions against "the danger ... of reading back contemporary

---

Abdelhamid El Ouali, "Territorial Integrity: Rethinking the Territorial Sovereign Right of the Existence of the States" (2006) 11(4) *Geopolitics* 630–650, 631.

76 Benno Teschke, *The Myth of 1648: Class, Geopolitics and the Making of Modern International Relations* (London, Verso, 2003) 230.

77 Elden 2013 (n 13), 3.

78 Ryngaert (n 75), 54 (talks about seventeenth century); Teschke (n 76), 230 (indicates it occurs in the nineteenth century).

79 Shalom Kassan, "Extraterritorial Jurisdiction in the Ancient World" (1935) 29 *American Journal of International Law* 237–247, 240.

80 ibid., 240.

81 Plato, *Complete Works*, edited by John M. Cooper (Indianapolis and Cambridge, Hackett Publishing Company, 1997) bk II, 369 b ff.

82 ibid., bk III, 676 a ff.

83 Elden 2013 (n 13), 21–52.

84 ibid., 38.

85 Jean Gottmann, "The Evolution of the Concept of Territory" (1975) 14(3) *Social Science Information* 29–47, 32.

Setting out the theoretical framework 17

notions into ancient thought."[86] Plato's most persuasive argument in favour of exclusive territoriality – be it in terms of the "doctrines of isolation, political and economic restraint and self-sufficiency"[87] – is his statement that "the legislator ... when he divides up the territory he must give these priority by setting aside plots of land for them, endowed with all the appropriate resources."[88] A line in Aristotle's *Politics* which recommends that "the city should be formidable not only to its citizens but to some of its neighbours ..."[89] confirms the principle of non-intervention.

The concept of *polis* is often translated as State but not strictly as we have it today. In Plato's *Republic* it's seen that mutual assistance is the kinetic force that propels the formation of *polis*.[90] A State (*polis*) is constituted so that citizens can access material or services which the other has or can render. In the *Laws*, Plato describes how States are formed "by the grouping of primitive families to form tribes, which in their turn eventually unite with one another to form the city."[91] The intriguing aspect of the Athenian's question in the *Laws* regarding *polis* is that it "concerns the location of the future city or, more generally, the nature of its territory."[92] Elden's argument that although *polis* has all the ingredients of a State, it should not be construed as such is persuasive.[93] Therefore, statements that refer to territory may not be interpreted as international borders.

2.3.2 Roman antiquity

In classical Latin, *territorium* refers to "Land belonging to a town or other community."[94] Until the mid-fourteenth century, it had no political connotations but that changed "with the discovery of Roman law in the Italian city-states" when "*territorium* became explicitly tied to that of jurisdiction."[95] In the Roman Empire, and unlike the Ancient Greece that advocated for a secure territory for *polis*, the political structure was a bit complex and mostly decentralised. What obtained, especially in the earlier periods, could be likened to "a two-level monarchy, in which quite large populations were subject both to local kings and, indirectly, to a distant superior monarch in Rome, the emperor."[96]

---

86 Elden 2013 (n 13), 38.
87 Gottmann 1975 (n 85), 32.
88 Plato (n 81), *Laws*, bk V, 738 d.
89 B. Jowett, "Politics" in Jonathan Barnes (ed.), *The Complete Works of Aristotle – The Revised Oxford Translation*, Volumes One and Two (Princeton, Princeton University Press, 1984) bk VII, 6.1327^{b}1.
90 Leo Ferrari, "The Origin of the State According to Plato" (1956) 12(2) *Laval theologique et philosophique* 145–151, 145.
91 ibid., 145.
92 Leo Strauss, *The Arguments and Actions of Plato's Laws* (Chicago, University of Chicago Press, 1975) 54.
93 Elden 2013 (n 13), 50.
94 Elden 2010 (n 13), 758.
95 ibid., 758.
96 Fergus Millar, *Rome, the Greek World and the East*, Volume 2 (Chapel Hill and London, The University of North Carolina Press, 2004) 229.

18 *Setting out the theoretical framework*

Territory had three connotations: the domain of kings, dynasts and *dekarchiai*. In Strabo's *Geography* Millar wrote "… kings and dynasts and *dekarchiai* belong to his (emperor's) portion, and always have done."[97] Millar interpreted this to mean that a three-tier political structure existed in Rome at the time and each had a peculiar territorial structure. First is *dynastai* comprising "minor rulers without the title of king," second is *basileis* which is the king and then the Emperor.[98] There were other layers of governance with territorial jurisdictional competence. For instance, there were "provincial territory," "free cities," "tribal heads" (*phylarchoi*) and "priests" (*hiereis*).[99] What you find in classical literature from "the early first century" is that Rome had a structure of governance based on "subordinate, or intermediate, monarchs."[100]

The evolution of territorial States in Continental Europe followed a certain pattern from the Middle Ages to the Early Modern Period.[101] First was a dualistic formation that favoured kings and emperors as territorial heads, and second was a decentralised system that recognised the powers of princes, cities and provinces.[102] The decentralised network is visible in the Peace of Westphalia which accords political powers to the Princes. Several cities "estimated at 3,000 to 4, 000 or even more"[103] were within the Roman Empire. Various factors, mostly economic and political, determined the development of micro and macro cities. For instance, "the bishop's cities West of the Rhine and South of the Danube, situated in 'Old Europe,' were at the origin of German urbanization."[104]

Consequently, megacities evolved with enormous demographic changes that affected the internal normative landscape of cities and their economic and political relations with other cities. Cities like Brabant, Prague, Liege and Cologne had an estimated 40,000 inhabitants while Paris, Milan and Venice had twice that number.[105] Imperial cities acquire more territories through wars to boost their economic and political fortune. Some examples were Bern and Zurich that acquired vast "cantons" or Nuremberg, whose expansionist drive extended to about "1,500 square kilometers, encompassing six towns and many villages."[106]

Be that as it may, feudalism was the mainstay of the medieval political landscape. It favoured "territorial princes." The word, "*territorium*" was first used in Germany for "representation of estates … of the imperial city Eger."[107] Conquest, communal crashes, instability and insecurity coupled with "an increasingly

---

97 ibid., 230.
98 ibid.
99 ibid.
100 ibid.
101 Peter Moraw, "Cities and Citizenry as Factors of State Formation in the Roman-German Empire of the Late Middle Ages" (1989) 18(5) *Theory and Society* (Special Issue on Cities and States in Europe, 1000–1800) 631–662, 635.
102 Moraw (n 101), 635.
103 ibid., 636.
104 ibid.
105 ibid., 637.
106 ibid., 639.
107 ibid.

Setting out the theoretical framework 19

legalistic Empire" resulted in the demand for "better organised territories."[108] In Germany, for instance, there were three kinds of cities; namely, "free cities," "imperial cities" and "territorial cities." The "free cities" refer to small communities that gained political autonomy from the control of bishops. As the name goes, "imperial cities" are cities of the emperor and other cities annexed to them, and the "territorial cities" are composed of communities under the control of the feudal lords.[109] These cities or communities were not States, yet each city had its laws and *modus operandi.*

Some political theorists have suggested that a decretal issued by Pope Innocent III in 1202, *Per Venerabilem,* triggered the debate on exclusive territoriality for kings within their domain. Count William of Montpellier requested the Pontiff to confer temporal rights of inheritance to his "bastard children" (*ex defectu natalium*) and the Pope refused.[110] Because Pope Innocent III had granted similar privileges to children born to King Philip II of France, Pope Innocent III defended his refusal by arguing that to the King belongs absolute and exclusive powers in temporal matters. In his words:

> *Insuper, cum rex ipse superiorem in temporalibus minime recognoscat, sine juris alterius laesione in eo se jurisdictioni nostrae subjicere potuit et subjecit, in quo forsitan videretur aliquibus quod per se ipsum, non tanquam pater cum filiis, sed tanquam princeps cum subditis, potuerit dispensare.*[111]

The royal jurists construed this to mean that the King's *potestas* within his territory paralleled "that of the Holy Roman Emperor."[112] The struggle for control gravitated to the theory of territorial sovereignty.[113]

2.4 State territory as a political construct of the twentieth century

There are no hard facts to evidence when State territory entered the lexicon of international relations. It evolved, but the gravitational pull was at its peak in the twentieth century. Territory was first a political construct which transformed into a legal concept. The twentieth century is remarkable for some reasons. It marked the end of the partition of Africa[114] and the conclusion of peace treaties that ended interminable warfare that engulfed Europe. In the Americas, the waves of

108 ibid.
109 ibid., 641–643.
110 Brian Tierney, "'Tria Quippe Distinguit Iudicia …' A Note on Innocent III's Decretal Per Venerabilem" (1962) 37(1) *Speculum* 48–59.
111 Pope Innocent III, *Nobili Viro, Willelmo, Domino Montispessulani. De Legitimatione Liberorum* in *Patrologia Latina Database,* Volume 214 (Alexandria, Chadwyck-Healey Inc., 1996) 475.
112 Elden 2010 (n 13), 759.
113 An example is power tussle between Pope Boniface VIII and King Philip IV, see Norman N. Erickson, "A Dispute between a Priest and a Knight" (1967) 111(5) *Proceedings of the American Philosophical Society* 288–309.
114 Roland Oliver and G. N. Sanderson (eds), *The Cambridge History of Africa from 1870 to 1905,* Volume 6 (Cambridge, Cambridge University Press, 1985) 96–158.

20 Setting out the theoretical framework

change started much earlier following the nineteenth century's Monroe Doctrine that resisted further forceful territorial acquisition.[115]

In defence of the Monroe Doctrine, President Roosevelt once said that "all that this country (United States of America) desires is to see the neighbouring countries stable, orderly, and prosperous ..."[116] In Southeast Asia, for instance, "[t]he personalistic and quasi-feudal complex of arrangements which had been the hallmark of earlier political systems was overridden and often eliminated."[117] In the early twentieth century, many internal boundaries transformed into political and national borders with domestic "laws, languages, currencies, and even weights and measures according to their respective European usages."[118]

Therefore, the barrage of international conventions concluded in the twentieth century played a significant role not only in safeguarding States' territory but also in solidifying the political construct known as State.[119] However, the last quarter of the twentieth century witnessed "The Balkanization of the West"[120] leading to the dissolution of the Soviet Union and the Former Yugoslavia. The ground-breaking political events of the twentieth century transformed the psyche of international political gladiators by engendering a system that recognises States as equals. Hence, before the comity of nations, every sovereign State has one vote. As Krasner put it, "[a]lmost all of the new states that emerged from the colonial empires after the Second World War were not only international legal sovereigns but also Westphalian sovereigns."[121]

2.5 Correlation between territory and sovereignty

What does Krasner mean by "Westphalian sovereign state model"?[122] The need to establish a link between territory and sovereignty is crucial when we talk about the Westphalian sovereign State model as it relates to political philosophy and legal discipline. To do this, readers are advised to take note of Elden's criticism of Foucault's attempt to equate territory with sovereignty.[123] First, we define and contextualise sovereignty before we attempt to establish the nexus.

115 Jay Sexton, *The Monroe Doctrine: Empire and Nation in Nineteenth-Century America* (Basingstoke, Macmillan, 2011) 15–16.
116 Edward J. Renehan, *The Monroe Doctrine: The Cornerstone of American Foreign Policy* (New York, Infobase Publishing, 2007) 103 (the phrase in the bracket is not in the original).
117 Carl A. Trocki, "Political Structures in the Nineteenth and Early Twentieth Centuries" in Nicholas Tarling (ed.), *The Cambridge History of Southeast Asia: The Nineteenth and Twentieth Centuries*, Volume 2 (Cambridge, Cambridge University Press, 1992) 79.
118 ibid., 79–81.
119 Chris Cook and John Paxton, *European Political Facts of the Twentieth Century*, Fifth Edition (New York, Palgrave, 2001) 1–37.
120 Stjepan G. Mestrovic, *The Balkanization of the West* (London, Routledge, 1994) 3.
121 Stephen D. Krasner, *Sovereignty: Organized Hypocrisy* (Princeton, Princeton University Press, 1999) 154.
122 Krasner 2001 (n 28), 17.
123 Stuart Elden, "How Should We do the History of Territory?" (2013) 1(1) *Territory, Politics, Governance* 5–20, 8–10 [hereinafter Elden 2013a].

Setting out the theoretical framework 21

2.5.1 Sovereignty as a political concept

Krasner has identified four kinds of sovereignty, namely: "international legal sovereignty, Westphalian sovereignty, domestic sovereignty, and interdependence sovereignty."[124] Further elaboration does not help our inquiry; it is good to note that they portray various perspectives. For instance, international legal sovereignty concerns "practices associated with mutual recognition, usually between territorial entities that have formal juridical independence" and "Westphalian sovereignty refers to political organization based on the exclusion of external actors from authority structures within a given territory."[125] The Westphalian sovereignty might not function appropriately without international legal sovereignty because both aspects deal with "authority and legitimacy." Diplomats attempt to restructure world order through conventions even when some of the conventions are hortatory.

The two other sovereignties which Krasner identifies are domestic and interdependence. The former "refers to the formal organization of political authority within the state and the ability of public authorities to exercise effective control within the borders of their own polity" and the latter "refers to the ability of public authorities to regulate the flow of information, ideas, goods, people, pollutants, or capital across the borders of their state."[126] What is at stake here is the capacity of a State to control activities within its territory.

Based on Krasner's classification, sovereignty falls into two broad categories: the capacity to have "authority and legitimacy" on the one hand and the ability to put the *auctoritas* into use through effective control on the other hand. Both elements are at play when we talk about sovereignty, vis-à-vis a defined territory. It seems weird to have one without the other as Krasner's categorisation might suggest.[127] However, a State might temporarily suspend an aspect of its sovereignty through a contract. No matter its shape or form, sovereignty – whether as a political construct or a legal certainty – implies some elements of *de jure* exclusivity. Therefore, inclusivity which derives from treaty regimes or the *de facto* approximation of some layers of sovereignty is concessionary and subject to other variables.[128] It is often said that nation-State is an old-fashioned idea.[129]

---

124 Krasner 1999 (n 121), 3.
125 ibid., 3–4.
126 ibid., 4.
127 ibid.
128 Antony Anghie, *Imperialism, Sovereignty and the Making of International Law* (Cambridge, Cambridge University Press, 2004) 101.
129 Kenichi Ohmae, *The End of the Nation State: The Rise of Regional Economies* (London, Harper Collins, 1995) 7; Stuart Elden, "Missing the Point: Globalization, Deterritorialization and the Space of the World" (2005) 30(1) *Transactions of the Institute of British Geographers* 8–19, 9.

22   Setting out the theoretical framework

2.5.2 Sovereignty as a legal concept

Law students in England will be familiar with Dicey's assertion that parliament can make or unmake law whatsoever.[130] It is similar to the Lotus Principle on the international stage. In that regard, legal sovereignty envisages the capacity of a State to legislate on any reasonable topic or an item and enforce its laws within a delimited territory to the exclusion of others. Without dabbling into the controversy surrounding John Austin's legal philosophy on sovereignty,[131] one could reasonably, though reluctantly, advance the view that the rule of law is sovereign in a functional democracy. Hans Kelsen equates State with the legal order as follows: "one of the distinctive results of the pure theory of law is its recognition that the coercive order which constitutes the political community we call a State, is a legal order."[132] A reservation regarding the import of Kelsen's position is in order because not all laws promote the common good or human rights. However, questions might be asked concerning laws that militate against the exclusivity of territorial sovereignty or the necessity of territorial sovereignty in a world that is becoming increasingly globalised. Yet, we uphold that profound disrespect of States' territory is inimical to international order. Hence, a coercive order could imply an undue interference.

2.5.3 The point of convergence

Arguments concerning the birth of territorial sovereignty in relation to modern State structure have been stiff and tensed. Authors like Osiander explains that the right conferred upon Princes by the Peace of Westphalia is *landeshoheit* which in German denotes "territorial jurisdiction."[133] English translators translated it as "territorial sovereignty."[134] However, the original texts of the treaties concluded in Westphalia were in Latin. The exact phrase used in Article 64 is *iuris territorialis* (territorial right), and its equivalent in French is *supériorité territoriale*.[135] While territorial sovereignty is not expressed in the Peace of Westphalia, the principle is implied.[136] As Croxton put it, "the peace of Westphalia legitimized the de

---

130 A. V. Dicey, *Introduction to the Study of the Law of the Constitution* (London, Macmillan and Co Ltd, 1959) 39–40; cf John McGarry, "The Principle of Parliamentary Sovereignty" (2012) 32(4) *Legal Studies* 577–599, 577.

131 For discussions see John Austin, *The Province of Jurisprudence Determined*, edited by Wilfred E. Rumble (Cambridge, Cambridge University Press, 1999) 10–105.

132 Hans Kelsen, "The Pure Theory of Law and Analytical Jurisprudence" (1941) 55(1) *Harvard Law Review* 44–70, 64–65; Hans Kelsen, "Recognition in International Law: Theoretical Observations" (1941) 35(4) *American Journal of International Law* 605–617, 606–610.

133 Andreas Osiander, "Sovereignty, International Relations, and the Westphalian Myth" (2001) 55(2) *International Organisation* 251–287, 272.

134 ibid.

135 Elden 2013 (n 13), 313.

136 F. H. Hinsley, *Sovereignty*, Second Edition (London, Cambridge University Press, 1986) 26; Derek Croxton, "The Peace of Westphalia of 1648 and the Origins of Sovereignty" (1999) 21(3) *International History Review* 569–591, 573–574.

Setting out the theoretical framework   23

facto independence of the German princes, and thus took a demonstrable step towards the formal recognition of sovereignty."[137] According to Elden, it is irrelevant whether it is called "right, jurisdiction or indeed sovereignty" insofar as "it is held over territory."[138]

Leibniz is perhaps the first political philosopher to attempt the unification of the two concepts while responding to Duke of Hanover's request "to clarify the position of the rulers within the Empire."[139] He distinguishes "Imperial *majestas*" from "sovereignty" – the former relates to "the power to demand obedience and loyalty, without being commanded themselves" and the latter is "stressed in the treaties of Westphalia, as concerned with territory."[140] Consequently, he defines sovereign as "he who is master of a territory," albeit not as a supreme authority in international affairs.[141] Hence, the Peace of Westphalia reserves certain powers to the Emperor. But Leibniz was more an "apologist for a German electorate" and his thesis "was to show that minor German princes were as 'sovereign' as the kings of France and Spain."[142] His work, "*De Jure Suprematus ac Legationis Principum Germaniae*" published in 1678 with a pseudonym, "Caesarini Furstenerii" equates the *potestas* of Princes to that of the Emperor. It states:

> *Hinc illud oritur quod Jurisconsulti Germani vocant Superioritatem territorialem vel sublime territorii jus ... Aliud enim est Dominus jurisdictionis, aliud Dominus territorii ... Haec qui accurate considerabit, Superioritatem territorialem in sumo cogendi sive coercendi Jure consistere, videbit, quae tantum a simplici coercendi facultate differ, quantum in Legibus Romanis vis publica a privata ... Hoc porro Jus non Principibus tantum Imperii, sed & Comitibus competit.*[143]

Many authors accept that his thesis became popular in Europe and facilitated the delimitation of international borders.[144] Authors such as Osiander are sceptical about the universal acceptability of this narrative. Yet it provides insight into the proximity between territory and sovereignty. According to the *Permanent Court of Arbitration*, "Territorial sovereignty cannot limit itself to its negative side, i.e. to excluding the activities of other States; for it serves to divide between nations the space upon which human activities are employed ..."[145] Primarily, territorial

---

137 Croxton 1999 (n 136), 574.
138 Elden 2005 (n 129), 13.
139 ibid., 14.
140 ibid.
141 ibid.
142 Patrick Riley, "Introduction" in Gottfried Wilhelm Leibniz, *Leibniz: Political Writings*, Second Edition (Cambridge, Cambridge University Press, 1988) 26–27.
143 Caesarini Furstenerii, *De Jure Suprematus Ac Legationis Principum Germaniae* (Londini, Passau, 1678) 48–50, available at <https://archive.org/details/bub_gb_5-jKZRjZmfUC/page/n73> accessed 7 July 2019.
144 John H. Herz, "Rise and Demise of the Territorial State" (1957) 9(4) *World Politics* 473–493, 479.
145 *Island of Palmas* case (n 21), 839.

24 Setting out the theoretical framework

sovereignty revolves around authority, power and control over a delimited portion of the earth surface. It is sometimes regarded as the power of jurisdiction.

2.6 Territorial jurisdiction

Another concept that explains territorial sovereignty is jurisdiction. The *Permanent Court of International Justice* in *S.S. Lotus* held that jurisdiction is territorial. Judge Max Huber in the *Island of Palmas* described jurisdiction as "a constituent element of territorial sovereignty."[146] In this regard, Ryngaert's monograph establishes how territorial sovereignty connects with jurisdiction and equally clarifies why jurisdiction in Continental Europe is perceived differently in common law countries and in civil law countries.[147] The distinction pre-existed modern sovereign States.

In Ancient Rome, "personality, and not territoriality, was the basic principle of jurisdiction."[148] The Peace of Westphalia reflects that sentiment. Thus, the doctrine of universal jurisdiction is contrary to the fundamental principle of sovereign equality of States.[149] This is because "jurisdiction under international law is considered the sum of external competences of the state deriving from sovereignty."[150] Jurisdiction is an integral element of sovereignty and equality dictates States relations. As the maxim goes: "*par in parem non habet imperium.*"[151]

Crawford describes jurisdiction as the capacity "to regulate the conduct of natural and juridical persons."[152] The US Supreme Court held that "jurisdiction of the nation within its own territory is necessarily exclusive and absolute" such that its unlawful external restriction "would imply a diminution of its sovereignty ..."[153]

2.6.1 Economic jurisdiction

Economic jurisdiction allows States to control "extractable minerals, oil and other natural resources and to profit from their sale."[154] This principle was initiated by the United Nations to protect economic interests of "colonial peoples and developing countries."[155] It is meant to address "inequitable legal arrangements, under which foreign investors had obtained title to exploit resources in the past, to be

---

146 ibid., 840.
147 Ryngaert (n 75), 50.
148 ibid.
149 Crawford 2012 (n 32) 447.
150 Aisling O'Sullivan, *Universal Jurisdiction in International Criminal Law: The Debate and the battle for Hegemony* (Abingdon and New York, Routledge, 2017) 79.
151 Crawford 2012 (n 32), 448.
152 ibid., 456.
153 *Schooner Exchange v McFaddon* (1812) 11 U.S. (7 Cranch) 116, 136.
154 Stilz 2011 (n 27), 573; Myres S. McDougal and William T. Burke, "Claims to Authority Over the Territorial Sea" (1962) 1(1) *Philippine International Law Journal* 29–138, 33.
155 Nico Schrijver, *Sovereignty over Natural Resources* (Cambridge, Cambridge University Press, 1997) 1.

Setting out the theoretical framework 25

altered or even to be annulled *ab initio* because they conflicted with the concept of permanent sovereignty."[156] This is a departure from the principle of *pacta sunt servanda*. However, the expropriation of foreign asset is not automatic but must comply with the international minimum standard. For instance, new States must reasonably compensate foreign investors or review the existing contract in a way that accommodates the interests of the parties.

A similar consideration applies to "residual sovereignty"[157] in which a contract determines the administration of a State and its resources. Claims over economic jurisdiction are sometimes difficult to justify because of the fluidity of some regions of State borders, especially in the *Exclusive Economic Zone*.[158] It creates conflict between States and indigenous peoples insofar as the latter have a right to profit from the natural resources on their land.[159] Nonetheless, international law bequeaths sovereign States with the power to control natural resources within their territory.

2.6.2 Border control

The right of a State to control its borders is a consequence of territorial sovereignty. In recent times, the exercise of this right has been constrained by many factors. First is the argument in favour of human rights as it relates to the migration crisis and second is the fluid character of cyberspace activities. Also, military and economic alliances have softened what used to be "physical presence;"[160] that is, a State's ability to control the influx of persons in and out of its territory.

In principle, States make laws and policies to determine or regulate who enters, remains or exits their territory. A State could evict or extradite violators of its domestic legislation or laws of other States or prosecute foreign nationals residing within their territory. This right may be subject to international human rights law.[161] Recently, the European Court of Human Rights held that the detention of irregular migrants and asylum seekers amounted to torture and inhuman treatment.[162]

Other issues confronting border control are globalisation, extraterritoriality, universal jurisdiction and most recently cyber-territory. Globalisation here means that States no longer control their internal affairs exclusively, whether politically or economically. Often people talk about global governance when referring to the function

---

156 ibid.
157 Crawford 2012 (n 32), 207.
158 *Guyana v Suriname*, Award PCA (2007) 30 *RIAA* 1–144, paras 425–447.
159 UNGA Res. A/RES/61/295 (2 October 2007), art. 26; Claire Charters, "Indigenous Peoples' Rights to Lands, Territories, and Resources in the UNDRIP: Articles 10, 25, 26, and 27" in Jessie Hohmann and Marc Weller (ed.), *The UN Declaration on the Rights of Indigenous Peoples: A Commentary* (Oxford, Oxford University Press, 2018) 395.
160 Miller 2012 (n 27), 265.
161 *Convention Relating to the Status of Refugees* (Signed at Geneva on 28 July 1951, entered into force on 22 April 1954) 189 UNTS 150, art. 33.
162 *Case of S.D. v Greece* (Application No. 53541/07) Judgment ECtHR (2009), paras 33–34; *Case of Tabesh v Greece* (Application No. 8256/07) Judgment ECtHR (2009), para. 44.

26 *Setting out the theoretical framework*

of the United Nations and some authors push for its democratisation. The regional blocs like the European Union and NATO are formed to provide services reserved initially for States. Hence, the supporters of Brexit want to reclaim the "sovereignty" of the United Kingdom.

Earlier, we said that States have control over citizens of other countries residing within their territory. Such powers are not exclusive because every State has residual sovereignty over its nationals abroad. Residual sovereignty equally applies when a foreign power occupies a sovereign territory of another State in peacetime based on a mutual agreement. This extraterritorial application of the law is "by virtue of a permissive rule derived from international custom or from a convention"[163] because jurisdiction is territorial. Therefore, extraterritoriality is conceptually an exciting topic but a complex phenomenon.

The Supreme Court of the United States has examined a lot of issues bordering on control. They include the "geographic scope of U.S. regulatory laws, the power of U.S. courts over foreign defendants, the rights of foreigners detained outside U.S. territory, or the ability of U.S. courts to entertain causes of action arising out of activity abroad."[164] Common to all scenarios is to assess whether the US courts have jurisdiction outside the US's territory either as "prescriptive jurisdiction," "adjudicative jurisdiction," or "enforcement jurisdiction."[165] Arguably, two elements stand out, namely: "the location of the conduct" and "the location of the party."[166] It may well be that domestic laws legitimise other States' intervention as often is the case in cyberspace disputes. Yet the burden of proof rests on the State that alleges. The case concerning *Military and Paramilitary Activities In and Against Nicaragua*[167] establishes a victim's threshold below which territorial interference is prohibited. It could apply if aimed at rescuing nationals abroad but on condition that the State in question lacks the capacity.[168]

Again, the concept of universal jurisdiction became popular following the arrest of Augusto Pinochet in 1998. In principle, it puts "everyone everywhere on notice that they can be held to account anywhere for certain serious offences against international law – such as piracy, torture, genocide, and terrorist acts ..."[169] It operates on the basis that such crimes are antihuman and affect the entire humanity. Yet its enforcement is contentious,[170] and not all States are a party to

163 The *Lotus* case (n 24), 19.
164 Anthony J. Colangelo, "What is Extraterritorial Jurisdiction?" (2013) 99(6) *Cornell Law Review* 1303–1352, 1303–1304.
165 ibid., 1304–1305.
166 ibid., 1305.
167 *Nicaragua* case (n 8), para. 195.
168 Stefan Talmon, "The Responsibility of Outside Powers for Acts of Secessionist Entities" (2009) 58(3)
   International and Comparative Law Quarterly 493–518, 499–500.
169 Colangelo (n 164), 1306–1307; Ryngaert (n 75), 120.
170 Daphne Richemond, "Normativity in International Law: The Case of Unilateral Humanitarian Intervention" (2003) 6 *Yale Human Rights & Development Law Journal* 45–80, 46–51.

the jurisdiction of the International Criminal Court. Despite the warrant for the arrest of Omar al-Bashir,[171] no State intervened in Sudan to effect the arrest. Instead, the legality of the said warrant has dominated legal discourse[172] to the extent that the States party to the ICC visited by al-Bashir failed to arrest and surrender him to The Hague.[173]

Perhaps in a restrictive sense, extraterritoriality refers to Conventions on Diplomatic Relations that protect the territory of diplomats, although the expulsion of the Russian diplomats from the United States over Russia's alleged meddling in the US's general elections suggests the contrary. One could say that border control remains a prerogative of States and can only be set aside by agreement.

2.7 Scope of State territory

Traditionally, State territory refers to land, territorial sea and airspace. Some decades ago, cyberspace was added to the list. Chapter 4 evaluates cyberspace in much detail, but this section focuses on land, territorial sea and airspace.

2.7.1 Land

The definition of land is settled at law.[174] Land includes subsoil, sea coast, internal waters, reefs and bays.[175] The internal waters refer not only to "waters on the landward side of the baseline of the territorial sea..."[176] but also lakes, rivers and similar substances landlocked within the boundaries of a State up to territorial sea.[177] It also includes the navigable inter-States waterways created

---

171 *The Prosecutor v Omar Hassan Ahmad Al Bashir* (ICC-02/05–01/09) (4 March 2009).

172 Manisuli Ssenyonjo, "The International Criminal Court Arrest Warrant Decision for President Al Bashir of Sudan" (2010) 59(1) *International and Comparative Law Quarterly* 205–225; Samar El-Masri, "The legality of the International Criminal Court's decision against Omar Al-Bashir of Sudan" (2011) 66(2) *International Journal* 371–390.

173 Dire Tladi, "The Duty on South Africa to Arrest and Surrender President Al-Bashir under South African and International Law" (2015) 13(5) *Journal of International Criminal Justice* 1027–1047.

174 *Mott v Palmer* 1 N Y (1848) 564, 569; Nicola Jackson, John Stevens and Robert Pearce, *Land Law*, Fourth Edition (London, Sweet and Maxwell, 2008) 11–12; K. J. Gray and P.D. Symes, *Real Property and Real People: Principles of Land Law* (London, Butterworths, 1981) 50–51.

175 Jennings and Watts (n 20), 572; Ian Brownlie, *International Law and the Use of Force by States* (New York, Oxford University Press, 1963) 203.

176 United Nations, *Convention on the Law of the Sea* (concluded at Montego Bay on 10 December 1982, entered into force on 16 November 1994) 1833 UNTS 397, art. 8, [hereinafter *UNCLOS*].

177 Jennings and Watts (n 20), 574; *UNCLOS* (n 176), art. 9; cf *Convention on the Law of the Non-Navigational Uses of International Watercourse* (concluded at New York on 21 May 1997, entered into force on 17 August 2014), art. 8, available at <https://treaties.un.org/doc/Publication/UNTS/No%20Volume/

28 Setting out the theoretical framework

by treaty[178] except for the "Danube and its mouth" created by the Treaty of Paris in 1856[179] and the Peace Treaties that transformed some rivers in Europe to free international waterways.[180] Equally included are canals, reefs, bays and straits[181] or any fixture, chattel or object stably erected on the land. A State's dominion over land extends to space above its land (including the airspace) and the strata beneath.[182]

2.7.2 Territorial Sea

"Territorial Sea" is used here in a generic sense to refer to maritime zones under States' control. The *Convention on the Law of the Sea* distinguishes four zones as follows: Territorial Sea,[183] Contiguous Zone,[184] Continental Shelf[185] and Exclusive

52106/Part/I-52106-0800000280025697.pdf> accessed 22 August 2017 (these waters do not fall within the definition of internal waters).

178 Jennings and Watts (n 20), 575.

179 *General Treaty of Peace between Great Britain, Austria, France, Prussia, Russia, Sardinia, and Turkey* (1856), art. 15, reproduced in Edward Hertslet, *The Map of Europe by Treaty: Showing the Various Political and Territorial Changes Which Have Taken Place since the General Peace of 1814; With Numerous Maps and Notes*, Volume 2 (London, Butterworths, 1875) 1257.

180 *The Treaty of Peace with Germany* (Signed at Versailles on 28 June 1919, entered into force on 10 January 1920) (1919) 13(3) *American Journal of International Law Supplement* 151, arts 331–337; *Convention and Statute on Freedom of Transit* (Concluded at Barcelona on 20 April 1921, entered into force on 31 October 1922) 7 LNTS 11, art. 2; United Nations, *Convention on the Protection and Use of Transboundary Watercourses and International Lakes* (Done at Helsinki on 17 March 1992, entered into force on 6 October 1996) 1936 UNTS 269, art. 14; *Final Act of the Congress of Vienna* (1815) reproduced in Hertslet *supra* n 179, Volume 1 (London, Butterworths, 1875) 269–270, arts 108–109; *Case Relating to the Territorial Jurisdiction of the International Commission of the River Order*, Judgment PCIJ Series A, No. 23 (1929) 26–27. In some cases, conditions were attached, see Jan H. W. Verzijl, *International Law in Historical Perspective*, Volume 3 (Leyden, A.W. Sijthoff, 1970) 122–25.

181 Jennings and Watts (n 20), 591–598, 626–660; Clive Parry (ed.), *A British Digest of International Law: Compiled Principally from the Archives of the Foreign Office*, Volume 2b (London, Stevens and Sons, 1967) 321–338.

182 Ben McFarlane *et al.*, *Land Law: Text, Cases and Materials*, Second Edition (Oxford, Oxford University Press, 2012) 42.

183 The territorial sea is a belt of the sea of 12 nautical miles in breadth adjacent to the territory of a coastal State, including land territory and internal waters and, in the case of an archipelagic State, its archipelagic waters. See *UNCLOS* (n 176), art. 3.

184 The contiguous zone is an area extending up to 24 nautical miles from the territorial sea baseline. See *UNCLOS* (n 176), art. 33(2); *Convention on the Territorial Sea and the Contiguous Zone* (Concluded at Geneva on 29 April 1958, entered into force on 10 September 1964) 516 UNTS 206, art. 24(1b) [hereinafter *Convention on the Territorial Sea*].

185 The Continental Shelf comprises the seabed and subsoil of the submarine areas that extend beyond the territorial sea to a distance of up to 350 nautical miles where the natural prolongation of the land territory extends up to or beyond that distance, or to 200 nautical miles where the natural prolongation of the land territory does not extend to that distance. See *UNCLOS* (n 176), art. 76; *Convention on the Continental*

Setting out the theoretical framework 29

Economic Zones (EEZ).[186] We refer to all as territorial sea because our thesis is that States have exclusive authority over them. Beyond these zones is designated "Area" or the "High Seas" not subject to States' jurisdiction.[187] How States exercise limited sovereignty over the High Seas is beyond our scope.[188]

Whether a State could extend its jurisdiction over the High Seas has been tested in the *Fisheries Jurisdiction* case.[189] Based on its laws, the *Coastal Fisheries Protection Act*[190] as amended,[191] Canada seized a Spanish fishing vessel on the High Seas. The international community condemns it as contrary to best practice.[192] The ICJ has identified four elements to be considered when deciding territorial sea disputes as follows: "the relevant coasts and baselines ... any pre-existing agreement relating to the delimitation of the maritime areas, delimiting the territorial sea (where requested) by applying the equidistance special circumstances rule, delimiting the continental shelf/EEZ applying the equitable principle – relevant circumstance rule."[193]

In most territorial sea disputes, the maxim that land dominates the sea applies.[194] If the Continental Shelf is adjacent to the territories of two or more States whose coasts are opposite each other, a special agreement is negotiated on an *ad hoc* basis.[195] Some authors contend that territorial sea disputes are about control of resources and not jurisdictional.[196] A case in point is Article 2 of the

Shelf (Done at Geneva on 29 April 1958, entered into force on 10 June 1964) 499 UNTS 311, art. 1 [hereinafter *Convention on the Continental Shelf*].

186 The Exclusive Economic Zone (EEZ) is an area beyond and adjacent to the territorial sea but may not extend beyond 200 nautical miles from the territorial sea baselines. See *UNCLOS* (n 176), art. 57. However, it has been suggested that EEZ does not fall within the territory of a state. UNCLOS Article 56 specifies the rights, jurisdiction and duties of the coastal state in the EEZ while Article 58 sets out the rights and duties of other States in the EEZ.

187 *UNCLOS* (n 176), arts 1, 89.

188 For details see Efthymios Papastavridis, *The Interception of Vessels on the High Seas: Contemporary Challenges to the Legal Order of the Oceans* (Oxford and Portland, Hart Publishing, 2013).

189 *Fisheries Jurisdiction* (Spain v Canada) (Jurisdiction of the Court) Judgment ICJ Reports (1998) p. 432 [hereinafter *Spain v Canada Fisheries Jurisdiction* case].

190 Canada, *Coastal Fisheries Protection Act* (R.S.C., 1985, c. C-33), section 3, available at <http://laws-lois.justice.gc.ca/eng/acts/C-33/> accessed 20 April 2017.

191 Canada, "Coastal Fisheries Protection Act as Amended in 1994" (Received Royal Assent on 12 May 1994) (1994) 33(5) *International Legal Materials* 1383–1388, sections 3 and 4.

192 *Spain v Canada Fisheries Jurisdiction* case (n 189), para. 20; Dino Kritsiotis, "When States Use Armed Force" in Christian Reus-Smit (ed.), *The Politics of International Law* (Cambridge, Cambridge University Press, 2004) 69.

193 Jiuyong SHI, "Maritime Delimitation in the Jurisprudence of the International Court of Justice" (2010) 9(2) *Chinese Journal of International Law* 271–291, 274; R. R. Churchill and A. V. Lowe, *The Law of the Sea*, Third Edition (Manchester, Manchester University Press, 1999) 182–183.

194 *Convention on the Continental Shelf* (n 185), arts 6(1) and 6(2); *Convention on the Territorial Sea* (n 184), art. 12(1).

195 *North Sea Continental Shelf* cases (n 23), para. 83.

196 Hersch Lauterpacht, "Sovereignty over Submarine Areas" (1950) 27 *British Yearbook of International Law* 376–433, 387.

30 *Setting out the theoretical framework*

treaty between the United Kingdom and Venezuela which makes sovereignty over some maritime regions hypothetical,[197] contrary to the existing law on the Continental Shelf that requires such frontiers be delimited.[198]

However, States have territorial rights which include: (1) "claims relating to control over access, (2) claims to apply authority to vessels belonging to other States, and (3) claims to prescribe policy for events in the territorial sea."[199] Others include (4) "claims to prescribe and apply policy to events aboard vessels, and (5) claims to an exclusive appropriation of resources."[200] These rights are broad and exclusive. It gives States sovereignty as well as jurisdiction over their territorial sea except for the "shared right" in the EEZ and the Continental Shelf. The exclusive right of a State to a maritime environment is customary[201] and can only be restricted by the right of innocent passage.[202] Nonetheless, Lauterpacht argues that such limitations are compatible with restrictions imposed by customary international law or undertaken by treaty.[203]

2.7.3 Airspace

Paul Fauchille's book *Le Domaine Aerien et Regime Juridique des Aerostats* promotes the "freedom of air" without abrogating the "right of self-defence of the territorial State."[204] In 1906, the International Law Institute adopted a resolution which provides as follows: "[t]he air is free. States have over it, in times of peace or war, just the rights necessary to their own protection."[205] According to Fauchille, "300 m of altitude" falls within a State territorial sovereignty; beyond which and up to 1, 500 m should be designated "intermediary zone" where a State could restrict flights to safeguard its national security.[206] Fauchille's thesis was flouted during the First World War. Consequently, authors like A. Vereschaguin postulate that States have exclusive right over their airspace.[207] At the time, the

---

197 *Treaty between Great Britain and Northern Ireland and Venezuela Relating to the Submarine Areas of the Gulf of Paria* (Done at Caracas on 26 February 1942, entered into force on 22 September 1942) 205 LNTS 121, art. 2.
198 Lauterpacht (n 196), 380; See also *In the Matter of the Bay of Bengal Maritime Boundary Arbitration Between the People's Republic of Bangladesh and the Republic of India*, Award PCA (The Hague, 7 July 2014) 156, para. 507; *UNCLOS* (n 176), arts 56, 58, 78 and 79.
199 McDougal and Burke (n 154), 33 (numbering not in the original).
200 ibid.
201 SHI (n 193), 275.
202 *UNCLOS* (n 176), arts 17–21.
203 Lauterpacht (n 196), 391. Note that a State can contract out its territorial right in lieu of other interests such as security through multilateral or bilateral treaties. See Elizabeth Samson, "Is Gaza Occupied: Redefining the Status of Gaza Under International Law" (2010) 25(5) *American University International Law Review* 915–968, 936–938.
204 Olavo de Oliviera Bittencourt Neto, *Defining the Limits of Outer Space for Regulatory Purposes* (Cham, Springer, 2015) 9.
205 ibid., 10.
206 ibid.
207 A. Vereschaguin, "Derecho Aéreo Internacional" in G. I. Tunkin, *Curso de Derecho Internacional: Manual* (Moscow, Russia: Progresso, 1979) 71; Neto (n 204), 10–11.

Setting out the theoretical framework 31

debate centred around the distinction between "air" common to all and "airspace" subject to States' sovereignty. In 1916, "the First Pan-American Aeronautical Conference held in Santiago, Chile ... defended categorically that State had sovereign rights over their respective air spaces."[208] Another conference held in 1919 shortly before the end of the First World War echoed the same sentiment. The tempo was sustained with treaties and writings of scholars like John Westlake.

The 1944 Convention on International Civil Aviation[209] (Chicago Convention) provides in Article 1: "the contracting States recognize that every State has complete and exclusive sovereignty over the airspace above its territory."[210] It is a breach of international law to fly over the airspace of another State without authorisation. Flagrant violation of this law has caused air mishaps in the past[211] until Lissitzyn suggested that the use of force against civil aircraft should be prohibited.[212] The International Civil Aviation Organisation[213] (ICAO) prohibits violation of civil aircraft in its *Standards, Practices and Procedures for the Rules of the Air*. In 1984, the ICAO adopted an amendment (Article 3*bis*) to the Chicago Convention[214] which authorises States to order intruding aircraft to land at a designated airport for proper checks.

The Chicago Convention does not set limits upon which States could exercise sovereignty in the airspace. It seems to have adopted the principle *cuius est solum, eius est usque ad coelum et ad inferos* ("for whoever owns the soil, it is theirs up to Heaven and down to Hell"). This maxim is no longer defensible[215] because the UN General Assembly's Resolution 2222 (XXI) designates the "outer space" as *res communis*.[216] Initially, the limit set by the international community was the lowest height of satellites placed in the

---

208 Neto (n 204), 11.
209 *Convention on International Civil Aviation* (Done at Chicago on 7 December 1944, entered into force on 4 April 1947) 15 UNTS 295 [hereinafter *Chicago Convention*].
210 ibid., art. 1.
211 Peter Malanczuk, *Akehurst's Modern Introduction to International Law*, Seventh Revised Edition (London and New York, Routledge, 1997) 198–99.
212 Oliver J. Lissitzyn, "The Treatment of Aerial Intruders in Recent Practice and International Law" (1953) 47(4) *American Journal of International Law* 559–589, 586.
213 International Civil Aviation Organisation, "Rules of the Air" (1983) 22 *International Legal Materials* 1154–1189, 1187; International Humanitarian Law Research Initiative, *Commentary on the HPCR Manual on International Law Applicable to Air and Missile Warfare* (Cambridge, Cambridge University Press, 2013) 146.
214 *Protocol Relating to an Amendment to the Convention on International Civil Aviation* (Signed at Montreal on 10 May 1984, entered into force on 1 October 1998) 2122 UNTS 337, art. 3*bis.*
215 Clement L. Bouve, "Private Ownership of Airspace" (1930) 1(2) *Air Law Review* 232–258, 246–248.
216 *Treaty on Principles Governing the Activities of States in the Exploration and Use of Outer Space, Including the Moon and Other Celestial Bodies* (Opened for signature at Moscow, London and Washington on 27 January 1966, entered into force on 10 October 1967) 610 UNTS 205, art. 2.

32   Setting out the theoretical framework

orbit.[217] The discoveries by the Committee on Space Research led to the adoption of 100 km as the lower boundary of the outer space.[218]

Unlike the "right of innocent passage," there is no consensus among States on whether the right of innocent overflight is permitted.[219] A report submitted by the Legal, Commercial and Financial Sub-commission to the Aeronautical Commission did not recommend it[220] although it was codified in Article 2 of the *Paris Convention* 1919,[221] Article 2 of the *Madrid Convention* 1926[222] and Article 4 of the *Havana Convention* 1928.[223] These provisions, in the opinion of the International Law Commission (ILC), do not evidence a custom.[224] Yet there is a tension between the "right of transit passage" in Article 38 of the UNCLOS and Article 39 which imposes duties upon vessels on transit not to violate the territorial sovereignty of a State.

The text of Article 1 of the three regional conventions is similar[225] to Article 1 of the *Chicago Convention*.[226] They emphasise that States have *complete and*

---

217 Bin Cheng, "The Legal Status of Outer Space and Relevant Issues: Delimitation of Outer Space and Definition of Peaceful Use" (1983) 11(1&2) *Journal of Space Law* 89–105, 92–94; Paul G. Dembling and Daniel M. Arons, "The Evolution of the Outer Space Treaty" (1967) 33(3) *Journal of Air Law and Commerce* 419–446, 432–436; D. Goedhuis, "Reflections on the Evolution of Space Law" (1966) 13(2) *Netherlands International Law Review* 109–149, 127.

218 He Qizhi, "The Problem of Definition and Delimitation of Outer Space" (1982) 10 (2) *Journal of Space Law* 157–164, 162; Cheng (n 217), 94; Stephen Hobe argues that "space activities" at an altitude of 100 km above sea level is in line with current international space law and state practice. See Committee on the Peaceful Uses of Outer Space, "Draft Model Law on National Space Legislation and Explanatory Notes" UN Doc. A/AC.105/C.2/2013/CRP.6 (26 March 2013) 4.

219 John Cobb Cooper, "The International Air Navigation Conference, Paris 1910" (1952) 19(2) *Journal of Air Law and Commerce* 127–143, 128; Marjorie M. Whiteman, *Digest of International Law*, Volume 4 (Washington D.C., Department of States, 1965) 460.

220 E. Pepin, *The Law of the Air and the Draft Articles Concerning the Law of the Sea* (Adopted by the International Law Commission at its eighth session) UN Doc. A/CONF.13/4 (4 October 1957) 64, see footnote 1 [hereinafter *ILC Report on Air*]; For further discussion see Stephen Latchford, "Freedom of the Air – Early Theories, Freedom, Zone, Sovereignty" (1948) 1(5) *Documents & State Papers* 303–322.

221 *Convention Relating to the Regulation of Aerial Navigation* (Signed at Paris on 13 October 1919, entered into force on 29 March 1922) 11 UNTS 173, art. 2.

222 The Spanish text of the *Convenio Ibero-Americano de Navegacion Aerea* 1926 is available at <www.sct.gob.mx/fileadmin/_migrated/content_uploads/3_Decreto_por_el_cual_se_promulga_el_Convenio_Iberoamericano.pdf> accessed 23 July 2019. Note that the *Madrid Convention* was not registered with any international body and was overlooked during the drafting of the Chicago Convention. For detail, visit <www.icao.int/secretaria t/PostalHistory/1926_the_Ibero_american_convention.htm> accessed 23 July 2019.

223 *Pan-American Convention on Commercial Aviation* (Signed at Havana on 20 February 1928) (1931) 1(1) *Revue Aeronautique Internationale* 77–82; *UNCLOS* (n 176), arts 17–22.

224 *ILC Report on Air* (n 220), 67.

225 ibid., 64–65.

226 *Chicago Convention* (n 209), art. 1.

exclusive sovereignty over their airspace. The ILC has explained that the phrase "complete and exclusive" means that the inviolability of the airspace is a customary rule of international law.[227] Perhaps, the ILC arrives at this conclusion having considered the *travaux preparatoires* of the *Chicago Convention* which did not permit innocent overflight.[228] Therefore, States could not justify trespassing the airspace of other States, except for defence of *force majeure*. Innocent overflight is permissible through agreements.[229]

2.7.4 Cyber-territory

The term "cyber-territory" seems ambiguous for some reasons. First, it is intangible. Second, how to exercise sovereignty in cyberspace is vague. Third, it is difficult to apply international law in cyberspace. However, cyberspace has become the mainstay of States' activities. Chapter 4 will examine that in much detail to buttress the inadequacy of maintaining the restrictive approach to Article 2, paragraph 4, of the Charter of the United Nations.

2.8 State territory – power-play in history

This section examines the power-play that paved the way for the evolution of State territory. The aim is to assess the impact of conquest in the evolution of delimitation of territory as the basis for inter-State relations.

2.8.1 Ancient world

By the ancient world, we intend to examine Ancient Greece and the Roman world. It is not meant to be exhaustive but a snapshot of the evolutionary trend; focusing attention on conquests that marked this period.

2.8.1.1 Ancient Greece

Our point of reference date back to the Bronze Age (around 3, 000–1,000 BC), early Iron Age (around 1,200–800 BC), the Archaic Age (around 776 BC) until the Later Ages (around 600 BC). Again, we shall not engage in a sequence of events on the evolution of State territory for none exists. We

---

227 *ILC Report on Air* (n 220), 65.
228 The provisions made in Part I and Article 68 in Part III of the Chicago Convention imply that the subjacent State enjoys complete and exclusive sovereignty. See *Chicago Convention* (n 209), arts 1–10 and 68.
229 *Peace Treaty Between Israel and Egypt* (Signed at Washington on 26 March 1979, entered into force on 25 April 1979) 1136 UNTS 115, Annex 1, art. 3; Dore Gold, "Legal Acrobatics: The Palestinian Claim that Gaza is Still 'Occupied' Even After Israel Withdraws" (2005) 5(3) *Jerusalem Issue Brief*, available at <http://jcpa.org/brief/brief005-3.htm> accessed 9 December 2019.

34   Setting out the theoretical framework

highlight the prevailing war of conquest[230] portrayed by virtually "all political theorists of classical Greece."[231]

The peak of the Bronze Age, that is, the Mycenaean era (roughly 1200–800 BC) was characterised by *palatial* societies. The *wanax* ("king") was sovereign and co-ordinated the social, economic, defence and political activities of versed agrarian city-States. More so, the palace was an industrial hub that produced bronze and manufactured weaponry.[232] Since *wanax* defended city-States from external invasion, the proprietary right primarily vested on him; second on *demos* (community); and lastly on individuals by way of compensation for their military services.[233] The Dorians were a dominant force in the Mycenaean era (late Bronze Age) because of their proficiency in the use of iron weaponry. The time frame is uncertain; some authors date it around the seventh to fifth centuries BC,[234] but archaeological findings indicate 1400 to 1000 BC.[235]

Ancient Greece's political history was characterised by conquest.[236] Tyrtaios depicted "the invasion and conquest of the Peloponnese by Herakleidai and Dorians" as follows:

> *Zeus gave the sons of Herakles this state* (polis).
> *Under their lead we left windswept Erineos*
> *and came to Pelops' broad sea-circled land.*[237]

The poem talks about Zeus bequeathing sons of Herakles a State; reminiscent of nationalist theory of State territory, but of divine origin. But they expanded to "Pelops' broad see-circled land." Conquest led to the fragmentation of political communities. Political communities "developed into independent city-states, most of them small in terms of their population and their territory."[238] For instance, the territory of the island city-State of Belbina was estimated at 8 s.km.[239] From the Archaic Age going forward, land grab, drive for territorial expansion, trade contacts and conquest were the mainstays of inter-polis politics in Greece.[240]

---

230 David M. Pritchard, "Public Finance and War in Ancient Greece" (2015) 62(1) *Greece & Rome* 48–59, 49.
231 Athanasios Samaras, "Aristotle's Best City in the Context of His Concept of *Aretē*" (2019) 36(1) *Polis, The Journal for Ancient Greek and Roman Political Thought* 139–152, 147.
232 Nicholas Kyriazis and Xenophon Paparrigopoulos, "War and Democracy in Ancient Greece" (2014) 38(1) *European Journal of Law and Economics* 163–183, 165.
233 Ibid., 165.
234 Jan Paul Crielaard, "The Ionians in the Archaic Period: Shifting Identities in a Changing World" in Ton Derks and Nico Roymans (eds), *Ethnic Constructs in Antiquity* (Amsterdam, Amsterdam University Press, 2009) 47–48.
235 C. Schuchhardt, "Art. V.- 1. Schliemann's Excavations: An Archaeological and Historical Study" (1892) 175(360) *The Edinburgh Review* 399–434, 410–411.
236 J. Murray, "Art. V.-1. The Mycenaean Age" (1898) 188(375) *The Quarterly Review* 90–112, 98.
237 Crielaard (n 234), 47-48.
238 Kyriazis and Paparrigopoulos (n 232), 167.
239 ibid.
240 ibid.

Setting out the theoretical framework 35

Polis means city-State. In dark ages, it could mean "a stronghold with or without a small hill-top settlement." In the classical era, "a political community of citizens, living in an urban centre and its hinterland, and united in governing the population of the territory through a number of developed political institutions."[241] The political institutions were based on kinship and tribal affiliations constantly besieged by crashes of various forms of government. Interestingly, "when the principal meaning is country ... *polis* almost invariably has the connotation 'territory,' and denotes the territory of a *polis* in the political sense."[242] On average, *polis* refers to territory, population and government. These connotations are reflected in Aristotle's definition as follows: "a partnership (*koinonia*) of citizens (*politai*) in a constitution (*politeia*)."[243]

According to Aristotle, State is the bonding of various communities.[244] The quest for dominance, power and supremacy as depicted in Homer's famous poem, *Iliad*[245] has always interrupted fledgling territorial sovereignty[246] within the *polis* and, indeed, most communities in the Ancient Near East were engulfed in endemic civil wars, often caused by territorial conquest or scramble for scarce material resources.[247] In fact, "by the death of Cyrus in 530 most of the Near East had passed under Persian control through a rapid series of conquests. Under Cyrus' son Cambyses Egypt and parts of Libya including the Greek city of Cyrene were subjugated."[248]

Why was it so? Aristotle posits that conflicts start when the powerful impose their will and rules upon the weaker.[249]

2.8.1.2 Roman antiquity

Italy came to history's limelight around 700 BC, populated by peoples from various cultures who spoke various languages. Settlers traded with the native Italians, whose primary occupation was agriculture (especially animal husbandry); hence, *Italia* means "calf land."[250]

The Ancient city of Rome was "a small town on the Tiber River in central Italy."[251] It "engaged in an eternal, and ever-obstinate war"[252] with its neighbours. Conquest was a means to greatness and some Roman kings disregarded the peace agreement concluded

---

241 Mogens Herman Hansen, *Polis and City-State: An Ancient Concept and its Modern Equivalent* (Munksgaard, Copenhagen, 1998) 10.
242 ibid., 52.
243 Barnes (n 89), section 1276[b]1 at p. 4347; Hansen (n 241), 53.
244 Barnes (n 89), section 1252[b]1 at p. 4268.
245 Michael M. Sage, *Warfare in Ancient Greece* (London, Routledge, 1996) 1–2, 81.
246 Hinsley 1986 (n 136), 28; Hansen (n 241), 67.
247 Barnes (n 89), section 1291[a]1 at p. 4397.
248 Sage (n 245), 81.
249 Barnes (n 89), section 1255[a]1 at pp. 4275–4276.
250 Ramsay MacMullen, "Ancient Rome" in *Encyclopaedia Britannica*, available at <https://academic-eb-com.kuleuven.ezproxy.kuleuven.be/levels/collegiate/article/ancient-Rome/106272> accessed 5 August 2019.
251 ibid.
252 Baron de Montesquieu, *Reflections on the Causes of the Rise and Fall of the Roman Empire*, Fourth Edition (Glasgow, Robert Urie, 1758) 30.

36 *Setting out the theoretical framework*

by their predecessors. During this period, the city of Rome was not well planned or organised like the Greece's *polis* in terms of political structure. Its earliest recorded social, political and military institutions were accredited to king Romulus; from whose reign going forward (753–509 BC), Rome expanded both in the size of the population and landmass.[253] Rome rose steadily from a small town on the Tiber River to an enviable empire through conquering "countries bordering the Mediterranean from Spain to Egypt" over three centuries.[254] When Rome became a *Republic*, the centuriated assembly mandated to decide issues relating to war and peace voted for war as a means to enrich themselves. In most cases, the insatiable appetite for land and dominance was the cause and wars authorised by *fetial* priests were considered just because such wars were adjudged sanctioned by Roman gods.

2.8.2 Medieval world

History is a continuum. The medieval period is not separate from the ancient world; neither is the present divorced from the past except that each epoch is distinguishable by specific events. Most authors accept that "Middle Ages" falls within the decline of the Western Roman Empire up until the discoveries of the New World. Others prefer a time frame dating back from 1150 to 1650 BC.[255] Therefore, to think of the "Medieval Ages" only in terms of the collapse of the Western Roman Empire is misleading because the Eastern wing had continued for yet another millennium.

The Medieval period can also be described in terms of the influence which religion had on politics. Then, Christianity played a significant role in political matters and the marriage between Church and State led to unhealthy tension between both. Christianity was blamed for Alaric and the Goths' conquest of Rome which happened in August 410. In defence, St. Augustine wrote his book on two cities. "He contrasts the two *civitates* – the *civitas* of God and the *civitas* of the Devil."[256] His choice of word, "city," was ambivalent and facilitated the ideological dualism between Church and State. Scholastics and Popes found his thoughts ideal to promote papal supremacy in temporal affairs. Pope Gregory VII had argued that to "the Pope, as God's Vicar, all mankind is subject, and all rulers responsible."[257] Popes had powers to depose or excommunicate secular leaders. The medieval canonists referred to *status generalis ecclesiae* as "the papal power to legislate and to dispense."[258] The assumption is that the sacred sphere is superior to the secular sphere. The consequence was that Pope ceded territories of *infidels*[259] to Christian kings. Against this backdrop,

---

253 ibid., 25–26.
254 Martin Goodman, *The Roman World 44 BC–AD 180* (London, Routledge, 1997) 8.
255 Elden 2013 (n 13), 99.
256 Norman H. Baynes, *The Political Ideas of St. Augustine's De Civitate Dei* (London, G. Bell and Sons, 1936) 5.
257 James Bryce, *The Holy Roman Empire* (London, Macmillan, 1901) 160.
258 John H. Hackett, "State of the Church: A Concept of the Medieval Canonists" (1963) 23(3) *The Jurist* 259–290, 259.
259 Pope Adrian IV authorised Henry II to conquer Ireland. For the text see "The Bull of Pope Adrian IV empowering Henry II to conquer Ireland A.D. 1155," available at

Setting out the theoretical framework 37

one appreciates that the clause, *cuius regio, eius religio* in the Peace of Augsburg was to safeguard territories of kings from external interferences. Within this context the Peace of Westphalia was concluded to grant political autonomy to Princes.

2.8.3 Modern world

From the viewpoint of public international law, Hugo Grotius, a widely acclaimed founder,[260] is a reference. As seen, the pre-modern societies concentrated political authority on Monarchs, Popes and Roman Emperors with a hierarchical decentralised power structure shared by Kings, Princes, Nobility, Bishops and Abbots.[261]

The practice of establishing international boundaries was shaped in the eighteenth century as "a basic rule of co-existence."[262] It became a standard for international relations in the first quarter of the nineteenth century. By the mid-nineteenth century, nationalism became too strong that annexation without the consent of the inhabitants was abrogated.[263] However, the sentiment around nationalism was high and destabilising. This is evident from wars of unification of the Germans and the Italians or the partitioning of the Ottoman empires into nation-States.[264] Between 1849 and 1914, industrialised societies had emerged with new forms of States based on diplomatic and military alliances.[265] Although independence was emphasised, the need for alliances was imperative.

<http://avalon.law.yale.edu/medieval/bullad.asp> accessed 17 August 2019. Pope Nicholas V issued *Dum Diversas* on 18 June 1452 which authorised Alfonso V of Portugal to reduce any Saracens and pagans and any other unbelievers to perpetual slavery. *Romanus Pontifex* was a follow-up on that, issued on 5 January 1455. It authorised the same Emperor to seize non-Christian lands and to enslave non-Christian peoples in Africa and the New World. In 1493 Alexander VI issued *Inter Caetera*, which prohibited a Christian nation from establishing dominion over lands previously dominated by another Christian nation but did not outlaw conquest. For the English translation of this text, visit <www.papalencyclicals.net/Nichol05/> accessed 17 August 2019.

260 Another school held that Francisco de Vitoria is the founder. See Anthony Pagden, "Introduction: Francisco de Vitoria and the Origins of the Modern Global Order" in Jose Maria Beneyto and Justo Corti Varela (eds), *At the Origins of Modernity: Francisco de Vitoria and the Discovery of International Law* (Cham, Springer, 2017) 2.

261 Charles Tilly, "Reflections on the History of European State-making" in Charles Tilly (ed.), *The Formation of National States in Western Europe* (Princeton, Princeton University Press, 1975) 21; Roland Axtmann, "The State of the State: The Model of the Modern State and its Contemporary Transformation" (2004) 25(3) *International Political Science Review* 259–279, 259.

262 Hedley Bull, *The Anarchical Society: A Study of Order in World Politics*, Fourth Edition (New York, Palgrave Macmillan, 2012) 35.

263 Sharon Korman, *The Right of Conquest: The Acquisition of Territory by Force in International Law and Practice* (Oxford, Clarendon Press, 1996) 93.

264 Mark W. Zacher, "The Territorial Integrity Norm: International Boundaries and the Use of Force" (2001) 55(2) *International Organization* 215–250, 218; Alfred Cobban, *The Nation State and National Self-Determination*, Revised Edition (London, Collins, 1969) 28.

265 William Woodruff, *A Concise History of the Modern World*, Fourth Edition (New York, Palgrave Macmillan, 2002) 136.

38 *Setting out the theoretical framework*

In the Americas, President Monroe's Seventh Annual Message to the Congress[266] declared that the United States would no longer recognise territorial acquisition of States in the Western Hemisphere. It did, however, pledge not to interfere with colonies or dependencies under the control of European powers.[267] Therefore, Monroe's Doctrine did not enhance the process of decolonisation because countries of Asia and Africa were *terra nullius,* technically.[268] However, it awakened the consciousness latent in the Peace of Westphalia such that treaties concluded in Europe during this time designated States' territory as inviolable.

2.9 Search for world peace and rethinking of State territory

The historical trappings discussed above add relevance to this work but the contexts to be mindful of are the two world wars. The preamble of the UN Charter seeks "to save succeeding generations from the scourge of war, which twice in our lifetime has brought untold sorrow to mankind."[269] Therefore, the understanding of State in the international arena should be guided by the norm and spirit of the UN Charter.

2.9.1 *Peace of Westphalia*

The view that the Peace of Westphalia implies exclusivity is premised on the suffix *torium* which denotes "belonging to."[270] When *torium* is suffixed to *terra* it reads *territorium.* The idea of "belonging to" should be interpreted as political governance and not proprietary right insofar as feudalism was a legitimate mode of acquisition of title. Gottmann describes territory as jurisdiction within which States exercise sovereignty.[271] Elden disagrees.[272]

The Peace of Westphalia comprises two peace treaties signed at Munster and Osnabruck in 1648 to end the Thirty Years' War in Europe.[273] The former was between the Roman Empire and France and their respective confederates and allies while the latter was between the Roman Empire and

---

266 James Monroe, "Seventh Annual Message to the US Congress" (2 December 1823), paras 61–62, available at <www.presidency.ucsb.edu/ws/index.php?pid=29465&st=&st1=> accessed 20 August 2019.

267 ibid., para. 61.

268 Woodruff (n 265), 44; *General Act of the Conference of Berlin Concerning the Congo* (1909) 3(1) *American Journal of International Law* Supplement 7–25, art. 10 (it declares certain parts of the territories in Africa neutral for free trade).

269 *UN Charter* (n 3), preamble para. 1.

270 Jean Gottmann, *The Significance of Territory* (Charlottesville, University Press of Virginia, 1973) 16.

271 ibid., 2.

272 Stuart Elden, "The Significance of Territory" (2013) 68(1) *Geographica Helvetica* 65–68, 66.

273 Nicholas Lanza, "The Thirty Years War" (2014) 1(1) *Histories* 43–51, 44; J. V. Polišenský, "The Thirty Years War" (1954) 6 *Past and Present* 31–43, 32.

Setting out the theoretical framework 39

Sweden. Both treaties affected the way authority was exercised over territory ever after. However, the primary constituent of these documents was to promote equality and religious tolerance between Protestants and Catholics.[274] As discussed in Section 2.8.2, Christianity was a dominant force in the Middle Ages such that the provisions of Articles 64 and 65 of the Treaty of Osnabruck were revolutionary.[275]

Article 64 provides as follows:

> And to prevent for the future any differences arising in the Politick State, all and every one of the Electors, Princes and States of the Roman Empire, are so established and confirmed in their ancient Rights, Prerogatives, Liberties, Privileges, free exercise of Territorial Right, as well Ecclesiastick, as Politick Lordships, Regales, by virtue of this present Transaction: that they never can or ought to be molested therein by any whomsoever upon any manner of pretence.[276]

This provision contains far-reaching rights which include exclusive authority in political and religious matters. Also, it allowed Electors, Princes and States within the Empire free exercise of "territorial right" and expressly prohibited contracting parties from molesting others "upon any manner of pretence." This conveys the impression of the duty to respect others. An objection might be that this provision did not envisage "Modern State" as we have it today. Relying on the work of Machiavelli, *The Prince*, Foucault posits that "… *la souveraineté dans le droit public, du Moyen Age au xvi siecle, ne s'exerce pas sur les choses, elle s'exerce d'abord sur un territoire et, par consequent, sur les sujets qui y habitent.*"[277] Elden disagrees with Foucault's equation of land with territory for lack of clarity.[278] Territory was not an object for governance, but people were.[279] How States acquire sovereignty over inanimate things becomes the issue.

Nonetheless, an English judge, Henry de Bracton once said, "*parem autem non habet rex in regno suo*"[280] to underscore the supremacy of the King within his realm. Hence, Article 65 of the Peace of Westphalia safeguards the "right of suffrage" for the heads of the political unit within the Empire. It is similar to the voting arrangement in the United Nations General Assembly. Before the Peace of Westphalia came into effect, no such right had existed in the legal

---

274 Leo Gross, "The Peace of Westphalia, 1648–1948" (1948) 42(1) *American Journal of International Law* 20–41, 22.
275 *Treaty of Westphalia* (1648), arts 64 and 65, available at <http://avalon.law.yale.edu/17th_century/westphal.asp> accessed 22 August 2019 [hereinafter *Treaty of Westphalia*].
276 ibid., art. 64.
277 Michel Foucault, *Sécurité, Territoire, Population: Cours au Collège de France (1977–1978)* (Paris, Gallimard/Seuil, 2004) 99.
278 Elden 2013a (n 123), 9.
279 ibid.
280 Henry de Bracton, *De Legibus et Consuetudinibus Angliae*, Volume II (Londini, Typis Milonis Flesher & Roberti Young, 1640) 33. Translated into English by the President and Fellows of Harvard College, available at <http://amesfoundation.law.harvard.edu/Bracton/> accessed 12 August 2019.

40 Setting out the theoretical framework

instrument of early Medieval Europe.[281] The Peace of Westphalia shielded political entities within the Empire from undue influence from the Church and the Roman Empire.[282]

Neither in the Treaty of Munster nor the Treaty of Osnabruck was the phrase "territorial integrity" used. Even the word "sovereignty" did not feature in any of them.[283] Yet Hinsley argues that it can be deduced from it.[284] Consequently, Westphalia inaugurates a world order which encourages respect for States' territory.[285] Earlier, the Treaties of Nuremberg (1532) and the Peace of Augsburg (1555)[286] safeguarded religious and political liberties. For instance, "*cuius regio, eius religio*" allowed Kings and Princes to adopt State religion without external interference. Equally, it enhanced the unification of political units and made each unit subject to no external authority.[287] The Peace of Westphalia is remarkable for separating political sphere from religious sphere as it relates to an external factor. Hence, it accords sovereignty to the "Dutch Republic and the Helvetian Confederation."[288]

That said, the claim that Westphalia is the origin of independent States is disputed. Croxton, for example, argues that the treaties did not refer to the United Provinces' independence or sovereignty.[289] Instead, the Peace of Westphalia referred to independence in a clause that excluded the Burgundian Circle (of which they were a part) from the provisions of the treaty until Spain made peace with France.[290] The conditionality of this clause, Croxton argues, indicates it was a diplomatic ploy to compel France to sue for peace with the Roman Empire since the treaty explicitly recognised that the Circle of Burgundy remained part of the Roman Empire.[291]

Additionally, Croxton has observed that the Peace of Westphalia is loosely drafted[292] such that its purpose is not easily discernible. On the one hand, it manifests the act of sequestration of people (vassals, subjects and people) and

---

281 Sir George Clark, *The Seventeenth Century*, Second Edition (London, Oxford University Press, 1947) 171–207; Alexander B. Murphy, "The Sovereign State System as Political-Territorial Ideal: Historical and Contemporary Considerations" in Thomas J. Biersteker and Cynthia Weber (eds), *State Sovereignty as Social Construct* (Cambridge, Cambridge University Press, 1996) 84.

282 Hinsley 1986 (n 136), 26; Kalevi J. Holsti, *Peace and War: Armed Conflicts and International Order, 1648–1989* (Cambridge, Cambridge University Press, 1991) 39.

283 Croxton 1999 (n 136), 577.

284 Hinsley 1986 (n 136), 26.

285 Derek Croxton, *Westphalia: The Last Christian Peace* (New York, Palgrave Macmillan, 2013) 3; Ronald G. Asch, *The Thirty Years War: The Holy Roman Empire and Europe 1618–1648* (London, Macmillan Press, 1997) 142–49.

286 Croxton 1999 (n 136), 570; F. H. Hinsley, "The Concept of Sovereignty and Relations Between States" in W. J. Stankiewicz (ed.), *In Defense of Sovereignty* (New York, Oxford University Press, 1969) 275–278.

287 Bruce Russett, Harvey Starr and David Kinsella, *World Politics: The Menu for Choice*, Ninth Edition (Boston, Wadsworth, 2010) 57–59.

288 Asch (n 285), 144.

289 ibid.

290 Croxton 1999 (n 136), 577.

291 *Treaty of Westphalia* (n 275), art. 4.

292 Croxton 1999 (n 136), 577–79.

Setting out the theoretical framework 41

territories.[293] In some instances, there were clauses requiring the Empire to transfer part of its territory to France.[294] On the other hand, some clauses seem to preserve rather than break off the Imperial tie.[295] Also to be noticed were clauses aimed at restoring territories to their previous owners.[296] Based on these weaknesses, some political scientists and historians do not think Westphalia envisaged a world order free from interference in the internal affairs of others.[297]

Therefore, the power it accords to kings and princes does not translate to outright abrogation of all forms of interference in any meaningful way. Territorial conquests had continued after the Peace of Westphalia came into force. However, aberration does not nullify the law. The principle of *cuius regio, eius religio* which it promotes, makes the rights of Princes and estates inviolable; albeit the rights so conferred seem *persona* than *territorial*. This explains why it allows the transfer of peoples and territories while vesting exclusive authority upon kings and princes.

The position adopted by France concerning the Peace of Westphalia was that the Thirty Years' War was necessary "to resist the Habsburgs' unlawful absolutism."[298] This could mean that the sanctity of State territory could be compromised in the event of gross human rights violations. On the contrary, Sweden prioritised independence during the negotiations. Therefore, the need to respect a constituted authority was crucial for negotiators seeking to evolve a paradigm for international relations. The negotiators did not dispute this *metanoia* in a way of rethinking territory except that Pope Innocent X considered the outcome as null and void.[299]

2.9.2 League of Nations

Uninviting pacifism might appear to some thinkers, the culture of war or violence has not promoted international peace and security. This line of thought came out eloquently in sessions held by the British diplomats to galvanise support for the League of Nations. In his lecture on 15 October 1919, Lord Eustace Percy traced incessant wars to imprecise territorial boundaries and vague agreements on expropriation of natural resources.[300] One message came out clear – States convert international diplomacy to parochial national interest – hence, the need to

293 *Treaty of Westphalia* (n 275), arts 9, 23, 30, 76 and 92.
294 ibid., arts 80 and 87.
295 Croxton 1999 (n 136), 581.
296 *Treaty of Westphalia* (n 275), arts 15, 18, 32 and 90.
297 Justin Rosenberg, "A Non-Realist Theory of Sovereignty?: Giddens' the Nation-State and Violence" (1990) 19(2) *Journal of International Studies* 249–259, 253.
298 Croxton 1999 (n 136), 583; Asch (n 285), 144–45; Murphy (n 281), 88–89.
299 Derek Croxton and Geoffrey Parker, "A Swift and Sure Peace: The Congress of Westphalia 1643–1648" in Williamson Murray and Jim Lacey (eds), *The Making of Peace: Rulers, States, and the Aftermath of War* (Cambridge, Cambridge University Press, 2009) 73.
300 Lord Eustace Percy, "The League of Nations" (1919) 64 *Journal of the Royal United Service Institution* 92–109.

42   *Setting out the theoretical framework*

establish the League of Nations to check States' excesses. Major C. W. Arnett concludes: "unless we can exclude war altogether, war will wipe out civilization – the next war – and that is the prime reason we must have a league which will prevent nations indulging in war."[301] As if a prophecy, there was yet another war.

In 1823, President James Monroe had pursued a policy of non-expansionism to safeguard fragile independent States.[302] The League of Nations was rightly conceived but failed, which, according to some authors, was due to inadequate implementation of the provisions relating to collective security.[303] We shall examine how Article 10 of the Covenant of the League of Nations attempted to tackle issues relating to State territory. Anghie has evaluated the League from the viewpoint of how the mandate system encouraged self-determination and decolonisation.[304]

Before the League of Nations came on board, Congress system delimited certain fluid borders in Europe to douse inter-States conflicts. The *Final Act of the Congress of Vienna*[305] and its *Protocol*[306] accorded full sovereignty to emerging States like Switzerland and barred Protecting Power from undue interference. In clear terms, the "Act" declares that the Powers acknowledge the "territorial integrity" and "inviolability" of Switzerland. Also, it affirms Switzerland's "independence of all foreign influence."[307] Similarly, Article 7 of the *Congress of Paris* states as follows: "… [t]heir Majesties engage, each on his part, to respect the Independence and the Territorial Integrity of the Ottoman Empire …"[308] The kingdoms in question were the United Kingdom of Great Britain and Ireland, Austria, France, Prussia, Russia and Sardinia. For D'Amato, the *respect clause* aims to prevent permanent loss of territory.[309]

---

301 ibid., 107.
302 T. Miller Maguire, "The War Policy of the United States" (1917) 62 *Journal of the Royal United Service Institution* 260–268.
303 C. G. Fenwick, "The 'Failure' of the League of Nations" (1936) 30(3) *American Journal of International Law* 506–509; Robert Kolb, "The Eternal Problem of Collective Security: From the League of Nations to the United Nations" (2007) 26(4) *Refugee Survey Quarterly* 220–226.
304 Anghie (n 128), 115.
305 *General Treaty Between Great Britain, Austria, France, Portugal, Prussia, Russia, Spain, and Sweden* (Signed at Vienna on 9 June 1815), arts 2, 4, 7 and 39, reproduced in Hertslet *supra* n 179 (Volume 1) 208.
306 *Protocol of Conference between Great Britain, Austria, Prussia, and Russia, Respecting the Territorial Arrangements, and Defensive System of the Germanic Confederation* (Signed at Paris on 20 November 1815), art. 4, reproduced in Hertslet *supra* n 179 (Volume 1) 326.
307 *Act, Signed by the Protecting Powers, Austria, France, Great Britain, Prussia and Russia, for the Acknowledgment and Guarantee of the Perpetual Neutrality of Switzerland, and the Inviolability of its Territory* (Concluded at Paris on 20 November 1815) reproduced in Hertslet *supra* n 179 (Volume 1) 370–371.
308 *General Treaty of Peace Between Great Britain, Austria, France, Prussia, Russia, Sardinia, and Turkey* (Signed at Paris on 30 March 1856) reproduced in Hertslet *supra* n 179, 1254–1255.
309 Anthony D'Amato, *International Law: Process and Prospect*, Second Edition (New York, Transnational Publishers, 1995) 58.

Setting out the theoretical framework   43

2.9.2.1 The Covenant of the League of Nations

Article 10 of the Covenant of the League of Nations obliges the participating States to "respect" and "preserve" "the territorial integrity and existing political independence of all Members of the League."[310] Both words, "respect" and "preserve" were contested as very broad, particularly the positive obligation to preserve the territory of other States.[311]

Although President Wilson had wanted to promote the inviolability of State territory, the involvement of the United States in the First World War facilitated the secession of Austria-Hungary.[312] The League was established to, *inter alia*, punish States that violated the territory of others,[313] but it failed to maintain peace[314] partly due to lack of political will.[315] It has been argued that Article 10 allows violation of States' territory by means short of aggression and equally legitimises aggression as a means of re-establishing territorial claims.[316] Moreover, the League System is not clear about how self-determination aligns with the duty to respect and preserve State territory given that the mandate system envisages changes to the existing international boundaries.

However, Thomas Franck believes that Article 25 of the Covenant of the League of Nations permits intervention insofar as self-determination mitigates human sufferings.[317] On the contrary, the Committee of Jurists in the *Aaland Islands Dispute* held: "the recognition of this principle in a certain number of international treaties cannot be considered as sufficient to put it upon the same footing as a positive rule of the law of Nations."[318] The ICJ in the *Burkina Faso v*

---

310 *The Covenant of the League of Nations* (Adopted at Paris on 29 April 1919, entered into force on 10 January 1920) (1919) 13(2) *American Journal of International Law Supplement* 128–139, art. 10.

311 Leland M. Goodrich and Edvard Hambro, *Charter of the United Nations: Commentary and Documents* (Boston, World Peace Foundation, 1946) 68.

312 Woodrow Wilson, "Address to a Joint Session of Congress on the Conditions of Peace" (8 January 1918), point 10, available at <www.presidency.ucsb.edu/> accessed 20 August 2019 [hereinafter *President Wilson's Fourteen Points*].

313 David Stevenson, *The First World War and International Politics* (Oxford, Clarendon Press, 1991) 244–251.

314 Goodrich and Hambro (n 311), 3–4; see generally, L. Oppenheim, *The League of Nations and its Problems: Three Lectures* (London, Longmans, Green and Co., 1919).

315 David Hunter Miller, *The Drafting of the Covenant* (New York, G. P. Putnams' Sons, 1928) 358.

316 D'Amato (n 309), 63.

317 Thomas M. Franck, *The Power of Legitimacy Among Nations* (New York, Oxford University Press 1990) 154–162.

318 League of Nations, "Report of the International Committee of Jurists Entrusted by the Council of the League of Nations With the Task of Giving an Advisory Opinion Upon the Legal Aspects of the Aaland Islands Question" (1920) 3 *League of Nations Official Journal Supplement* 3–19, 5; Philip Marshall Brown, "Self-Determination in Central Europe" (1920) 14(1) *American Journal of International Law* 235–239. *Cf* League of Nations, "The Aaland Islands Question: Report Submitted to the Council of the League of Nations by the Commission of Rapporteurs" LN Council Doc. B7.21/68/106 (1921) 318 (the Committee of Rapporteurs argues that a State territory could be breached as a last resort).

44 Setting out the theoretical framework

Mali case[319] upheld this. A fair calculus is that the League's scope is broad but defaulted on implementation due to political apathy by world powers. The prize for that negligence is the Second World War.

2.9.3 United Nations

The formation of the United Nations was precipitated by inter-State territory-related conflicts and wars.[320] After the conquest of Manchuria by Japan in 1931, then US Secretary of State, Henry Stimson declared that the United States would no longer recognise the acquisition of territory by force.[321] In 1939, Nazi Germany compelled Poland to cede the Rhineland, the *Anschluss* and the Sudetenland to it.[322] It also invaded the Soviet Union in 1941 barely two years after both parties signed a peace accord. Justifying the need to establish the United Nations, President Roosevelt said, "Aggressors like Hitler and the Japanese war lords organize for years for the day when they can launch their evil strength against weaker nations devoted to their peaceful pursuits."[323] While commenting on the phrase, "sovereign equality ... enshrined in principle number one of the Dumbarton Oaks Proposals," then US Secretary of State said that "it means that every peace-loving state, however small, has the same supreme authority over its own territory as any other state, however large."[324]

The repeated territorial crises between the Anglo-German and Franco-German allies predated the Treaty of Versailles. The United Nations inaugurates a world order that promotes respect of State territory as a benchmark for harmonious co-existence.[325] President Roosevelt thought of establishing a supranational organisation of a three-tier hierarchical structure, consisting of State Parties, the "Executive Committee" and four Great Powers (United States, Britain, USSR and China) to serve as the world "Four Policemen."[326] The current structure of the General Assembly and Security Council (where some States have veto power) was adopted to reduce inequality insofar as reasonably practicable.

The debate on earlier drafts of the UN Charter focused attention on the member States' equality before the law. The Panamanian delegation recommended that the

---

319 *Frontier Dispute* (Burkina Faso/Republic of Mali) Judgment ICJ Reports (1986) p. 554, para. 23.
320 Holsti (n 282), 306–34; John A. Vasquez, *The War Puzzle* (Cambridge, Cambridge University Press, 2009) 136–45; Zacher (n 264), 215–16.
321 Arnold D. McNair, "The Stimson Doctrine of Non-Recognition" (1933) 14 *British Yearbook of International Law* 65–75, 65.
322 John A. Vasquez, "The Causes of the Second War in Europe: A New Scientific Explanation" (1996) 17(2) *International Political Science Review* 161–178, 164.
323 United States Department of State, "Washington Conversations on International Organization" (1944) 11(276) *The Department of State Bulletin* 365.
324 United States Department of State, "What the Dumbarton Oaks Peace Means" (1945) 12(292) *The Department of State Bulletin* 115–148, 115.
325 Justin Morris, "Origins of the United Nations" in Thomas G. Weiss and Sam Daws (eds), *The Oxford Handbook on the United Nations*, Second Edition (Oxford, Oxford University Press, 2018) 44–46.
326 ibid., 46.

phrase "international law" be included in the purposes and principles of the UN to safeguard equality.[327] Besides, the Four Great Powers at San Francisco Conference discussed two concerns raised during the drafting of the Dumbarton Oaks proposals; namely, the "purposes" and "principles" of the UN and the definition of aggression. It was resolved that any interference in the internal affairs of State must be "with due regard for principles of justice and international law."[328] Article 1 of the Charter empowers the UN and its Organs to conduct its affairs "... in conformity with the principles of justice and international law ..."[329] Hence, only collective intervention is permitted. Moreover, an action taken by a State or group of States intervening in the internal affairs of another State must be geared towards restoring or maintaining peace.[330] The General Assembly may recommend such a measure if the circumstance so demands for matters not seized by the Security Council.[331]

2.10 Territory – a heartbeat of State sovereignty

Territory is "that definite portion of the surface of the globe which is subjected to the sovereignty of the State."[332] While adjudicating territorial disputes in the *Island of Palmas*,[333] Max Huber explains that within a defined territory, States have the right to exercise the functions of a State to the exclusion of any other State. In a democracy, functions of a State relate to the three arms of government. This should be borne in mind when interpreting territory as a criterion of Statehood. According to Franz Von Liszt, "independence (*selbstandigkeit*) and supremacy over territory (*landeshoheit*) were indispensable attributes of the State."[334] The idea of "independence" or "supremacy" does not negate contractual arrangements but buttresses the fact that "concepts like 'sovereignty' and 'title' are historically associated with the patrimony of states."[335]

However, *a defined portion* could be ambiguous because some States lack delimited boundaries.[336] The Security Council denied the Former Socialist Federal Republic of Yugoslavia (FRY) *locus standi* for lack of a defined territory[337] although

---

327 United Nations, *Documents of the United Nations Conference on International Organization San Francisco, 1945*, Volume 6 (New York, United Nations, 1955) 79 [hereinafter *UNCIO*].
328 *UNCIO*, Vol. 3, 622.
329 *UN Charter* (n 3), art 1(1).
330 *UNCIO*, Vol. 6, 25–26, 29–31, 80–81.
331 *UNCIO*, Vol. 9, 108–110.
332 Oppenheim 1963 (n 20), 305; Jennings and Watts (n 20), 563.
333 *Island of Palmas* case (n 21), 838.
334 Grant (n 15), 409.
335 Crawford 2012 (n 32), 206.
336 Vidmar (n 22), 702; Jaafar (n 22), 1–10.
337 UNSC Res. S/RES/757 (30 May 1992), preamble para. 10; UNSC Res. S/RES/777 (16 September 1992), operative para. 1.

46 *Setting out the theoretical framework*

the ICJ allowed it to appear before it in the Bosnian genocide case.[338] On the balance of probabilities, the FRY was a State at the material time because the ICJ's jurisdiction applies to State parties.[339] As held by the ICJ in the *North Sea Continental Shelf* cases,[340] "there is no rule that the land frontiers of a State must be fully delimited and defined." This *obiter* was upheld in a dispute between Libya and Chad.[341] States are bound by their obligations under international law in respect of other States undergoing the process of dissolution or self-determination.[342]

Territory remains the heartbeat of States because it creates a domain within which States act lawfully and can only be changed from within. This explained why dissolution did not obliterate the legal status of the FRY in the eyes of the law. A "defined portion of the surface of the globe" traditionally refers to the legal "title" which every State possesses over land, territorial sea and the airspace.[343] In the *Burkina Faso v Mali* case,[344] the ICJ held that the word "title" "comprehends both any evidence which may establish the existence of a right and the actual source of that right."[345] Shaw traces the source of State's territorial right to the Roman rules dealing with property[346] and Crawford argues that States by nature are territorial entities.[347] A defined territory is the circumscribed portion of the earth's surface within which States have the right to display their activities to the exclusion of others.[348]

2.11 Treaty regime and residual sovereignty

Treaty regime deals with the effect of bilateral and multilateral agreements on territorial sovereignty while residual sovereignty discusses territorial occupation.

338 *Application of Convention on Prevention and Punishment of Crime of Genocide* (Bosnia & Herzegovina v Yugoslavia) Preliminary Objections ICJ Reports (1996) pp. 595, 596.
339 *Statute of the International Court of Justice* (Adopted at San Francisco on 26 June 1945, entered into force on 24 October 1945) (1945) 39(3) *American Journal of International Law Supplement* 215–229, art. 34(1).
340 *North Sea Continental Shelf* cases (n 23), para. 46.
341 *Territorial Dispute* (Libyan Arab Jamahiriya/Chad) Judgment ICJ Reports (1994) p. 6, paras 44, 52.
342 UNGA Res. A/RES/46/238 (22 May 1992) (admission of Croatia to the United Nations); UNGA Res. A/RES/46/236 (22 May 1992) (admission of Slovenia to the United Nations); UNGA Res. A/RES/46/237 (22 May 1992) (admission of Bosnia-Herzegovina to the United Nations).
343 Malcolm N. Shaw, *International Law*, Seventh Edition (Cambridge, Cambridge University Press, 2014) 354.
344 *Frontier Dispute* (Burkina Faso/Republic of Mali) Judgment ICJ Reports (1986) p. 554, para. 18.
345 *Case Concerning the Land, Island and Maritime Frontier Dispute* (El Salvador v Honduras: Nicaragua intervening) Judgment ICJ Reports (1992) p. 351, para. 45.
346 Shaw 2014 (n 343), 354.
347 Crawford 2006 (n 16), 46; Oppenheim 1963 (n 20), 452.
348 *Island of Palmas* case (n 21), 839; Jennings and Watts (n 20), 564; the *Lotus* case (n 24), 18; *Legal Status of Eastern Greenland* (Denmark v Norway) Judgment PCIJ Series A/B, No. 53 (1933) pp. 21, 82 (Dissenting opinion of Judge M. Anzilotti).

Setting out the theoretical framework 47

A treaty regime does not abrogate territorial sovereignty but suspends it. As subjects of international law, States have a right to enter into contracts and are bound by it. Hence, international law creates rights and obligations.[349] States exercise rights within the ambit of the law, subject to the principle of *pacta sunt servanda*. Therefore, neither the UN nor any of its organs are above States. Instead, both the UN and its organs are an emanation of States' consent and must operate on four guiding principles. First, matters are decided in the General Assembly based on "one-state-one-vote."[350] Second, all votes cast are equal. Third, no State can claim jurisdiction over another, and fourth, domestic courts' jurisdiction is territorial.[351]

Therefore, residual competencies exercised by the UN and its organs would have no effect but for a mutual agreement. An exception might be the defunct mandate system under the League or Trusteeship under the UN. But both were transitory. For States that operate a federal system of governance, the ICJ in *LaGrand* and *Avena*[352] held that the central government is vicariously liable for international wrongs of the federating units. For cases involving occupation in times of peace, the occupying power is bound by international law[353] and cannot alter the territorial borders of the State[354] and must maintain the *status quo*.[355] The occupying power enjoys the *de facto* sovereignty[356] which can be revoked by *de iure* sovereign. After the dissolution of the Baltic States, the Helsinki District Court held that Estonia was not liable for the debt resulting from a contract entered into by an occupying power with Skop bank.[357]

349 Alan James, "Comment on J. D. B. Miller" (1986) 12(2) *Review of International Studies* 91–93, 92; J. D. B. Miller, "Sovereignty as a Source of Vitality for the State" (1986) 12(2) *Review of International Studies* 79–89; Ben Chigara, *Legitimacy Deficit in Custom: A Deconstructionist Critique* (Farnham, Ashgate Publishing 2001) 73.
350 For the voting system for the UN Member States, see *UN Charter* (n 3), art. 18. For the Security Council Members voting system, see *UN Charter* (n 3), art. 27. For the ECOSOC Members voting system, see *UN Charter* (n 3), art. 67. For the Trustee Council Members voting system (now suspended), see *UN Charter* (n 3), art. 89.
351 Herbert Weinschel, "The Doctrine of the Equality of States and Its Recent Modifications" (1951) 45(3) *American Journal of International Law* 417–442, 419; Jennings and Watts (n 20), 339; *Nicaragua* case (n 8), paras 59, 70, 202 and 284; *Chae Chan Ping v* United States, Supreme Court of the United States (1888) 130 U.S. 581, 604.
352 *LaGrand (Germany v US)*, ICJ Reports 2001 pp. 466, 514; *Avena and Other Mexican Nationals* (Mexico v United States of America) Judgment ICJ Reports (2004) pp. 12, 65–66.
353 *Convention (IV) Respecting the Laws and Customs of War on Land and its Annex: Regulations Concerning the Laws and Customs of War on Land* (The Hague, 18 October 1907), art. 42, available at <http://avalon.law.yale.edu/20th_century/hague04.asp> accessed 23 August 2019 [hereinafter *Hague Regulations*].
354 Martti Koskenniemi, "Occupied Zone – A Zone of Reasonableness" (2008) 41(1 & 2) *Israel Law Review* 13–40, 30.
355 *Hague Regulations* (n 353), art. 43.
356 Crawford 2012 (n 32), 207.
357 Tarja Langstrom, *Transformation in Russia and International Law* (Leiden and Boston, Martinus Nijhoff Publishers, 2003) 195–196.

3 Inviolability of State territory and Article 2(4) of the UN Charter

3.0 Introduction

This chapter seeks to deconstruct Article 2(4) to tease out the doctrine of respect for the inviolability of State territory. The word "inviolability" was neither expressed in the UN Charter nor Article 2(4) and "respect" was not used in Article 2(4) either. By "respect" is meant an obligation to refrain from conducts which could undermine the territorial integrity of another State for whatever reasons except in accordance with statutory exceptions, namely: self-defence or when authorised by the Security Council. This interpretive approach hinges on the exclusive nature of sovereign territoriality as discussed in Chapter 2. This chapter explores the legislative history of Article 2(4) carefully in conjunction with Article 2(7) of the UN Charter as well as other instruments at universal,[1] regional,[2] and national levels[3] to establish that respect for the inviolability of State territory is directly and principally intended.

---

1 UNGA Res. A/RES/25/2625 (24 October 1970), principle 1 [hereinafter *Declaration on Friendly Relations*]; UNGA Res. A/RES/29/3314 (14 December 1974), art. 3 [hereinafter *GA Definition of Aggression*]; *Convention (IV) Relative to the Protection of Civilian Persons in Time of War* (Done at Geneva on 12 August 1949, entered into force on 21 October 1950) 75 UNTS 287, arts 47 and 54 [hereinafter *The 1949 Geneva Convention IV*]; *Hague Convention (II) respecting the Laws and Customs of War on Land and its annex: Regulations concerning the Laws and Customs of War on Land* (Concluded at The Hague on 29 July 1899, entered into force on 4 September 1900) 32 Stat. 1803, arts 43 and 55 [hereinafter *The Hague Regulation II*].
2 *Charter of the Organization of American States* (Signed at Bogotá on 30 April 1948, entered into force on 13 December 1951) 119 UNTS 3, arts 21, 24 [hereinafter *OAS Charter*]; *Charter of the Organisation of African Unity* (Done at Addis Ababa on 25 May 1963, entered into force on 13 September 1963) 479 UNTS 39, art. 3 [hereinafter *OAU Charter*]; *Conference on Security and Co-operation in Europe Final Act* (Signed at Helsinki on 1 August 1975) (1975) 73(1888) *Department of State Bulletin* 323–350, arts 3 and 4, [hereinafter *Helsinki Final Act*].
3 *The Constitution of the Russian Federation* (Ratified on 12 December 1993), art. 4(3), available at <www.departments.bucknell.edu/russian/const/constit.html> accessed 29 September 2019; *Constitution of the Azerbaijan Republic as amended through 1995* (Enacted on 21 April 1978), art. 11, available at <www.constituteproject.org/> accessed 29 September 2019.

3.1 Clarification of methodology

The report issued by the ILC has shown that the ICJ interprets treaty "contemporaneously" or "evolutionary."[4] The ICJ applies the former whenever it wants to unravel meanings attached to a specific term or clause in a treaty[5] and the latter when it construes "terms that are by definition evolutionary."[6] In the *Legal Consequences for States of the Continued Presence of South Africa in Namibia (South West Africa) Notwithstanding Security Council Resolution 276 (1970)*, the ICJ reasoned that "the strenuous conditions of the modern world" and "the well-being and development of the peoples concerned" in Article 22 of the Covenant of the League of Nations are non-static phrases but must progressively address the desire for self-determination.[7] The ICJ shows that the doctrine of intertemporality plays out in varying degrees.

An evolutive interpretive approach is neither disingenuous nor contrary to best practice.[8] Again, the Advisory Opinion of the *International Tribunal for the Law of the Sea* affirms that international obligations are subject to flux.[9] This "occurs when the meaning of the text of the treaty changes over time"[10] due to a substantial change in circumstance. It could be said that the inclusion of cyberspace within the scope of State territory is significant. Hence, the *Vienna Convention on the Law of Treaties* (VCLT) accommodates layers of interpretation.[11]

Legal texts are brought to bear on contemporary *sitz im leben* through "interpretative practice and methodology."[12] "Methodology is the scholarly reflection of interpretative method and practice is its application."[13] The doctrine of evolutive interpretation could be analysed from two perspectives. First is to analyse the meaning when there is no *consensus ad idem* "on the object and purpose of the treaty or on the generic terms it uses."[14] Luigi Crema finds this technique useful

4 International Law Commission, *Report of the International Law Commission: Sixty-Eighth Session (2 May–10 June and 4 July–12 August 2016)*, UN Doc. A/71/10 (2016), 182–183 [hereinafter *ILC Report 2016*].
5 *Case Concerning a Boundary Dispute Between Argentina and Chile Concerning the Delimitation of the Frontier Line Between Boundary Post 62 and Mount Fitzroy* (Argentina v Chile) 22 RIAA 3–149, p. 43, para. 130.
6 *ILC Report 2016* (n 4), 182.
7 *Legal Consequences for States of the Continued Presence of South Africa in Namibia (South West Africa) Notwithstanding Security Council Resolution 276 (1970)*, Advisory Opinion ICJ Reports (1971) p. 16, para. 53 [hereinafter *Namibia Advisory Opinion*].
8 Gabrielle Marceau, "Evolutive Interpretation by the WTO Adjudicator" (2018) 21(4) *Journal of International Economic Law* 791–813.
9 *Responsibilities and Obligations of States with Respect to Activities in the Area*, Advisory Opinion, ITLOS Reports (2011) p. 10, para. 117.
10 Christian Djeffal, *Static and Evolutive Treaty Interpretation: A Functional Reconstruction* (Cambridge, Cambridge University Press, 2016) 347.
11 United Nations, *Vienna Convention on the Law of Treaties* (Done at Vienna on 23 May 1969, entered into force on 28 January 1980) 1155 UNTS 331, arts 31–33 [hereinafter VCLT].
12 Djeffal (n 10), 348.
13 ibid.
14 Marceau (n 8), 794.

50 *Inviolability of State territory*

when there are "changes in the meaning of a term, systemic changes, or new considerations linked to the object and purpose of the treaty."[15] When these changes occur, the courts are required to redefine the norm without tampering with its nature.[16] While the ordinary meaning of the term used in Article 2(4) is unambiguous linguistically, changes in the scope of territory might require adaptation. However, a closer evaluation of the context in which the Charter of the United Nations evolved suggests that States are, at least, not against a broader meaning.

Another school approaches evolutive interpretation from the viewpoint of what the parties intended. For authors like Bjorge, it is used "to establish the intention of the parties."[17] Intention helps to unlock agreements and can be gleaned from submissions made by States as contained in the *travaux préparatoires*. What the parties intend can be corroborated by State practice or other instruments concluded consequent upon the legal instrument entering into force. While Pellet encourages the ICJ to take *sitz im leben* into account when interpreting treaties, Simma is critical of evolutive interpretation and Crawford cautions against inappropriate application of laws.[18] This chapter takes evolutive interpretation seriously when analysing Article 2(4). Arguably, "war" and the "search for world peace" are contexts that should inform reasonable interpretation of Article 2(4).

3.1.1 Deductive reasoning

The methodology described above requires a bit of deductive reasoning. This approach might discomfort black-letter law theorists, according to whom legal reasoning should be preoccupied with the application of the law. Yet application is not that simple but involves making a value judgment through a process of "identifying the range of possible or plausible interpretations of the relevant rule(s), text(s) or other objects of interpretation, and constructing arguments in favour of and against each of the main candidates"[19] or facts. Thus, the expression, *apply the law*, goes with justifiable deductions applied to the facts. Besides, the socio-legal research has shown gross inadequacy of ignoring the social contexts when teaching or practising law.[20]

Deduction is derived from Latin feminine noun *deductio*; a "noun of action from past participle stem of *deducere* ..., from *de* 'down' + *ducere* 'to lead'."[21]

---

15 ibid.
16 Panos Merkouris, "(Inter)Temporal Considerations in the Interpretive Process of the VCLT: Do Treaties Endure, Perdure or Exdure?" (2014) 45 *Netherlands Yearbook of International Law* 121–156, 131.
17 Marceau (n 8), 794.
18 ibid., 795.
19 William Twining and David Miers, *How to Do Things with Rules*, Fifth Edition (Cambridge, Cambridge University Press, 2014) 337.
20 Fiona Cownie, *Legal Academics: Culture and Identities* (Oxford, Hart Publishing, 2004) 55.
21 Douglas Harper, *Online Etymology Dictionary*, available at <www.etymonline.com/> accessed 1 September 2019.

Inviolability of State territory 51

According to Aristotle, deduction is "an argument in which, certain things being laid down, something other than these necessarily comes about through them."[22] He likened the distinction between demonstration and dialectical deduction to knowledge and opinion respectively. In the *Prior Analytics*, he distinguishes between a "demonstration," "a proposition," "a term" and "a deduction."[23] A proposition "is a statement affirming or denying something of something."[24] "A demonstrative proposition is the assumption of one of two contradictory statements ... whereas a dialectical proposition choice between two contradictories."[25] A "term" is "that into which the proposition is resolved, i.e. both the predicate and that of which it is predicated."[26] Therefore, "a deduction is a discourse in which, certain things being stated, something other than what is stated follows of necessity from their being so."[27]

Aristotle stresses that deductions are necessary but distinguishes perfect deduction from an imperfect deduction. The former "needs nothing other than what has been stated to make the necessity evident" while the latter "needs either one or more things, which are indeed the necessary consequences of the terms set down but have not been assumed in the propositions."[28] Therefore, "a conclusion is deducible when it has been necessarily inferred from its premises."[29] The idea of inferential necessity reinforces the need for a reverse application of the common law doctrine of necessity. The dilemma is this – stick with a narrow interpretation of Article 2(4) and risk another world war. The danger with a positivistic reading of Article 2(4) is that it obscures the explosive effect of *de minimis* breaches. It seems reasonable and proportionate sometimes to apply judicial activism in a way that enhances the overall objective of a text.

3.2 Substantive norm

Before we discuss Article 2(4), we recall that the charter drafters wanted to put forward viable standards that regulate international conducts. The *vinculo iuris* is expressed in the preamble, namely, to "save succeeding generations from the scourge of war, which twice in our lifetime has brought untold sorrow to mankind." To this end, Article 2 has been described as "the heart of the Charter's proscriptions of international violence ..." without which "the delicate superstructure of the Charter would lack a crucial normative foundation."[30]

22 W. A. Pickard-Cambridge, "Topics" in Jonathan Barnes (ed.), *The Complete Works of Aristotle – The Revised Oxford Translation* (Princeton, Princeton University Press, 1984) Book I, para. 100^{a}20–25 at p. 381.
23 A. J. Jenkinson, "Prior Analytics" in Barnes (n 22), Book I, para. 24^{a}10 at p. 103.
24 ibid.
25 ibid., 104.
26 ibid.
27 ibid.
28 ibid., 105.
29 Jean-Louis Hudry, "Aristotle on Deduction and Inferential Necessity" (2013) 67(1) *The Review of Metaphysics* 29–54, 30.
30 Kevin T. Baine, "The Use of Nonviolent Coercion: A Study in Legality Under Article 2(4) of the Charter of the United Nations" (1974) 122(4) *University of Pennsylvania Law Review* 983–1011, 985–986.

52 *Inviolability of State territory*

3.2.1 *Article 2(4) of the United Nations Charter*

Article 2(4) of the UN Charter was a response to the Moscow Declaration of 1943[31] seeking a lasting solution to international peace and security. It provides as follows:

> All Members shall refrain in their international relations from the threat or use of force against the territorial integrity or political independence of any state, or in any other manner inconsistent with the Purposes of the United Nations.[32]

This provision has been described as customary international law.[33] If the text is restricted to "the threat or use of force," what distinguishes it from the previous peace treaties? The Kellogg-Briand Pact expressly prohibits "recourse to war" as a means of settling international disputes or as an "instrument of national policy."[34] Article 10 of the Covenant of the League of Nations[35] obliges State Parties to "respect and preserve as against external aggression the territorial integrity and existing political independence of all Members ..." It equally prohibits the member States from resorting to war if conditions stated in Articles 12, 13 and 15 of the Covenant of the League of Nations were not met.[36]

The omission of phrases such as "respect and preserve" in Article 2(4) is a bit disconcerting.[37] Admittedly, "preserve" creates positive obligations for States[38] but

---

31 James Frederick Green, "The Dumbarton Oaks Conversations" (1944) 11(278) *The Department of State Bulletin* 462–643; *The Moscow Conference of 1943*, "Joint Four-Nation Declaration," arts 5–6, available at <http://avalon.law.yale.edu/wwii/moscow. asp> accessed 4 September 2019.

32 United Nations, *Charter of the United Nations* (Signed at San Francisco on 26 June 1945, entered into force on 24 October 1945) 1 UNTS XVI, art. 2(4) [hereinafter *UN Charter*].

33 *Case Concerning Military and Paramilitary Activities In and Against Nicaragua* (Nicaragua v United States of America) Judgment ICJ Reports (1986) p. 14, paras 98–101, 190–191, 227 [hereinafter *Nicaragua* case]; *Legality of the Threat or Use of Nuclear Weapons*, Advisory Opinion ICJ Reports (1996) p. 226, para. 105 [hereinafter *Legality of the Threat or Use of Nuclear Weapons*]; *Legal Consequences of the Construction of a Wall in the Occupied Palestinian Territory*, Advisory Opinion ICJ Reports (2004) p. 136, paras 86–88; *Armed Activities on the Territory of the Congo* (Democratic Republic of the Congo v Uganda) Judgment ICJ Reports (2005) p. 168, para. 162 [hereinafter *DRC v Uganda*]; *The Case of the S.S. "Lotus"* (France v Turkey) Judgment PCIJ Series A, No. 10 (1927), 18–19.

34 *General Treaty for Renunciation of War as Instrument of National Policy* (Signed at Paris on 27 August 1928, entered into force on 25 July 1929) 94 UNTS 57, art. 1.

35 *The Covenant of the League of Nations* (Adopted at Paris on 29 April 1919, entered into force on 10 January 1920) (1919) 13(2) *American Journal of International Law Supplement* 128–139, art. 10 [hereinafter *The Covenant of the League of Nations*].

36 ibid., arts 12, 13 and 15. Bruno Simma describes the conditions as the "cooling-off period." See Bruno Simma *et al.* (eds), *The Charter of the United Nations: A Commentary*, Second Edition (New York, Oxford University Press, 2002) 115.

37 Leland M. Goodrich, Edvard Hambro and Anne Patricia Simons, *Charter of the United Nations: Commentary and Documents*, Third and Revised Edition (New York, Columbia University Press, 1969) 45.

38 Leland M. Goodrich and Edvard Hambro, *Charter of the United Nations: Commentary and Documents* (Boston, World Peace Foundation, 1946) 68.

Inviolability of State territory   53

what of "respect" which imposes a negative obligation to refrain from violating the territory of other States? If treaties that pre-existed the UN Charter abrogated war and aggression, such as, the *Locarno Pact*,[39] of what novelty is Article 2(4)? The omission of the word "inviolability" in the text of Article 2(4) is disturbing because some founding member States (such as the United States and the Soviet Union) had used that expression in their bilateral treaties with other States.[40]

3.2.2 Travaux préparatoires *of Article 2(4) – States' submissions*

The Dumbarton Oaks Proposals read: "All members of the Organisation shall refrain in their international relations from the threat or use of force in any manner inconsistent with the purposes of the Organisation."[41] Some countries made recommendations to this proposal. Australia requested that the phrase "against the territorial integrity or political independence of any member or state, or in any other manner inconsistent with the purposes of the United Nations" should be inserted after the phrase, "use of force."[42] Bolivia expanded the draft proposal to include acts of violence and aggression and added a new paragraph on the "inviolability of State territory."[43] Brazil considers that interference which threatens the national security of a State – whether directly or indirectly – should form part of Article 2(4).[44] Czechoslovakia wanted a revised text to read: "respect for the territorial integrity and political independence of States-members."[45] The word "respect" appears in the documents submitted by Egypt,[46] Ethiopia[47] and Mexico.[48] Honduras accepted the Dumbarton Oaks

---

39 *Treaty of Mutual Guarantee between Germany, Belgium, France, Great Britain and Italy* (Done at Locarno on 16 October 1925, entered into force on 14 September 1926) 54 LNTS 289, arts 1–2 [hereinafter *Locarno Pact*].

40 *U.S.S.R. – Estonia: Treaty of Non-Aggression and Peaceful Settlement of Dispute* (Signed at Moscow on 4 May 1932; ratifications exchanged on 18 August 1932) (1933) 27(4) *American Journal of International Law Supplement* 167–169, art. 1; *U.S.S.R. – Poland: Treaty of Non-Aggression* (Signed at Moscow on 25 July 1932; ratifications exchanged on 23 December 1932) (1933) 27(4) *American Journal of International Law Supplement* 188–190, art. 1; Inter-American Conference on War and Peace, "Act of Chapultepec" (Concluded at Mexico on 3 March 1945) (1945) 12(297) *Department of State Bulletin* 339–340, 340 [see in particular, Part 1, Third declaration]; *U.S.S.R. – Estonia: Treaty of Non-Aggression and Peaceful Settlement of Dispute* (Signed at Moscow on 4 May 1932; ratifications exchanged on 18 August 1932) (1933) 27(4) *American Journal of International Law Supplement* 167–169, art. 1.

41 United Nations, *Documents of the United Nations Conference on International Organization San Francisco, 1945*, Volume 3 (New York, United Nations, 1955) 3 [hereinafter *UNCIO*].

42 ibid., 543.

43 ibid., 578, 582–583.

44 ibid., 237.

45 ibid., 467.

46 ibid., 454.

47 ibid., 558.

48 ibid., 65.

54 *Inviolability of State territory*

Proposals,[49] New Zealand requested that any measure to be taken against State aggressor should be collective[50] and Norway argued that the Security Council must authorise all interventions.[51] The Netherlands pointed out that the criterion for settlement of disputes should be clear and "on the basis of respect for law...."[52]

While some States applauded the establishment of the United Nations, some States were wary of its effects on their territorial sovereignty.[53] Chile, for instance, proposed a list of norms clarifying what State sovereignty entailed.[54] The amendment submitted to Committee I/1 by the Peruvian government reads in part "the Organization is based on the respect for the personality, sovereignty, independence, juridical equality and territorial integrity of States "[55] The need to protect States' territorial sovereignty informed the insertion of the phrase, "in conformity with the principles of justice and international law" in Article 1.[56]

Again, the idea of sovereign equality of States undoubtedly means, among other things, that States are free and sovereign to the extent not limited by the Charter.[57] To this end, the then US Secretary of State, Edward Stettinius Jr., said that the Charter would have a mechanism that protected the integrity of States.[58] Hence, delegations at San Francisco knew that Article 2 was not inimical to sovereign equality of States.[59] The phrase "territorial integrity" was inserted to calm the nerves of apprehensive weaker States,[60] although it was not defined.[61]

3.2.3 Essential components of Article 2(4)

Before we proceed further with our analysis, we shall first briefly examine some essential components of Article 2(4).

---

49 ibid., 349–350.
50 ibid., 487.
51 ibid., 366.
52 ibid., 312.
53 Anthony D'Amato, *International Law: Process and Prospect*, Second Edition (New York, Transnational Publishers, 1995) 69.
54 *UNCIO*, Vol. 3, 293.
55 *UNCIO*, Vol. 6, 304.
56 Goodrich and Hambro 1946 (n 38), 60–61.
57 ibid., 64.
58 Edward Stettinius, "What the Dumbarton Oaks Peace Plan means" (1945) 12(292) *The Department of State Bulletin* 115–119, 117.
59 Goodrich and Hambro 1946 (n 38), 19.
60 Ian Brownlie, *International Law and the Use of Force by States* (New York, Oxford University Press, 1963) 267; *UNCIO*, Vol. 6, 304.
61 S. Akweenda, "Territorial Integrity: A Brief Analysis of a Complex Concept" (1989) 1 (3) *African Journal of International and Comparative Law* 500–506, 502.

3.2.3.1 Threat of force

The "threat of force" is expressly prohibited in Article 2(4) and other instruments[62] but was not defined[63] in the Charter. It has a weak literary antecedent[64] and was referred to indirectly previously[65] but was formerly codified in the Dumbarton Oaks Proposals.[66]

The ICJ's Advisory Opinion on the *Legality of the Threat or Use of Nuclear Weapons* addresses some crucial questions relating to the threat of force. It held,

> the notions of "threat" and "use" of force under Article 2, paragraph 4, of the Charter stand together in the sense that if the use of force itself in a given case is illegal … the threat to use such force will likewise be illegal.[67]

Authors have criticised this opinion for making a threat of force a non-substantive offence.[68] According to the United States, a breach of a State's airspace by a military aircraft "may constitute a sufficient threat to justify the use of force in self-defence."[69] In other words, a threat of force is independent of the actual use of force. This argument is credible considering the devastating effects of the actual use of force (such as weapons of mass destruction) could have on a State's territory.

The ILC defined the threat of force as "acts undertaken with a view to making a state believe that force will be used against it if certain demands are not met by that state."[70] Note that this definition did not say military threat or threat with

---

62 *Declaration on Friendly Relations* (n 1), principle 1; *GA Definition of Aggression* (n 1), art. 3; UNGA Res. A/RES/42/22 (18 November 1987), operative para. 1.

63 Olivier Corten, *The Law Against War: The Prohibition on the Use of Force in Contemporary International Law* (Oxford and Portland, Hart Publishing, 2010) 93; James A. Green and Francis Grimal, "The Threat of Force as an Action in Self-Defense under International Law" (2011) 44(2) *Vanderbilt Journal of Transnational Law* 285–329, 291.

64 Romana Sadurska, "Threats of Force" (1988) 82(2) *American Journal of International Law* 239–268, 248; Marco Roscini, "Threats of Armed Force and Contemporary International Law" (2007) 54(2) *Netherlands International Law Review* 229–277, 231; Green and Grimal (n 63), 285.

65 Josef L. Kunz, "*Bellum justum* and *bellum legale*" (1951) 45(3) *American Journal of International Law* 528–534, 533.

66 Corten (n 63), 92.

67 *Legality of the Threat or Use of Nuclear Weapons* (n 33), para. 47.

68 Sadurska (n 64), 250; Roscini (n 64), 230; The 2001 Report of the International Law Commission explains that threat of conduct, incitement or attempt to incite threat constitute in themselves wrongful acts, see UNGAOR, UN Doc. A/56/10(SUPP) (23 April–1 June and 2 July–10 August 2001), 143.

69 United States Department of Homeland Security, *The Commander's Handbook on the Law of Naval Operations* (July 2007 Edition), para. 4.4.2, available at <www.jag.navy.mil/documents/NWP_1-14M_Commanders_Handbook.pdf> accessed 29 September 2019.

70 International Law Commission, *Document A/44/10: Report of the International Law Commission on work of its Forty-first session* (Volume II, Part II, *Yearbook of the International Law Commission*, 1989) 68.

56 Inviolability of State territory

military hardware. Brownlie observes that a threat of force could be "express or implied."[71] At San Francisco, Brazil had proposed that economic coercion be included as a form of threat, but it was rejected. Czechoslovakia and Yugoslavia resuscitated the debate in their proposals to the *Special Committee on Principles of International Law Concerning Friendly Relations and Co-operation among States.*[72] What constituted a threat of force remained contentious and was again challenged in the *Corfu Channel* case.[73]

3.2.3.2 Use of force

How Article 2(4) relates to the Use of Force has been widely discussed[74] and shall not be repeated. Our project is to explore other reasonings which support a broad interpretation even while discussing the narrow interpretive approach.

3.2.3.2A ARGUMENT IN FAVOUR OF RESTRICTIVE READING OF ARTICLE 2(4)

Brazil recommended that a clause "… from the threat or use of economic measures in any manner inconsistent …"[75] should be added to the Dumbarton Oaks Proposals on Article 2(4). The amendment was rejected. In a debate which preceded voting on Brazil's amendment, the Belgian delegation said that Brazil underestimated the scope of the phrase "in any other manner" in the Dumbarton Oaks Proposals.[76] Similarly, a delegate from the United States said: "the intention of the authors of the original text was to state in the broadest terms an absolute all-inclusive prohibition; the phrase 'or in any other manner' was designed to insure that there should be no loopholes."[77] This is a strong statement which might include economic coercion even though the amendment was rejected.

Some factors contributed to the rejection of Brazil's amendment. One factor is "the vagueness of the notion of an 'impermissible' use of economic force."[78] To clarify, when Czechoslovakia and Yugoslavia pressed for the inclusion of "political and other forms of pressure or coercion" as part of the prohibited conducts under Article 2(4), it was rejected because the articles of the Charter should be read in

---

71 Brownlie 1963 (n 60), 241; Sadurska (n 64), 241.
72 UN Doc. A/5746 (16 November 1964) 30.
73 *Corfu Channel* (United Kingdom v Albania) (Merits) Judgment ICJ Reports (1949) pp. 4, 35 [hereinafter *Corfu Channel* case].
74 See generally Brownlie 1963 (n 60); Corten (n 63), 51; Yoram Dinstein, *War Aggression and Self-Defence*, Fifth Edition (Cambridge, Cambridge University Press, 2011) 95; Christine Gray, *International Law and the Use of Force*, Third Edition (Oxford, Oxford University Press, 2008) 42; Rosalyn Higgins, *Problems and Process: International Law and How We Use It* (Oxford, Oxford University Press, 1994) 240; Thomas M. Franck, *Recourse to Force: State Action Against Threats and Armed Attack* (Cambridge, Cambridge University Press, 2002) 20.
75 *UNCIO*, Vol. 3, 253.
76 *UNCIO*, Vol. 6, 334.
77 ibid., 335.
78 Baine (n 30), 995.

connection with other related articles.[79] Anything to the contrary will render Articles 41 and 51 ineffectual.[80] While cross-referencing is the way to go, it might as well support an absolute all-inclusive prohibition when read in conjunction with the preamble, Article 1(1) and Article 2(7). Moreover, sponsoring an armed attack against a State amounts to intervention in the internal affairs of a State.[81] This applies to the UN and its organs which enjoy statutory immunity while exercising their functions "in conformity with the principles of justice and international law."[82] Nonetheless, the phrase, "use of force" traditionally applies to "physical force or armed force and does not include economic or political pressure."[83]

3.2.3.2B ARGUMENT IN FAVOUR OF EXPANDED READING OF ARTICLE 2(4)

Three reasons in favour of an expanded reading of Article 2(4) are summarised as follows:

> the inclusion of these coercions is legitimate within the textual confines of the Charter; that other international documents drafted since the Charter came into effect demonstrate a growing world sensitivity to the problem posed by the use of political and economic weapons; and that outlawing this genre of coercion can have only a salutary effect on international relations, and may well constitute a necessary step in the evolution of normative standards of international coercive conduct.[84]

These reasons shall be revisited later. To pick up on the textual reading of Article 2(4), it says, "the threat or use of force" and did not say "physical force or armed force." To this end, the text is clear and unequivocal; otherwise, the preamble and Article 46 would not have specified "armed force." Similarly, Article 51 allows self-defence when "an armed attack occurs" to forestall any "pre-emptive or anticipatory attacks."[85] Therefore, expanded reading supports the purposes and principles of the Charter. The current tension between the United States and Iran cannot be absolved of economic and political underpinnings.[86] However, the major criticism against expanded reading is that it blurs acceptable diplomatic channels available to States.[87]

79 UN Doc. A/5746 (16 November 1964), 30.
80 ibid., 31–32.
81 *Nicaragua* case (n 33), para. 195.
82 *UN Charter* (n 32), art. 1(1).
83 UN Doc. A/AC.119/L.8 (31 August 1964), 3, para. 2.
84 Baine (n 30), 997.
85 ibid., 997–998.
86 Millie Bull, "US-IRAN tensions erupt as Tehran accuses Washington Think Tank of 'Economic Terrorism'" (UK, Express Newspapers, 26 August 2019) A1.
87 Baine (n 30), 996.

58   *Inviolability of State territory*

3.2.3.3 Territorial integrity and political independence

The phrase, "territorial integrity and political independence" was not in the Dumbarton Oaks Proposals. It was introduced *per* Australian amendment to "preclude interference with the enforcement clauses of Chapter VIII of the Charter."[88] However, a delegate from Peru strongly objected to the Commission's refusal to accept its proposal which would have included "personality," "juridical equality" and "sovereignty" among the protected rights. He contends that the inclusion of "territorial integrity and political independence" does not safeguard "the absolute respect"[89] which would have been otherwise established. In defence, the Rapporteur to Commission I, Farid Zeineddine outlined four elements of "sovereign equality" one of which is "that the personality of the state is respected as well as its territorial integrity and political independence."[90] In his words, this explains why "respect for territorial integrity and political independence went into Article 4 as amended by the Australian Delegation."[91] A similar expression, "respect" was used by the Minister of Foreign Affairs of Brazil.[92] Why the word "respect" was not codified in Article 2(4) is unclear given its legal antecedents.

Further, the meaning of the phrase "against territorial integrity or political independence of any State" was debated during the drafting of the *Declaration on Friendly Relations*. Delegates agreed that "it had been inserted at San Francisco in order to guarantee the territorial integrity and political independence of small and weak States …"[93] Discussants emphasised that force is not used in the abstract but is always directed *against* the territorial integrity or political independence of a State. Hence, States cannot resort to the use of force as a defence nor claim it is "to maintain the establish constitutional order or to protect a minority, or on any other pretext."[94] Consequently, the phrase, "any State" applies to "both members of the United Nations and non-members" alike.[95]

3.2.3.4 In any other manner inconsistent with the purposes of the United Nations

According to the delegate from the United States, "the intention of the authors of the original text was to state in the broadest terms an absolute all-inclusive prohibition; the phrase 'or in any other manner' was designed to insure that there should be no loopholes."[96] Wright argues that the US quarantine of Cuba is inconsistent with the purposes of the UN Charter.[97] It is immaterial that the said interdiction is an "offensive"

---

88   *UNCIO*, Vol. 6, 335.
89   ibid., 68.
90   ibid., 69.
91   ibid., 69.
92   *UNCIO*, Vol. 1, 671.
93   UN Doc. A/5746 (16 November 1964), 26.
94   ibid.
95   ibid., 27.
96   *UNCIO*, Vol. 6, 335.
97   Quincy Wright, "The Cuban Quarantine" (1963) 57(3) *American Journal of International Law* 546–565, 555.

Inviolability of State territory   59

or a "defensive" measure.[98] Interestingly, the phrase "in any other manner" embraces many issues that catalyse intervention nowadays. Cassese regards them as exceptional conditions like the right of peoples to self-determination during the decolonisation era[99] or when there is a gross violation of human rights.[100] As held by the ICJ, the core human rights acquire the status of *jus cogens* as well as customary international law.[101]

As shall be seen, there is no credible evidence to suggest that State practice accepts that the said conditions override the *jus cogens* character of Article 2(4). Unilateral interventions, even for just causes, are inconsistent with the purposes of the UN Charter.[102] The primary purpose of the UN is to maintain international peace and security and to foster peace in accordance with the principles of justice and international law through peaceful resolution of international disputes.[103] States' conducts directed against the territory of other States which do not enhance this objective contravene Article 2(4).[104]

3.3 Article 2(7) of the United Nations

Article 2, paragraph 7 provides as follows:

> Nothing contained in the present Charter shall authorize the United Nations to intervene in matters which are essentially within the domestic jurisdiction of any state or shall require the Members to submit such matters to settlement under the present Charter; but this principle shall not prejudice the application of enforcement measures under Chapter VII.[105]

98 Brunson argues that the lawfulness of the act should be assessed based on the values sought in light of threat facing international community. See Brunson MacChesney, "Some Comments on the 'Quarantine' of Cuba" (1963) 57(3) *American Journal of International Law* 592–597, 594–595.

99 Antonio Cassese, *Self-determination of Peoples: A Legal Reappraisal* (Cambridge, Cambridge University Press, 1995) 174–176; Antonio Cassese, *International Law in a Divided World* (New York, Oxford University Press, 1986) 131–136; *Western Sahara*, Advisory Opinion ICJ Reports (1975) pp. 12, 122 (Separate Opinion of Judge Dillard states: "It is for the people to determine the destiny of the territory and not the territory the destiny of the people.")

100 Joshua Castellino, "International Law and Self-determination: Peoples, Indigenous Peoples, and Minorities" in Christian Walter *et al.* (eds), *Self-determination and Secession in International Law* (Oxford, Oxford University Press, 2014) 31; George Nolte, "Secession and External Intervention" in Marcelo G. Kohen (ed.), *Secession: International Law Perspectives* (Cambridge, Cambridge University Press, 2006) 73; *UN Charter* (n 32), art. 1(3).

101 *Barcelona Traction, Light and Power Co. Ltd* (Belgium v Spain) Judgment ICJ Reports (1970) p. 3, paras 33–34; *United States Diplomatic and Consular Staff in Tehran* (United States of America v Iran) Judgment ICJ Reports (1980) p. 3, para. 91.

102 David Luban, "Just War and Human Rights" (1980) 9(2) *Philosophy & Public Affairs* 160–181, 162.

103 *UN Charter* (n 32), art. 1(1).

104 Wright (n 97), 557.

105 UN Charter (n 32), art. 2(7).

60 *Inviolability of State territory*

This article insulates States from undue intervention from the Organs of the United Nations. The principle codified in Article 2(7) appears to have started when the US Senate amended the *Olney-Pauncefote Arbitration Treaty of 1897* so that disputants did not submit to the arbitration committee any material it considered could harm its foreign or domestic policy.[106] It was later codified in Article 15, paragraph 8 of the Covenant of the League of Nations. States are competent to reserve matters to their domestic jurisdiction before signing up to treaties.

The difficulty is how to balance States' right with the responsibilities of the United Nations. Before the UN was born, the position of the Permanent Court of International Justice (PCIJ) on the matter was not determinate but subject to "the development of international relation."[107] At present, there is no list outlining the nature and content of issues that fall outside States' domestic jurisdiction. The word, "intervene" in Article 2(7) is ambiguous and the conditions that could trigger it controversial.[108] Tsagourias has explored a viewpoint that suggests that the principle of subsidiarity could explain it.[109] However, caution should be applied not to construe States' *potestas* as subsidiary to or derives from the United Nations. A careful reading of the *Report of the Special Committee on Principles of International Law Concerning Friendly Relations and Co-operation Among States* left no doubt that Article 2(7) encapsulates the principle of non-intervention.[110] In document A/AC.199/L.26, the United States "makes clear that the obligation referred to springs from Article 2, paragraph 4, of the Charter ..."[111] It follows that interventions must conform with the principles enunciated in Article 1(1) of the Charter.

3.3.1 *Is Article 2(7) a clawback article?*

The connection between Article 2(7) and Article 2(4) is rather curious. Could this be double protection against unlawful interventions? Recall that the United States explains that the link "makes clear that the obligation (it) referred to springs from Article 2, paragraph 4, of the Charter."[112] Additionally, two Resolutions[113]

---

106 Leland M. Goodrich, "The United Nations and Domestic Jurisdiction" (1949) *International Organization* 14–28, 14–15.
107 *Nationality Decree Issued in Tunis and Morocco*, Advisory Opinion, PCIJ Series B, No. 4 (1923) p. 7, 24.
108 D. R. Gilmour, "The Meaning of 'Intervene' Within Article 2(7) of the United Nations Charter – An Historical Perspective" (1967) 16(2) *International and Comparative Law Quarterly* 330–351, 332–333.
109 Nicholas Tsagourias, "Security Council Legislation, Article 2(7) of the UN Charter, and the Principle of Subsidiarity" (2011) 24 *Leiden Journal of International Law* 539–559, 548.
110 UN Doc. A/5746 (16 November 1964), 109–140.
111 ibid., 112.
112 ibid., 112 (emphasis added).
113 UNGA Res. A/RES/36/103 (9 December 1981), operative para. 1 [hereinafter *Inadmissibility of Intervention in States' Affairs*]; UNGA Res. A/RES/20/2131 (21 December 1965), operative para. 1 [hereinafter *Inadmissibility of Intervention in Domestic Affairs*].

Inviolability of State territory   61

adopted by the United Nations General Assembly prohibit intervention in the internal affairs of other States.

The word "intervention" has been analysed in much detail here.[114] In the *Case Concerning Military and Paramilitary Activities In and Against Nicaragua*, the ICJ held that Article 2(7) is meant to protect the sovereignty of States[115] from unauthorised unilateral interventions, whether by individual or groups. The court also said that States are at liberty to decide on "a political, economic, social and cultural system, and the formulation of foreign policy."[116] It implies that intervention may not always be through physical armed force. When a State faces an internal crisis, how to ascertain "unacceptable limits"[117] that require the response of the UN could be ambiguous[118] due to several competing factors such as cultural sensitivity.

Two deductions are possible. First, the prohibition of the "threat or use of force" in paragraph 4 and "intervention" in paragraph 7 are examples of the requirement to respect the inviolability of State territory. As Cassese opines,

> [a] radical turning point was the adoption of the UN Charter, which in Article 2.4 proscribes any threat or use of force, thus creating *inter alia* a right of all member states ... to non-intervention in their internal or external relations by the threat or use of force.[119]

In other words, Article 2(4) is implicated whenever the intervenor uses threat or force. *Argumentum a fortiori*, all other interventions do not involve the threat or use of force. Hence, peaceful entry into a State territory on invitation might turn out to be a threat, use of force or an unlawful intervention if an invitee refuses to withdraw its troops when instructed to do so.[120] Initially, Article 2(7) was restricted to acts of the United Nations but was later interpreted as embodying the general principle of non-intervention.[121]

Second, the text of Article 2(7) expressly refers to "matters which are essentially within the domestic jurisdiction of any state."[122] Two Resolutions of the UN General Assembly mentioned earlier refer to civil strife. Both resolutions condemn "all other forms of interference" directed against the political, economic and cultural elements

---

114 Gilmour (n 108), 330–351.
115 *Nicaragua* case (n 33), para. 205; Nolte 2006 (n 100), 69; Gray (n 74), 67; Robert Jennings and Arthur Watts (eds), *Oppenheim's International Law*, Ninth Edition (London and New York, Longman, 1996) 428.
116 *Nicaragua* case (n 33), para. 205.
117 George Nolte, "Article 2(7)" in Simma *et al.* (n 36), 152.
118 Gilmour (n 108), 330; Luke T. Lee, "The Mexico City Conference of the United Nations Special Committee on Principles of International Law Concerning Friendly Relations and Co-Operation among States" (1965) 14(4) *International and Comparative Law Quarterly* 1296–1313, 1305–1306.
119 Cassese 1986 (n 99), 145.
120 *DRC v Uganda* (n 33), para. 53.
121 Nolte 2002 (n 117), 153.
122 *UN Charter* (n 32), art 2(7).

62 *Inviolability of State territory*

of a State.[123] These Resolutions post-UN Charter adopted inclusive language in terms of territorial sovereignty. According to Nolte, the idea of "domestic jurisdiction" in Article 2(7) is not limited to physically delimited boundaries of a State[124] but also includes extra-territorial jurisdiction.

As shall be seen, the boundary between Article 2(4) and Article 2(7) is fluid, mostly in cases dealing with the enforcement of rights in the Exclusive Economic Zone.[125] This makes Article 2(7) looks more like a clawback article. Article 2(7) would not have been necessary if the phrase, *respect for the inviolability of a State territory* were codified in Article 2(4) of the UN Charter.[126] The proposals of the delegation from Czechoslovakia[127] and Yugoslavia[128] prohibit "direct or indirect intervention … in the internal or external affairs of any other State through threat or exerting pressure (whether political, economic or diplomatic) to change the target State's social or political order."[129] A joint proposal submitted by Ghana, India and Yugoslavia lists the following conducts as examples of the prohibited interference:

(a) organise, assist, foment, incite or tolerate subversive or terrorist activities against another state or interfere in civil strife in another State;
(b) interfere with or hinder, in any form or manner, the promulgation or execution of laws in regard to matters essentially within the competence of any State;
(c) use duress to obtain or maintain territorial agreements or special advantages of any kind; and
(d) recognise territorial acquisitions or special advantages obtained by duress of any kind by another State.[130]

---

123 *Inadmissibility of Intervention in Domestic Affairs* (n 113), operative paras 1–2; *Inadmissibility of Intervention in States Affairs* (n 113), art. 1(b).
124 Nolte 2002 (n 117), 157.
125 *Guyana v Suriname* (Arbitral Tribunal constituted pursuant to Article 287, and in accordance with Annex VII, of the United Nations Convention on the Law of the Sea) Award PCA (2007) 30 *RIAA* 1–144, paras 425–447.
126 Yugoslavia's proposal includes a broad range of rights in the text of Article 2(7). See Special Committee on Principles of International Law Concerning Friendly Relations and Co-operation Among States, "Yugoslavia's Proposal" UN Doc. A/AC.119/L.7 (31 August 1964) 2 [hereinafter *Yugoslavia's Proposal on Non-intervention*].
127 Special Committee on Principles of International Law Concerning Friendly Relations and Co-operation Among States, "Czechoslovakia's Proposal" UN Doc. A/AC.119/L.6 (29 August 1964), 2.
128 *Yugoslavia's Proposal on Non-intervention* (n 126), 2–3.
129 Edward McWhinney, "The New Countries and the New International Law: The United Nations' Special Conference on Friendly Relations and Co-Operation among States" (1966) 60(1) *American Journal of International Law* 1–33, 21 (the quotation is modified).
130 Special Committee on Principles of International Law Concerning Friendly Relations and Co-operation Among States, "Ghana, India and Yugoslavia's Proposal" UN Doc. A/AC.119/L.27 (21 September 1964), 1.

Inviolability of State territory   63

The United Kingdom objected to zero tolerance in influencing the policies and actions of other States in an interdependent world.[131] Such law, the UK argues, is beyond the objective of the international law insofar as it does not conflict with the principles of self-determination of peoples or the sovereign equality of States.[132] These proposals show the uneasiness between the positions taken by powerful States on the one hand and the weaker States on the other hand. The troubling aspect of the viewpoint of the powerful States is how to measure the degree of influence that would be permitted given the asymmetric bargaining power of the weaker States. Equally troubling from the viewpoint of the weaker States is how to evolve an exhaustive list of what constitutes intervention.[133]

3.3.2 Adjudicating humanitarian intervention in light of Article 2(7)

The upsurge in humanitarian crisis has led to the evolution of theories on humanitarian intervention.[134] Its legitimacy is contested[135] although there are treaty provisions that allow it on certain conditions.[136] Such matters arise because of the inefficiency of the Security Council. Take the fiduciary theory as an example, the *Report of the Independent Inquiry into the Actions of the United Nations During the Genocide in Rwanda* regrets the failure of the United Nations to prevent or stop the genocide.[137] Collective failure paves the way for unlawful unilateralism based on the principle of the "Responsibility to Protect."[138] What is needed is a revamped Security Council.

131 Special Committee on Principles of International Law Concerning Friendly Relations and Co-operation Among States, "The United Kingdom's Proposal" UN Doc. A/AC.119/L.8 (31 August 1964), 7.
132 ibid., 7.
133 Mexico's draft contains eight different categories of prohibited intervention. See Special Committee on Principles of International Law Concerning Friendly Relations and Co-operation Among States, "Mexico's Proposal" UN Doc. A/AC.119/L.24 (21 September 1964), 1–2.
134 Nicholas J. Wheeler, *Saving Strangers: Humanitarian Intervention in International Society* (Oxford, Oxford University Press, 2000) 21–52.
135 Ethan J. Leib and Stephen R. Galoob, "Fiduciary Political Theory: A Critique" (2016) 125(7) *Yale Law Journal* 1820–1878, 1820.
136 VCLT (n 11), art. 64.
137 UN Doc. S/1999/1257 (15 December 1999), 3.
138 Monica Hakimi, "State Bystander Responsibility" (2010) 21(2) *European Journal of International Law* 341–385; Bruno Simma, "NATO, the UN and the Use of Force: Legal Aspects" (1999) 10(1) *European Journal of International Law* 1–22, 2; Eyal Benvenisti, "Sovereigns as Trustees of Humanity: On the Accountability of States to Foreign Stakeholders" (2013) 107(2) *American Journal of International Law* 295–333; Evan J. Criddle, "A Sacred Trust of Civilization: Fiduciary Foundations of International Law" in Andrew S. Gold and Paul B. Miller (eds), *Philosophical Foundations of Fiduciary Law* (Oxford, Oxford University Press, 2014) 404; Evan J. Criddle, "Proportionality in Counterinsurgency: A Relational Theory" (2012) 87(3) *Notre Dame Law Review* 1073–1112, 1077; Evan J. Criddle, "Standing for Human Rights Abroad" (2015) 100(2) *Cornell Law Review* 269–334, 274; Evan J. Criddle and Evan Fox-Decent, "A Fiduciary Theory of Jus Cogens" (2009) 34(1) *Yale Journal of*

64   *Inviolability of State territory*

Conceptually, sovereignty applies to States and not to "officeholders" who enjoy immunity while in office.[139] The line between territorial sovereignty and accountability for the officeholders should not be blurred. Otherwise, the vision of the UN could be jeopardised. In some cases, interventions create more sufferings for those to be rescued.[140] A case in point is the failed policy of "quickly in and quickly out" applied in Cambodia.[141] In Libya, lousy timing was to blame for the worsening humanitarian situation after the intervention.[142] Sometimes, factors motivating unilateral interventions are not altruistic and to apply the liberal manifesto to all cases of freedom fighters is a recipe for anarchy.[143] While a "sit and watch" scenario is morally detestable, a reformed Security Council is recommendable.[144] The Public International Law should not dabble into the jurisdiction of the International Human Rights Law which has mechanisms for holding violators of human rights accountable.

3.4 Other documents from the United Nations

We move on to examine how post Charter instruments and State practice understood State territory.

3.4.1 *The decolonisation period*

The General Assembly's Resolution on the *Declaration on the Granting of Independence to Colonial Countries and Peoples*[145] deals with territorial issues. The

> *International Law* 331–388; Evan Fox-Decent and Evan J. Criddle, "The Fiduciary Constitution of Human Rights" (2009) 15(4) *Legal Theory* 301–336, 309.
>
> 139 G.W.F. Hegel, *Philosophy of Right*, translated by S.W Dyde (Kitchener, Batoche Books, 2001) 195.
> 140 Ben Chigara, "Humanitarian Intervention Missions: Elementary Considerations, Humanity and the Good Samaritans" (2001) *Australian International Law Journal* 66–89.
> 141 Richard A. Falk, "The Cambodian Operation and International Law" (1971) 65(1) *American Journal of International Law* 1–25; Wolfgang Friedmann, "Comments on the Articles on the Legality of the United States Action in Cambodia" (1971) 65(1) *American Journal of International Law* 77–79, 78; Robert H. Bork, "Comments on the Articles on the Legality of the United States Action in Cambodia" (1971) 65(1) *American Journal of International Law* 79–81, 79. *Cf* John N. Moore, "Legal Dimensions of the Decision to Intercede in Cambodia" (1971) 65(1) *American Journal of International Law* 38–75.
> 142 Tim Walker and Nigel Morris, "Barack Obama says David Cameron allowed Libya to Become a Shit Show" (*Independent*, 10 March 2016), available at <www.independent.co.uk/news/uk/politics/barack-obama-says-david-cameron-allowed-libya-to-become-a-s-show-a6923976.html> accessed 22 October 2019.
> 143 Michael J. Smith, "Humanitarian Intervention: An Overview of the Ethical Issues" (1998) 12(1) *Ethics and International Affairs* 63–79, 70.
> 144 Louis Henkin, "Kosovo and the Law of Humanitarian Intervention" (1999) 93(4) *American Journal of International Law* 824–828, 826.
> 145 UNGA Res. A/RES/1514(XV) (14 December 1960), preamble para. 11, declarations 4, 6 and 7.

relevant section declares: "any attempt aimed at the partial or total disruption of the national unity and the territorial integrity of a country is incompatible with the purposes and principles of the Charter of the United Nations."[146] The word "disruption" does not only occur through armed intervention but could embrace other forms of interference which might be covert. The ICJ in the *Frontier Dispute* case[147] holds that *uti possidetis* protects new States from "fratricidal struggles" that could result from the "withdrawal of the administering power." The *Treaty of Peace with Germany*[148] reversed territories of Alsace-Lorraine forcefully ceded to Germany back to France. The African heads of State and government have agreed to "respect the borders existing on their achievement of national independence."[149]

Therefore, State practice encourages collegial acts that facilitate self-determination for peoples under colonial powers.[150] The UN supervised referendum led to political independence for most territories between 1945 and 1979[151] and many others afterwards.[152] The UN General Assembly declared 1990 through 2000 an International Decade for the Eradication of Colonialism.[153] Consequently, the General Assembly's Resolution 65/119[154] calls on member States to "implement the plan of action for the Second International Decade for the Eradication of Colonialism...." These instruments call for collective measures and not unilateral actions.

3.4.2 During the period of military occupation

Article 43 of The Hague Regulations IV (1907)[155] obliges the occupying power to respect the laws in force in a country it occupies. The occupying power must protect the territory of the State.[156] Article 43 applies equally to the UN whenever its organ or agency embarks upon a peacekeeping mission. The occupying power

---

146 ibid., declaration 6.
147 *Frontier Dispute* (Burkina Faso/Republic of Mali) Judgment ICJ Reports (1986) p. 554, para. 20.
148 *The Treaty of Peace with Germany* (Signed at Versailles on 28 June 1919, entered into force on 10 January 1920) (1919) 13(3) *American Journal of International Law Supplement* 151, section V, art. 51.
149 Organisation of African Unity, "Border Disputes Among African States" (Cairo, 17–21 July 1964) AHG/Res.16(I), para. 2 [hereinafter *OAU Resolution on Border Disputes Among African States*].
150 Cassese 1995 (n 99), 90; UNGA Res. A/RES/1514 (XV), preamble para. 6.
151 Hector G. Espiell, "Implementation of United Nations Resolutions Relating to the Right of Peoples Under Colonial and Alien Domination to Self-Determination" UN Doc. E/CN.4/Sub.2/405/Rev.1 (1 January 1980), 46.
152 Cassese 1995 (n 99), 75.
153 UNGA Res. A/RES/43/47 (22 November 1988), operative para. 1.
154 UNGA Res. A/RES/65/119 (10 December 2010), operative para. 2.
155 *The Hague Regulation II* (n 1), art. 43.
156 James Crawford, *Brownlie's Principles of Public International Law*, Eighth Edition (Oxford, Oxford University Press, 2012) 599.

66   *Inviolability of State territory*

assumes the duty of care and is bound by Article 55 to safeguard the State's properties and administer them following "the rules of usufruct."[157]

Similarly, Article 54 of the Geneva Conventions IV (1949)[158] prohibits the occupying power from altering the legal or administrative status in the occupied territories. Instead, the occupying power must take the necessary step to safeguard the rights of the "protected persons" should there be any change in the institutions of government between an occupying power and the State.[159] These laws protect not only the territorial integrity of the occupied States but also the fundamental human rights of the citizens. It leads to the conclusion that a war situation does not diminish or abrogate the sanctity of a State's territory. The occupying power may introduce changes that are necessary for the welfare of the State and its populace.[160]

3.4.3 Treaty regime and State territory

A treaty would bind Contracting Parties if facts were substantially the same.[161] After Palau's independence in 1993, the Security Council terminated the United Nations Trusteeship Agreement because of the substantial change in the circumstance.[162] However, the doctrine of *rebus sic stantibus*[163] does not apply to boundaries established by treaties.[164] Hence, the *Vienna Convention on Succession of States in Respect of Treaties*[165] echoes the same sentiment. James L. Brierly agrees with the judgment of the PCIJ that the doctrine of *rebus sic stantibus* does not defeat the "presumed intention of the parties" but merely fulfils it.[166]

---

157 *The Hague Regulation II* (n 1), art. 55.
158 *The 1949 Geneva Convention IV* (n 1), art. 54.
159 ibid., art. 47.
160 Eyal Benvenisti, *The International Law of Occupation* (Princeton, Princeton University Press, 1993) 11; Yoram Dinstein, *The International Law of Belligerent Occupation* (Cambridge, Cambridge University Press, 2009) 115.
161 Riaz Mohammad Khan, "Vienna Convention on Law of Treaties — Article 62 (Fundamental Change of Circumstances)" (1973) 26(1) *Pakistan Horizon* 16–28, 17.
162 The United Nations and Decolonization, "International Trusteeship System," available at <www.un.org/en/decolonization/its.shtml> accessed 27 September 2019.
163 For further discussion, see Oliver J. Lissitzyn, "Treaties and Changed Circumstances (*Rebus Sic Stantibus*)" (1967) 61(4) *American Journal of International Law* 895–922; J. W. Garner, "The Doctrine of *Rebus Sic Stantibus* and the Termination of Treaties" (1927) 21(3) *American Journal of International Law* 509–516; Herbert W. Briggs, "*Rebus Sic Stantibus* Before the Security Council: The Anglo-Egyptian Question" (1949) 43(4) *American Journal of International Law* 762–769.
164 VCLT (n 11), art. 62(2).
165 *Vienna Convention on Succession of States in Respect of Treaties* (Done at Vienna on 23 August 1978, entered into force on 6 November 1996) 1946 UNTS 3, art. 11.
166 James L. Brierly, *The Law of Nations: An Introduction to the International Law of Peace*, Sixth Edition (Oxford, Clarendon Press, 1963) 336–337.

3.4.4 Soft law and State territory

The adoption of the *Declaration on Principles of International Law Concerning Friendly Relations and Co-operation Among States in Accordance with the Charter of the United Nations* has been described as an attempt by the international community to re-engage with the debate on the specificity of the concept of coexistence as articulated in the "old international law doctrine."[167]

Before that, Resolution 1966 (XVIII) adopted in 1963 established a Special Committee on the Declaration on Friendly Relations.[168] The preambular paragraph recalled the previous Resolutions[169] of the General Assembly which encouraged "making it (the provision of the Charter) a more effective means of furthering the purposes and principles set forth in Articles 1 and 2 of the Charter."[170] The Special Committee was to study the proposed Declaration to ascertain "their progressive development and codification, so as to secure their more effective application."[171] Substantive paragraphs 3(a) and 4 of Resolution 1815 (XVII) invite the UN member States to submit their proposals on the aforesaid Declaration to the Secretary-General.[172]

The degree of divergence of submissions made by States was illuminating. On policy, the top priorities revolved around respect for human rights, economic exploration and exploitation, cultural preservation and the need to put an end to colonialism.[173] The Sixth Committee was to extract a legal instrument acceptable to the UN Member States from complex politically sensitive issues. While the delegates of the developed world interpreted the mandate of the Commission as strengthening the existing principle, some of the representatives of the developing world were thinking about rewriting Article 2(4).[174]

The proposal submitted by Czechoslovakia broadened the scope of Article 2(4) to include "planning, preparation, initiation and waging of a war of aggression ..."[175] Additionally, Czechoslovakia argues that States shall "refrain from economic, political or any other form of pressure aimed against the political independence or territorial integrity of any State."[176] Also, proposals with broad scope were tendered by Yugoslavia[177] and a draft co-authored by Ghana, India and

---

167 McWhinney (n 129), 2.
168 UNGA Res. A/RES/18/1966 (16 December 1963), operative para. 1.
169 UNGA Res. A/RES/15/1505 (12 December 1960), preamble para. 3; UNGA Res. A/RES/16/1686 (18 December 1961), preamble para. 1; UNGA Res. A/RES/17/1815 (18 December 1962), preamble para. 1.
170 UNGA Res. A/RES/1966 (XVIII) (16 December 1963), preamble para. 3 (emphasis added).
171 ibid., preamble para. 4; UNGA Res. A/RES/17/1815 (18 December 1962), operative para. 2.
172 UNGA Res. A/RES/17/1815 (18 December 1962), operative paras 3(a) and 4.
173 John N. Hazard, "The Sixth Committee and New Law" (1963) 57(3) *American Journal of International Law* 604–613, 604.
174 McWhinney (n 129), 3.
175 UN Doc. A/AC.119/L.6 (29 August 1964), 1.
176 ibid., 1.
177 UN Doc. A/AC.119/L.7 (31 August 1964), 1.

68 Inviolability of State territory

Yugoslavia.[178] Other States that extended the reach of the prohibited act to include coercion, whether military, economic or political were "Afghanistan, Algeria, Cambodia, Ceylon, Ethiopia, ... Indonesia, Mali, Morocco, Somalia, Syria, and United Arab Republic."[179] According to the Syrian delegate, Article 2 (4) "should not be construed in the narrow sense to mean only 'armed force'; it should encompass all forms of pressure, avowed or unavowed, direct or indirect, against the territorial integrity or political independence of a State."[180]

In the same vein, "Cameroon, Canada, Central African Republic, Chile, Colombia, Congo (Leopoldville), Dahomey, Denmark, Japan, Liberia, Nigeria, Pakistan, Sierra Leone and Tanganyika" maintain that States are obliged to "respect the territorial integrity and political independence of states ..."[181] Some States commented on proposals submitted by others, some called for clarifications or made observations on written submissions. For Sweden, the principle inherent in Article 2(4) relates to the fundamental questions about "customary international law and of interpretation of the United Nations Charter and the practice under the Charter."[182] Hence, it is unclear whether the "threat or use of force" is "confined to armed physical force" or "covers various types of economic coercion, subversion, revolutionary propaganda, etc ..."[183] According to the United States, the scope of Article 2(4) is broad but the increase in the number of acts brought under its control exceeds what the drafters could have articulated.[184]

Again, the push for the expansion of the scope of Article 2(4) failed but not the desire. The United Kingdom relied upon the *travaux préparatoires* of Article 2(4) to argue that political and economic coercions were beyond what was decided at San Francisco. However, other violations could come under the principle of non-intervention.[185] The representative of the Soviet Union highlighted the difficulty in defining "war propaganda"[186] in the proposal submitted by Czechoslovakia. Guatemala's representative was sceptical that the political pressure of the powerful States might collapse the internal structure of small States.[187] It seems that the inclusion of economic and political coercion within the scope of the prohibited conduct under Article 2(4) again failed because powerful States saw both as instruments of diplomacy. Yet, weaker States were sceptical of their effect on their territorial sovereignty.

Again, this haggling captures the debate that took place when Article 2(4) was drafted. If the binary interpretation suffices, why have another discussion on it? It

---

178 UN Doc. A/AC.119/L.27 (21 September 1964), para. 1.
179 UN Doc. A/AC.119/L.1 (24 June 1964), 10, para. 8.
180 UNGAOR, "Eighteenth Session – Sixth Committee, 812th Meeting" UN Doc. A/C.6/SR.812 (15 November 1963) p. 168, para. 10.
181 UN Doc. A/AC.119/L.1 (24 June 1964) 9, para. 7.
182 ibid., 12, para. 15.
183 ibid.
184 ibid., 12, para. 17.
185 UN Doc. A/AC.119/L.8 (31 August 1964), 3, para. 2.
186 McWhinney (n 129), 10.
187 Hazard (n 173), 609.

Inviolability of State territory 69

should be recalled that the General Assembly Resolution 2625 (XXV) is meant to evaluate "progressive development and codification of" certain principles; one of which is Article 2(4).[188] A regurgitation of the existing norm makes fun of its progressive character. If our initial argument that the line between Articles 2(4) and 2(7) is fluid stands, then the differentiation is unnecessary. Arguably, Vienna Conventions and soft law attest to uneasiness to retain narrow interpretation. This might explain the insertion of the word "inviolability" in some regional instruments as shall be discussed next.

3.4.5 Regional instruments post UN Charter

The words, "respect" or "inviolability" of State territory were expressly codified in some regional instruments. They are the *Charter of the Organization of American States (1948)*,[189] the *Charter of the Organisation of African Unity* (1963)[190] and the *Conference on Security and Cooperation in Europe Helsinki Final Act* (1975).[191] The idea was implied in the Charter of the Arab League (1945),[192] although the founding member States did not highlight it.[193]

The African Heads of State and Government in 1964 committed to "respect the borders existing on their achievement of national independence."[194] The reason is simple. Most Africa countries inherited colonial boundaries, and respect for the *status quo* is adjudged an antidote to crisis and instability on the continent.[195] Consequently, the doctrine of *uti possidetis* helped to avert anarchy from territory-related disputes in Africa. The Organisation of African Unity considers "respect for the sovereignty and territorial integrity of each state and for its inalienable right to independent existence"[196] as a fundamental principle of coexistence. A similar text is found in the *Constitutive Act of the African Union*[197] although Article 4(h) of the Act authorises collective intervention to prevent "war crimes, genocide and crimes against humanity."[198]

---

188 *Declaration on Friendly Relations* (n 1), preamble paras 17–18.
189 *OAS Charter* (n 2), arts 17, 24 and 25.
190 ibid., art. 3.
191 *Helsinki Final Act* (n 2), arts 3 and 4.
192 League of Arab States, *Charter of Arab League* (Done at Cairo on 22 March 1945, entered into force on 10 May 1945) 70 UNTS 248, art. 5.
193 Mark W. Zacher, *International Conflicts and Collective Security, 1946–77: The* United Nations, *Organization of American States, Organization of African Unity and Arab League* (New York, Praeger, 1979) 165, 189.
194 See *OAU Resolution on Border Disputes Among African States* (n 149), operative para. 2.
195 Robert O. Matthews, "Interstate Conflicts in Africa: A Review" (1970) 24(2) *International Organisation* 335–360, 336.
196 *OAU Charter* (n 2), art. III(3).
197 Organisation of African Unity, *Constitutive Act of the African Union* (Adopted on 11 July 2000, entered into force on 26 May 2001) 2158 UNTS 3, art. 4(b) [hereinafter *Constitutive Act of the African Union*]; Organisation of African Unity, "The Territorial Integrity of Basutoland, Bechuanaland and Swaziland" (Adopted by the Assembly of Heads of State and Government in its first Ordinary Session in Cairo, UAR, from 17 to 21 July 1964) AHG/Res.12(I), operative para. 1.
198 *Constitutive Act of the African Union* (n 197), art. 4(h).

70 *Inviolability of State territory*

In Europe, a couple of treaties had safeguarded States' territory before the adoption of the *Conference on Security and Cooperation in Europe Helsinki Final Act* (Helsinki Final Act) in 1975.[199] The bilateral agreements between West Germany and its Communist neighbours obliged the parties "to respect without restriction the territorial integrity of each state."[200] The *1990 Charter of Paris for A New Europe* was founded on two democratic principles of "respect and co-operation."[201] The *General Framework Agreement for Peace in Bosnia and Herzegovina*[202] obliges State parties to "fully respect the sovereign equality of one another." Even when self-determination is at issue, the Badinter Arbitration Committee held that "the right to self-determination must not involve changes to existing frontiers."[203]

However, the most robust instrument that expressly contains the requirement of the inviolability of State territory is the *Helsinki Final Act*.[204] Principle 3 provides as follows: "the participating States regard as inviolable all one another's frontiers as well as the frontiers of all States in Europe and therefore they will refrain now and in the future from assaulting these frontiers."[205] The text of this instrument concluded nearly three decades after the UN Charter is remarkable. Principle 4 obliges the participating States to "respect the territorial integrity of each participating State."[206] The prohibition of physical force by way of military actions is found in Principle 4(3).[207] Hierarchically, the threat or use of force dissipates if respect and inviolability were upheld.

The exclusive right of a sovereign State to its territory can only be modified by agreement.[208] Therefore, the status of Kosovo[209] *vis-à-vis* Martti Ahtisaari's

---

199 *Helsinki Final Act* (n 2), art. 3.
200 John J. Maresca, *To Helsinki: The Conference on Security and Cooperation in Europe, 1973–1975* (Durham, Duke University Press, 1985) 86–87.
201 *Charter of Paris for a New Europe* (Done at Paris on 21 November 1990), preamble para. 1, available at <www.osce.org/mc/39516?download=true> accessed 11 September 2019.
202 Dayton Peace Accords, *General Framework Agreement for Peace in Bosnia and Herzegovina* (Done at Paris on 21 November 1995, entered into force on 14 December 1995), art. 1, available at <http://avalon.law.yale.edu/20th_century/day01.asp> accessed 29 September 2019.
203 Alain Pellet, "The Opinions of the Badinter Arbitration Committee: A Second Breath for the Self-Determination of Peoples" (1992) 3(1) *European Journal of International Law* 178–185, 180.
204 *Helsinki Final Act* (n 2), art. 3.
205 ibid., art. 3(1).
206 ibid., art. 4(1).
207 ibid., art. 4(3).
208 Malcolm N. Shaw, *International Law*, Seventh Edition (Cambridge, Cambridge University Press, 2014) 718.
209 Andreas Zimmermann and Carsten Stahn, "Yugoslav Territory, United Nations Trusteeship or Sovereign State? Reflection on the Current and Future Legal Status of Kosovo" (2001) 70(4) *Nordic Journal of International Law* 423–460.

Inviolability of State territory 71

recommendation[210] and the Security Council Resolutions[211] affirming the territorial integrity of the Federal Republic of Yugoslavia remains ambiguous. The written statements submitted to the ICJ by States that participated in the *Kosovo Advisory Proceedings*[212] appear to favour self-determination. About 37 member States justified Kosovo's secession attempt. Although 37 out of the 193[213] current members of the UN are not widespread to evidence a new custom, it may well signal that States' territories are not inviolable.[214] Edwin has pointed out that Kosovo sets a precedent which undermines the requirement to respect the inviolability of State territory[215] even as the States that supported NATO's activities perceive Kosovo as a case *sui generis*.

However, the dissolution of Yugoslavia in the early 1990s did not persuade the European Community (EC) and the Conference on Security and Co-operation in Europe to change their position on the inviolability of Yugoslavia's territory.[216] The "troika" of the EC Foreign Ministers (Italy, Luxemburg and the Netherlands) initiated peace negotiations while upholding the territorial integrity of Yugoslavia.

The European Council's meetings held in 1991[217] were to determine for the first time the interpretation of the principles enunciated in the Helsinki Final Act as it relates to the principles of territorial integrity, self-determination and non-intervention. The British Foreign Secretary, Douglas Hurd's initial reaction was that the "integrity of Yugoslavia" must be respected.[218] The Secretary-General of

---

210 United Nations Secretary-General, "Report of the Special Envoy of the Secretary-General on Kosovo's Future Status" UN Doc. S/2007/168 (26 March 2007), para. 5 (the report states, "I have come to the conclusion that the only viable option for Kosovo is independence").

211 UNSC Res. S/RES/1160 (31 March 1998), preamble para. 8; UNSC Res. S/RES/1199 (23 September 1998), preamble para. 14.

212 *Accordance with International Law of the Unilateral Declaration of Independence in Respect of Kosovo*, Advisory Opinion ICJ Reports (2010) p. 403. See in particular the written statements of the following states: Albania at pp. 23–24, Estonia at p. 15, Finland at p. 10, Germany at p. 26, the Netherlands at p. 13, Switzerland at pp. 17–18, Ireland at p. 12, Poland at p. 22, Latvia at p. 2, Luxembourg at pp. 1–3, Maldives at pp. 1–2, Slovenia at p. 2, France at pp. 25–26, Japan at pp. 5–6, and the United Kingdom at p. 9.

213 As of September 2019.

214 Daniel H. Meester, "The International Court of Justice's Kosovo Case: Assessing the Current State of International Legal Opinion on Remedial Secession" (2010) 48 *Canadian Yearbook of International Law* 215–254, 246.

215 Edwin Bakker, "The Recognition of Kosovo: Violating Territorial Integrity is a Recipe for Trouble" (2008) 19(3) *Security and Human Rights* 183–186, 185; Svante E. Cornell, S. Frederick Starr and Mamuka Tsereteli, *A Western Strategy for the South Caucasus* (Washington D.C., The Central Asia-Caucasus Institute and Silk Road Studies Program, 2015) 27.

216 Marc Weller, "The International Response to the Dissolution of the Socialist Federal Republic of Yugoslavia" (1992) 86(3) *American Journal of International Law* 569–607, 570.

217 ibid., 571.

218 ibid., 572.

72   Inviolability of State territory

the Western European Union, Willem van Eekelen suggested that troops could be sent not to defend the territory of Yugoslavia but to understudy the sources of the crisis and observe the process. Still, the Soviet Union construed that as intervention.[219] In short, Yugoslavia was a case of dissolution[220] such that a unilateral external intervention would be unlawful.[221] According to the Arbitration Commission chaired by Robert Badinter,[222] the established principle of international law does not admit changes to the existing frontiers at the time of independence except where the parent State consents to its alteration.[223]

Consequently, the guideline issued by the EC for recognising new States provides that "respect for the inviolability of all frontiers ... can only be changed by peaceful means and by common agreement."[224] The guideline is silent on whether third States could facilitate self-determination but expressly obliges State parties to respect the UN Charter and the Helsinki Final Act.[225] It follows that respect for the inviolability of States' territory has become a "general principle of law recognised by civilized nations" in accordance with Article 38(c) of the Statute of the ICJ. Article 3 of the *Charter of the Commonwealth of Independent States*[226] uses the word "inviolability" interchangeably with the phrase "respect for the sovereignty of member states."

In the Americas, the cumulative effect of President Woodrow Wilson's Fourteen Point Agenda and Monroe's Doctrine is geared toward respecting territorial sovereignty. This view is articulated in Articles 17, 24 and 25 of the Charter of the Organisation of American States.[227] Unfortunately, the United States and the Soviet Union have been accused of not being altruistically committed to those noble ideals.[228] We conclude that the insertion of "inviolability" and "respect" in most if not all regional instruments after the UN Charter had entered into force shows that respect for the inviolability of State territory has a universal appeal.

219 ibid., 575.
220 Robert Badinter, "Conference on Yugoslavia Arbitration Committee – Opinions" (1991) 31(6) *International Legal Materials* 1494–1526, 1497, para. 3(b).
221 Commission of the European Communities, "Joint Statement on Yugoslavia – 28 August 1991" (1991) 24(7/8) *Bulletin of the European Communities* 115–116.
222 For legal issues and the opinion of the Commission, see Maurizo Ragazzi, "Conference on Yugoslavia Arbitration Commission: Opinions on Questions Arising from the Dissolution of Yugoslavia" (1992) 31(6) *International Legal Materials* 1488–1493.
223 Badinter (n 220), 1498, para. 1(b).
224 The European Community, "Declaration on Yugoslavia and on the Guidelines on the Recognition of New States" (1992) 31(6) *International Legal Materials* 1485–1487, 1487, operative para. 3 (emphasis mine).
225 ibid., 1487, para. 1.
226 *Charter of the Commonwealth of Independent States (with Declaration and Decisions)* (Adopted at Minsk on 22 January 1993, entered into force on 24 January 1994) 1819 UNTS 58, art. 3; Michael B. Bishku, "The South Caucasus Republics: Relations with the U.S. and the EU" (2015) 22(2) *Middle East Policy* 40–57.
227 *OAS Charter* (n 2), arts 17, 24 and 25.
228 Ryan Griffiths, "The Future of Self-Determination and Territorial Integrity in the Asian Century" (2014) 27(3) *The Pacific Review* 457–478, 460.

Inviolability of State territory 73

3.5 Respect and inviolability: a retrospective exegesis of Article 2(4)

As seen, the *travaux préparatoires* favour narrow construction because the drafters were preoccupied with saving "succeeding generations from the scourge of war." However, it seems that political considerations played a palliative role in reconciling contradictory views. Before the UN was born, foreign policy was conducted "through force or the threat of the imposition of force."[229] Nation-bullying became so intolerable for Latin Americans that "the Inter-American Commission of Jurists recommended the adoption of a principle of non-interference" in 1927.[230] By 1933 the *Montevideo Convention* was adopted and "a defined territory" became a condition for Statehood. The Inter-American Conference held at Buenos Aires in 1936 outlawed "intervention of any one of them, directly or indirectly, and for whatever reason, in the internal or external affairs of the parties."[231]

The principle of non-intervention was also enshrined in the Act of Chapultepec. No doubt, the desire to evolve a functional supranational organisation with the backup of the United States, unlike the defunct League of Nations, may have influenced negotiations during the drafting of the UN Charter. Nonetheless, Baine contends that Article 2(4) is expandable for the following reasons: first, documents contemporaneous to the UN Charter adopted an all-inclusive phrase; second, the provision of the Charter that permits self-defence when there is an armed attack (Article 51) is not inconsistent with broad interpretation; third, the broad reading agrees with the purposes of the UN as enshrined in Article 1(1) of the Charter; fourth, submissions made by States when the General Assembly Resolution 2625 (XXV) was drafted support a broad interpretation; fifth, the definition of aggression recommends that circumstantial evidence less physical armed force should be taken into account.[232]

3.5.1 Contextualising the use of force in the post-1945 world

The restrictive interpretation of Article 2(4) trivialises the fact that force does not happen unexpectedly. Physical force belongs to the family of coercion and is often undertaken as a last resort. The Latin word *coercere* means "to control, restrain."[233] This is the primary purpose of threat or use of force. Coercion has been defined as "the use of threatened force, including the limited use of actual force to back up the threat, to induce an adversary to behave differently than it otherwise would."[234] Therefore, force is coercion of military nature and "...

---

229 Edward Gordon, "Article 2(4) and Permissive Pragmatism" (1984) 78 *Proceedings of the Annual Meeting (American Society of International Law)* 87–99, 90.
230 ibid., 91.
231 ibid.
232 Baine (n 30), 997–999.
233 Online Etymology Dictionary, "Coercion," available at <www.etymonline.com/search?q=coercion> accessed 13 September 2019.
234 Daniel L. Byman, Matthew C. Waxman and Eric Larson, *Air Power as a Coercive Instrument* (Washington D.C., Rand Corporation, 1999) 10.

74 *Inviolability of State territory*

consists of military conflict between nations or groups of nations and is often accompanied by undisguised invasion of another's territory either for aggression or defensive purposes."[235] Such measures are activated to enforce a frustrating diplomatic, ideological or economic coercion. Recall that the ICJ in the *Nicaragua* case said that a State could adopt any political ideology of its choice. That States are not at war with each other does not necessarily mean that they are at peace. Surprisingly, ideological coercion by way of hostile propaganda directed against the territorial integrity of a State is beyond the reach of Article 2(4). Even when no armed intervention is involved, such acts undermine the territorial integrity or political independence of the affected State. It is part of what the ILC describes as "indirect aggression."[236]

When evaluating any coercive measures, factors that should be considered are intensity and purpose. Take ideological coercion as an example: actions could range from comments on internal affairs of a State, adverse and severe public criticism of another government "to extraterritorial broadcasting"[237] and "dropping propaganda leaflets ..."[238] to incite revolution. Hans Kelsen once said, "every state may resort to war against another state for any reason whatsoever without violating international law, unless a state has assumed an obligation in a treaty which restricts its freedom of action in this respect."[239] The notion of lawful and unlawful coercions is recent. It started from the time of Bodin and Hobbes when "force" was limited to coercions that could ignite a global war.[240] Although not all military coercion or use of force leads to war, armed force is multilayer as buttresses by *de minimis* rule. Yet Article 2(4) makes no such exemption.

After the *Carolin* incident, the United States and the United Kingdom agreed that necessity could trigger armed self-defence. The *Convention (II) Respecting the Limitation of the Employment of Force for the Recovery of Contract Debts*[241] prohibited armed force as a means of debt recovery. The *Treaty for the Renunciation of War* condemns "recourse to war for the solution of international controversies, and renounce it as an instrument of national policy in their relations with one another."[242] The Nuremberg Charter expanded the scope of "crime against

---

235 Baine (n 30), 989.
236 UNGAOR – Sixth Session Supplement No. 9, UN Doc. A/1858 (16 May – 27 July 1951) 9, para. 47.
237 Baine (n 30), 992.
238 UNSCOR S/3232 (19 June 1954) 1–3.
239 Hans Kelsen, "Collective Security Under General International Law" (1954) 49 *International Law Studies Series. US Naval War College* 34–52, 35.
240 W. Michael Reisman, "Article 2(4): The use of force in Contemporary International Law" (1984) 78 *Proceedings of the Annual Meeting (American Society of International Law)* 74–87, 74–75.
241 *Convention Respecting the Limitation of the Employment of Force for the Recovery of Contract Debts* (1908) 2(1/2) *American Journal of International Law (Supplement)* 81–85, art. 1.
242 *Treaty for the Renunciation of War* (Signed at Paris 27 August 1928), art. 1, available at <https://avalon.law.yale.edu/20th_century/kbpact.asp> accessed 13 September 2019.

Inviolability of State territory 75

peace" to include "… planning, preparation, initiation, or waging of a war of aggression, or a war in violation of international treaties, agreements or assurances, or participation in a common plan or conspiracy for the accomplishment of any of the foregoing."[243] The resolution of the General Assembly provides that a case of aggression is determined having regard to "… all the circumstances of each particular case …"[244]

3.5.2 Balancing opposing views on the scope of Article 2(4)

Two reasons have been adduced to downplay attempts to expand Article 2(4): First is the difficulty in measuring motives, purpose and intensity in a manner that accommodates economic and political coercion without introducing ambiguity in the law. Second, if uncertainty were introduced, it might lead to noncompliance because the prohibition of armed force will no longer be imperative.[245] Though credible, these objections are not overwhelming to discharge the relevance of a broad interpretation. Concerning the question of clarity, arguments are not formidable that "balancing in regard to economic and political coercion would taint the consideration of clear military violation of article 2(4)."[246] The proposals of Czechoslovakia and Yugoslavia merely expanded the scope. Regarding the second objection, State parties knew that Article 2(4) prohibits armed force. The inclusion of other elements strengthens this purpose rather than weakens it.[247] Therefore, the definition of aggression is elastic to include "… planning, preparation, initiation …" *et cetera*.

The broad meaning is recognised at a regional level. First, Article 15 of the 1948 Charter of the Organisation of American States[248] prohibits "any other form of interference or attempted threat against the personality of a State." Similarly, Article 16 prohibits the "use of coercive measures of an economic or political character to force the sovereign will of another state."[249] Second, the *communiqué* issued by the African-Asian World Peace Conference in 1955 requires States to abstain "from exerting pressures on other countries."[250] Third, the Belgrade

---

243 *Charter of the International Military Tribunal* (Nuremberg Trial Proceedings, Volume 1), art. 6(a), available at <https://avalon.law.yale.edu/imt/imtconst.asp> accessed 13 September 2019.

244 UNGA Res. A/RES/3314 (XXIX) (14 December 1974), Annex, preamble para. 11.

245 Louis Henkin analysed a similar demand for broadening the scope of Article 51 of the UN Charter. See Louis Henkin, "Force, Intervention, and Neutrality in Contemporary International Law" (1963) 57 *Proceedings of the American Society of International Law at Its Annual Meeting* 147–173; Baine (n 30), 1005.

246 Baine (n 30), 1005.

247 For the definition of respect for the inviolability of State territory as put forward by Hyde, see Derek W. Bowett, *Self-Defence in International Law* (Manchester, Manchester University Press, 1958) 39.

248 *OAS Charter* (n 2), art. 15.

249 ibid., art. 16.

250 *Final Communique of the Asian-African Conference of Bandung* (24 April 1955), art. 6(b), available at <http://franke.uchicago.edu/Final_Communique_Bandung_1955. pdf> accessed 28 September 2019.

76 Inviolability of State territory

Declaration[251] recognises that the reduction in the growth of military blocs will enhance world peace and international relations. Fourth, virtually all regional instruments[252] adopted either the word "inviolability" or "respect" or both concepts.

As State practice shows, member States resist economic or political coercion. When Egypt interdicted Israeli vessels in the Suez Canal, Egypt was held in breach of armistice agreements that allow non-interference "... with the rights of nations to navigate the seas and to trade freely with one another, including the Arab States and Israel."[253] In 1960, Cuba equated economic coercion with military aggression while protesting against the United States' decision to reduce the quota of sugar it supplied to it. According to the Cuban delegate to the Security Council "... the punitive measures proposed [by the United States] have ... ranged from the elimination of the sugar quota – economic aggression – to the landing of marines – military aggression ..."[254] In response, the United States argued that Cuba engaged in "provocative actions" against her; some of which included "Cuban propaganda activity in the diplomatic sphere" and "false allegations by Cuban press and radio."[255] No matter how both arguments are looked at, neither States accepted conduct less than armed force.

Ecuador accused the United States of economic bullying in contravention of Article 19 of the OAS Charter when the latter suspended sales of military hardware to it in retaliation for the former's interdiction of its vessels within its claimed territorial waters.[256] Economic espionage which has been a subject for intense

---

251 *Belgrade Declaration of Non-Aligned Countries* (Adopted at the first conference of Head of State or Government of Non-Aligned Countries, Belgrade, 6 September 1961), part 1, para. 9, available at <http://cns.miis.edu/nam/documents/Official_Document/1st_Summit_FD_Belgrade_Declaration_1961.pdf> accessed 29 September 2019; Hans Blix, "Report of the Special Committee on Principles of International Law Concerning Friendly Relations and Co-operation among States – Nineteenth Session" UN Doc. A/5746 (16 November 1964) 34–35.

252 *Locarno Pact* (n 39), art. 1. Some authors have argued that the Locarno Pact permits adjustment of boundaries through peaceful negotiations, see Philip M. H. Bell, *The Origins of the Second World War in Europe*, Second Edition (New York, Longman, 1997) 36–37. Other authors argue that the boundaries delimited by the pact were meant to be final, see Felix Gilbert, *The End of the European Era, 1890 to the Present*, Second Edition (New York and London, Norton, 1984) 221–222; *OAU Charter* (n 2), arts 2 and 3; Jeffrey Herbst, "The Creation and Maintenance of National Boundaries in Africa" (1989) 43(4) *International Organization* 673–692, 674–677; Peter Malanczuk, *Akehurst's Modern Introduction to International Law*, Seventh Revised Edition (London and New York, Routledge, 1997) 162; Steven R. Ratner, "Drawing a Better Line: *Uti Possidetis* and the Borders of New States" (1996) 90(4) *American Journal of International Law* 590–624, 595–596; Mark W. Zacher, "The Territorial Integrity Norm: International Boundaries and the Use of Force" (2001) 55(2) *International Organisation* 215–250, 221–223; *Helsinki Final Act* (n 2), art. 3(1).

253 UNSCOR, UN Doc. S/2298/Rev.1 (15 August 1951), para. 9.

254 As quoted in Baine (n 30), 1007; see also UNSCOR, UN Doc. S/4378 (11 July 1960) 1–3.

255 UNSCOR, UN Doc. S/4388 (15 July 1960), Annex Memorandum, pp. 8–9.

256 Joseph John Jova, "A Review of the Progress and Problems of the Organization of American States" (1971) 65 *Department of State Bulletin* 284–294, 287.

Inviolability of State territory 77

discussion[257] has strained the relationship between the United States and China due to trade war.[258] It has been suggested that economic coercion directed against a State is to "provoke a domestic social crisis that could lead to either the overthrow ... or the discrediting of the government."[259] It is a deliberate fiscal policy enforced through economic sanctions, denial of access to international funds, embargo and restriction on trade and so forth. Does it further international peace and security?

3.5.3 Economic and political coercion v States' sovereignty

States are not duty-bound to assist others, even financially. However, *mala fide* contracts are voidable. Therefore, States are expected to engage in fair business practices according to established standard for corporate development.[260] A "cumulative list of published disputes"[261] from the World Trade Organisation shows how unfair business practices strain international relations. However, only economic coercion deployed against the territorial integrity and political independence of a State could trigger Article 2(4). While the line between "smart negotiation" and intimidation might be fluid, the difference lies in purposes to which domestic fiscal policies are directed. There is no gainsaying that a State crippled by economic coercion might resort to self-help if it has the capability.[262]

3.6 Dual meaning of Article 2(4) of the UN Charter

From what has been said, the narrow interpretation which has dominated the discourse on Article 2(4)[263] neglects unlawful means by which the territory of

257 Anonymous, "United States and China Reach Agreement Regarding Economic Espionage and International Cybersecurity Norms" (2015) 109(4) *American Journal of International Law* 878–882.
258 Kara Loridas, "United States-China Trade War: Signs of Protectionism in a Globalised Economy" (2011) 34(2) *Suffolk Transnational Law Review* 403–427.
259 James F. Petras and Robert LaPorte, "Can We Do Business with Radical Nationalists? Chile: No" (1972) 7 *Foreign Policy* 132–158, 139.
260 Joseph E. Stiglitz and Andrew Charlton, *Fair Trade for All: How Trade can Promote Development* (Oxford, Oxford University Press, 2005) 4–6.
261 World Trade Organisation, *Dispute Settlement Reports 2017: Volume VIII Papers 3767 to 4372* (Cambridge, Cambridge University Press, 2018) 4343–4372.
262 Baine (n 30), 1009–1010.
263 Cassese 1986 (n 99), 137; Paul R. Hensel, Michael E. Allison and Ahmed Khanani, "Territorial Integrity Treaties and Armed Conflict over Territory" (2009) 26(2) *Conflict Management and Peace Science* 120–143, 123; *The Covenant of the League of Nations* (n 35), art. 10; *Anti-war Treaty of Non-aggression and Conciliation* (Adopted at Rio de Janeiro Brazil on 10 October 1933), art. 2, available at <http://avalon.law. yale.edu/20th_century/intam01.asp> accessed 17 September 2019 (note that this Treaty has been superseded by the American Treaty on Pacific Settlement (Pact of Bogotá 1948). Now it applies if the parties to a dispute have ratified the Pact of Bogotá 1948; *Convention on Rights and Duties of States Adopted by the Seventh International Conference of American States* (Signed at Montevideo on 16 December

78 *Inviolability of State territory*

States could be violated. Presently, cyberattacks pose significant threats to international peace and security.[264] The Council of Europe "reiterates that any country that relies extensively on cyberspace might be influenced by cyberattacks the same way as by conventional acts of aggression."[265] Chapter 4 focuses attention on the impact of cyberspace on State territory. Next to consider is the effect of *de minimis* rule on the classical interpretation of Article 2(4).

3.6.1 *The* de minimis *rule and issues regarding broad interpretation*

The *de minimis* rule originates from the Roman Law and has two aspects: namely, procedural and substantive.[266] The procedural element deals with the practice by which the *praetor* does not concern himself with triviality (*de minimis non curat praetor*). The substantive element is derived from the *de minimis non curat lex* maxim, which means that the law does not deal with triviality.[267]

The ICJ uses the phrase "mere frontier incidents" to refer to minimal incursions[268] that do not trigger the right to self-defence. This interpretation is widely debated.[269] Again, we see such a debate in the Eritrea/Ethiopia Claims Commission Award on Ethiopia's *jus ad bellum* Claims 1–8.[270] In fact, the Commission was to determine

> 1933, entered into force on 26 December 1934) 165 LNTS 19, art. 11; *UN Charter* (n 32), art. 2(4); *OAS Charter* (n 2), art. 21; *Protocol on Non-Aggression* (Concluded at Lagos on 22 April 1978, entered into force provisionally on 13 May 1982) 1690 UNTS 39, arts 1, 2; *SADC Protocol on Politics, Defense and Security Co-operation* (Done at Blantyre on 14 August 2001, entered into force on 2 March 2004), art. 11, available at <www.sadc.int/files/3613/5292/8367/Protocol_on_Politics_Defence_and_Security20001.pdf> accessed 17 September 2019.
>
> 264 Organisation for Security and Co-operation in Europe Parliamentary Assembly, "Resolution on Cyber Security" paras 1–4, available at <www.oscepa.org/meetings/annual-sessions/2013-istanbul-annual-session/2013-istanbul-final-declaration/1652-15> accessed 29 September 2019 [hereinafter *Council of Europe Resolution on Cyber Security*]; UNSC Res. S/RES/2341 (13 February 2017), preamble para. 15; UNGA Res. A/RES/57/239 (31 January 2003), preamble para. 2.
>
> 265 *Council of Europe Resolution on Cyber Security* (n 264), para. 5.
>
> 266 Janja Hojnik, "De Minimis Rule within the EU Internal Market Freedoms: Towards a More Mature and Legitimate Market?" (2013) 6(1) *European Journal of Legal Studies* 25–45, 26.
>
> 267 ibid., 26–27.
>
> 268 *Nicaragua* case (n 33), paras 191, 195 and 247; *Corfu Channel* case (n 73), 30–31 (the Court's opinion that the passage of the Royal Navy could "demonstrate such force" means that it constitutes a threat but not sufficient to constitute a violation of Albania's sovereignty).
>
> 269 Corten (n 63), 55, 77; Mary Ellen O'Connell, "The True Meaning of Force" (2014) 108 *American Journal of International Law Unbound* 141–144; Gray (n 74), 148; Independent International Fact-Finding Mission on the Conflict in Georgia, *Reports* (Volume II, September 2009) 242, available at <www.mpil.de/en/pub/publications/archive/independent_international_fact.cfm> accessed 28 September 2019 [hereinafter *Report on the Conflict in Georgia*].
>
> 270 *Eritrea/Ethiopia Claims Commission Partial Award – Jus Ad Bellum – Ethiopia's Claims 1–8* (2006) 45 *International Legal Materials* 430–435, para. 11.

Inviolability of State territory 79

who fired the first shot in May and in June 1998 and whether the supposed victim State could rely on the right to self-defence. On facts as presented, the Commission was unable to make such a determination but instead held that the incursions were relatively minor incidents that did not qualify as an armed attack.[271]

In 1970, Thomas Franck reported that Article 2(4) had been murdered[272] but was reassured that it was instead in a coma and could be resuscitated.[273] It seems that the time for resuscitation is running out. In the view of some authors, the right to self-defence "covers all physical force which surpasses a minimum threshold of intensity."[274] It excludes "targeted Killing of single individuals, forcible abductions of individual persons, or the interception of a single aircraft."[275] Some authors argue that "operations aimed at rescuing nationals abroad, 'hot pursuit' operations, small-scale counterterrorist operations abroad, and localized hostile encounter between military units"[276] were not covered by Article 2(4).

Tom Ruys has reappraised the effects of *de minimis* rule on State territory.[277] According to him, since the prohibition of the use of force is a *jus cogens* norm, "no consideration of whatever nature may be invoked to warrant resorting to the threat or use of force in violation of the Charter."[278] For Sharp, Article 2(4) prohibits unarmed physical force such as the spreading of fire across a State

---

271 ibid., para. 12.
272 Thomas M. Franck, "Who Killed Article 2(4) or: Changing Norms Governing the Use of Force by States" (1970) 64(4) *American Journal of International Law* 809–837.
273 Louis Henkin, "The Reports of the Death of Article 2(4) are Greatly Exaggerated" (1971) 65 *American Journal of International Law* 544–548.
274 *Report on the Conflict in Georgia* (n 269), 242; Corten (n 63), 77.
275 *Report on the Conflict in Georgia* (n 269), 242 (footnote 49).
276 Tom Ruys, "The Meaning of 'Force' and the Boundaries of the *Jus ad bellum*: Are Minimal Uses of Force Excluded from UN Charter 2(4)?" (2014) 108(2) *American Journal of International Law* 159–210, 159.
277 ibid., 159–210.
278 ibid., 161–162; UNGA Res. A/RES/42/22 (18 November 1987), Annex – Section I, para. 3. For whether the use of force is permitted as a countermeasure operation, see Josef Mrazek, "Prohibition of the Use and Threat of Force: Self-Defence and Self-Help in International Law" (1989) 27 *Canadian Yearbook of International Law* 81–112, 90; *Draft Articles on Responsibility of States for Internationally Wrongful Acts* (Adopted by the International Law Commission at its Fifty-Third Session in 2001, Volume II, Part II, *Yearbook of the International Law Commission*, 2001) 26, art. 66 [hereinafter *Articles on Responsibility of States*]; *Arbitral Tribunal Constituted Pursuant to Article 287, and in Accordance with Annex VII, of the United Nations Convention on the Law of the Sea in the Matter of an Arbitration Between Guyana and Suriname* (Permanent Court of Arbitration, The Hague 17 September 2007) 30 RIAA 1–144, para. 446 [hereinafter *Guyana/Suriname Award*]; For argument against necessity, see Gray (n 74), 217–19; Roberto Ago, "Addendum to the Eighth Report on State Responsibility" (Volume II, Part I, *Yearbook of International Law Commission*, 1980) 13, paras 7, 8, 18, 56, 40–41, 58–59, 44 and 66; *cf* Jens David Ohlin, "The Bounds of Necessity" (2008) 6(2) *Journal of International Criminal Justice* 289–308; *Articles on Responsibility of States*, art. 25(2).

80 Inviolability of State territory

frontier.[279] Hence, the conjunctive phrase, "inconsistent with the purposes of the United Nations" is a comprehensive ban.[280]

However, some judicial decisions consider rescue operations kept within the ambit of reasonableness and necessity as lawful.[281] Judge Simma supports proportionate countermeasures undertaken by a victim State to stop ongoing violation.[282] While self-defence is allowed, enforcement could be a complicated process. For instance, was the abduction of Adolf Eichmann from Argentina's territory, the kidnapping of Herr Lampersberger from the Czechoslovakian territory and the abduction of Herr Berthold Jacob-Salomon from Swiss territory lawful without prior authorisation?[283] Although exceptions to the law are premised on "practicality and common sense,"[284] it must be admitted that a State's conduct which strains its relations with another State does not enhance international peace and security. Respect entails attitudinal change towards accepting the sovereignty of other States. It must be acknowledged that persistent minimal incursions into the territory of other States could endanger international peace and security.[285]

279 Walter Gary Sharp, *Cyberspace and the Use of Force* (Falls Church, Aegis Research Corporation, 1999) 101; Daniel B. Silver, "Computer Network Attack as a Use of Force Under Article 2(4) of the United Nations Charter" in Michael N. Schmitt and Brian T. O'Donnell (eds), *Computer Network Attack and International Law* (Newport, US Naval War College, 2002) 82–83.
280 Louis Henkin, *How Nations Behave: Law and Foreign Policy*, Second Edition (New York, Columbia University Press, 1968) 136–138; Sean D. Murphy, "Terrorism and the Concept of Armed Attack in Article 51 of the U.N. Charter" (2002) 43(1) *Harvard International Law Journal* 41–52, 42; Dino Kritsiotis, "When States Use Armed Force" in Christian Reus-Smit (ed.), *The Politics of International Law* (Cambridge, Cambridge University Press, 2004) 58–59.
281 International Tribunal for the Law of the Sea, *The M/V "Saiga" (No. 2)* case (Saint Vincent and Grenadines v Guinea) Judgment (1999) 38 *International Legal Materials* 1323–1364, para. 155; *Guyana/Suriname Award* (n 278), para. 445; *S.S. "I'm Alone"* (Canada v United States) Award (1933) 3 RIAA 1609–1618, 1615.
282 *Oil Platforms* (Islamic Republic of Iran v United States of America) Judgment ICJ Reports (2003) p. 161 [hereinafter *Oil Platforms* case] (see the Separate Opinion of Judge Simma at p. 331, para. 12).
283 For analysis see Edwin D. Dickinson, "Jurisdiction Following Seizure or Arrest in Violation of International Law" (1934) 28(2) *American Journal of International Law* 231–245; Lawrence Preuss, "Kidnaping of Fugitives from Justice on Foreign Territory" (1935) 29(3) *American Journal of International Law* 502–507; Hans W. Baade, "The Eichmann Trial: Some Legal Aspects" (1961) 10(3) *Duke Law Journal* 400–420; Felice Morgenstern, "Jurisdiction in Seizures Effected in Violation of International Law" (1952) 29 *British Yearbook of International Law* 265–282.
284 O'Connell (n 269), 143.
285 Mario Amadeo, "Letter Dated 15 June 1960 from the Representative of Argentina Addressed to the President of the Security Council" UN Doc. S/4336 (15 June 1960) 1–3; UNSC Res. S/138 (23 June 1960), para. 1; see generally, UNSCOR, UN Doc. S/PV.865 (22 June 1960); UNSCOR, UN Doc. S/PV.868 (23 June 1960).

3.6.2 Jus cogens *character of Article 2(4)*

According to the ILC, "the law of the Charter concerning the prohibition of the use of force in itself constitutes a conspicuous example of a rule in international law having the character of *jus cogens*."[286] The ICJ's jurisprudence[287] and scholarship[288] endorse this interpretation. Article 53 of the VCLT[289] designates a peremptory norm as a norm "accepted and recognised by the international community of States as a whole as a norm from which no derogation is permitted." By "derogation" is meant that no treaty can modify or set aside a peremptory norm,[290] except a sub-

---

286 See "Report of the International Law Commission on the Work of its eighteenth session – Geneva, 4 May–19 July 1966," Vol. II, Part II (*Yearbook of the International Law Commission,* 1966) 247.

287 *Nicaragua* case (n 33), para. 190; *Oil Platforms* case (n 282), 378 (Separate Opinion of Judge Rigaux); *DRC v Uganda* (n 33), 223–225 (the Court described the prohibited act under Article 2(4) as a cornerstone of the United Nations Charter).

288 Alexander Orakhelashvili, *Peremptory Norms in International Law* (Oxford, Oxford University Press, 2006) 51; Ian D. Seiderman, *Hierarchy in International Law: The Human Rights Dimension* (Antwerp, Intersentia, 2001) 61; Corten (n 63), 200–213; James Crawford, *The Creation of International Law*, Second Edition (New York, Oxford University Press, 2006) 146; Dinstein 2011 (n 74), 99–104; Wheeler (n 134), 44–45; Mohammad Taghi Karoubi, *Just or Unjust War? International Law and Unilateral Use of Armed Force by States at the Turn of the 20th Century* (Burlington, Ashgate Publishing Company, 2004) 108–109; Lindsay Moir, *Reappraising the Resort to Force: International Law, Jus Ad Bellum and the War on Terror* (Oxford, Hart Publishing, 2010) 9; Lauri Hannikainen, *Peremptory Norms (Jus Cogens) in International Law: Historical Development, Criteria, Present Status* (Helsinki, Finnish Lawyers Publication Co., 1988) 323, 356; Ian Sinclair, *The Vienna Convention on the Law of Treaties*, Second Edition (Manchester, Manchester University Press, 1984) 215–216, 222–223; Robert Kolb, *Peremptory International Law – Jus Cogens: A General Inventory* (Oxford, Hart Publishing, 2015) 124; Dino Kritsiotis, "Reappraising Policy Objections to Humanitarian Intervention" (1998) 19(4) *Michigan Journal of International Law* 1005–1050, 1042–1043; Carin Kahgan, "Jus Cogens and the Inherent Right to Self- Defense" (1997) 3(3) *ILSA Journal of International & Comparative Law* 767–828, 777–781; Jonathan I. Charney, "Anticipatory Humanitarian Intervention in Kosovo" (1999) 93(4) *American Journal of International Law* 834–841, 837; Michael N. Schmitt, "Computer Network Attack and the Use of Force in International Law: Thoughts on a Normative Framework" (1999) 37(3) *Columbia Journal of Transnational Law* 885–938, 922; Oscar Schachter, "In Defense of International Rules on the Use of Force" (1986) 53(1) *University of Chicago Law Review* 113–146, 129; Egon Schwelb, "Some Aspects of International *Jus Cogens* as Formulated by the International Law Commission" (1967) 61(4) *American Journal of International Law* 946–975, 952; Pamela J. Stephens, "A Categorical Approach to Human Rights Claims: Jus Cogens as a Limitation on Enforcement?" (2004) 22(2) *Wisconsin International Law Journal* 245–272, 253–254; Alfred Verdross, "Jus Dispositivum and Jus Cogens in International Law" 60(1) *American Journal of International Law* 55–63, 60; Simma 1999 (n 138), 3; Marjorie M. Whiteman, "Jus Cogens in International Law, with a Projected List" (1977) 7(2) *Georgia Journal of International & Comparative Law* 609–628, 625.

289 VCLT (n 11), art. 53.

290 Corten (n 63), 200.

82 Inviolability of State territory

sequent peremptory norm having the same character.[291] Even the distinction between aggression and the lesser form of the use of force does not affect the peremptory character of Article 2(4).[292]

A peremptory norm is a "concern of all States."[293] States "have a legal interest in their protection."[294] In the *Case Concerning Armed Activities on the Territory of the Congo*,[295] Judge Simma said, "if there ever was a military activity before the Court that deserves to be qualified as an act of aggression, it is the Ugandan invasion of the DRC."[296] It shows the difficulty in compartmentalising Article 2 (4) into the "use of force," "armed attack" or "aggression." Admittedly, there is a disconnect between the conceptual designation of Article 2(4) as a peremptory norm on the one hand and conducts that undermine other States' territory on the other hand. This is without prejudice to contending issues such as human rights, self-determination, humanitarian intervention, *et cetera*.[297]

Arguably, it is not proven whether human rights are capable of modifying or abrogating Article 2(4).[298] It would indeed appear not to be so. Although the ICJ in the *East Timor* case affirms that the right to self-determination has an *erga omnes* character,[299] not all *erga omnes* obligations derive from peremptory norms.[300] The benefits accruing from the *de minimis* breaches of States' territory are not worth disrupting international peace and security. Strict compliance with the UN Charter in matters of collective action is still a credible option.

291 VCLT (n 11), art. 53; Ruys (n 276), 160.
292 Corten (n 63), 200.
293 *Barcelona Traction, Light and Power Company, Limited* (Second Phase) Judgment ICJ Reports (1970) p. 3, para. 33.
294 ibid., para. 33.
295 *DRC v Uganda* (n 33), 334–335 (Separate Opinion of Judge Simma).
296 ibid., 335 (Separate Opinion of Judge Simma).
297 Simma 1999 (n 138), 2–3; *Application of the Convention on the Prevention and Punishment of the Crime of Genocide* (Bosnia and Herzegovina v Serbia and Montenegro) Judgment ICJ Reports (2007) p. 43, paras 163, 165; Anthony D'Amato, "The Invasion of Panama was a Lawful Response to Tyranny" (1990) 84(2) *American Journal of International Law* 516–524, 516, 520; W. Michael Reisman, "Coercion and Self-determination: Construing Charter Article 2(4)" (1984) 78(3) *American Journal of International Law* 642–645, 643; *cf* Louis Henkin, "The Use of Force: Law and U.S. Policy" in Louis Henkin *et al.* (eds), *Right v. Might: International Law and the Use of Force* (New York and London, Council on Foreign Relations Press, 1989) 38 (Henkin argues that these other objectives must be sought via other means other than the use of force); Cassese 1995 (n 99), 199–200; Oscar Schachter, "The Legality of Pro-democratic Invasion" (1984) 78(3) *American Journal of International Law* 645–650, 649.
298 David Wippman, "Treaty-Based Intervention: Who Can Say No" (1995) 62(2) *University of Chicago Law Review* 607–688, 619.
299 *Case Concerning East Timor* (Portugal v Australia) Judgment ICJ Reports (1995) p. 90, para. 29.
300 Alain Pellet, "Can a State Commit a Crime? Definitely, Yes!" (1999) 10(2) *European Journal of International Law* 425–434, 429.

3.7 Effects of the supranational bodies on territorial sovereignty

Supranational bodies refer to the United Nations and its organs.[301] It is supposed that a State territorial sovereignty may be affected by agreements to which it is a party. Therefore, an analysis that follows could apply to instruments concluded at regional levels.[302]

3.7.1 The UN General Assembly

The decision to establish the United Nations was reached at the World Conference held in Moscow[303] in 1943. The Commission II that worked on the section of the Charter on the General Assembly was divided into four subcommittees. Committee II/1 worked on "structure and procedures;" Committee II/2 worked on "political and security Functions;" Committee II/3 worked on "Economic and Social Co-operation" and Committee II/4 worked on "Trusteeship System."[304] The Dumbarton Oaks Proposals confer on the General Assembly "the right to consider the general principles of cooperation in the maintenance of international peace and security ..."[305] It could also make "recommendations" or *refer* "any such principles or questions" to the Security Council.[306]

A couple of issues that may have direct implications for territorial sovereignty need to be mentioned. First, the question of whether the General Assembly has powers to "expel" and "suspend" a State was discussed and approved. Therefore, States must align their internal affairs in accordance with the principles of the UN. Technically, the UN is supreme in matters relating to the affairs of the comity of nations. But "expulsion" and "suspension" are a strategy to safeguard the primary purpose of the UN. Hence, it was pointed out that the aim of establishing the UN was not to form a universal democratic system.[307] States retain their territorial sovereignty.

Regarding "functions and Powers" of the General Assembly, Committee II/2 made a vital recommendation leading to the adoption of Article 10 of the UN Charter. The General Assembly "may discuss any questions or any matters within the scope of the present Charter or relating to the powers" of any other organs of the UN and make "recommendations" accordingly.[308] Article 11 empowers the

---

301 For a flowchart of the agencies within the United Nations, see *Yearbook of the United Nations*, 1960 (New York, United Nations, 1960 vi [further citation from Yearbooks will be as follows: "*UN Yearbook*, year of publication, pagination"]; *UN Charter* (n 32), art. 7.

302 Cuba had argued persuasively before the Security Council that it has the prerogative right to determine which international body – whether regional or United Nations – will adjudicate its dispute. See *UN Yearbook*, 1960, 155–159.

303 The Moscow Conference of October 1943, "Joint Four-Nation Declaration" declaration 4, available at <http://avalon.law.yale.edu/wwii/moscow.asp> accessed 29 September 2019.

304 *UN Yearbook*, 1946–47, 13.

305 *UNCIO*, Vol. 3, 3.

306 ibid.

307 *UN Yearbook*, 1946–47, 21.

308 UN Charter (n 32), art. 10; *UN Yearbook*, 1946–47, 22.

84 Inviolability of State territory

UN General Assembly to "consider the general principles of co-operation in the maintenance of international peace and security ..." Suffice to say that the General Assembly can "discuss"[309] matters affecting international peace and security and make recommendations insofar as the Security Council has not seized of the matter.

That States are *subject* of international law does not make them subservient to an *absolute sovereign UN* in Austinian sense[310] or as defined by Bodin.[311] It does mean, however, that the UN is a mechanism for States' accountability. To that end, there is a contractual limitation to States' sovereignty. Arguably, *subject* is a nomenclature for artificial legal entities eligible for membership of the UN, sharing equal rights and obligations.[312] Thus, "subject" signals a *locus standi* in the international arena.[313] A State's territory remains inviolable insofar as it exercises its sovereignty in line with internationally recognised standards. Its territoriality is not compromised as such since the UN's system operates the principle of sovereign equality of States.[314]

The sovereign equality of States entails that: (1) any matter raised on the floor of the UN, which has to be settled by consent, must be decided by the doctrine of "one-state-one-vote,"[315] (2) all votes are of equal weight, (3) no State can claim jurisdiction over another, and (4) the jurisdiction of domestic courts is territorial.[316] However, Brierly[317] has reservation regarding the legal ramification of this doctrine. It is reasonable if it refers to rights protected by law but does not mean that all States have equal rights.[318] A case in point is the voting arrangement in the

---

309 *UNCIO*, Vol. 9, 412.

310 H. L. A. Hart, *The Concept of Law*, Second Edition (Oxford, Oxford University Press, 1994) 28; Thomas M. Franck, *The Power of Legitimacy Among Nations* (New York, Oxford University Press, 1990) 35.

311 W. J. Rees, "The Theory of Sovereignty Restated" (1950) 59(236) *Mind* 495–521, 499.

312 Alan James, "Comment on J. D. B. Miller" (1986) 12(2) *Review of International Studies* 91–93, 92; J. D. B. Miller, "Sovereignty as a Source of Vitality for the State" (1986) 12(2) *Review of International Studies* 79–89; Ben Chigara, *Legitimacy Deficit in Custom: A Deconstructionist Critique* (Farnham, Ashgate Publishing, 2001) 73.

313 Hans Kelsen, "The Principle of Sovereign Equality of States as a Basis for International Organisation" (1944) 53(2) *Yale Law Journal* 207–220, 208.

314 UN Charter (n 32), art. 2(1); *OAS Charter* (n 2), art. 6; *OAU Charter* (n 2), art. 3; *Corfu Channel* case (n 73), 35.

315 For voting system in the General Assembly, see *UN Charter* (n 32), art. 18; for the Security Council, see *UN Charter* (n 32), art. 27; for ECOSOC, see *UN Charter* (n 32), art. 67; for Trusteeship Council (now suspended), see *UN Charter* (n 32), art. 89.

316 Herbert Weinschel, "The Doctrine of the Equality of States and Its Recent Modifications" (1951) 45(3) *American Journal of International Law* 417–442, 419; Jennings and Watts (n 115), 339; *Nicaragua* case (n 33), paras 59, 70, 202 and 284; *Chae Chan Ping v* United States, Supreme Court of the United States (1888) 130 U.S. 581, 604.

317 Brierly (n 166), 131–32.

318 ibid., 131–32; Jennings and Watts (n 115), 339; Edwin D. Dickinson, *The Equality of States in International Law* (Cambridge, Harvard University Press, 1920) 334–335; Weinschel (n 316), 438.

Security Council that gives veto powers to the permanent members which non-permanent members do not have.[319]

Sovereign equality of States is a controversial topic, especially regarding the inequitable application of laws. For instance, the Advisory Opinion of the ICJ in the *Legality of the Threat or Use of Nuclear Weapons* is binding[320] upon States that have nuclear arsenals and are a party to *Treaty on Non-proliferation of Nuclear Weapons*.[321] Be that as it may, formal equality connotes uniformity in the application of the law.

3.7.2 Security Council

The Security Council (SC) is an organ of the United Nations with statutory powers to maintain international peace and security. How such powers affect territorial sovereignty is our concern and not the procedural matters and voting arrangement hotly contested when the Charter was drafted.[322] Pursuant to powers under Chapter VII and Chapter VIII, the SC can take decisions that directly or indirectly affect the territorial integrity or political independence of a State. It could authorise economic sanctions against a State[323] or permit a supervised plebiscite leading to the dissolution of a State[324] or sanction the use of physical force against a State.[325] The interpretation of the SC's resolutions purporting to authorise intervention in the internal affairs of States could be complicated.[326] Consequently, the ICJ has advised that "the language of a resolution of the Security Council should be carefully analysed before a conclusion can be made as to its binding effect."[327] To authorise coercive measures, the SC must make a determination of the "existence of threat to the peace, breach of the peace, or an act of aggression within the meaning of Article 39 of the Charter."[328]

319 *UN Charter* (n 32), art. 27(3).
320 Note that the ICJ Advisory opinions have no binding effect but they have legal weight and moral authority. See International Court of Justice, "Jurisdiction – Advisory Opinion," available at <www.icj-cij.org/jurisdiction/index.php?p1=5&p2=2> accessed 19 September 2019.
321 An example is the *Treaty on the Non-Proliferation of Nuclear Weapons* (Adopted at London on 1 July 1968, entered into force on 5 March 1970) 729 UNTS 161. For other instruments, visit the website of the United Nations Office for Disarmament Affairs at <www.un.org/disarmament/about/> accessed 7 August 2019.
322 For a discussion on procedural matters and voting arrangement, see *UN Yearbook*, 1946–47, 23–24.
323 UNSC Res. S/RES/1160 (31 March 1998), operative para. 10.
324 UN Doc. E/CN.4/Sub.2/405/Rev.1 (1 January 1980), 46ff.
325 UNSC Res. S/RES/1973 (17 March 2011), operative para. 4; UNSC Res. S/RES/169 (24 November 1961), operative para. 4.
326 For further analysis, see Josephat Chukwuemeka Ezenwajiaku, *Respect for the Inviolability of State Territory* (Unpublished Doctoral Thesis submitted to Brunel University London, 2017) 282–290.
327 *Namibia Advisory Opinion* (n 7), para. 114.
328 Erika de Wet, *The Chapter VII Powers of the United Nations Security Council* (Oxford, Hart Publishing, 2004) 133.

86   Inviolability of State territory

In the area of law-making, the SC has established two *ad hoc* Tribunals that tried war crimes committed in the former Yugoslavia[329] and Rwanda.[330] Koskenniemi describes such actions as tantamount to "international legislation."[331] After the 9/11 terrorist attacks on the United States, the SC adopted Resolution 1373 (2001)[332] which Costa Rica describes as "the first time in history, the Security Council enacted legislation for the rest of the international community."[333] It portrays the SC as "World legislator"[334] contrary to its statutory powers.[335] Thus, the Appeals Chamber in the *Tadić* case argues that the SC lacks binding legislative powers.[336]

Another issue to consider is how the voting arrangement could affect the sovereign equality of States. That law is made for or enforced against some States does not undermine the principle of the sovereign equality of States. The critical factor in determining "equality" in this regard is whether, given "the same conditions States have the same duties and the same rights."[337] In the Security Council exists stratified equality – first among the P5 and second among the elected members.[338] The justification for this disparity is that it makes for fast and effective enforcement of the mandate of the SC.[339]

That said, a treaty sometimes imposes an obligation upon States against their consent. A State that abstains from voting or votes against a resolution which passed will still be bound by it.[340] Some treaties bind States irrespective of their consent, such as the *Convention Abolishing International Servitudes*.[341] Besides,

---

329   UNSC Res. S/RES/827 (25 May 1993), operative para. 2.
330   UNSC Res. S/RES/955 (8 November 1994), operative para. 1.
331   Martti Koskenniemi, "The Police in the Temple Order, Justice and the UN: A Dialectical View" (1995) 6(3) *European Journal of International Law* 325–348, 326.
332   UNSC Res. S/RES/1373 (28 September 2001), operative para. 1.
333   UNGAOR, UN Doc. A/56/PV.25 (15 October 2001), 3 (speech by Mr. Niehaus, the representative of Costa Rica).
334   Stefan Talmon, "The Security Council as World Legislature" (2005) 99(1) *American Journal of International Law* 175–193, 175; Matthew Happold, "Security Council Resolution 1373 and the Constitution of the United Nations" (2003) 16(3) *Leiden Journal of International Law* 593–610, 596; Jose E. Alvarez, "The UN's War on Terrorism" (2003) 31(2) *International Journal of Legal Information* 238–250, 241; Jose E. Alvarez, "Hegemonic International Law Revisited" (2003) 97(4) *American Journal of International Law* 873–887, 874.
335   *Statute of the International Court of Justice* (Adopted at San Francisco on 26 June 1945, entered into force on 24 October 1945) (1945) 39(3) *American Journal of International Law Supplement* 215–229, art. 38 [hereinafter *ICJ Statute*] (enumerates the sources of international law).
336   *The Prosecutor v Duško Tadić a/k/a "Dule"* (Case No. IT 94–1-AR72) (Decision on the Defence Motion for Interlocutory Appeal on Jurisdiction) ICTY (2 October 1995), para. 43.
337   Kelsen 1944 (n 313), 209.
338   Weinschel (n 316), 438–440.
339   Hans Kelsen, "Organization and Procedure of the Security Council of the United Nations" (1946) 59(7) *Harvard Law Review* 1087–1121, 1102–1103.
340   *UN Charter* (n 32), art. 25; Weinschel (n 316), 428; see also Cassese 1995 (n 99), 188 (he argues that sovereign power does not enjoy unfettered rights).
341   These treaties oblige *erga omnes*. For a detailed discussion see Office of the United Nations High Commissioner for Human Rights, *Abolishing Slavery and its*

Inviolability of State territory 87

an agreement entered by the agent, provided it does not act *ultra vires*, binds the sovereign State.[342] But these instruments are contractual. Supposedly, if and only if the P5 acts within its mandate,[343] their privileged position does not undermine the sovereign equality of States.[344] Therefore, there is no legal order that safeguards absolute equality in a heterogeneous society.

3.7.3 Judicial institution

The United Nations adopted the ICJ as its "principal judicial organ."[345] Article 93 of the UN Charter makes all member States *ipso facto* parties to the ICJ's Statute.[346] Article 94 declares that the ICJ has jurisdiction over the member States and obliges them to comply with the decisions of the Court.[347] Article 35(1) of the ICJ's Statute provides that the Court has jurisdiction over States that are party to its Statute.[348] It acquires jurisdiction over cases submitted to it in accordance with the provision of Article 38 of its Statute.[349] The ICJ's Statute "is based upon the Statute of the Permanent Court of International Justice and forms an integral part of the Charter."[350]

The Informal Inter-Allied Committee of Jurists that revised the Statute of the PCIJ considered whether the ICJ should contain a provision making the jurisdiction of the Court compulsory for States' parties.[351] It recommends that States' parties should be allowed to accept the jurisdiction of the ICJ in general or in defined cases.[352] The ICJ's compulsory jurisdiction as provided for in Article 36 of the ICJ's Statute[353] kicks in under two conditions: (1) when a State signs a special agreement referring a dispute to the ICJ or are parties to a treaty providing for the ICJ's dispute resolution, and (2) when in accordance with Article 36(2), a State

---

Contemporary Forms (New York; Geneva, United Nations, 2002) UN Doc. HR/PUB/02/4 (2002), 3, para. 7.
342 Kelsen 1944 (n 313), 210.
343 *UN Charter* (n 32), arts 24–27.
344 ibid., art. 39; Peter Hulsroj, "The Legal Function of the Security Council" (2002) 1 (1) *Chinese Journal of International Law* 59–93, 60
345 *UN Charter* (n 32), art. 92.
346 ibid., art. 93.
347 ibid., art. 94.
348 *ICJ Statute* (n 335), art. 35(1).
349 ibid., art. 38.
350 *UN Yearbook*, 1946–47, 591.
351 United States Department of State, *The International Court of Justice: Selected Documents Relating to the Drafting of the Statute* (Washington D.C., Government Printing Office, 1946) 33 [hereinafter *The US Department of State Draft of the ICJ Statute*]; Lucius C. Caflisch, "The Recent Judgment of the International Court of Justice in the Case Concerning the Aerial Incident of July 27, 1955, and the Interpretation of Article 36(5) of the Statute of the Court" (1960) 54(4) *American Journal of International Law* 855–868, 586–587.
352 *The US Department of State Draft of the ICJ Statute* (n 351), 33.
353 *ICJ Statute* (n 335), art. 36.

88 *Inviolability of State territory*

makes a declaration to the effect that it agrees to be sued by any State depositing a similar declaration.[354]

3.7.4 Compulsory jurisdiction's historical antecedent – the League of Nations

Article 14 of the Covenant of the League of Nations[355] authorised the establishment of the PCIJ.[356] Article 36(2) of the Statute of the PCIJ contains a clause on the compulsory jurisdiction. This article was adopted by the First Assembly of the League of Nations as a compromise between the draft proposal of the Committee of Jurists and an amendment proposed by the Council of the League of Nations.[357]

Hudson explains that it is the English text that translates the French word *obligatoire* to read compulsory.[358] Ordinarily, "obligatory" is most appropriate and should mean that the PCIJ exercises jurisdiction not as an "external compulsion, but as a result of the assumption of an obligation by the State concerned."[359] Besides, the ICJ acquires jurisdiction when the parties have submitted a special agreement referring a dispute to it[360] or when a State accepts the Court's compulsory jurisdiction through an express declaration.[361] Moreover, a State can make a reservation when depositing its acceptance[362] or opt out of the compulsory jurisdiction.[363] The enforcement of the compulsory jurisdiction was unsuccessful under the League of Nations[364] as bolstered by the case of *Belgium v China*.[365]

---

354 George P. Shultz, "U.S. Terminates Acceptance of ICJ Compulsory Jurisdiction" (1986) 86(2106) *Department of State Bulletin* 67–71, 68.

355 *The Covenant of the League of Nations* (n 35), art. 14.

356 See generally, *Statute for the Permanent Court of International Justice* (Done at Geneva on 16 December 1920, entered into force on 8 October 1921) 6 LNTS 390.

357 Manley O. Hudson, "Obligatory Jurisdiction Under Article 36 of the Statute of the Permanent Court of International Justice" (1933–1934) 19(2) *Iowa Law Review* 190–217, 190.

358 ibid., 191 (see footnote number 1).

359 ibid.; Kelsen 1944 (n 313), 214.

360 Cullen Bryant Gosnell, "The Compulsory Jurisdiction of the World Court" (1927–1928) 14(8) *Virginia Law Review* 618–643, 620–621; Manley O. Hudson, "Permanent Court of International Justice" (1921–1922) 35(3) *Harvard Law Review* 245–275, 259; *The Covenant of the League of Nations* (n 35), art. 12.

361 Hudson 1921–1922 (n 360), 259. For example, Lithuania accepted the compulsory jurisdiction for a period of five years. See *Protocol of Signature Relating to the Statute of the Permanent Court of International Justice Provided for by Article 14 of the Covenant of the League of Nations* (Done at Geneva on 16 December 1920), 6 LNTS 380, 387 [hereinafter *Reservations on Compulsory Jurisdiction of Article 36 of the PCIJ Statute*].

362 States such as Switzerland, Denmark, Salvador, Costa Rica, Uruguay, Luxemburg, Finland, the Netherlands, Liberia, Sweden, Norway, Panama, Brazil, Austria and China accepted the compulsory clause on the condition of reciprocity. See *Reservations on Compulsory Jurisdiction of Article 36 of the PCIJ Statute* (n 361), 384–388.

363 Hudson 1933–1934 (n 357), 191

364 Gosnell (n 360), 623–624.

365 *Denunciation of the Treaty of November 2nd, 1865 between China and Belgium* (Belgium v China) Orders of 8 January, 15 February and 18 June 1927 PCIJ Series A,

Essentially, the ICJ's compulsory jurisdiction is contractual. The grey area is that State parties acceding to it lack the foreknowledge of whom or on what issue a suit may be brought against them. This is because a declaration covers any issue of international law.[366] However, States rely on reservations,[367] the "principle of reciprocity" (exclusion clause in their opponent's declaration)[368] to defeat compulsory jurisdiction requirement. Additionally, an aggrieved State could raise non-jurisdictional objections to the Court mediating a dispute or withdraw from the Court's compulsory jurisdiction.[369] The United States terminated the Court's compulsory jurisdiction in the *Nicaragua* case for what it called the defect in the Court's procedure.[370]

Justice Oda has observed that States are disinterested in adjudicating their legal disputes before the ICJ.[371] The ICJ has been accused of being a propaganda instrument that legitimises the political agenda of some States.[372] In criminal matters, some African States wanted to withdraw from the jurisdiction of the International Criminal Court.[373]

As such, the jurisdiction of World Courts depends on the member States' willingness to be bound by it. Currently, the number of the UN member States that are parties to the compulsory jurisdiction of the ICJ is 73.[374] Kelsen has recommended that the compulsory jurisdiction should apply to all cases and for all member States to avoid disputes being classified as nonjusticiable.[375] He argues that taking such a measure is compatible with the sovereign equality of States, provided States consent to new obligations.[376] Kelsen's advice is well-

No. 8 (1927), 5; *Denunciation of the Treaty of November 2nd, 1865 between China and Belgium* (Belgium v China) Orders of 25 May 1929 PCIJ Series A, Nos 18/19 (1929) 7; L. H. Woolsey, "China's Termination of Unequal Treaties" (1927) 21(2) *American Journal of International Law* 289–294.

366 *ICJ Statute* (n 335), art. 38.
367 VCLT (n 11), arts 19–23; Shultz (n 354), 68.
368 Shultz (n 354), 68.
369 ibid.; *Declaration Recognizing as Compulsory the Jurisdiction of the Court, in Conformity with Article 36, Paragraph 2, of the Statute of the International Court of Justice* (Washington D.C., 14 August 1946) 1 UNTS 11, 11–12 (the declaration made by the United States).
370 Shultz (n 354), 68–71.
371 Shigeru Oda, "The Compulsory Jurisdiction of the International Court of Justice: A Myth? A Statistical Analysis of Contentious Cases" (2000) 49(2) *International and Comparative Law Quarterly* 251–277, 252.
372 Gary L. Scott and Karen D. Csajko, "Compulsory Jurisdiction and Defiance in the World Court: A Comparison of the PCIJ and the ICJ" (1988) 16(2&3) *Denver Journal of International Law and Policy* 377–392, 388.
373 See BBC News, "African Union Backs Mass Withdrawal from ICC" (1 February 2017), available at <www.bbc.co.uk/news/world-africa-38826073> accessed 9 April 2017.
374 International Court of Justice, "Declarations Recognising the Jurisdiction of the Court as Compulsory – Status as at 30 September 2019," available at <www.icj-cij.org/en/declarations> accessed 30 September 2019.
375 Kelsen 1944 (n 313), 216.
376 ibid.

90 *Inviolability of State territory*

founded to the extent that he strikes a balance between respect of a State territory and the need to hold States accountable for their wrongful acts. However,
the conditionality of future consent to new obligations might inhibit the entire
judicial process.

The ICJ assumes jurisdiction when cases are referred to it by States or when an
authorised UN organ[377] seeks its advisory opinion on any legal matter. Strictly,
powers exercised by judicial institutions or indeed by any organ of the United
Nations are delegated. Laws emanating therefrom do not diminish States' sovereignty as such. Article 38 of the ICJ's Statute recognises that States are major
actors in the creation of rules of customary international law.

---

377 *UN Charter* (n 32), art. 96.

4 Expanding the frontiers of Article 2(4) to cyberspace

4.0 Introduction

The issue to be addressed in this chapter is whether cyberspace is part of a State's territory. Traditionally, the answer is no but the contemporary political discourse has expanded the scope of a State territory to include cyberspace.[1] However, to apply Article 2(4) to cyberspace requires a broadening of its interpretive scope. While territorial sovereignty is exclusive in character such that actions directed against a State's personality may constitute a delict, it is contentious whether the non-kinetic character of such infringements on cyber-territory[2] could qualify as physical force or be classified as an armed attack.[3] This chapter observes that respect for the inviolability of State territory is a better way to address such issues instead of attempts to apply international legal instruments directly to cyberspace.

4.1 The definition of cyberspace

The rule of engagement published by the United States Joint Chief of Staff defines cyberspace as "[a] global domain within the information environment consisting of the interdependent networks of information technology infrastructures and resident data, including the Internet, telecommunications networks, computer systems, and embedded processors and controllers."[4] The cyberspace is such that it is difficult to have one definition that satisfies curious minds.[5] It "is not a physical place ... but a term that refers to an environment created by the confluence

---

1 Wolff Heintschel von Heinegg, "Territorial Sovereignty and Neutrality in Cyberspace" (2013) 89 *International Law Studies* 123–156, 123–124.
2 Cyber-territory may be defined as territory in cyberspace.
3 Ryan Jenkins argues that this kind of consideration is irrelevant. See Ryan Jenkins, "Is Stuxnet Physical? Does it Matter?" (2013) 12(1) *Journal of Military Ethics* 68–79, 68.
4 Joint Chiefs of Staff, *Department of Defense Dictionary of Military and Associated Terms* (as amended October 2019) 55, available at <www.jcs.mil/Doctrine/> accessed 24 October 2019.
5 For other definitions, see Jason Andress and Steve Winterfeld, *Cyber Warfare: Techniques, Tactics and Tools for Security Practitioners*, Second Edition (Amsterdam, Elsevier, 2014) 3; Kristen E. Eichensehr, "The Cyber-Law of Nations" (2015) 103(2) *Georgetown Law Journal* 317–380, 324.

92 *Expanding the frontiers of Article 2(4)*

of cooperative networks of computers, information systems, and telecommunication infrastructures commonly referred to as the World Wide Web."[6] A significant obstacle to delimiting cyberspace is its placelessness,[7] making its status equivalent to *res communis omnium* beyond the exclusive jurisdiction or sovereignty of a State.[8] However, international law allows a State to exercise relative or transient exclusive authority over its vessels in *res communis omnium*. Therefore, the desire to extend legal instruments that apply in the physical territory to cyber-territory is reasonable if it were on a temporary basis. Besides, to impose the current interpretation of Article 2(4) on cyberspace might be hindered by the non-kinetic nature of the cyber atmosphere.

4.2 Contextualising Article 2(4) of the UN Charter in cyberspace

At present, in Europe, a comprehensive document that seeks to apply international law to cyberspace is a work titled, the *Tallinn Manual on the International Law Applicable to Cyber Warfare*.[9] It is a non-binding academic document that makes invaluable contributions on virtually all aspects of international law with plausible suggestions on how international law might be applied in cyberspace. In 2011, the Barack Obama's administration argued that the existing international laws apply in cyberspace.[10] As the ICJ affirms in the *Military and Paramilitary Activities In and Against Nicaragua*, the prohibition of the threat or use of force is of customary international law.[11] Therefore, Article 2(4) is both a positive law as well as a customary international law. We do not intend to review the *Tallinn Manual* here but will abstract from it relevant guidance for further analysis. While the *Tallinn Manual* touches on pertinent topics in international law, we shall analyse three principles here, namely: sovereignty, jurisdiction and the use of force.

---

6 Thomas C. Wingfield, *The Law of Information Conflict: National Security Law in Cyberspace* (Falls Church, Aegis Research Corporation 2000) 17; Derek S. Reveron, "An Introduction to National Security and Cyberspace" in Derek S. Reveron (ed.), *Cyberspace and National Security: Threats, Opportunity, and Power in a Virtual World* (Washington D.C., Georgetown University Press, 2012) 5; Heinegg (n 1), 125.
7 Geoffrey L. Herrera, "Cyberspace and Sovereignty: Thought on Physical Space and Digital Space" in Myriam D. Cavelty *et al.* (eds), *Power and Security in the Information Age: Investigating the Role of the State in Cyberspace* (Farnham, Ashgate Publishing, 2007) 69.
8 Heinegg (n 1), 125–126.
9 See generally Michael N. Schmitt (ed.), *Tallinn Manual on the International Law Applicable to Cyber Warfare* (New York, Cambridge University Press, 2013); Michael N. Schmitt and Liis Vihul (eds), *Tallinn Manual 2.0 on the International Law Applicable to Cyber Operations* (Cambridge, Cambridge University Press, 2017).
10 The White House, *International Strategy for Cyberspace: Prosperity, Security, and Openness in a Networked World* (Washington D.C., May 2011) 9, available at <https://obamawhite house.archives.gov/sites/default/files/rss_viewer/international_strategy_for_cyberspace. pdf > accessed 23 October 2019 [hereinafter *International Strategy for Cyberspace*].
11 ICJ Reports (1986) p. 14, paras 188, 190.

4.2.1 Sovereignty in cyberspace

The definition of sovereignty as provided for in the *Tallinn Manual* is "*sui juris, esse suae potestatis, superanus* or *summa potestas.*"[12] The *summa potestas* was bequeathed to princes by the Peace of Westphalia. Going by the principle, the *Tallinn Manual* provides that "States enjoy sovereignty over any cyber infrastructure located on their territory and activities associated with that cyber infrastructure."[13] It further says that "[a]lthough territoriality lies at the heart of the principle of sovereignty, in certain circumstances, States may also exercise sovereign prerogatives such as jurisdiction over cyber infrastructure and activities abroad, as well as over certain persons engaged in those activities."[14] With this doctrine of *ratione loci*,[15] the *Tallinn Manual* debunks the disingenuous placelessness argument that defeats sovereignty. It seems that the overarching principle is *la terre domine la mer*. In other words, cyber infrastructure domiciled in a physical geographical territory confers legitimacy and sovereignty on cyberspace. Thus, States acquire rights and supposedly responsibilities over such infrastructures. Another ramification of this doctrine is a possible vicarious liability for wrongful acts committed by non-State actors against the integrity of a State insofar as the cyberspace infrastructure used for the commission of an unlawful act is located within the territory of the accused State.[16]

The *Tallinn Manual* based its analysis on the exclusive character of the functions of a State as enumerated in the *Island of Palmas* case.[17] In *The South China Sea Arbitration*,[18] for instance, the Permanent Court of Arbitration noted China's submission that "permanent sovereignty over … resources … should be respected by other countries." The argument based on *ratione loci* applies not only to the legal definition of land but also to such infrastructures installed on movable properties (aircraft and ships) belonging to a State. The *Tallinn Manual* identifies three areas in which territorial sovereignty is exercised in cyberspace. First is the "physical layer" which comprises "the physical network components (i.e., hardware and other infrastructure, such as cables,

---

12 Schmitt and Vihul (n 9), 11.
13 ibid.
14 ibid.
15 For the application of the doctrine see Wolff Heintschel von Heinegg, "Legal Implications of Territorial Sovereignty in Cyberspace" in C. Czosseck *et al.* (eds), *2012 4th International Conference on Cyber Conflict Proceedings* (Tallinn, NATO CCD COE Publications, 2012) 7–19.
16 Nicholas Tsagourias argues that self-defence should be available against non-State actors to avoid creating a gap in legal instrument that should protect State territory. See Nicholas Tsagourias, "The Tallinn Manual on the International Law Applicable to Cyber Warfare: A Commentary on Chapter II – The Use of Force" (2012) 15 *Yearbook of International Humanitarian Law* 19–43, 21.
17 *Island of Palmas* case (The Netherlands v USA) (The Hague, 1928) II RIAA 829–871, 838 [hereinafter *Island of Palmas* case].
18 *Case No. 2013–19 In the Matter of the South China Sea Arbitration between the Republic of the Philippines and the Peoples Republic of China*, Award PCA (12 July 2016), paras 251–252.

94 *Expanding the frontiers of Article 2(4)*

routers, servers and computers)."[19] Second is "logical layer" which "consists of the connections that exist between network devices. It includes applications, data, and protocols that allow the exchange of data across the physical layer."[20] The third is "social layer" which "encompasses individuals and groups engaged in cyber activities."[21] It follows from this finding that all aspects of cyberspace are subject to State's sovereignty. However, sovereignty might overlap due to the cobweb nature of cyberspace interface. Yet lack of delimitation does not gravely undermine territorial sovereignty.

For the sake of clarity, we have to distinguish between territorial sovereignty and territorial integrity. The latter applies if unlawful intervention, threat or force is directed against the territory of a State.[22] The former is breached in all other cases of illegal acts or when a State performs functions of a State in a foreign land without authorisation. When *Stuxnet* worm was deployed against Iran's cyber infrastructure, some authors contend that a breach could be established when "the effect caused by a State on the territory of another State, notwithstanding their scale or intensity, must be of either physical nature or perceptible as the exercise of a foreign State's authority."[23] The exclusivity character of territorial sovereignty could rebut the effect, intensity and physical elements. Also, it may be difficult to equate physical damage caused by cyber-attacks to "armed" physical attacks.

4.2.2 Jurisdiction in cyberspace

One area in which territorial sovereignty applies in cyberspace is to regulate the movement of peoples and goods across borders. As established in the *Lotus* case, jurisdiction is territorial and in rare cases extraterritorial, in accordance with international law. The *Tallinn Manual* acquiesces to this principle and observes that States have three jurisdictional competences, namely: legislative, executive and judicial.[24] A monograph on jurisdiction is in the public domain[25] and shall not be repeated. However, "Rule 9" allows States to exercise "territorial jurisdiction over (a) cyber infrastructure and persons engaged in cyber activities on its territory; (b) cyber activities originating in, or completed on, its territory; or (c) cyber activities having a substantial effect in its territory."[26] In summary, "territorial jurisdiction applies to persons, natural and legal, involved in cyber activities that are present within a State's territory and to cyber infrastructure and data that

19 Schmitt and Vihul (n 9), 12.
20 ibid.
21 ibid.
22 Malcolm N. Shaw, *International Law*, Sixth Edition (Cambridge, Cambridge University Press, 2008) 522.
23 Katharina Ziolkowski, "Stuxnet – Legal Considerations" 19, available at <https://ccdcoe.org/library/publications/stuxnet-legal-considerations/> accessed 25 October 2019.
24 Schmitt and Vihul (n 9), 51–52.
25 See generally Cedric Ryngaert, *Jurisdiction in International Law*, Second Edition (Oxford, Oxford University Press, 2015).
26 Schmitt and Vihul (n 9), 55.

Expanding the frontiers of Article 2(4) 95

are located on that territory."[27] It could happen that multiple States may have territorial jurisdiction over an action initiated in one State that has effects on other States. But no consensus exists among experts as to whether *de minimis* cyber-attacks expunge territorial jurisdiction.[28]

Concerning extraterritorial jurisdiction, much depends on certain variables. Rules 10 to 11 provide the necessary conditions. For example, under Rule 10, a State acquires extraterritorial prescriptive jurisdiction when cyber activities are "conducted by its nationals" or "committed on board vessels and aircraft possessing its nationality"[29] among others. The principles of *cause* and *effect* establish the required nexus for applying extraterritorial jurisdiction. It could be that the initiator of a cyber act has some proximity with the State seeking to enforce territorial sovereignty either as its citizen or by the person's mere presence within its territory or due to the effect which the person's action has on a State territory. As shall be seen, many States have laws regulating cyberspace. It is a recent, unprecedented and welcome development. Also, commendable is the attempt to apply the existing legal framework to cyberspace. However, such an evolutive approach supports broad interpretation in relation to Article 2(4) of the UN Charter as shall be shown later.

4.2.3 Use of force in cyberspace

In Chapter 3, we showed how States (especially weak States) wanted Article 2(4) to be construed broadly. This can be gleaned from the purposes of the Charter and submissions made by States seeking to extend its scope to include economic coercion. However, the interpretation of Article 2(4) that has survived decades indicates that it prohibits physical armed force. The *Tallinn Manual* uses the ICJ's *Advisory Opinion on the Legality of the Threat or Use of Nuclear Weapons* as the basis for its analysis. From paragraph 37 going forward, the ICJ analysed Article 2(4) and at paragraph 39 held that "these provisions … apply to any use of force, regardless of the weapons employed."[30] Note that the legal question before the ICJ was as follows: "Is the threat or use of nuclear weapons in any circumstance permitted under international law?"[31] According to the view of experts, what matters "is not the instrument used … but rather, as described in Rule 69, the consequences of the operation and its surrounding circumstances."[32] Rule 69 provides as follows, "a cyber operation constitutes a use of force when its scale and effects are comparable to non-cyber operations rising to the level of a use of force."[33] It seems that this is an attempt to replicate the controversial *de minimis* principle in cyber-territory. Hence, experts are of the view that cyber intrusion would still be unlawful even when the effects are not grave to constitute the use of force.[34]

27 ibid.
28 ibid.
29 ibid., 60.
30 ICJ Reports (1996) p. 226, para. 39.
31 UNGA Res. A/RES/49/75K (15 December 1994), preamble para. 12.
32 Schmitt and Vihul (n 9), 328.
33 ibid., 330.
34 ibid., 330.

96 *Expanding the frontiers of Article 2(4)*

First and foremost, a few questions beg for clarifications. First, what is the conventional understanding of weapon? Second, what does physical armed force means? Third, what does ICJ mean when it says that self-defence is available only when a State is a victim of an armed attack? In our times when States' lives are cyberspace-based, what happens if a victim State is unable to recover from the effects of a cyber-attack? Tsagourias' commentary on the views expressed in the *Tallinn Manual* on the use of force is instructive. He observes, *inter alia*, that the *Tallinn Manual* "rejects an instrument-based approach to force and adopts an effects-based one."[35] If that is correct, one is left in doubt why economic sanctions capable of producing adverse humanitarian consequences should be left out. Besides, the *Tallinn Manual* excludes "the manipulation of a state's economic data" from the prohibited conduct. Tsagourias asks, and rightly too, should this be the case if tampering with a State cyberspace infrastructure "may have serious repercussions on the state's economic and political well being ..."?[36] We see in the *Tallinn Manual* an attempt to transplant the existing norms to cyberspace without a proper dissection of peculiarities of the cyberspace environment. For instance, weaponry as traditionally conceived, cannot be equated with what Rowe calls "cyberweapons" which consist of "just bit patterns."[37] While Jenkins argues that there could be instances of physicality in virtue of the "physical location"[38] of the computer hardware, yet laws are enacted not for rare exceptions.

As this chapter progresses, some of these issues will be monitored closely. It seeks to argue that, (1) exclusive character of territorial sovereignty imposes the duty of respect upon States, and (2) *opinio juris* that attempts to include cyber-territory within the scope of Article 2(4) may have informed the evolution of domestic legislation by which States assert full control in cyber-territory. Most importantly, it shows that Article 2(4) is expandable insofar as it accommodates the purposes of the United Nations. Otherwise, a direct application of the existing norm to cyberspace might seem excessive.

4.3 Areas of concern for States in cyberspace

The invention of the Internet[39] brought significant changes to the traditional notion of State territory as articulated by the Peace of Westphalia. It dismantled the conceptual barriers posed by the idea of territorial sovereignty. As defined by the *Oxford English Dictionary*, the Internet is "the global network comprising a loose confederation of interconnected networks using standardized communication protocols, which facilitates various information and communication systems such as the World

---

35 Tsagourias (n 16), 22.
36 ibid.
37 Neil C. Rowe, "The Ethics of Cyberweapons in Warfare" (2010) 1(1) *International Journal of Technoethics* 20–31, 21–22.
38 Jenkins (n 3), 70.
39 The internet is defined as "a communications network that is part of the further electronic circle called cyberspace." See Georgios I. Zekos, "Cyber-territory and Jurisdiction of Nations" (2012) 15(12) *Journal of Internet Law* 3–23, 5.

Expanding the frontiers of Article 2(4) 97

Wide Web and email."[40] It provides a platform for the exchange of ideas, revolutionises the ease of doing business, facilitates the process of globalisation and enhances transnational free flow of information and cyber-crimes. Not only is the invention fascinating but also cyberspace is thought "beyond the reach of laws"[41] even when the activities that go on in it pose a threat to States' territorial sovereignty. It is a primary responsibility of a State to protect the life and properties of its citizens both in hard and soft copies. Since the thrust of our position hinges on respect for the inviolability of State territory, we shall focus our attention on three unlawful cyberspace activities that hinder international peace and security, namely: cyberwar, cyberespionage and cybercrime.[42] According to Eichensehr, they are low points in inter-State relations and in most cases defy domestic regulation.[43]

4.3.1 Cyberwar

The concept of "cyberwar" or "cyberwarfare" is borrowed from the conventional terminology associated with *jus ad bellum*[44] to describe malicious attacks on cyberspace "critical infrastructure"[45] of a State. We use *cyberwar* and *cyberwarfare* to mean the same thing. Some authors prefer "information warfare" (IW) or "information operation" (IO)[46] instead of cyberwarfare. But such ascriptions could be mistaken because "information warfare" is akin to propaganda. Cyberwarfare has been defined as:

> the offensive and defensive use of information and communication systems to gain adversarial advantage by denying use of information or system on which such information is created, resides, or is transmitted, by copying, altering, or destroying information or the means to communicate by electronic means.[47]

---

40 See *Internet, n.*, Oxford English Dictionary (Oxford University Press, 2019), available at <www.oed.com/view/Entry/248411?rskey=o37NIC&result=2&isAdvanced-false#eid> accessed 25 October 2019.

41 Zekos (n 39), 5.

42 For other cyber-related offences, see Andress and Winterfeld (n 5), 212.

43 Eichensehr (n 5), 320.

44 *Jus ad bellum* deals with laws regulating armed conflicts. It provides guidelines on how war may be fought, stipulates legitimate reasons under which a State might choose to wage war. Under the regime of Article 2(4), war is prohibited but for self-defence or authorised by the Security Council.

45 Critical infrastructures refer to computer hardware or system. If destroyed by malware this could lead to malfunction and negatively impact on the entire system. Robert S. Owen, "Infrastructures of Cyber Warfare" in Lech J. Janczewski and Andrew M. Colarik (eds), *Cyber Warfare and Cyber Terrorism* (Hershey and New York, Information Science Reference, 2008) 36.

46 Roland Heickero, *Emerging Cyber Threats and Russian Views on Information Warfare and Information Operations* (Stockholm, Swedish Defence Research Agency, 2010) 13–18, available at <www.highseclabs.com/data/foir2970.pdf> accessed 26 October 2019; John H. Nugent and Mahesh Raisinghani, "Bits and Bytes vs Bullets and Bombs: A New Form of Warfare" in Janczewski and Colarik (n 45), 33.

47 Nugent and Raisinghani (n 46), 33.

98 Expanding the frontiers of Article 2(4)

What this really means is unclear and in practical terms contentious and controversial to implement.[48] We are referring to events that take place in the virtual world. Technically, cyberwarfare "includes things like the networks, computers, hardware (this includes weapon systems with embedded computer chips), software (commercial and government developed), applications (like command and control systems), protocols, mobile devices, and the people that run them."[49] Defensive cyberwarfare requires a secure network, firewall and antivirus software capable of detecting malicious malware and of preventing its effect on a State's critical infrastructure. Offensive cyberwarfare is designed to penetrate the cyber-defence-wall to extract useful information from such an infrastructure or to cause severe damage or destroy it. Sometimes cyber warfare is a strategy to outsmart an enemy in conventional warfare just like the 2008 attack on Georgia's cyber infrastructure. For instance, "Operation Orchard" targeted "Syria's air defense systems," and "Operation Cast Lead" disabled Israeli websites and so forth.[50]

The *Tallinn Manual* introduces "scale and effects" threshold "similar to an armed attack"[51] to establish that cyberwar of offensive nature has occurred so that self-defence might be available. Tsagourias faults this proposal for lack of "further explanation or criteria for measuring the gravity of a particular force."[52] Some factors were proposed such as "severity, immediacy, directness, invasiveness, measurability of effects, military character, state involvement, and presumptive legality."[53] But there is no indication that those criteria drive States' policy on cyber warfare. As Tsagourias substantiates with the criterion of severity, it is estimated that Stuxnet worm "destroyed approximately 1,000 centrifuges" but it is totally unclear whether this exceeds the "*de minimis* threshold."[54] Although the attack retarded the Iranian nuclear programme, Tsagourias insists that it does not amount to "physical destruction."[55]

Moreover, "cyberattacks should be conducted with a distinction between military and civilian targets, consider the proportionality principle as well as the possibility of secondary and tertiary effects."[56] Currently, there is no consensus on how to classify information and communications technology infrastructure as "purely civilian" or State-owned.[57] Schmitt recommends surgical targeting to mitigate civilian casualties.[58] How to achieve that in a cobweb computer network

---

48 Alexander Klimburg and Heli Tirmaa-Klaar, *Cybersecurity and Cyberpower: Concepts, Conditions and Capabilities for Cooperation for Action Within the EU* (Brussels, European Parliament, 2011) 13–14.
49 Andress and Winterfeld (n 5), 36.
50 ibid., 12.
51 Klimburg and Tirmaa-Klaar (n 48), 13.
52 Tsagourias (n 16), 23.
53 Schmitt and Vihul (n 9), 334–336.
54 Tsagourias (n 16), 23.
55 ibid., 23.
56 Klimburg and Tirmaa-Klaar (n 48), 13.
57 ibid.
58 Michael N. Schmitt, "The Law of Cyber Targeting" (2015) 68(2) *Naval War College Review* 10–29, 13.

Expanding the frontiers of Article 2(4) 99

system remains a considerable challenge. "To date, no nation has declared a cyber war ..."[59] and we need not speculate so much about the form it might take.

4.3.2 Cyberwarfare military strategies

A quick overview of cyber warfare strategies which have been adopted by States shows a lack of coherence in policy and approach. Russia's method is "to attack an adversary's centres of gravity and critical vulnerabilities" in order to "win against an opponent, militarily as well as politically, at a low cost without necessarily occupying the territory of the enemy."[60] Similarly, the People's Republic of China operates the policy of "offensive operations exploiting the vulnerabilities and dependence of nations on ICT and the internet ."[61] While the United States of America excludes "attacks on confidentiality ... *that is*, 'probe' or espionage" from its definition, Germany makes no distinction "between a probe and a cyber attack."[62]

4.3.2.1 Chinese cyberwarfare model

The People's Republic of China has evolved a military command structure for cyberwarfare. It consists of different levels of operation, namely: strategic planning and general operations (comprising defensive and offensive units). At the level of strategic planning, the Ministry of State Security gathers intelligence and evaluates the risk of cyber-attacks. The People's Liberation Army (PLA) performs multiple integrated operations known as the C4ISR. The C4ISR is an acronym which represents "command, control, communications, computers, intelligence, surveillance and reconnaissance."[63] It is designed to enhance information and intelligence sharing among other units. The Strategic Support Force "is responsible for the PLA's space, cyber, and electronic warfare missions."[64] Each level in cyber operation has battalions "that are integrated into military district and field-army structures"[65] and some units carry out surgical and strategic strikes on the enemy's critical infrastructure.

---

59 Andress and Winterfeld (n 5), 10.
60 Melissa E. Hathaway and Alexander Klimburg "Preliminary Considerations: On National Cyber Security" in Alexander Klimburg (ed.), *National Cyber Security Framework Manual* (Tallinn, NATO CCD COE Publication, 2012) 17.
61 ibid.
62 ibid., 18 (emphasis added).
63 Elsa Kania, "PLA Strategy Support Force: The Information Umbrella for China's Military" (*The Diplomat*, 1 April 2017), available at <https://thediplomat.com/2017/04/pla-strategic-support-force-the-information-umbrella-for-chinas-military/> accessed 26 October 2019.
64 John Costello, "The Strategic Support Force: Update and Overview" (2016) 16(19) *China Brief*, available at <https://jamestown.org/program/strategic-support-force-update-overview/> accessed 26 October 2019.
65 Klimburg and Tirmaa-Klaar (n 48), 16.

100 *Expanding the frontiers of Article 2(4)*

4.3.2.2 Russian cyberwarfare model

As a matter of policy, Russia strives to develop independent State-owned and managed hardware and software programmes.[66] The rationale is to create a safe computer operating system and a search engine that could replace Google. Operationally, Russia conducts cyberwar through a decentralised system that operates within the intelligence community.[67] The Committee for State Security (*Komitet gosudarstvennoy bezopasnosti*) led the intelligence agency before the dissolution of the Soviet Union in 1991. Its functions were taken over by the Federal Security Services. Initially, Russia enacted a law (System for Ensuring Investigative Activities Legislation).[68] which authorises the secret security agencies to intercept mobile telephone communications of individuals without a prior notification. That strategy failed when the European Court of Human Rights ruled that it violated the individual's right to privacy.[69]

Additionally, Russia operates multiple cyberspace intelligence gathering and analysis units such as the "Foreign Intelligence Services," and the "Main Directorate of Electronic Intelligence," which monitor and scrutinise socio-political structures around the world *et cetera*.[70] Russia operates a sophisticated Cyber Security Network and there are strong indications that Russia's armed forces partner with "hacker patriots" while conducting cyberwar.[71] This was the case in the cyberattack on Georgia and Estonia alleged to have been orchestrated by Russia.[72]

4.3.2.3 The US cyberwarfare model

The United States of America's cyberwarfare strategy is elaborate and includes cyber command structure with full operational capacities.[73] A sub-unit of the US Cyber Command (USCYBERCOM), the US Army Cyber Command (ARCYBER) published its mission statement as follows:

> U.S. Army Cyber Command integrates and conducts full-spectrum cyberspace operations, electronic warfare, and information operations, ensuring freedom

---

66 ibid., 16–17.
67 Andrei Soldatov and Irina Borogan, "The Mutation of the Russian Secret Services," available at <www.agentura.ru/english/dosie/mutation/> accessed 27 October 2019.
68 Russian Federation, *Order of the Russian Federation Communications Ministry No. 25 of February 18, 1997, on Cooperation between Communications Organizations and the Federal Security Service in Conducting Investigative Activities over Electronic Communications Network.* The text in Russian language is available at <www.lawmix.ru/prof/76083> accessed 27 October 2019, art. 5.
69 *Case of Roman Zakharov v Russia* (Application No. 47143/06) Grand Chamber, Judgment ECtHR (2015), paras 165, 175, 179 and 297.
70 Soldatov and Borogan (n 67).
71 Klimburg and Tirmaa-Klaar (n 48), 17.
72 Jon Swaine, "Georgia: Russia 'Conducting Cyber War'" (*The Telegraph*, 11 August 2008), available at <www.telegraph.co.uk/news/worldnews/europe/georgia/2539157/Georgia-Russia-conducting-cyber-war.html> accessed 27 October 2019.
73 For details, visit U.S. Cyber Command at <www.cybercom.mil/> accessed 27 October 2019.

of action for friendly forces in and through the cyber domain and the information environment, while denying the same to our adversaries.[74]

In September 2018, an updated *National Cyber Strategy of the United States of America* was published. It condemns the rate at which some States engage in "pernicious economic espionage and malicious cyber activities" against the United States and other nations across the world.[75] The US strategy was designed to "defend," "promote," "preserve" and "expand" American interests in cyberspace.[76]

The USCYBERCOM is the "10th Unified Combatant Command" which "directs, synchronizes, and coordinates cyberspace planning and operations in defense of the U.S. and its interests." It is made up of "133 Cyber Mission Force (CMF) teams consisting of Cyber Protection Teams, Combat Mission Teams and National Mission Teams for a total of about 6,200 uniformed and civilian personnel."[77] By every standard, the United States has an advanced cyberspace strategy, and the largest cyberspace domain is domiciled in the US.[78] It could shut down cyberspace or deny its adversaries access to it.[79] Yet the US is still vulnerable to cyberattacks and has alleged that some countries have broken its cyber-wall.[80]

4.4 Cybercrime

There is no universally accepted definition of cybercrimes. Yet cybercrimes increase at an alarming rate.[81] Consequently, how States define and approach cybercrimes differ significantly and could be a source of conflicts. The UN General Assembly's attempt to evolve a universally acceptable definition of cybercrime and how to tackle it is yet to materialise.[82] But States are advised to put in place legislation that facilitates timely prosecution of cyber-offenders.[83] However, cybercrimes fall

---

74 For details, visit U.S. Army Cyber Command at <www.arcyber.army.mil/> accessed 27 October 2019.
75 White House, *National Cyber Strategy of the United States of America* (Washington D.C., White House, 2018) 1, available at <www.whitehouse.gov/wp-content/uploads/2018/09/National-Cyber-Strategy.pdf> accessed 27 October 2019 [hereinafter *US National Strategy*].
76 ibid., 3.
77 Department of Defence, "U.S. Cyber Command History," available at <www.cyber com.mil/About/History/> accessed 10 December 2019.
78 Klimburg and Tirmaa-Klaar (n 48), 18.
79 President Donald Trump had suggested that the US could shut down cyberspace because of the threat extremist ideologies disseminated through the Internet pose to its national security. See Sean Lawson, "The Law That Could Allow Trump to Shut Down the US Internet" (*Forbes*, 2 December 2016), available at <www.forbes.com/sites/seanlawson/2016/12/02/the-law-that-could-allow-trump-to-shut-down-the-u-s-internet/> accessed 27 October 2019.
80 *US National Strategy* (n 75), 2.
81 Hathaway and Klimburg (n 60), 13.
82 UNGA Res. A/Res/60/230 (1 April 2011), operative para. 9; UNGA Res. A/Res/45/121 (14 December 1990), preamble para. 5.
83 UNGA Res. A/Res/67/189 (27 March 2013), operative paras 7–8, 20.

102 *Expanding the frontiers of Article 2(4)*

within one of the following: "i) offences against the confidentiality, integrity and availability of computer data and systems; ii) computer-related offences; iii) content-related offences; iv) offences related to infringements of copyright and related rights."[84]

Kierkegaard has defined cybercrime as "any illegal act involving a computer and all activities done with criminal intent in cyberspace or which are computer-related."[85] Kierkegaard's definition is broad and makes no distinction between such acts as may be perpetrated by individuals, corporate bodies or States. But it contains two elements of a crime, namely, the *actus reus* and *mens rea*. But some attacks cannot be classified as espionage, crime or an act of war. This was the case when Google was attacked in 2010.[86] This might result in legal imprecision. In 1996, Russia amended Chapter 28 of its Penal Code to accommodate cybercrimes.[87] A year later, China followed suit.[88] On 1 July 2004, the European Council's *Convention on Cybercrime* entered into force.[89] At present, most if not all States have laws prohibiting cyber-related offences. As shall be argued later, legislative jurisdiction is an exercise of territorial sovereignty as established in the *Lotus* case. Cyber-related crimes were not envisaged in 1945 when the Charter came into force and the principle of *nullum crimen nulla poena sine praevia lege poenali* may defeat any attempt to apply the provision of Article 2(4) of the UN Charter directly in cyberspace.

4.5 Cyber espionage

The cyberspace strategy of the US condemns in strong terms the "pernicious economic espionage and malicious cyber activities, causing significant economic disruption and harm to individuals, commercial and non-commercial interests, and governments across the world."[90] This policy statement suggests that such conducts fall short of the acceptable standard of behaviour. We do know, however, that the status of espionage under international law is ambivalent. According to

---

84 United Nations Office on Drugs and Crime, "Cybercrime," available at <www.unodc.org/unodc/en/cybercrime/global-programme-cybercrime.html> accessed 28 October 2019.

85 Sylvia Mercado Kierkegaard, "EU Tackles Cybercrime" in Janczewski and Colarik (n 45), 438.

86 Andress and Winterfeld (n 5), 13.

87 Russian Federation, *The Criminal Code of the Russian Federation No. 63-FZ of June 13 1996* (Adopted by the State of Duma on 24 May 1996, adopted by the Federation Council on 5 June 1996), art. 272, available at <www.wipo.int/edocs/lexdocs/laws/en/ru/ru006en.pdf> accessed 28 October 2019.

88 The People's Republic of China, *Criminal Law of the People's Republic of China* (Adopted at the Second Session of the Fifth National People's Congress on 1 July 1997, revised at the Fifth Session of the Eighth National People's Congress on 14 March 1997), arts 285–288, available at <www.warnathgroup.com/wp-content/uploads/2015/03/China-Criminal-Code.pdf> accessed 28 October 2019.

89 Council of Europe, *Convention on Cybercrime* (concluded at Budapest on 23 November 2001, entered into force on 1 July 2004) 2296 UNTS 167 [hereinafter *Convention on Cybercrime*].

90 *US National Strategy* (n 75), 1.

Wright, espionage in peacetime is illegal but legal in wartime.[91] Delupis premises lawfulness or otherwise of espionage on the means used.[92] For others still, espionage is illegal when it involves trespassing the territory of others.[93] Why espionage should be tolerated is mind-boggling. Time is ripe for the international community to meaningfully engage in a robust debate on its lawfulness and other forms of breaches of States' territory below the threshold of the threat or use of force.

Espionage could be defined as "the practice of spying or obtaining secrets from rivals or enemies for military, political, or business advantage."[94] Such practices amount to theft of intellectual property and there have been reported cases of massive "State-sponsored industrial espionage."[95] The question that should be addressed by the international community is the lawfulness of punishing individuals found guilty of theft if States get away with it. The *Tallinn Manual* criminal element is met if in the process the critical infrastructure of a State is damaged.

4.6 Policing the "unknown" – attempts to delimit the cyberspace

A couple of factors hinder States from exercising exclusive control over the cyberspace. First is its virtual nature. Second is the difficulty in attributing responsibility to States with certainty. The third is the absence of extant international law applicable to cyberspace.

Herrera refers to cyberspace as "no place."[96] Therefore, delimitation of territory in law or in fact will be difficult where every computer could be a point of entry.[97] Andress and Winterfeld suggest that demarcation is possible along the line of the "Internet extension such as.gov or .mil which is the blend between the physical and logical."[98] But given the high level of cyberspace traffic coupled with the fact that users are geographically dispersed, effective policing remains a challenge. Moreover, the effective policing of cyberspace is capital intensive which not all States could afford.

Other factors worth considering are the hardware and software configuration that allows free flow of data. The cyberspace hardware is designed in a way that "permits the circulation of bits[99] – whether reified as radio-frequency (RF) energy, electric signals or photons."[100] To stampede the flow of information with

---

91 Quincy Wright, "Legal Aspect of the U-2 Incident" (1960) 54(4) *American Journal of International Law* 836–854, 849.
92 Ingrid Delupis, "Foreign Warships and Immunity for Espionage" (1984) 78(1) *American Journal of International Law* 53–75, 67.
93 ibid.
94 Kenneth J. Knapp and William R. Boulton, "Ten Information Warfare Trends" in Janczewski and Colarik (n 45), 25.
95 Hathaway and Klimburg (n 60), 16.
96 Herrera (n 7), 69.
97 Paul Rosenzweig, *Cyber Warfare: How Conflicts in Cyberspace are Challenging America and Changing the World* (Santa Barbara, Praeger, 2013) 201.
98 Andress and Winterfeld (n 5), 35–36.
99 A bit is a digit in the binary numeral system. See Janczewski and Colarik (n 45), 33.
100 Martin C. Libicki, *Conquest in Cyberspace: Natural Security and Information Warfare* (New York, Cambridge University Press, 2007) 24.

104 Expanding the frontiers of Article 2(4)

legislation or an inbuilt firewall will harm the cyberspace DNA designed to allow cross-border information dissemination. Besides, most cyberspace attacks the world has so far witnessed were not successfully attributed to States with certainty. The Estonian government classified the much publicised Estonian cyber-attack as "criminal act as opposed to a use of force by another state" and the Iranian government never came out openly to admit "to have been cyber attacked."[101] Consequently, most cyber-attacks are regarded as "the actions of criminal gangs or recreational hackers" that "do not set precedent for international law."[102]

4.7 Territorialising the cyberspace

The Permanent Court of International Justice in the *Legal Status of Eastern Greenland* highlights two elements in addition to "title such as a treaty of cession" by which sovereignty over territory can be proven. They are, "the intention and will to act as sovereign, and some actual exercise or display of such authority."[103] This section demonstrates how territorialisation has achieved that in cyberspace through the three arms of government. The last part of this chapter will evaluate Article 2(4) in light of the discourse on direct application of international law.

4.7.1 The political discourse – executive

The Soviet Union is believed to have been attacked in 1982 when "a trans-Siberian pipeline exploded."[104] In 1986, the "Brain" virus was detected[105] and two years later, the "Morris worm" was discovered.[106] In 2007, Estonia's military and government computers were disabled with "distributed denial-of-service (DDoS)."[107] The attacks almost ground Estonia's executive and legislative affairs to a halt. The cyber-attack on Estonia has been described as "a mild version of a new form of digital violence that could halt public services, commerce and government operations."[108] Indeed it was mild in comparison with the 2010 cyber-attacks on Iran's nuclear reactor infrastructure.

---

101 Gary Brown and Keira Poellet, "The Customary International Law of Cyberspace" (2012) 6(3) *Strategic Studies Quarterly* 126–145, 132–133.
102 ibid., 133.
103 *Legal Status of Eastern Greenland* (Denmark v Norway) Judgment PCIJ Series A/B, No. 53 (1933) pp. 21, 45–46 [hereinafter *Legal Status of Eastern Greenland*].
104 Brown and Poellet (n 101), 130.
105 Jeremy Paquette, "A History of Viruses" (Symantec Corporation, 16 July 2000), available at <www.symantec.com/connect/articles/history-viruses> accessed 29 October 2019.
106 Paul Schmehl, "Malware Infection Vectors: Past, Present and Future" (Symantec Corporation, 5 August 2002), available at <www.symantec.com/connect/articles/malware-infection-vectors-past-present-and-future> accessed 29 October 2019.
107 Stephen Herzog, "Revisiting the Estonian Cyber Attacks: Digital Threats and Multinational Responses" (2011) 4(2) *Journal of Strategic Security* 49–60, 51–52.
108 ibid., 54.

Expanding the frontiers of Article 2(4) 105

In 2008, President George W. Bush's directives on Cyberspace Policy Review[109] identified areas of concern that required urgent State protection. The Obama's administration solidified Bush's "Comprehensive National Cybersecurity Initiative"[110] with a view to "establish a front line of defence against today's immediate threats;" "to defend against the full spectrum of threats;" and "to strengthen the future cybersecurity environment." In Europe, the attack on Estonia led NATO to establish "the government Computer Emergency Response Team (CERT)"[111] and "new directions for cyber security and the appropriate punishments for states found to have engaged in digital warfare."[112] It was suggested that Article 5, which allows for collective defence in the event of an armed attack, be extended to cyberspace. Eventually, "NATO adopted a unified Policy on Cyber Defence and created the Brussels-based Cyber Defence Management Authority (CDMA)" for its member States. Tallinn became the headquarters of "NATO Cooperative Cyber Defence Centre of Excellence (CCD CoE)" as well as for "the Atlantic Alliance."[113] These bodies entrusted with the Internal Security Strategy have recommended "integrated border management" to check cyber-security threats.[114]

Since 2008, cyber security has become a recurring issue discussed in the UN General Assembly.[115] Overall, the debate revolves around a joint effort to tackle, curb and if possible, eliminate the threats posed to national security by cyber-related offences. As said earlier, there is neither a universally accepted definition of cyberspace nor a mode of behaviour in cyberspace.[116] Hence, President Barack Obama argued that international law is applicable in cyberspace.[117] In September 2014, 60 world leaders (including the NATO member States) issued a *communiqué* which specifies, *inter alia*, that "international law including international humanitarian law and the UN Charter, applies in cyberspace."[118]

---

109 The White House, *National Security Presidential Directive/NSPD-54: Homeland Security Presidential Directive/HSPD-23* (Washington D.C., 8 January 2008), available at <https://fas.org/irp/offdocs/nspd/index.html> accessed 30 October 2019.

110 The White House, *The Comprehensive National Cybersecurity Initiative*, available at <https://obamawhitehouse.archives.gov/sites/default/files/cybersecurity.pdf> accessed 30 October 2019.

111 Herzog (n 107), 54.

112 ibid.

113 ibid., 54–55.

114 European Commission, *The EU Internal Security Strategy in Action: Five Steps Toward a More Secure Europe* (Brussels, 22 November 2010), para. 9, available at <https://europa.eu/rapid/press-release_MEMO-10-598_en.htm> accessed 30 October 2019.

115 UN Doc. A/68/98 (24 June 2013) p. 6, para. 1; UN Doc. A/65/201 (16 July 2010), para. 1; UNGA Res. A/60/45 (6 July 2006), operative para. 1; UN Doc. A/71/172 (19 July 2016).

116 Detlev Wolter, "The UN Takes a Big Step Forward on Cybersecurity" (posted on Arms Control Association website on 4 September 2013), available at <www.armscontrol.org/act/2013-09/un-takes-big-step-forward-cybersecurity> accessed 30 October 2019.

117 *International Strategy for Cyberspace* (n 10), 9.

118 NATO Summit 2014, *Wales Summit Declaration* (Issued by the Heads of State and Government participating in the Meeting of the North Atlantic Council in Wales from

106   *Expanding the frontiers of Article 2(4)*

During that period, the African Union adopted the *Convention on Cyber Security and Personal Data Protection.*[119] While this political synergy is helpful, we await a UN-sponsored convention to that effect. According to Demchak and Dombrowski, the current political currency is aimed at encouraging States to extend "their sovereign control in the virtual world in the name of security and economic sustainability."[120]

4.7.2 Two elements of cyber-territorial sovereignty

One can interpret the current moves by States to delimit cyberspace from the viewpoint of government as a condition for Statehood. A peaceful and continuous display of State authority over a certain portion of the earth's surface confers good title.[121] This criterion is in line with the "intention and will to act as sovereign" as established in the *Legal Status of Eastern Greenland.*[122] These conditions seem to drive the desire to delimit cyberspace. How it works out in principle is still evolving. But it seems very unlikely that States will be capable to exercise exclusive sovereignty in cyberspace because of its peculiar characteristics. Therefore, the cobweb character of cyberspace portrays it more as a pooled sovereignty because States' capacity to exercise their functions in cyberspace (like enforcement) could be hampered but for a collegial approach. Let us substantiate that by examining the notion of *de facto* and *de iure* sovereignty.

4.7.2.1 De facto *cyber-sovereignty*

Some transnational crimes are prosecuted if there is a nexus between the accused and prosecuting State or if the alleged crime affects the territory of the prosecuting State. States exercise extraterritorial jurisdiction over their nationals abroad and the doctrine of effect applies when a State is a victim of an attack committed by foreign nationals abroad. An attempt to apply the existing international law to cyberspace may not surmount the rigour of the Westphalian notion of defined borders. However, the *de facto* sovereignty contains an effective control model. For instance, in disputes over territories not delimited by treaties, the doctrine of effective control receives more weight than other criteria.[123] An exception applied during the period of decolonisation when *uti possidetis* was prioritised.[124] In the *Burkina Faso v Mali* case, the ICJ ruled that *effectivités* plays a

---

4 to 5 September 2014), para. 72, available at <www.nato.int/cps/en/natohq/index.htm> accessed 30 October 2019.

119 African Union, *Convention on Cyber Security and Personal Data Protection* (Adopted by the Twenty-third Ordinary Session of the Assembly, held in Malabo, Equatorial Guinea, 27 June 2014), available at <https://au.int/en/treaties/african-union-convention-cyber-security-and-personal-data-protection> accessed 30 October 2019.

120 Chris C. Demchak and Peter Dombrowski, "Rise of a Cybered Westphalian Age" (2011) 5(1) *Strategic Studies Quarterly* 32–61, 32.

121 *Island of Palmas* case (n 17), 839.

122 *Legal Status of Eastern Greenland* (n 103), 45–46.

123 *Island of Palmas* case (n 17), 846, 838–839.

124 For a meaningful discussion on the criteria see: Brian Taylor Summer, "Territorial Disputes at the International Court of Justice" (2004) 53(6) *Duke Law Journal*

Expanding the frontiers of Article 2(4)   107

supportive role but comes to prominence when other modes of acquisition are absent.[125]

The Supreme Court of the United States in the *Lakhdar Boumediene, et al., v George W. Bush, President of the United States* case[126] handed down a landmark judgment on *de facto* sovereignty. The Court was asked to determine whether Guantanamo Bay detainees were within the territory of the United States. Some Justices recalled their previous judgment which held that "Guantanamo was under the complete control and jurisdiction of the United States."[127] They further submit that

> [a]t common law, courts exercised habeas jurisdiction over the claims of aliens detained within sovereign territory of the realm, as well as the claims of persons detained in the so-called exempt jurisdictions, where ordinary writs did not run, and all other dominions under the sovereign's control ...[128]

The cyberspace is an excellent example of "exempt jurisdiction" or what Colangelo calls "concurrent sovereignty."[129] While a State on whose territory the cyberspace infrastructure is located enjoys *de jure* sovereignty, other States whose interest might be affected by its use enjoy *de facto* sovereignty.

In the opinion of the Justices that dissented, "Guantanamo Bay is in every practical respect a United States territory"[130] because it is under the US "complete control and jurisdiction."[131] According to Colangelo, "practical sovereignty means practical control over a territory" and "*de facto* sovereignty means *both* practical control *and* jurisdiction over a territory, such that the de facto sovereign's laws and legal system govern the territory."[132] Based on its objective assessment, the US Supreme Court held that while Cuba "retains *de jure* sovereignty over Guantanamo," the US "maintains *de facto* sovereignty" over that territory.[133] Under the principles established in *S.S. Lotus*, consent allows for extraterritorial application of laws. Effective control not only evidence sovereignty but also is a condition for attributing responsibility to States for actions of non-State actors.[134] Therefore, "overlapping sovereignties"[135] do not bar States from exercising *de facto* sovereignty in cyberspace.

1779–1812.; Andrew F. Burghardt, "The Bases of Territorial Claims" (1973) 63(2) *Geographical Review* 225–245.
125 ICJ Reports (Judgment) (1986) p. 554, para. 63.
126 127 S.Ct. 1478 (2007).
127 ibid., 1479 (per Justice Breyer *et al.*, dissenting opinion).
128 ibid.
129 Anthony J. Colangelo, "De Facto Sovereignty: Boumediene and Beyond" (2009) 77 (3) *The George Washington Law Review* 632–676, 625.
130 127 S.Ct. 1478 (2007), 1479.
131 ibid.
132 Colangelo (n 129), 626.
133 ibid., 625.
134 International Law Commission, *Draft Articles on Responsibility of States for Internationally Wrongful Acts* (Vol. II, Part II, *Yearbook of the International Law Commission*, 2001), art. 8.
135 Colangelo (n 129), 624.

108 *Expanding the frontiers of Article 2(4)*

4.7.2.2 De jure *cyber-sovereignty*

In simple terms, "*de jure* sovereignty means 'formal' or 'technical' sovereignty in the sense of formal recognition of sovereignty by the government *vis-à-vis* other governments, and is a political question immune from judicial inquiry."[136] This chapter in its entirely partly argues that *de jure* cyber-sovereignty is a relatively new development that was not part of States' territory when the UN Charter came into force in 1945. While it is a welcome development and indeed a necessity given new forms of threats which cyberspace poses to international peace and security, direct application of Article 2(4) is untenable unless its scope is broadened to read respect for the inviolability of State territory.

4.8 Factors enabling *de jure* cyber-territorial rights

Traditionally, cyberspace was ranked as *res communis omnium* like the Outer Space, High Seas or Antarctica. A conversation regarding the possibility of subjecting *res communis omnium* to States' sovereignty started when Neil Armstrong hoisted "a US flag on the moon in 1969."[137] But it was not sustained because the *Outer Space Treaty* prohibits it.[138] Yet the conversation is not over considering States' encroachment to those sacred areas. It is not inconceivable to see domestic laws purporting to exercise sovereignty in those areas in future; although their peculiarities might favour overlapping sovereignty. It is unlikely that exclusivity which characterises territoriality will apply in a cyber-domain where States have competing interests.

Nonetheless, the US has indicated its commitment to exercise such functions as might be reasonably necessary to protect its territorial integrity.[139] Most commentators on matters relating to cyberspace do not contest that States could exercise sovereignty in cyberspace. Thus, the *Group of Governmental Experts on Developments in the Field of Information and Telecommunications in the Context of International Security* favours the doctrine of *Ratione loci.*[140] The report it issued in 2013 says, *inter alia*, "State sovereignty and international norms and principles that flow from sovereignty apply to the conduct by States of ICT-related activities and to their jurisdiction over ICT infrastructure within their territory."[141] It further clarifies as follows:

---

136 ibid., 626.
137 Yasmin Ali, "Who Owns Outer Space?" (BBC News, 25 September 2015), available at <www.bbc.co.uk/news/science-environment-34324443> accessed 1 November 2019.
138 *Treaty on Principles Governing the Activities of States in the Exploration and Use of Outer Space, Including the Moon and Other Celestial Bodies* (Concluded at Washington, Moscow and London on 27 January 1967, entered into Force on 10 October 1967) 610 UNTS 206, art. 2.
139 United States Department of Defense, "A Report to the Congress Pursuant to the National Defense Authorisation Act for Fiscal Year 2011, Section 934" (November 2011) 7–9, available at <https://nsarchive2.gwu.edu//NSAEBB/NSAEBB424/docs/Cyber-059.pdf> accessed 2 November 2019.
140 UN Doc. A/70/174 (22 July 2015), paras 27–29.
141 ibid., para. 27.

(a) States have jurisdiction over the ICT infrastructure located within their territory;

(b) In their use of ICTs, States must observe, among other principles of international law, State sovereignty, sovereign equality, the settlement of disputes by peaceful means and non-intervention in the internal affairs of other States. Existing obligations under international law are applicable to State use of ICTs. States must comply with their obligations under international law to respect and protect human rights and fundamental freedoms;

(c) Underscoring the aspirations of the international community to the peaceful use of ICTs for the common good of mankind, and recalling that the Charter applies in its entirety, the Group noted the inherent right of States to take measures consistent with international law and as recognized in the Charter. The Group recognized the need for further study on this matter;

(d) The Group notes the established international legal principles, including, where applicable, the principles of humanity, necessity, proportionality and distinction;

(e) States must not use proxies to commit internationally wrongful acts using ICTs, and should seek to ensure that their territory is not used by non-State actors to commit such acts;

(f) States must meet their international obligations regarding internationally wrongful acts attributable to them under international law. However, the indication that an ICT activity was launched or otherwise originates from the territory or the ICT infrastructure of a State may be insufficient in itself to attribute the activity to that State. The Group noted that the accusations of organizing and implementing wrongful acts brought against States should be substantiated.[142]

In summary, this text advocates for the inviolability of State territory in cyberspace. A caveat that ought to be acknowledged is that the application of international law in cyberspace is subject to qualification. As observed, cyber-attacks are non-kinetic and may not constitute the physical armed attack as traditionally intended for Article 2(4) of the UN Charter. Besides, States that are major players in the evolution of cyberlaw have not reached a consensus on what the detailed technicalities should be. In the area of cyberspace governance, for instance, the "questions of 'who participates' and 'who controls'" remain contentious and are conditioned by national interests of "Russia, China and the United States."[143] While China and Russia support a "state-based model," "the United States and its allies" prefer "a multistakeholder model" which incorporates "the private sector, civil society, academia, and individuals, in addition to governments."[144]

142 ibid., para. 28.
143 Eichensehr (n 5), 346.
144 ibid.

110 *Expanding the frontiers of Article 2(4)*

4.8.1 UN – International Code of Conduct for Information Security

In 2011, China, Russia, Tajikistan and Uzbekistan proposed an "International Code of Conduct for Information Security"[145] (Draft Code of Conduct) to the United Nations. It consists of three parts, namely: preamble, purpose and scope and the Code of Conduct. The preamble discusses, among other things, economic and information advantages of cyberspace and highlights the need not to put its use to nefarious ends. Part two adumbrates purposes and scope of the Draft Code of Conduct as well as identifies the rights and responsibilities of States in cyberspace to harmonise States' approaches to achieving those objectives. Part three enumerates pledges to which intending State Parties would be committed. Worthy of note is that the operative paragraph (a) obliges States to have "… respect for the sovereignty, territorial and political independence of all States."[146] The choice of the word respect is commendable and perhaps buttresses the non-kinetic character of the virtual world."

The United Nations Group of Governmental Experts on Development in the Field of Information and Telecommunications in the Context of International Security[147] was constituted in 2004 to create means of tackling cyberspace threats. Its reports[148] explain the "norms, rules and principles for responsible behaviour of States" in cyberspace. It also elaborates on how international law could be applied to the use of ICT.[149] Presently, brainstorming and discussions are underway within the United Nations and it is hoped that a multilateral *Convention on Cyberspace* might be a reality someday.

4.8.2 World Summit on Information Society

The international community held two World Summits on the Information Society in Geneva and Tunis in 2003 and 2005 respectively and issued a *communiqué* afterwards.[150] Paragraph 36 of the *communiqué* authorises the United Nations to interfere with the integrity of cyberspace infrastructure domiciled in a State to prevent its use "for purposes that are inconsistent with the objectives of maintaining international stability and security."[151] Paragraph 39 recommends a "regulatory framework reflecting national realities,"[152] and equally affirms that "policy authority for internet-related public policy issues is the sovereign right of

---

145 UN Doc. A/66/359 (14 September 2011) Annex, 3ff; UNGA Res. A/RES/53/70 (4 December 1998), operative para 2.
146 UN Doc. A/66/359 (14 September 2011), operative para. (a).
147 UNGA Res. A/RES/58/32 (8 December 2003), operative para. 5.
148 UN Doc. A/70/174 (22 July 2015), operative paras 9–15; UN Doc. A/68/98 (24 June 2013), operative para. 20.
149 UN Doc. A/70/174 (22 July 2015), operative paras 24–29.
150 United Nations World Summit on the Information Society Geneva 2003 – Tunis 2005, "Declaration of Principles, Building the Information Society: A Global Challenge in the New Millennium" UN Doc. WSIS-03/GENEVA/DOC/4-E (12 December 2003) [hereinafter *World Summit on Information Technology*].
151 ibid., para. 36.
152 ibid., para. 39; UNGA Res. A/RES/56/121 (19 December 2001), operative para. 1.

Expanding the frontiers of Article 2(4) 111

States."[153] Importantly, these Summits encourage international agencies, regions and States with the requisite capabilities to evolve mechanisms to tackle cyberspace offences. Responses have been impressive because many States have enacted laws which allow them to exercise sovereignty in cyberspace.

4.8.3 The view of Group of Seven (G7) on cyberspace

The Group of Seven (G7) Industrialised Democracies, formerly known as G8 but for the suspension of Russia in 2014 over its annexation of Crimea, had taken a position on the matter when they met in Japan in 2016. A joint *communiqué* issued by their Information and Communication Technology Ministers affirmed their resolve "to strengthen international collaboration, capacity building and public-private partnership" in the fight against cyber-attacks as well as to "support risk management based approaches to cybersecurity."[154] Their shared "common values and principles" include "democracy, respect for the rule of law, free, fair and open markets, respect for territorial integrity, and respect for human rights and international humanitarian law."[155] They emphasise the need for States to partner with "the private sector, civil society and communities in investigating, disrupting and prosecuting terrorists' illegal activities online."[156] Collegiality is the benchmark of G7's strategy to curbing cyber-related offences. It confirms the overlapping character of cyber-territorial sovereignty. The head of government for G7 echoes that sentiment in the policy document tagged the *Principles and Actions on Cyber*,[157] although it argues "that international law, including the United Nations Charter, is applicable in cyberspace."[158] Yet it does not further explain how that is feasible but "looks forward to the work of the new GGE, including further discussions on how existing international law applies to cyberspace ..."[159] On this premise, the *Tallinn Manual* discussed earlier in part is an ambitious, comprehensive, non-binding academic work attempting to develop a blueprint on the subject matter. However, our analysis has revealed some of the weaknesses inherent in the direct application of Article 2(4) to cyberspace.

---

153 *World Summit on Information Technology* (n 150), para. 49.
154 The G7, "Joint Declaration by G7 ICT Ministers" (Action Plan on Implementing the Charter, adopted by the G7 Information and Communication Technology Ministers at Japan on 29–30 April 2016), para. 19, available at <www.g8.utoronto.ca/ict/2016-ict-declaration.html> accessed 2 November 2019.
155 The G7, "Joint *communiqué*" (Adopted by the G7 Foreign Ministers at Hiroshima Japan on 10–11 April 2016), preamble, available at <www.mofa.go.jp/ms/is_s/page24e_000138.html> accessed 2 November 2019.
156 ibid., 3–4.
157 The G7, "The Principles of Actions on Cyber" (Adopted at the G7 Summit held at Ise-Chima Japan on 26–27 May 2016) 1–3, available at <www.mofa.go.jp/ecm/ec/page24e_000148.html> accessed 3 November 2019.
158 ibid., 1.
159 ibid.

112 *Expanding the frontiers of Article 2(4)*

4.8.4 International Telecommunications Union

"Founded in 1865 to facilitate international connectivity in communications networks,"[160] the International Telecommunications Union (ITU) weighed into the debate on cybersecurity. It has adopted seven strategic goals in its "Global Cybersecurity Agenda."[161] The first strategic goal deals with an "elaboration of strategies for the development of a model cybercrime legislation that is globally applicable and interoperable with existing national and regional legislative measures."[162] This recognises the need for legislation suited to cyberspace. Later, the United Nations General Assembly "encourages Member States and relevant regional and international organizations" to share their technical know-how and best practice in cybersecurity with other Stakeholders.[163]

After Edward Snowden's revelation of a mass surveillance programme by the National Security Agency, Deutsche Telekom "put forward the idea of a national and eventual Schengen routing of Internet traffic."[164] By "national routing" it is meant "that information exchanged between domestic servers and computers should travel only over domestic infrastructure and therefore remain within territorial borders."[165] If this initiative succeeds, it will put cyberspace on a par with the Westphalian sovereignty structure. The purpose is to ensure data security, to protect such data from prying eyes of cyber-spies and to delimit Internet traffic routes. The downside is that it subjects cyberspace to State's authority in breach of Barlow's formal *"Declaration of the Independence of Cyberspace."*[166]

ITU has developed,

> (i) Combatting Cybercrime toolkit … (ii) partnership with the United Nations Office on Drugs and Crime (UNODC) on mitigating the risks posed by cybercrime, and the secure use of ICT through various joint initiatives and capacity building to benefit countries worldwide; as well as (iii) customized

---

160 See *About International Telecommunication Union (ITU)*, available at <www.itu.int/en/about/Pages/default.aspx> accessed 3 November 2019.

161 This was launched by Dr Hamadoun Touré in 2007 as a response to a request made by the World Summit on the Information Society (WSIS) after its 2005 Convention in Tunis. It consists of five strategic pillars – "legal framework; technical measures; organizational structures; capacity building and international cooperation." See International Telecommunication Union, *ITU Global Cybersecurity Agenda (GCA): A Framework for International Cooperation in Cybersecurity*, at p. 15, available at <www.intgovforum.org/Substantive_2nd_IGF/ITU_GCA_E.pdf> accessed 4 November 2019.

162 ibid.

163 UNGA Res. A/Res/64/211 (17 March 2010), operative para. 2.

164 Andreas Baur-Ahrens, "The Power of Cyberspace Centralisation: Analysing the Example of Data Territorialisation" in Matthias Leese and Stef Wittendorp (eds), *Security/Mobility* (Manchester, Manchester United Press, 2017) 37.

165 ibid., 37.

166 John Perry Barlow, *A Declaration of the Independence of Cyberspace* (San Francisco, Electronic Frontier Foundation, 1996), available at <www.eff.org/cyberspace-independence> accessed 4 November 2019.

support and technical assistance to ITU membership designed to meet the individual requirements of the country.[167]

"Combatting cybercrime toolkit" exposes various forms of cybercrimes and how they have been addressed in national laws.[168] The ITU also assists governments in building up capacity that meets the contemporary challenges they face in cyberspace.[169] There are visible signs of cooperation at international, national and regional levels to tackle cyber-related offences.

4.9 Substantive cyberlaw – legislature

The capacity building in terms of a substantive national cyberlaw[170] has an impressive record. Available statistics from the United Nations Conference on Trade and Development shows that "138 States have adopted a law on cybercrimes and fourteen have a draft law."[171] The figure is encouraging and shows States' determination to exercise legislative jurisdiction in cyberspace. Yet more needs to be done to ensure that such cyberlaws and policies are operational at regional and international spheres through cooperation with law enforcement agents. As said earlier, the nature of cyberspace supports overlapping sovereignty, and cross-border effect of cyber-related offences requires cooperation among States for proper implementation of cyberlaws.

4.9.1 *The Council of Europe* Convention on Cybercrime

The Council of Europe adopted the *Convention on Cybercrime*[172] in November 2001 and it went into force in July 2004. It is a model of how to regulate cyberspace at the regional level and many States in Europe have domesticated it. Other regions have adopted similar instruments.[173] The preambular paragraph 4 of the Council of Europe's *Convention on Cybercrime* calls for "a common criminal policy aimed at the protection of society against cybercrime, *inter alia*, by adopting

---

167 For details visit <www.itu.int/en/ITU-D/Cybersecurity/Pages/legislation.aspx> accessed 4 November 2019.
168 See *Combatting Cybercrime: Tools and Capacity Building for Emerging Economies* (Washington D.C., United Nations and International Bank for Reconstitution and Development, 2017) 158–169 [hereinafter *ITU on Combatting Cybercrime*].
169 ITU, *Understanding Cybercrime: Phenomena, Challenges and Legal Response Report* (2014), iii, available at <www.itu.int/en/ITU-D/Cybersecurity/Documents/Cyber crime2014_E.pdf> accessed 4 November 2019.
170 By "cyberlaw" we mean criminal code prohibiting cyber-related offences.
171 *ITU on Combatting Cybercrime* (n 168), 226.
172 See generally, *Convention on Cybercrime* (n 89); Council of Europe, *Additional Protocol to the Convention on Cybercrime, Concerning the Criminalisation of Acts of a Racist and Xenophobic Nature Committed Through Computer Systems* (Concluded at Strasbourg on 28 January 2003, entered into force on 1 March 2006) 2466 UNTS 205.
173 Asia-Pacific Economic Cooperation, *APEC Principles for Action Against Spam* (Adopted by the 2005 APEC Telecommunications and Information Ministerial Meeting at Lima, Peru on 1 June 2005), para. B, available at <http://apec.org/> accessed 5 November 2019.

114   *Expanding the frontiers of Article 2(4)*

appropriate legislation and fostering international co-operation."[174] The emphasis on "appropriate legislation" underscores the uniqueness of cyberspace contrary to the popular notion that existing international laws apply in cyberspace.

The *Convention on Cybercrime* consists of three sections – substantive, procedural and jurisdiction. Each section is thematised in titles with a dropdown menu of prohibited acts as articulated in the articles. For instance, the section on substantive cyberlaw prohibits a broad range of activities categorised into five titles. They are: (1) "offences against the confidentiality, integrity and availability of computer data and systems;"[175] (2) "computer-related offences;"[176] (3) "content-related offences;"[177] (4) "offences related to infringements of copyright and related rights;"[178] and (5) "ancillary liability and sanctions."[179] Further analysis is not necessary insofar as our objective is to show that legislative jurisdiction is a State's function.[180] As established in *S.S. Lotus*, such a jurisdiction is territorial.

However, Article 22 is essential because it sets out conditions under which States could exercise jurisdiction in cyberspace. It allows State parties to assume jurisdiction over such acts

> when the offence is committed: (a) in its territory; or (b) on board a ship flying the flag of that party; or (c) on board an aircraft registered under the laws of that Party; or (d) by one of its nationals, if the offence is punishable under criminal law where it was committed or if the offence is committed outside the territorial jurisdiction of any State.[181]

It also calls for international cooperation in the prosecution of cyber-related offences. Article 4 mandates member States of the European Council to domesticate the Convention. In summary, the Council of Europe Convention on Cybercrime is an attempt to delimit cyberspace despite criticisms that it erodes individuals' rights to privacy[182] or lacks universal application.[183]

---

174 *Convention on Cybercrime* (n 89), preamble para. 4 (appropriate legislation emphasised).
175 ibid., arts 2–6.
176 ibid., arts 7–8.
177 ibid., art. 9.
178 ibid., art. 10.
179 ibid., arts 11–13.
180 For further analysis, see Miriam F. Miquelson-Weismann, "The Convention on Cybercrime: A Harmonized Implementation of International Penal Law: What Prospects for Procedural Due Process" (2005) 23(2) *John Marshall Journal of Computer and Information Law* 329–362.
181 *Convention on Cybercrime* (n 89), art. 22(1).
182 Kierkegaard (n 85), 433.
183 Stein Schjolberg and Solange Ghernaouti-Helie, *A Global Treaty on Cybersecurity and Cybercrime*, Second Edition (Oslo, AiTOslo, 2011), ii, available at <https://pircenter.org/en/articles/530-a-global-treaty-on-cybersecurity-and-cybercrime> accessed 5 November 2019.

Expanding the frontiers of Article 2(4) 115

4.9.2 Domestication of cyberlaw – emerging State practice?

The fact that about 138 States from across the globe have extant cyberlaw and about 14 have draft cyberlaw is a good sign of the development of State practice. The international community is committed to secure cyberspace in order to promote mutual economic benefits. The substantive section of most domestic cyberlaws is similar in content. In broad terms, they proscribe,

> (A) the unauthorized access to a computer system, or hacking, (B) illegal acquisition of computer data, (C) illegal interception of computer data, (D) illegal access to, and interfering with, computer data, (E) illegal system interference, (F) misuse of devices, (G) fraud, (H) forgery, (I) spamming, (J) child pornography and (K) copyright and trademark offenses.[184]

Let us illustrate further by examining the first three criminalised conducts.

4.9.2.1 Unlawful access

Unlawful access, also known as "hacking," covers a wide range of illegal means used to gain access to "an ICT device or network" and by which "the cybercriminal may target information and data, or may turn to target systems."[185] A hacking tool is mostly "malware," which is a generic word that covers "malicious code or software, including viruses, worms, Trojan horses, ransomware, spyware, adware and scareware."[186] The terminology used to designate cybercrimes could vary from State to State. It could be "unlawful access," "unauthorised access" "intrusion," "illegal access" and so forth. In some States, hacking might be specified while in others, it will be included as part of the prohibited conducts. Similarly, what constitutes *actus reus* and *mens rea* is determined by States. While some States might consider illegal access as dispositive of cybercrime, others might include "continued or remained access to the computer system beyond that initial unauthorized trespass."[187] According to the USA Patriot Act, "protected computer" includes "… a computer located outside the United States that is used in a manner that affects interstate or foreign commerce or communication of the United States."[188]

4.9.2.2 Illegal acquisition of computer data

A person will be guilty of an offence for possessing computer data intentionally acquired illegally. Kazakhstan's criminal code prohibits an illegal acquisition of such

> … information on a storage medium, in a computer, computer system, or computer network, and equally violation of the rules for operation of a

184 *ITU on Combatting Cybercrime* (n 168), 159.
185 ibid., 79.
186 ibid.
187 ibid., 159.
188 18-U.S.C. §1030(e)(2)(B) (2001).

116 *Expanding the frontiers of Article 2(4)*

computer, computer system or their network by persons who have access to the computer, computer system or their network, if this action entailed destruction, blocking, modification, or copying of information, or disruption of the work of a given computer, computer system, or computer network ... [189]

The phrase "if this action entailed destruction ..." refers to *mens rea* but under the German Criminal Code, a crime would have been committed irrespective of the intent.[190] Under the *Computer Fraud and Abuse Act* of the United States, a crime is committed when the trespasser accesses a computer "without authorization" or "exceeds authorized access."[191]

4.9.2.3 Illegal interception of computer data

As the name suggests, an unauthorised interception of "computer data during transmission"[192] is a criminal offence. According to the Penal Code of Botswana,

[a] person who intentionally and by technical means, without lawful excuse or justification intercepts (a) any non-public transmission to, from or within a computer or computer system; or (b) electromagnetic emissions that are carrying data, from a computer or computer system ...[193]

is guilty of an offence on conviction.

In summary, cyberlaws cover virtually all misconducts in cyberspace carried out by persons or group of persons if the conduct is directed against the ICT, network, data, computer or its software domiciled within a State. The threshold seems to have shifted since the international law does not allow a State to "extend the criminal jurisdiction of its courts to include a crime or offence committed by a foreigner abroad solely in consequence of the fact that one of its nationals has been a victim of the crime or offence."[194] This may no longer be the case with cybercrimes; the effectiveness of cyberlaws will largely depend on enforcement. For instance, section 11, subsection 3 of the penal code of the Bahamas authorises its courts to prosecute cyber criminals from any part of

---

189 Kazakhstan, *Law No. 167 of 16 July 1997 to Adopt the Criminal Code (as amended)*, art. 227.1, available at <www.ilo.org/dyn/natlex/natlex4.detail?p_isn=65070> accessed 5 November 2019.
190 See German Criminal Code, art. 202a, available at <www.gesetze-im-internet.de/eng lisch_stgb/> accessed 5 November 2019.
191 18 U.S.C. §§ 1030(a)(1), (a)(2), (a)(4) (some modifications made).
192 *ITU on Combatting Cybercrime* (n 168), 161.
193 Botswana, *Chapter 08:06 Cybercrime and Computer Related Crimes*, section 9, available at <www.itu.int/ITU-D/projects/ITU_EC_ACP/hipssa/Activities/SA/docs/ SA-1_Legislations/Botswana/CYBERCRIMES.pdf> accessed 5 November 2019.
194 *The Case of the S.S. "Lotus"* (France v Turkey) Judgment PCIJ Series A, No. 10 (1927) 7 [hereinafter *Lotus* case].

Expanding the frontiers of Article 2(4) 117

the world if the said offence is directed against the Bahamas. Can this type of law be enforced if there were no treaty between the parties?

4.10 Enforcement of cyberlaws – judiciary

As stated above, Iran brought no formal complaint before the ICJ when its nuclear reactor was attacked; neither did Georgia nor Estonia. The reasons, perhaps, could be the difficulty to prove such charges or lack of evidence. Consequently, there is no case law precedent to rely upon. Most commentators argue that self-defence could be available if the effects as a result of the attack were grave. When Georgia was attacked in 2008, a report issued by an independent international fact-finding mission condemned it[195] as deplorable but did not classify it as the use of force. It concludes that "the nature of defence against cyber attacks at this stage of its development means that such attacks are easy to carry out, but difficult to prevent, and to attribute to a source."[196] But suppose that the *Lockerbie* incident was caused by a cyberattack? Could it be classified as an armed attack? In our view, not likely because of its non-kinetic nature, although the effect is grave. A peaceful coexistence should not be based on the havoc caused but avoidance of antagonism between nations. But the crucial question for the courts is whether States have jurisdiction over cyberspace offences? Jurisprudence on how domestic courts approach various elements in cyber-related offences abound.[197] We turn to examine some of them.

4.10.1 Without authorisation[198]

Concerning unlawful access to a "protected computer," the court in the *United States v Drew* held that the threshold "will always be met when an individual using a computer contacts or communicates with an Internet website."[199] Later, it is required that the trespasser has observed or obtained information from the computer hacked, or that his or her actions have effects on the territory of a State. In the *United States v Ivanov*,[200] a Russian citizen hacked into the Online Information Bureau company based in Vernon, Connecticut. The court assumed jurisdiction on two grounds: first, "the intended and actual detrimental effects of Ivanov's actions in Russia occurred

195 Independent International Fact-Finding Mission on the Conflict in Georgia, "Reports" (Volume II, September 2009) 217–219, available at <www.mpil.de/en/pub/publications/archive/independent_international_fact.cfm> accessed 5 November 2019.
196 ibid., 219.
197 For cases decided by the US courts, see Department of Justice, *Prosecuting Computer Crimes Manual* (Washington D.C., Office of Legal Education, 2010) 4, available at <www.justice.gov/criminal-ccips> accessed 6 November 2019.
198 The meaning of "without authorization" is elusive in the jurisprudence of the United States. See U.S. v Drew, 259 F.R.D. 449 (C.D.Cal. 2009), 458.
199 ibid., 457.
200 175 F.Supp.2d 367 (D.Conn. 2001).

118 *Expanding the frontiers of Article 2(4)*

within the United States, and second, because each of the statutes under which Ivanov was charged with a substantive offense was intended by congress to apply extra-territorially."[201] Similarly, the Supreme Court of Victoria convicted an Australian citizen stalking a Canadian actress residing in Toronto through telephone calls. The Australian court observes that one cannot rebut the presumption that the penal code is intended to apply extraterritorially.[202] The UK court held that it has jurisdiction when a substantial part of the offence is committed in its territory or the offender resides within the UK.[203] In the *United States v Drew*, the court explains that the "actual aspiration ... need not be proved in order to establish a violation."[204] It is sufficient to establish that data is "knowingly" or "intentionally" obtained as against "mistaken, inadvertent, or careless ones."[205]

4.11 Direct application of Article 2(4) to cyberspace

So far, this chapter covers the following points: (1) Cyberspace is traditionally a *res communis omnium* but that has changed with the increase in cyber-related offences; (2) that States enact laws to regulate activities in cyberspace or to criminalise same is an exercise of State function. Thus, cyberspace has become a part of States' territory; (3) Cyberspace attacks are by nature non-kinetic and may not be construed as physical armed force strictly speaking. The next section will evaluate the debate regarding the direct application of international law in cyberspace.

The idea that international law is applicable in cyberspace is not sustainable because there is neither customary cyberlaw,[206] universal treaty or convention regulating States' behaviour in cyberspace nor jurisprudence from international judicial bodies. In fact, Brown and Poellet highlight the difficulty to evolve a customary cyberlaw because "actions and effects available to nations and nonstate actors in cyberspace do not necessarily match up neatly with the principles governing armed conflict."[207] What is available is *opinio juris* and nascent State practice. Therefore, States are bound by the provision of Article 2(4); to "be performed ... in good faith"[208] "in accordance with the ordinary meaning."[209] An evolutive interpretation which accommodates respect of the inviolability of States' territory takes care of cyber-related offences and is in accordance with the war context under which the Charter was drafted, purposes of the Charter as well as the *travaux préparatoires*.

---

201 ibid., 370.
202 *Director of Public Prosecution v Brian Andrew Sutcliffe* (in a matter of an appeal on a question of law pursuant to section 92 Magistrates' Court Act 1989) [2001] VSC 43, para. 43.
203 *R v Smith (Wallace Duncan) (No. 4)* [2004] EWCA Crim 631, para. 47.
204 259 F.R.D. 449, 457 (C.D. Cal. 2009), 457.
205 ibid., 459.
206 Brown and Poellet (n 101), 127.
207 ibid.
208 United Nations, *Vienna Convention on the Law of Treaties* (Concluded at Vienna on 23 May 1969, entered into force on 28 January 1980) 1155 UNTS 331, art. 26.
209 ibid., art. 31.

Expanding the frontiers of Article 2(4) 119

A treaty is binding upon the parties when facts on which it is contracted are the same.[210] Ambiguity undermines legality. In the *Diggs v Richardson* case, the plaintiff requested the US Court to order the US government to comply with the SC resolution 301 (1971) and the court held that the "U.N. resolution underlying that obligation does not confer rights on the citizens of the United States that are enforceable in court in the absence of implementing legislation."[211] Some States apply dual legislative system such that universal legal instruments must be domesticated afterwards. While Chapter 7 argues that the narrow interpretation of Article 2(4) does not enhance full realisation of the purpose of the UN Charter, it is unsustainable to stretch physical force to include non-kinetic attack. Irrespective of the strategies which States have adopted, the classical notions of *jus ad bellum* and *jus in bello* defy direct application of conventional warfare terminology to cyberspace.

4.11.1 *The effect test*

As observed above, an Independent International Fact-Finding Mission neither classifies cyber-attack on Georgia as an armed attack even though it is alleged to have aided conventional military combat. Again, none of the countries that have witnessed cyber war, attack or crimes resorted to physical armed attack in self-defence. None petitioned the ICJ in protest of a violation of Article 2(4).

The argument based on the effect test runs as follows: "aggressive cyber activities resulting in kinetic effects (i.e., physical destruction, damage, or injury) are covered by the law regarding the use of force and armed attack."[212] The *Lockerbie* incident would have been a good example if a cyber-attack had caused it. The U. S. Department of Homeland Security has conducted an experiment to demonstrate that cyber-attacks could physically destroy national power plants.[213] In the *United States v Robert Thomas* case,[214] the court was to determine a case that had a cross-border effect. The defendants from California had disseminated electronic graphic images across the United States. However, the online materials could only be accessed or downloaded by those that subscribed and paid their subscription fee. An undercover agent from Tennessee subscribed to and downloaded the material from Tennessee. The defendants were charged to court in Tennessee for violating the Federal Obscenity Statute. In defence, they argued that Tennessee lacked jurisdiction over an act perpetrated in California. The Sixth Circuit held that "the effects of the Defendants' criminal conduct reached

---

210 Riaz Mohammad Khan, "Vienna Convention on Law of Treaties – Article 62 (Fundamental Change of Circumstances)" (1973) 26(1) *Pakistan Horizon* 16–28, 17.
211 *Charles Coles Diggs Jr., et al., v Elliot L. Richardson* 555 F.2d 848 (1976), 850.
212 Brown and Poellet (n 101), 137.
213 CNN, "Staged Cyber Attack Reveals Vulnerability in Power Grid" (26 September 2007), available at <https://edition.cnn.com/2007/US/09/26/power.at.risk/index.html> accessed 7 November 2019.
214 74 F.3d 701 (6th Cir. 1996).

120 *Expanding the frontiers of Article 2(4)*

the Western District of Tennessee, and that district was suitable for accurate fact-finding."[215]

In general, an argument based on effect appears simplistic in a globalised world where actions performed in our continent could have ripple effects on others. Does the circulation of such materials cause physical damage to a State's critical infrastructure? One could argue that the dissemination of obscene pictures of minors through the Internet is prohibited. In the *Playboy Enterprises, Inc., v Chuckleberry Publishing Inc.* case,[216] "effect" (passing off) was the reason why a US court stopped the circulation of online publication of a magazine that was registered in Italy. The Attorney General of Minnesota has issued a general "warning to all Internet users and providers" that the State of Minnesota will exercise jurisdiction over acts that have an effect on Minnesota.[217] The controversial universal jurisdiction is also anchored on the "effect" theory.[218] Therefore, an argument based on effect is multifaceted. As it stands, the degree of the impact or damage that could trigger self-defence is unclear. Although it is almost settled that States' jurisdiction in cyberspace is triggered by harmful effects,[219] the limits to that right are debated.[220]

4.11.2 *Cyber-related offences and the law of armed conflict*

If international law were applicable in cyberspace, then a distinction is to be made between civilian computers (both hardware and software) and States' computers. The laws and customs of war require that the right of civilians be respected.[221] If only electronic operation were to be conducted, why refer to current international law as if physical armed defensive attack is an option? Besides, views vary as to what constitutes self-defence in cyberspace.[222] Civilians are not armed combatants and their computers and Internet network system should not be damaged in the

---

215 ibid., 710.
216 486 F.Supp. 414 (1980) 434–435; *United States v Aluminium Co. of America*, 148 F.2d 416 (2nd Cir. 1945) 444.
217 The Office of Minnesota Attorney General, "Statement of Minnesota Attorney General on Internet Jurisdiction," available at <https://cyber.harvard.edu/ilaw/Jurisdiction/Minnesota_Full.html> accessed 7 November 2019.
218 The concern is that cyberspace globalises cybercrimes such that prosecution of cyberspace offenders applies *erga omnes*. See Stephen Wilske and Teresa Schiller, "International Jurisdiction in Cyberspace: Which States May Regulate the Internet" (1997) 50 (1) *Federal Communications Law Journal* 117–178, 143.
219 Jason Coppel, "A Hard Look at the Effects Doctrine of Jurisdiction in Public International Law" (1993) 6(1) *Leiden Journal of International Law* 73–90, 73; Margaret Loo, "IBM v Commissioner: The Effects Test in the EEC" (1987) 10(1) *Boston College of International and Comparative Law Review* 125–133, 125.
220 Wilske and Schiller (n 218), 133.
221 *Protocol Additional to the Geneva Convention of 12 August 1949, and Relating to the Protection of Victims of International Armed Conflicts (Protocol II)* (Concluded at Geneva on 8 June 1977, entered into force on 7 December 1978) 1125 UNTS 609, art. 13.
222 Oona A. Hathaway *et al.*, "The Law of Cyber-Attack" (2012) 100(4) *California Law Review* 817–886.

Expanding the frontiers of Article 2(4)   121

process. Perhaps a rethink of what enemy combatants in the context of cyberwarfare means is crucial and should conform with the norms established by the Hague Regulations of 1907,[223] the Geneva Conventions[224] and the First Protocol Additional to the Geneva Conventions.[225]

Klimburg and Tirmaa-Klaar suggest that "cyberattacks should be conducted with a distinction between military and civilian targets, consider the proportionality principle as well as the possibility of secondary and tertiary effects."[226] However, they concede that what this means in practical terms is "subject of vigorous debate." Equally debatable is what might constitute appropriate countermeasures.[227] The United Nations has embarked upon creating "a global culture of cybersecurity" to sensitise its member States on the cyberspace behavioural norms.[228] Such a campaign should leverage capacity building to impress upon States their obligation to protect the territorial integrity of others and to confront cyber-related offences that could emanate from their territory. States should not be preoccupied with debating whether cyber-related offences fall within the prohibited conduct in Article 2(4) but imbibe a holistic approach to peaceful coexistence. The effort to fit cyber-related offences into the existing model may not be the best option.

4.12 The nature of States' obligations in cyberspace

There is no consensus on what States' obligation in cyberspace should be. Some people might prefer every State to take full control and responsibility of cyber activities originating from its territory while others would like a decentralised power structure that incorporates private bodies. Oppenheim talks about States assuming responsibility for their conduct that results in material damage in another State.[229] As seen, the nature of cyberspace has made attribution a near impossibility. Heinegg thinks that damage is irrelevant insofar as a State has unlawfully accessed the cyberspace infrastructure of another State[230] But some provisions of cyberlaws as examined do not require the prosecutor to prove malicious intent. It seems that criminal intent

---

223 *Hague Convention IV – Laws and Customs of War on Land* (Signed at The Hague on 18 October 1907, entered into force on 26 January 1910) 36 Stat. 2277, Annex Regulation, art. 1.
224 *Convention (IV) Relating to the Protection of Civilian Persons in Time of War* (Done at Geneva on 12 August 1949, entered into force on 21 October 1950) 75 UNTS 287, arts 15, 29–31.
225 *Protocol Additional to the Geneva Conventions of 12 August 1949, and Relating to the Protection of Victims of International Armed Conflicts (Protocol I)* (concluded at Geneva on 8 June 1977, entered into force on 7 December 1978) 1125 UNTS 3, art. 46.
226 Klimburg and Tirmaa-Klaar (n 48), 13.
227 ibid.
228 UNGA Res. A/RES/57/239 (20 December 2002), operative para. 2 and annex document; UN Doc. A/70/174 (22 July 2015), paras 9–15.
229 Robert Jennings and Arthur Watts (eds), *Oppenheim's International Law*, Ninth Edition, Volume 1: Peace, Parts 2–4 (London and New York, Longman, 1996) 385.
230 Heinegg (n 1), 129.

122 Expanding the frontiers of Article 2(4)

is established when the trespasser knowingly accesses a protected computer without authorisation. According to the Permanent Court of International Justice,

> ... the first and foremost restriction imposed by international law upon a State is that – failing the existence of a permissive rule to the contrary – it may not exercise its power in any form in the territory of another State.[231]

On this authority, any unauthorised cyber activity initiated or sponsored by a State against another is unacceptable. Hence, the *Corfu Channel* case avers that "[b]etween independent States, respect for territorial sovereignty is an essential foundation of international relations."[232]

Respect for the inviolability of State territory imposes upon States the duty to respect the territory of other States. It might appear trivial but when a State sets ablaze the national flag of another State in a live television broadcast, it may result in armed conflict between both States. States are duty-bound to refrain from applying non-kinetic force against critical infrastructure of other States. It includes but is not limited to such infrastructures as may be located on land, aircrafts, ships and possibly in airspace and other facilities that enjoy sovereign immunity.[233] Equally, States have the duty to safeguard critical infrastructures of other States domiciled in their territory and to prevent non-State actors from causing harm to such infrastructures. A State may not be liable for cybercrimes committed by non-State actors provided it co-operates with the Security Council charged with the "primary responsibility for the maintenance of international peace and security"[234] in good faith.

---

231 *Lotus* case (n 194), 18.
232 *Corfu Channel* (United Kingdom v Albania) (Merits) Judgment ICJ Reports (1949) pp. 4, 35.
233 Heinegg (n 1), 129; United Nations, *Convention on the Law of the Sea* (Concluded at Montego Bay on 10 December 1982, entered into force on 16 November 1994) 1833 UNTS 397, arts 95–96. Civilian aircraft enjoys some immunities. See International Humanitarian Law Research Initiative, *Commentary on the HPCR Manual on International Law Applicable to Air and Missile Warfare* (Cambridge, Cambridge University Press, 2013) 174.
234 *Legal Consequences of the Construction of a Wall in the Occupied Palestinian Territory*, Advisory Opinion ICJ Reports (2004) p. 136, para. 26.

5 Breaches of State territory

5.0 Introduction

In 1970, Thomas Franck wrote an article lamenting the demise of Article 2(4).[1] Statistics from the Uppsala Conflict Data Program revealed that between 1975 to 2018, there were 52 cases of "State-based violence;" 78 of "non-state violence" and 35 cases of "one-sided violence."[2] Franck's post-mortem on what caused the death of Article 2(4) is intriguing; he suggests that the reasons included the dysfunctional Security Council, the emergence of "new forms of attack," States' exploitation of "exceptions and ambiguities" in the Charter *et cetera*.[3] Henkin agrees with Franck's prognosis but argues that Article 2(4) is in comatose and could be revived.[4] Both views are not diametrically opposed to each other. This chapter seeks to evaluate breaches of State territory on land, airspace and territorial sea. The purpose is to determine how those breaches, especially conduct short of the threat or use of force, have impacted on the overall project of the maintenance of international peace and security.

5.1 Where is the UN Security Council?

The legislative history of the United Nations Charter (UN Charter) shows that the Security Council (SC) is designed to promptly and quickly respond to breaches of peace and acts of aggression. Chapter VII of the UN Charter authorises the SC to initiate, coordinate and supervise collective action to arrest situations that might endanger international peace and security. "Such action may include demonstrations, blockade and other operations by air, sea or land forces of Members of the United Nations."[5] The

---

1 Thomas M. Franck, "Who Killed Article 2(4) or: Changing Norms Governing the Use of Force by States" (1970) 64(4) *American Journal of International Law* 809–837.
2 Uppsala University Department of Peace and Conflict Research, "Uppsala Conflict Data Program," available at <https://ucdp.uu.se/encyclopedia> accessed 7 November 2019.
3 Franck (n 1), 809–810.
4 Louis Henkin, "The Reports of the Death of Article 2(4) are Greatly Exaggerated" (1971) 65(3) *American Journal of International Law* 544–548, 544.
5 United Nations, *Charter of the United Nations* (Signed at San Francisco on 26 June 1945, entered into force on 24 October 1945) 1 UNTS XVI, art. 42.

124 Breaches of State territory

UN Charter obliges member States to "hold immediately available national air-force contingents for combined international enforcement action."[6] The SC has the support of the international community but has erred in delivering on its mandate.

According to Franck, "with the exception of the U.N. action in defence of South Korea, it has never been possible to invoke these collective enforcement provisions."[7] Franck further says that this lone successful incident would not have happened "but for a fortuitous absence of the Soviet Union from the Security Council."[8] This claim touches on the fundamental issue undermining the effectiveness of the SC; namely, the crippling effect of veto arrangement. Since the Syrian Civil War started in 2011, the SC has been unable to authorise collective intervention due to negative votes from some permanent members. The latest casualty at the time of writing is a draft resolution co-sponsored by Kuwait, Germany and Belgium.[9] Whether the SC still retains its legitimacy has been a recurring issue in academic debates for decades.[10] To some writers, the legitimacy of the SC is not under threat.[11] Yet the recent study conducted in the UN General Assembly by Binder and Heupel reports legitimacy deficit.[12] Hence, some States are calling for a reform of the SC.[13] Kazakhstan laments the inability of the SC "to respond in a timely and effective manner to emerging security concerns."[14] For example, the Rwandan Genocide occurred without the intervention of the SC. The SC's failure to prevent conflicts in places like Libya, South Sudan, Ukraine, Darfur and Israel/Palestine is regrettable. According to Pollock, "It is harder to get a clear picture of conflicts the Security Council has

---

6 ibid., art. 45.
7 Franck (n 1), 810.
8 ibid.
9 UN Doc. S/2019/756 (19 September 2019).
10 See generally, Hilary Charlesworth and Jean-Marc Coicaud (eds), *Fault Lines of International Legitimacy* (New York, Cambridge University Press, 2010).
11 Inis L. Claude, "Collective Legitimization as a Political Function of the United Nations" (1966) 20(3) *International Organization* 367–379, 374; Ian Hurd, *After Anarchy: Legitimacy and Power in the United Nations Security Council* (Princeton, Princeton University Press, 2007) 176; Ian Hurd, "Legitimacy, Power, and the Symbolic Life of the UN Security Council" (2002) 8(1) *Global Governance* 35–52, 38–39; Martha Finnemore, *The Purpose of Intervention: Changing Beliefs About the Use of Force* (Ithaca, Cornell University Press, 2003) 81–82; Wayne Sandholtz and Alec Stone Sweet, "Law, Politics and International Governance" in Christian Reus-Smit (ed.), *The Politics of International Law* (Cambridge, Cambridge University Press, 2004) 238–271.
12 Martin Binder and Monika Heupel, "The Legitimacy of the UN Security Council: Evidence from Recent General Assembly Debates" (2015) 59(2) *International Studies Quarterly* 238–250; Thomas L. Brewer, "Collective Legitimization in International Organizations Concept and Practice" (1972) 2(1) *Denver Journal of International Law and Policy* 73–88, 80.
13 UNGAOR, UN Doc. A/55/PV.28 (22 September 2000), 12 (Venezuela argues that the SC should be reformed to ensure its credibility as a democratic, transparent and impartial organ); Yehuda Z. Blum, "Proposals for UN Security Council Reform" (2005) 99(3) *The American Journal of International Law* 632–649.
14 UNGAOR, UN Doc. A/61/PV.75 (12 December 2006), 7.

Breaches of State territory 125

prevented as they have left no searing memories in our collective conscious-ness."[15] Given the increase in the number of conflicts published by the Uppsala Conflict Data Program, it is pertinent to ask where is the SC?

5.1.1 New forms of attack

According to Franck, "new forms of attack" refers to other means of interference in the internal affairs of other States. It includes sponsoring "small-scale internal wars," supporting "national liberation" movements and "encouraging and aiding the guerrilla movements in occupied countries."[16] Strictly, these kind of breaches cannot be categorised as an armed attack; "the more subtle and indirect the encouragement, the more tenuous becomes the analogy to an 'armed attack.'"[17] As seen in Chapter 3, the weaker States' proposal for all forms of interference to be included within the scope of Article 2(4) failed. Sadly, self-defence is not available to victims of *de minimis* breaches and States sometimes take advantage of this gap in law. When Czechoslovakia engaged in armed conflict with the Com-munist minority in 1948, its representative informed the UN Secretary-General "… that the coup by the Communist minority by force was effectuated success-fully only because of official participation of representatives of the Union of Soviet Socialist Republics …"[18] The ICJ in the *Case Concerning Military and Para-military Activities In and Against Nicaragua* (Nicaragua v United States of America)[19] held that such help "may be regarded as a threat or use of force, or amount to intervention in the internal or external affairs of other States." The ICJ prescribes no remedies for such violations. While Article 2(4) was being drafted, the suggestion to include war propaganda within the scope of Article 2(4) failed. Yet, Franck observes that "one has only to experience a revolution in Africa or the Middle East to know that an effective, powerful radio transmitter may be worth more than its weight in grenades and pistols."[20] Although the regime of Article 2 (4) has reduced inter-States' wars,[21] mere frontier incidents appear to have increased.[22] Is the world today more secure and peaceful? Certainly not.

15 John Pollock, "70 Years of Successful Security and Fatal Failures at the UNSC" (International Policy Digest, 1 November 2016), available at <https://intpolicydigest. org/2016/01/11/70-years-of-successful-security-and-fatal-failures-at-the-unsc/>.
16 Franck (n 1), 812.
17 ibid.
18 See "Letter from the Permanent Representative of Chile to the United Nations Dated 15 March 1948 addressed to the Secretary-General" U.N. Doc. S/696 (16 March 1948), 2.
19 Judgment ICJ Reports (1986) p. 14, para. 195 [hereinafter *Nicaragua* case].
20 Franck (n 1), 814.
21 Henkin (n 4), 546.
22 Tom Ruys, "Of Arms, Funding and 'Non-lethal Assistance' – Issues Surrounding Third-State Intervention in the Syrian Civil War" (2014) 13(1) *Chinese Journal of International Law* 13–53.

126 *Breaches of State territory*

5.1.2 *Interventions to aid self-determination*

A society that promotes the rights of groups and individuals must find a way to preach tolerance. Agitation for self-determination of people may constitute a threat to international peace and security, especially when it is clothed with the garment of ethnic or tribal sentiments. There seems to be no blueprint on what an appropriate response from third parties (States) should be. For example, self-determination is a norm *jus cogens*[23] which obliges *erga omnes*.[24] Chigara opines that assistance may be necessary when the rights of the people are subdued.[25] But the view of the Supreme Court of Canada in *Reference re Secession of Quebec*[26] is that unilateral secession is a right of last resort for a people "blocked from the meaningful exercise of its right to self-determination internally." Yet the court did not allow third parties to initiate, instigate, finance or support it. Similarly, the International Commission of Jurists in the *Aaland Islands Question* believes that revolution and insurgency are domestic matters.[27] However, the Jurists recognise that the League of Nations could intervene if the situation arising therefrom "comes within the sphere of action of the League of Nations."[28] It implies collective measure duly authorised.

Therefore, NATO's intervention in Serbia, leading to the secession of Kosovo was condemned as illegal as well as Russia's intervention in Ukraine.[29] That said, States facilitated secession during the decolonisation era with the authorisation of the SC[30] but unilateral intervention is unacceptable.[31] When Russia aided the secession of South Ossetia and Abkhazia from Georgia, the international community made no pronouncement on it but urged the parties involved to de-escalate

---

23 Antonio Cassese's opinion is that self-determination could be facilitated. see Antonio Cassese, *Self-determination of Peoples: A Legal Reappraisal* (Cambridge, Cambridge University Press, 1995) 133–140.

24 *Case Concerning East Timor* (Portugal v Australia) Judgment ICJ Reports (1995) p. 90, para. 29.

25 Ben Chigara, "Humanitarian Intervention Missions – Elementary Considerations, Humanity and the Good Samaritans" (2001) 2001 *Australian International Law Journal* 66–89, 73; *Western Sahara*, Advisory Opinion ICJ Reports (1975) p. 12, paras 54–56.

26 [1998] 2 SCR 217, para. 134 [hereinafter *Reference re Secession of Quebec*]; See also "Report presented to the Council of the League of Nations by the Commission of Rapporteurs" LN Doc. B7 21/68/106 (1921), 1–14, 4, available at <www.ilsa.org/jessup/jessup10/basicmats/aaland2.pdf> accessed 9 November 2019.

27 The League of Nations, "Report of the International Committee of Jurists Entrusted by the Council of the League of Nations with the task of giving Advisory Opinion Upon the Legal Aspect of the Aaland Islands Question" (1920) *League of Nations Official Journal* (Special Supplement No. 3), 6.

28 ibid., 5.

29 UNGA Res. A/RES/68/262 (1 April 2014), operative para 1.

30 UNGA Res. A/RES/2105 (XX) (20 December 1965), operative para. 10.

31 Christine Gray, *International Law and the Use of Force by State*, Third Edition (Oxford, Oxford University Press, 2008) 56; Thomas M. Franck, *Recourse to Force: State Action Against Threats and Armed Attack* (Cambridge, Cambridge University Press 2002) 136.

Breaches of State territory 127

tensions.[32] Typically, self-determination is a domestic affair[33] but international law recognises "*de facto secession*."[34] However, the position of the ICJ is that intervention on request is only available to States.[35] On this basis, a unilateral and unauthorised intervention in favour of self-determination violates international law.

5.1.3 An unauthorised intervention for humanitarian reasons

Unauthorised intervention for humanitarian reason is another contentious area being closely monitored by policymakers, diplomats and academics. Hence, the emerging concept of Responsibility to Protect (R2P) advocates that human rights be salvaged from an abusive sovereign. Perhaps, this informs NATO's intervention in Yugoslavia and Iraq in favour of the Kosovars and Kurds respectively. The Economic Community of West African States intervened in Liberia in the 1990s. Uganda intervened in South Sudan and the African Union wanted to intervene in South Sudan in 2016.[36] We do not intend to explore this further. However, the Security Council's authorisation is a preferred option.

5.1.4 Misapplication of the Security Council's Resolution

When an explicit mandate of the SC is misapplied, it breeds mistrust and distrust in the polity and hinders the adoption of subsequent resolution when the need arises. When a draft resolution co-sponsored by Belgium, Germany and Kuwait regarding the humanitarian situation in Syria was debated in the SC, the representative of Russia warned against "hidden objectives of any kind."[37] In 1958, Lebanon petitioned the SC about "illegal and unprovoked intervention in the affairs of Lebanon by the United Arab Republic"[38] and informed the SC about its resolve to invite the United States to help preserve "Lebanon's integrity and independence."[39] The representative of the United States condemned not only

---

32 *Independent International Fact-Finding Mission on the Conflict in Georgia Report* (Volume I, 2009) 22, available at <www.mpil.de/en/pub/publications/archive/ independent_international_fact.cfm> accessed 8 November 2019.
33 Georg Nolte, "Secession and External Intervention" in Marcelo G. Kohen (ed.), *Secession: International Law Perspectives* (Cambridge, Cambridge University Press 2006) 72.
34 *Reference re Secession of Quebec* (n 26), paras 140, 154–155.
35 *Nicaragua* case (n 19), para. 246.
36 African Union, "Decision on the situation in South Sudan" Assembly/AU/Dec.613 (XXVII), para. 8; UNSC Res. S/RES/2304 (12 August 2016), operative para. 11; *cf* Tito Justin, "South Sudan Rejects Regional Troop Deployment by UN" (*Voice of America News*, 10 August 2016), available at <www.voanews.com/a/southsudan-rejects-regional-troop -deployment-united-nations/3459401.html> accessed 16 November 2019.
37 UN Doc. S/PV.8623 (19 September 2019), 2.
38 UN Doc. S/PV.827 (15 July 1958), 13.
39 ibid., 6.

128 Breaches of State territory

the "insurrection stimulated and assisted from outside" but also the "plots against the Kingdom of Jordan" and "the overthrow in an exceptionally brutal and revolting manner of the legally established Government of Iraq."[40] Therefore, Lebanon needs assistance from friendly nations to tackle "a ruthlessness of aggressive purposes."[41] The initial call for military assistance to protect the territorial integrity of Lebanon was later converted to collective self-defence.

According to Franck, Article 51 was not at issue because there were no cases of military invasion or an "armed attack."[42] The representative of Lebanon later clarified that what Lebanon meant by "massive intervention in the internal affairs of Lebanon" was "the supply of arms, training of personnel, radio propaganda, propaganda by the press, etc."[43] Is there a difference from what States suggested at the time of the drafting of Article 2(4)? The invasion of Iraq in 2003 was partly premised on continuing material breach contrary to the SC resolution 678 even when resolution 1441[44] does not expressly permit it. In 2011, then Prime Minister of the United Kingdom, David Cameron argued that regime change was not the purpose for intervention in the Libyan crisis, yet it was the eventual outcome.[45]

5.1.5 Textual ambiguity or regional enforcement?

The regional security mechanism is another area that requires careful evaluation. Article 51 allows for individual and collective self-defence in the event of an armed attack. The aspect of "collective self-defence" was not contained in the Dumbarton Oaks Proposals but was sponsored by the inter-American region. The fact that self-defence could commence "until the Security Council has taken the measures necessary to maintain international peace and security" appears textually clumsy. The yardstick to trigger collective measures is not spelt out. Therefore, Franck's submission that the veto arrangement "operates to perpetuate rather than to prevent use of force as long as the action is technically taken under Article 51" is persuasive.[46] The understanding that collective self-defence applies "exclusively in terms of regional defence by allied states"[47] is not explicit in Article 51. Yet the Charter does not define regional organisation nor stipulate conditions to establish same. Over time, States tactically merged collective measures in Article 51 with Article 52 which allows peaceful means. Moreover, an ideological difference catalysed by

40 ibid.
41 ibid., 8.
42 Franck (n 1), 816.
43 UN Doc. S/PV.828 (15 July 1958), 10.
44 UNSC Res. S/RES/1441 (8 November 2002), operative paras 1 and 4; Mahmoud Hmoud, "The Use of Force Against Iraq: Occupation and Security Council Resolution 1483" (2004) 36(3) *Cornell International Law Journal* 435–453, 436.
45 See BBC News, "Libya Removing Gaddafi Not Allowed, Says David Cameron" (21 March 2011), available at <www.bbc.co.uk/news/uk-politics-12802749> accessed 9 November 2019; UNSC Res. S/RES/1973 (17 March 2011), operative para. 4.
46 Franck (n 1), 824.
47 ibid.

national interest has made the components of "peaceful settlement" vague. Consequently, Article 52 that should promote peaceful settlement of disputes often ends in a disaster. Besides, the complex structure of some regional organisations "effectively *undermines* Article 2(4)."[48] In other words, States use regional organisation to shield the United Nations from performing its statutory duties in what came to be known as the doctrine of "overriding right of a region to demand conformity to regional standards."[49]

5.2 Land

This section examines modes of territorial acquisition in relation to possible breaches of States' territory on land.

5.2.1 A brief comment on the mode of acquisition of territory

The five traditional modes of acquisition are "occupation, accretion, cession, conquest, and prescription."[50] Modern scholarship considers this classification as obsolete and inadequate.[51] Shaw, for example, observes that "a special kind of treaty" could "establish an objective territorial regime valid *erga omnes*."[52] Since this section seeks to ascertain how States' territory is breached on land, we shall follow Shaw's line of thought. He says "… many boundary disputes in fact revolve around the question of treaty interpretation."[53] We acknowledge, however, that occupation and *dereliction* are sources of conflict between States as buttressed by the dispute over the Falkland Islands between the United Kingdom and Spain.

5.2.2 Identifying common elements

An article written by Brian Taylor Sumner, "Territorial Disputes at the International Court of Justice"[54] identifies nine categories on which territorial claims are brought before the ICJ. They are: "treaties, geography, economy, culture, effective control, history, *uti possidetis*, elitism, and ideology."[55] Each of the elements is sufficient to consummate a title but in most cases, these elements are not mutually exclusive. For example, treaty and effective control were prominent in the *Legal Status of Eastern Greenland* case.[56] Therefore, the judicial scale may be applied

48 ibid., 832 (emphasised word modified).
49 ibid., 833–834.
50 James Crawford, *Brownlie's Principles of Public International Law*, Eighth Edition (Oxford, Oxford University Press, 2012) 220.
51 ibid.
52 Malcolm N. Shaw, *International Law*, Sixth Edition (Cambridge, Cambridge University Press, 2008) 495–496.
53 ibid., 496.
54 Brian Taylor Sumner, "Territorial Disputes at the International Court of Justice" (2004) 53(6) *Duke Law Journal* 1779–1812.
55 ibid., 1779.
56 (Denmark v Norway) Judgment PCIJ Series A/B, No. 53 (1933) p. 21.

130 *Breaches of State territory*

when there are conflicts of elements. How each element confers a valid legal title has been discussed by Sumner and merits no further consideration. However, it seems that the most frequent elements are "effective control ... historical right to title, *uti possidetis*, geography, treaty law, and cultural homogeneity."[57] For instance, Russia's annexation of, or "reunification"[58] with Crimea may be legitimised on the basis of a treaty signed by both parties or classified as conquest, depending on the viewpoint of the person analysing. However, the notion of "reunification" could be based on historical right or perhaps cultural homogeneity if "one people" argument is sustainable. That said, we will focus on treaty law because of the Crimean incident. Besides, Sumner's article mentioned earlier has evaluated all the elements with examples.

5.2.2.1 Treaty law and claim to legal title

As a general rule, States are bound to observe in good faith a treaty which they have signed and ratified[59] insofar as facts are substantially the same.[60] The Security Council abrogated the Trusteeship Agreement when Palau gained independence in 1993 because of the change in circumstance. Yet, *rebus sic stantibus* does not always apply to boundaries established by treaties.[61] The problem is that the ICJ in the *North Sea Continental Shelf*[62] held that "there is no rule that the land frontiers of a State must be fully delimited and defined." This is because of the fluid nature of certain boundaries such as cyberspace. But where borders are delimited by treaty, a State seeking to exercise functions of a State in a foreign territory without its consent or authorisation may likely breach the latter's territorial sovereignty. While adjudicating disputes, the ICJ is to take into account treaties signed by the parties.[63]

---

57 Sumner (n 54), 1780.
58 The exact word which President Vladimir Putin used. See UN Doc. A/68/803-S/ 2014/202 (20 March 2014), 10 [hereinafter *President Putin's Address on Crimea*].
59 United Nations, *Vienna Convention on the Law of Treaties* (Concluded at Vienna on 23 May 1969, entered into force on 27 January 1980) 1155 UNTS 331, preamble para. 4, art. 26 [hereinafter *VCLT*].
60 Riaz Mohammad Khan, "Vienna Convention on Law of Treaties — Article 62 (Fundamental Change of Circumstances)" (1973) 26(1) *Pakistan Horizon* 16–28, 17.
61 *VCLT* (n 59), art. 62(2)(a); *Vienna Convention on Succession of States in Respect of Treaties* (Done at Vienna on 23 August 1978, entered into force on 6 November 1996) 1946 UNTS 3, art. 11.
62 *North Sea Continental Shelf* cases (Federal Republic of Germany/Denmark; Federal Republic of Germany/Netherlands) Judgment ICJ Reports (1969) p. 3, para. 46; *Territorial Dispute* (Libyan Arab Jamahiriya/Chad) Judgment ICJ Reports (1994) p. 6, paras 44, 52.
63 *Statute of the International Court of Justice* (Adopted at San Francisco on 26 June 1945, entered into force on 24 October 1945) (1945) 39(3) *American Journal of International Law Supplement* 215–229, art. 38(a).

5.2.2.1A UKRAINE V RUSSIA OVER CRIMEA

The collapse of the Soviet Union in 1991 effectuated the independence of Ukraine[64] following a positive outcome in a referendum conducted. Consequently, Russia signed and ratified bilateral and multilateral treaties, some of which avowed to respect Ukraine's territory.[65] Agreements are binding on the parties except those procured under threat or use of force.[66] After the dissolution of the Former Soviet Union, both States were signatories to the Helsinki Final Act, which was concluded in 1975. Principle 1 requires "participating States ... to respect each other's sovereign equality... including... territorial integrity and to freedom and political independence."[67]

On 17 March 2014, President Vladimir Putin issued an "Executive Order on recognising Republic of Crimea"[68] following a referendum conducted in Crimea on 16 March 2014. By that act, Russia recognised Crimea as "a sovereign and independent State." The question is whether that recognition is enough to legitimise the reunification? Yet it paved the way for "the accession of the Republic of Crimea" with the Russian Federation.[69] The Russian Constitutional Court classified this agreement as an "international treaty."[70] The fundamental question is whether Crimea at the material time has the *locus standi* to conduct such a referendum in which other parts of Ukraine did not participate and against the wish of the government of Ukraine and in the presence of the Russian military? Thomas Grant argues that the Crimean State Council does not possess the plenary competence to conclude a treaty of cession or annexation under the Ukrainian Constitution.[71] In the absence of such

---

64 Mark R. Beissinger, *Nationalist Mobilization and the Collapse of the Soviet State* (Cambridge, Cambridge University Press, 2002) 197.

65 See *The Alma-Ata Declaration* (Done on 21 December 1991) (1992) 31(1) *International Legal Materials* 147–154, 148, preamble para. 4; *Accord on the Creation of the Commonwealth of Independent States* (1996) 20 *Harvard Ukrainian Studies* 297–301, art. 5; *Treaty Between the Ukrainian Soviet Socialist Republic and the Russian Soviet Federative Socialist Republic* (1996) 20 *Harvard Ukrainian Studies* 291–296, art. 6; *Treaty on Friendship, Cooperation and Partnership between Ukraine and the Russian Federation* (1996) 20 *Harvard Ukrainian Studies* 319–329, arts 2 and 3.

66 *VCLT* (n 59), art. 52.

67 *Conference on Security and Co-operation in Europe Final Act* (Signed at Helsinki on 1 August 1975) (1975)73(1888) Department of State Bulletin 323–350, principle 1 ('to' not in the original).

68 See President of Russia Press Release, "Executive Order on Recognising Republic of Crimea" (17 March 2014), available at <http://en.kremlin.ru/events/president/news/20596> accessed 11 November 2019.

69 President of Russia Press Release, "Agreement on the Accession of the Republic of Crimea to the Russian Federation signed" (18 March 2014), available at <www.en.kremlin.ru/events/president/news/20604> accessed 11 November 2019.

70 A State could enter into an agreement with other subjects of international law that are not States. See *VCLT* (n 59), arts 2(1)(a) and 3(c); James Crawford, *The Creation of States in International Law*, Second Edition (Oxford, Oxford University Press, 2006) 28 (he refers to such entity as international personality).

71 Thomas D. Grant, "Current Developments: Annexation of Crimea" (2015) 109 *American Journal of International Law* 68–95, 71.

132   Breaches of State territory

authority, Lauterpacht writes that an entity that enters into such an agreement acts *ultra vires*.[72]

"Cession of a state territory is the transfer of sovereignty over the state territory by the owner-state to another state."[73] The right to cede part of a State's territory to another State is a prerogative of independent States.[74] Russia's recognition of Crimea as an independent State may not be enough; otherwise, powerful States may reinvent conquest through coerced cession. A valid cession requires full and lawfully given consent by the owner-State.[75] In the *Island of Palmas* case, Max Huber held that "Spain could not transfer more rights than she herself possessed."[76] Crimeans could have qualified to contract out their territory if they meet criteria set out by the General Assembly Resolution 1541 (1960).[77]

5.2.2.1B TREATY REGIME AND THE EFFECT OF LEX SPECIALIS

An interesting legal twist from the Crimean incident is the effect of law purporting to repeal the existing order when there is a political crisis. The political crisis in Ukraine seems to have stimulated the agitation for a referendum. When a State experiences an internal political crisis, unsolicited foreign intervention is not permitted.[78] Although Russia is authorised to reinforce its military presence in Ukraine,[79] the timing is of the

72 Tom Grant, "Who Can Make Treaties? Other Subjects of International Law" in Duncan B. Hollis, *The Oxford Guide to Treaties* (Oxford, Oxford University Press, 2012) 28.
73 Robert Jennings and Arthur Watts, *Oppenheim's International Law*, Ninth Edition, Volume 1: Peace (Oxford, Oxford University Press, 1996) 679.
74 *Island of Palmas* case (The Netherlands v USA) (The Hague, 1928) II RIAA 829–871, 838 [hereinafter *Island of Palmas* case].
75 Georg Schwarzenberger, *International Law*, Volume 1 (London, Stevens and Sons, 1957) 303; *VCLT* (n 59), art. 52 ("A treaty is void if its conclusion has been procured by the threat or use of force in violation of the principles of international law embodied in the Charter of the United Nations").
76 *Island of Palmas* case (n 74), 842.
77 It provides as follows: "A Non-Self-Governing Territory can be said to have reached a full measure of self government by (a) Emergence as a sovereign independent State; (b) Free association with an independent State; or (c) Integration with an independent State." See UNGA Res. A/RES/1541 (XV) (15 December 1960), Annex, principle VI.
78 Riikka Koskenmaki, "Legal Implications Resulting from State Failure in Light of the Case of Somalia" (2004) 73(1) *Nordic Journal of International Law* 1–36, 6; Daniel Thurer, "The 'Failed State' and International Law" (1999) 81(836) *International Review of the Red Cross* 731–761, 738.
79 *Agreement Between the Russian Federation and Ukraine on the Status and Conditions of the Russian Federation Black Sea Fleet's Stay on Ukrainian Territory* (28 May 1997), art. 4 [hereinafter *Black Sea Fleet's Stay Agreement*]; *Agreement Between the Russian Federation and Ukraine on the Parameters for the Division of the Black Sea Fleet* (28 May 1997); *Agreement Between the Russian Federation Government and the Government of Ukraine on Clearing Operations Associated with the Division of the Black Sea Fleet and the Russian Federation Black Sea Fleet's Stay on Ukrainian Territory* (28 May 1997). None of these agreements were registered in accordance with Article 102 of the UN Charter and therefore not readily accessible in English language. However, they are available in the Ukrainian Language at <https://zakon4.ra

Breaches of State territory 133

essence. If a quick military response were meant to create an enabling environment for the safe conduct of referendum, it sounds like "*Operation Retail*" in the *Corfu Channel* case which the ICJ said was unlawful.[80] The reinforcement was probably ill-founded since it prevented Ukraine's armed forces from taking reasonable steps to stop the referendum.[81] Sadly, Russia appears to have gained territory because of the said intervention. One lesson from the Crimea's political standoff is that conformism with the letter of the law may not always enhance harmonious coexistence.

Concerning unstable and failed States, Judge Hobhouse says, "a loss of control by a constitutional government may not immediately deprive it of its status, whereas an insurgent regime will require to establish control before it can exist as a government."[82] Besides, the SC would be required to make a statutory determination in accordance with Article 39 and to authorise intervention accordingly, unless it falls within the jurisdiction of the regional organisation.

5.2.2.1C ILLEGAL OCCUPATION

The Crimean scenario might constitute an illegal occupation. The relevant laws are *The Hague Conventions* and their annexed *Regulations*.[83] Occupation, as defined in Article 42 of the annexed Regulation of 1907, provides that a "[t]erritory is considered occupied when it is actually placed under the authority of the hostile army."[84] Occupation is proven when the occupying power is in effective control of a part or whole of a territory belonging to another sovereign State. There is, however, no consensus on what "actually placed under the authority of the hostile army" means. But Article 2 of the *Project of an International Declaration Concerning the Laws and Customs of War*[85]

---

    da.gov.ua/laws/%20show/643_076> accessed 11 November 2019. The unofficial translation into English language of the *Black Sea Fleet's Stay Agreement* is available at <https://en.wikisource.org/wiki/Partition_Treaty_on_the_Status_and_Conditions_of_the_Black_Sea_Fleet> accessed 11 November 2019.

80 *Corfu Channel* case (United Kingdom v Albania) (Merits) Judgment ICJ Reports (1949) p. 4, 35 [hereinafter *Corfu Channel* case].

81 *President Putin's Address on Crimea* (n 58), 5 (President Putin argues that it was meant to provide Crimeans the enabling atmosphere to decide their own future freely); The ICJ held that possession of a nuclear weapon could justify the inference of preparedness to use them. See *Legality of the Threat or Use of Nuclear Weapons,* Advisory Opinion ICJ Reports (1996) p. 226, para. 48 [hereinafter *ICJ Opinion on Nuclear Weapons*].

82 *Republic of Somalia v Woodhouse Drake & Carey (Suisse) S.A. and Others* [1993] 1 QB 54, 67.

83 *Convention (IV) Respecting the Laws and Customs of War on Land and its Annex: Regulations Concerning the Laws and Customs of War on Land* (The Hague, 18 October 1907), available at <http://avalon.law.yale.edu/20th_century/hague04.asp> accessed 11 November 2019 [hereinafter *Hague Regulations*].

84 ibid., art. 42.

85 *Project of an International Declaration Concerning the Laws and Customs of War* (Done at Brussels on 27 August 1874), art. 2, available at <www.icrc.org/applic/ihl/ihl.nsf/Article.xsp?action=openDocument&documentId=337371A4C94194E8C125 63CD005154B1> accessed 11 November 2019.

134 *Breaches of State territory*

(PDC) refers to the suspension of the authority of a legitimate government. It is irrelevant that occupation is temporary or that there are no hostilities or armed resistance from the occupied State.[86] The European Union has classified Crimea as a case of an illegal occupation.[87] It is not justified even when the purpose is to uphold human rights[88] or when the occupation is classified as "peaceful possession."[89] In the *Armed Activities on the Territory of the Congo*,[90] the ICJ held that friendly invitation could turn into an occupation when the invitee refuses to withdraw its troops if instructed to do so.

5.3 Territorial waters

The choice of "waters" instead of "sea" is intended to capture violations (though not exhaustive) that occur in an aquatic environment under the exclusive control of a State. Marine or maritime environment refers, but is not limited, to Internal Waters, Territorial Sea, Exclusive Economic Zone and the Continental Shelf. A pilot approach is adopted in dealing with breaches that relate to territorial waters. However, the rights available to States in each might vary[91] only that subject to treaties, conventions and customs applicable, a breach of any of the instruments is a breach of the territory of the affected State.

5.3.1 Applicable law

The *United Nations Convention on the Law of the Sea*[92] (UNCLOS) is the regime that applies to territorial waters. Article 301 substantially replicates Article 2(4) of the UN Charter as follows:

---

86 *Geneva Convention Relative to the Protection of Civilian Persons in Time of War* (Done at Geneva on 12 August 1949, entered into force on 21 October 1950) 75 UNTS 287, art. 2.
87 European Union, "OSCE Permanent Council No. 1231 Vienna, 6 June 2019," available at <www.osce.org/permanent-council/423137?download=true> accessed 11 November 2019.
88 UN Doc. A/57/366 (29 August 2002), paras 2, 15–23.
89 *Land and Maritime Boundary between Cameroon and Nigeria* (Cameroon v Nigeria: Equatorial Guinea intervening) Judgment ICJ Reports (2002) p. 303, paras 66, 70 [hereinafter *Cameroon v Nigeria*].
90 *Armed Activities on the Territory of the Congo* (Democratic Republic of the Congo v Uganda) Judgment ICJ Reports (2005) p. 168, paras 105ff [hereinafter *DRC v Uganda*].
91 See "Report of the International Law Commission Covering the Work of its Fifth Session, 1 June – 14 August 1953, Official Records of the General Assembly, Eighth Session, Supplement No. 9 (A/2456)" in *Yearbook of the International Law Commission*, Volume II (New York, United Nations, 1953) 212–220.
92 United Nations, *Convention on the Law of the Sea* (Concluded at Montego Bay on 10 December 1982, entered into force on 16 November 1994) 1833 UNTS 397 [hereinafter *UNCLOS*].

[i]n exercising their rights and performing their duties under this Convention, States Parties shall refrain from any threat or use of force against the territorial integrity or political independence of any State, or in any other manner inconsistent with the principles of international law embodied in the Charter of the United Nations.[93]

This provision can apply either way. That is, it protects vessels and warships[94] from being attacked by coastal States and as well prohibits vessels and warships sailing innocently[95] through a State's territorial waters from attacking coastal States. However, when Article 301 is breached, the procedural matters might seem a bit confusing. For example, Article 286[96] of the UNCLOS designates court and tribunal as competent to adjudicate disputes as may be submitted to it, but Article 298(b)[97] allows States to opt out of that procedure in respect of disputes concerning military activities. Oxman questions what remains of Article 301[98] given the opt-out clause that insulates military vessels from the compulsory regime of the UNCLOS. Another issue to highlight very quickly is the right of "innocent passage of foreign ships" through coastal States territorial waters.[99] It limits the exclusive sovereign right of States over their territory. Given the ICJ's observation that "[p]ossession of nuclear weapons may justify an inference of preparedness to

---

93 ibid., art. 301.
94 The term "warship" refers to

> a ship belonging to the naval forces of a State and bearing the external marks distinguishing warships of its nationality, under the command of an officer duly commissioned by the government and whose name appears in the Navy List, and manned by a crew who are under regular naval discipline.

> See *Convention on the High Seas* (Concluded at Geneva on 29 April 1958, entered into force on 30 September 1962) 450 UNTS 11, art. 8(2) [hereinafter *Convention on the High Seas*].

95 Article 8 paragraph 1 of the *Convention on the High Seas* states: "Warships on the high seas have complete immunity from the jurisdiction of any State other than the flag State" and Article 30 states: "The provisions of this Convention shall not affect conventions or other international agreements already in force, as between States Parties to them;" Article 14 of the *Convention on the Territorial Sea and the Contiguous Zone* provides as follows: "Subject to the provisions of these articles, ships of all States, whether coastal or not, shall enjoy the right of innocent passage through the territorial sea." See *Convention on the Territorial Sea and the Contiguous Zone* (Concluded at Geneva on 29 April 1958, entered into force on 10 September 1964) 516 UNTS 206, art. 14 [hereinafter *Convention on Sea and Contiguous Zone*].
96 *UNCLOS* (n 92), art. 286.
97 ibid., art. 298(b).
98 Bernard H. Oxman, "The Regime of Warships under the United Nations Convention on the Law of the Sea" (1984) 24(4) *Virginia Journal of International Law* 809–864, 814–815.
99 *UNCLOS* (n 92), art. 24; *Convention on Sea and Contiguous Zone* (n 95), arts 14–23; Lawrence Juda, "Innocent Passage by Warships in the Territorial Seas of the Soviet Union: Changing Doctrine" (1990) 21(1) *Ocean Development & International Law* 111–116.

136 Breaches of State territory

use them,"[100] Jessup and Brownlie's observation that the right of innocent passage contradicts the sovereignty of the coastal States[101] is credible. Another issue which shall not be investigated here is the immunity clause for warships.[102] However, a vessel or warship exercising the right of innocent passage will still breach a littoral State's territory if it fails to comply with the stringent conditions.[103]

5.3.2 Judicial interpretation of Article 301 of the UNCLOS

Territorial waters have a high record of cases on violation of States' territory. In *the Kingdom of the Netherlands v the Russian Federation*,[104] the Permanent Court of Arbitration (PCA) buttresses the need for judicial organs "to rely on primary rules of international law" when they "interpret and apply particular provisions of the Convention." Article 2(4), according to the ICJ, is "a cornerstone of the United Nations Charter."[105] No other law can be more fundamental in safeguarding the purposes of the United Nations. In *M/V "SAIGA" No. 2*,[106] the International Tribunal for the Law of the Sea (ITLOS) held that Article 293 of the UNCLOS "requires that the use of force must be avoided as far as possible and, where force is unavoidable, it must not go beyond what is reasonable and necessary in the circumstances." A similar restriction on the use of force during enforcement is found in the *I'm Alone* case[107] and the *Red Crusader* case.[108]

Against this backdrop, the PCA explains that Article 301 of the UNCLOS is triggered when a State violates the integrity of other States or exceeds a reasonableness threshold of force while enforcing compliance.[109] In the *South China Sea*

---

100 *ICJ Opinion on Nuclear Weapons* (n 81), para. 48.
101 Phillip C. Jessup, "'The Law of Territorial Waters and Maritime Jurisdiction' in Harvard Law School's Draft Convention on Territorial Waters" (1929) 23 *American Journal of International Law* (Special Supplement) 243–380, 295; Ian Brownlie, *Principles of Public International Law*, Seventh Edition (Oxford, Oxford University Press, 2008) 188–190.
102 *UNCLOS* (n 92), art. 32; *Convention on Sea and Contiguous Zone* (n 95), art. 22; *Jurisdictional Immunities of the State* (Germany v Italy: Greece intervening) Judgment ICJ Reports (2012) p. 99, para. 72.
103 The UNCLOS prohibits warships from engaging in any military activities that might constitute a threat or use of force to other States. See *UNCLOS* (n 92), art. 19(2). Article 20 requires submarines and other underwater vehicles to navigate on the surface and to show their flag. See *UNCLOS* (n 92), art. 20.
104 *The Kingdom of the Netherlands v the Russia Federation*, Award on the Merits, PCA (14 August 2015), para. 191 [hereinafter *PCA Award on Greenpeace*].
105 *DRC v Uganda* (n 90), para. 148.
106 *M/V "SAIGA" (No. 2)* (Saint Vincent and the Grenadines v Guinea) Judgment ITLOS Reports (1999) p. 10, para. 155 [hereinafter *SAIGA No. 2*].
107 *S.S. "I'm Alone"* (Canada v the United States) Award (1935) 3 RIAA 1609–1618, 1615, 1617 [hereinafter *I'm Alone* case].
108 *Investigation of Certain Incidents Affecting the British Trawler Red Crusader* (1962) 29 RIAA 521–539, 538 [hereinafter *Red Crusader* case].
109 *Award in the Arbitration Regarding the Delimitation of the Maritime Boundaries between Guyana v Suriname* (Award of 17 September 2007) 30 RIAA 1–144, para. 445 [hereinafter *Guyana v Suriname*].

dispute,[110] China stresses that using "warship to harass unarmed Chinese fishermen" is a display of force.

5.3.3 Causes of conflicts in territorial waters

Many factors account for why States clash in territorial waters. It could be to claim a title, to exercise the rights of exploitation and exploration, law enforcement, to exercise sovereignty, research, to exercise the right of innocent passage, extraterritorial application of domestic law, security and so forth. We shall limit our discussion to four factors; namely, to claim the title, to exercise the right of exploitation, to exercise the right of exploration and law enforcement.

5.3.3.1 A claim to title based on historic right

A primary reason why States clash in territorial waters is to claim a legal title in order to exercise control over it. A paper presented by Niels Andersen *et al.*, during a conference organised by the Offshore Technology in the United States in 2014 provides an overview of maritime boundary disputes globally.[111] It argues that "three-quarters of the potential acreage remains to be explored and/or exploited" and "about 14% of the areas available for exploration cover deep and ultra-deep waters of the Extended Continental Shelf or 'ECS'."[112] Moreover, the technology required by States to extend their ECS to "350 nautical miles from a country's 'normal' or 'straight' baselines and/or 100 nautical miles from their 2,500 depth isobath contour" is not readily available.[113] Currently, there are about 155 coastal States globally, about 209 maritime boundary agreements and about 311 disputed maritime boundaries.[114]

The international judicial institutions adjudicated ten maritime disputes in the first two decades of the twenty-first century. It is predicted to rise exponentially because of inexcusable boundary agreements in Africa.[115] Consequently, claims of ownership in undelimited maritime boundaries are mostly based on historicity or effective control. Although it is difficult to make a value judgment on this, we shall analyse how courts and tribunals interpret such claims.

---

110 *An Arbitral Tribunal Constituted Under Annex VII to the 1982 United Nations Convention on the Law of the Sea Between the Republic of the Philippines and the People's Republic of China*, Award PCA (12 July 2016), para. 790 [hereinafter *Philippines v China*].
111 Niels Andersen *et al.*, "International Boundary Disputes: An Unfinished Tale of Geology, Technology, Money, Law, History, Politics and Diplomacy" (Offshore Technology Conference, Houston, Texas, USA, 5–8 May 2014) 1–22.
112 ibid., 2.
113 ibid.
114 ibid., 2–3.
115 Wendell Roelf, "Spike Seen in African Offshore Disputes, Oil Companies Watching" (*Reuters*, 6 November 2014), available at <http://uk.reuters.com/article/uk-africa-oil-disputes-idUKKBN0IQ1OL20141106> accessed 12 November 2019.

138   *Breaches of State territory*

5.3.3.1A HISTORIC RIGHTS

On 22 January 2013, the Republic of the Philippines petitioned the PCA and accused the People's Republic of China of breaching its obligations under UNCLOS as follows: (1) interfered with its sovereign rights to exploit "the living and non-living resources of its EEZ and continental shelf;" (2) exhibited dangerous and unlawful conduct harmful to "ecosystems at Scarborough Shoal and Second Thomas Shoal;" (3) interdicted Philippine nationals from carrying on with their legitimate fishery occupation.[116] China made no formal submission to the PCA and was not represented during the proceedings. However, in the *notes verbales* which China deposited with the PCA, it claimed that historically it had a valid legal title over the disputed area, that is - "nine-dash line."[117]

By a mutual agreement, El Salvador and Honduras filed a complaint with the ICJ on 11 December 1986 requesting the court to determine the status of island and maritime boundary between them.[118] The court was required to take various elements into account such as treaties, history, effective control, elitism and economics. The court prioritised *uti possidetis juris*[119] as the basis for evaluating the State that exercised *effectivités* after the colonial era. At paragraph 58 of the judgment, the court provides an insight of how it balances conflicting elements:

> El Salvador claims that such an inequality existed even before independence, and that its ancient possession of the territories in dispute, "based on historic titles, is also based on reasons of crucial human necessity". The Chamber will not lose sight of this dimension of the matter; but it is one without direct legal incidence. For the *uti possidetis juris*, the question is not whether the colonial province needed wide boundaries to accommodate its population, but where those boundaries actually were; and post-independence *effectivités*, where relevant, have to be assessed in terms of actual events, not their social origins. As to the argument of inequality of natural resources, the Court, in the case concerning the *Continental Shelf (Tunisia/Libyan Arab Jamahiriya)*, took the view that economic considerations of this kind could not be taken into account for the delimitation of the continental shelf areas appertaining to two States (*I.C.J. Reports* 1982, p. 77, para. 107); still less can they be relevant for the determination of a land frontier which came into existence on independence.[120]

---

116 *Republic of the Philippines v People's Republic of China* (Memorial of the Philippines, Volume 1, 30 March 2014) 161 [hereinafter *Memorial of the Philippines*].

117 The "nine-dash line" refers to nine dotted lines on the map as reproduced by China representing the Islands over which China claims sovereignty. See Zhiguo Gao and Bing Bing Jia, "The Nine-Dash Line in the South China Sea: History, Status, and Implications" (2013) 107(1) *American Journal of International Law* 98–124. For the map, see *Memorial of the Philippines*, ibid., Figure 1.1.

118 *Land, Island and Maritime Frontier Dispute* (El Salvador/Honduras: Nicaragua intervening) Judgment ICJ Reports (1992) p. 350, para. 3.

119 ibid., paras 48–58.

120 ibid., para. 58.

Breaches of State territory 139

On 29 March 1994, the Republic of Cameroon lodged a complaint against the Federal Republic of Nigeria before the ICJ, alleging that Nigeria had violated , among others, its territory when its armed forces occupied Lake Chad.[121] In response, Nigeria pleaded the court to dismiss the claim, observing that it had acquired good title over the disputed area for various reasons, one of which it called "historical consolidation of title and the acquiescence of Cameroon."[122] The ICJ was not persuaded by that argument and found Nigeria in breach of its obligations under international law.

5.3.3.1B HISTORIC RIGHTS AND INVIOLABILITY OF STATE TERRITORY

The three cases mentioned above alluded to historic right in full or in part.[123] It accounts for the disputes between Libya and Tunisia over the Gulf of Tunis and the Gulf of Gabes in the 1980s.[124] Libya posited that "[a]t no stage prior to 1973, did Tunisia claim the 'Gulf of Gabes' as territorial waters, let alone internal waters."[125] Historic rights were a factor in Eritrea-Yemen disputes.[126] The parties requested the PCA to decide the matter "in accordance with the principles, rules and practices of international law applicable to the matter, and on the basis, in particular, of historic titles."[127]

Traditionally, a claim to title appreciates over time when there are no counterclaims.[128] Although Tunisia had persuaded the court to admit that historic rights *ipso facto* confer good titles,[129] attempt to trace the first occupants might result in an infinite regress. The name "South China Sea" presumes that China may have had historic rights in the disputed areas.[130] If that is the case, the doctrine of "inherency" preserves such rights.[131] One might

---

121 *Cameroon v Nigeria* (n 89), para. 25.

122 ibid., para. 26.

123 A widely accepted description by Blum denotes it as the possession by a State, over certain land or maritime areas, of rights that would not normally accrue to it under the general rules of international law, such rights having been acquired by that State through a process of historical consolidation. See Yehuda Z. Blum, "Historic Rights" in Rudolf Bernhardt (ed.), *Encyclopaedia of Public International Law*, Instalment 7 (The Netherlands, Elsevier Science Publishers B.V., 1984) 120.

124 Andrea Gioia, "Tunisia's Claims Over Adjacent Seas and the Doctrine of 'Historic Rights'" (1984) 11(2) *Syracuse Journal of International Law and Commerce* 327–376, 340–341.

125 *Continental Shelf* (Tunisia/Libyan Arab Jamahiriya) (Memorial of Libyan Arab Jamahiriya) Pleading ICJ Reports (1980) pp. 455, 506; *Continental Shelf* (Tunisia/Libyan Arab Jamahiriya) (Reply of the Libyan Arab Jamahiriya) Pleading ICJ Reports (1981) p. 103, para. 29.

126 *Territorial Sovereignty and Scope of the Dispute* (Eritrea v Yemen) (1998) 22 RIAA 209–332, 244.

127 ibid., para. 2.

128 Sumner (n 54), 1789.

129 *Tunisia v Libya Continental Shelf* case (Reply of Tunisia) Pleading ICJ Reports (15 July 1981), Volume IV, para. 3.13.

130 Jianming Shen, "China's Sovereignty Over the South China Sea: A Historical Perspective" (2002) 1(1) *Chinese Journal of International Law* 94–157.

131 Daniel P. O'Connell, *The International Law of the Sea*, Volume 2 (Oxford, Clarendon Press, 1984) 713; Zou Keyuan, "Historic Rights in International Law and in China's Practice" (2001) 32(2) *Ocean Development and International Law* 149–168, 165.

140   *Breaches of State territory*

argue that historic rights take precedence over treaty law but Judge Jimenez de Arechaga holds a contrary view.[132]

Historic rights were adopted in 1958 at the Geneva Conference to safeguard yet-to-be declared rights which coastal States had over their Continental Shelf, and was never intended to abrogate any acquired or existing rights.[133] The *Abyei Arbitration* held that the "traditional rights" remain unaffected by any territorial delimitation in the absence of any explicit agreement to the contrary.[134] However, the Abyei Arbitration Tribunal's understanding of "traditional rights" reflects entitlements. The PCA in the South China Sea's dispute clarifies that "historic rights" unlike "historic title" could mean benefits short of a claim to sovereignty.[135] The possession of historic rights does not eclipse sovereignty which coastal States have in their EEZ.[136] On that basis, China's conduct in the South China Sea which inhibited the Philippines from exercising exclusive right over the "nine-dash line" contravenes the UNCLOS.[137]

5.3.3.1C EXERCISE OF RIGHTS OF EXPLORATION AND EXPLOITATION

The UNCLOS bequeaths to coastal States, the right to explore, exploit, conserve and manage the natural resources, whether living or non-living in their EEZ and/or Continental Shelf.[138] Article 57 of the UNCLOS provides as follows, "[t]he exclusive economic zone shall not extend beyond 200 nautical miles from the baselines from which the breadth of the territorial sea is measured."[139] Similarly, Article 76 of the UNCLOS states:

> The continental shelf of a coastal State comprises the seabed and subsoil of the submarine areas that extend beyond its territorial sea throughout the natural prolongation of its land territory to the outer edge of the continental margin, or to a distance of 200 nautical miles from the baselines from which the breadth of the territorial sea is measured where the outer edge of the continental margin does not extend up to that distance.[140]

---

132 *Tunisia v Libya Continental Shelf* case, Judgment ICJ Reports (1982) p. 18, para. 82 (Separate Opinion of Judge Jimenez de Arechaga).

133 ibid., para. 82.

134 *Abyei Arbitration* (Government of Sudan v Sudan People's Liberation Movement/ Army) Final Award (2009) 30 RIAA 145–416, para. 766 [hereinafter *Abyei Arbitration*]; *Award Between the United States and the United Kingdom Relating to the Rights of Jurisdiction of United States in the Bering's Sea and the Preservation of Fur Seals* (United Kingdom v United States) Award (1893) 28 RIAA 263–276, 271 [hereinafter *Award Between the US and the UK on Indigenous Indians*] (this award exempts indigenous Indians from hunting of fur seals in the Bering Sea).

135 *Philippines v China* (n 110), para. 225.

136 ibid., para. 243.

137 ibid., para. 261; *UNCLOS* (n 92), arts 77, 81.

138 *UNCLOS* (n 92), arts 56(1), 77(1).

139 ibid., art. 57.

140 ibid., art. 76(1).

Breaches of State territory 141

The word "exclusive" means that only coastal States possess the sovereign rights[141] to explore or exploit the resources thereof.[142] Perhaps, an exception is that international law recognises that the exclusive right which States have does not extinguish "traditional rights" or "private rights."[143] Private rights refer to the natural right of indigenous peoples[144] to explore and exploit their ancestral land which States must respect and protect.[145] This is a departure from the Westphalian State-centric model.[146]

In the *South China Sea* dispute, the Philippines alleged that China interfered with its sovereign rights and jurisdiction over all the waters, seabed and subsoil within the "nine-dash line."[147] Regarding the non-living resources, China objected "to the conversion of the Philippines' contract with Sterling Energy for exploration of oil and gas deposits" within the Spratly Islands.[148] Regarding living resources, China had prevented the Philippines' vessels from fishing at the Mischief Reef since 1995.[149] China's position is that it has indisputable sovereignty, sovereign rights and jurisdiction over the disputed area.[150] The PCA thinks

---

141 UNCLOS did not define sovereign rights, but some of its provisions give the impression that sovereign rights are territorial. Compare the provisions of the following Articles of the *UNCLOS*: Articles 56, 73, 77, 194 and 246 with Article 137. The Permanent Court of Arbitration held that the notion that a State has sovereign rights over the living and non-living resources in the EEZ appears incompatible with the idea that another State could have historic rights over the same resources. See *Philippines v China* (n 110), para. 243.

142 *UNCLOS* (n 92), art. 77(2).

143 *Abyei Arbitration* (n 134), para. 766; *Award Between the US and the UK on Indigenous Indians* (n 134), 271; *Philippines v China* (n 110), para. 799.

144 *International Convention on Civil and Political Rights* (Concluded at New York on 16 December 1966, entered into force on 23 March 1976) 999 UNTS 171, art. 1; *International Convention on Economic, Social and Cultural Rights* (Concluded at New York on 16 December 1966, entered into force on 3 January 1976) 993 UNTS 3, art. 1; *United Nations Declaration on the Rights of Indigenous Peoples* (Adopted by the General Assembly on 2 October 2007) UNGA Res. A/RES/61/295 (2 October 2007), art. 4 [hereinafter *UNDRIP*].

145 *UNDRIP* (n 144), art. 8; International Labour Organization (ILO), *Indigenous and Tribal Peoples Convention* (Done at Geneva on 27 June 1989, entered into force on 5 September 1991), art. 4, available at <www.refworld.org/docid/3ddb6d514.html> accessed 1 June 2017; Joji Carino, "Indigenous Peoples' Right to Free, Prior, Informed Consent: Reflections on Concepts and Practice" (2005) 22(1) *Arizona Journal of International and Comparative Law* 19–40, 20; Committee on the Elimination of Racial Discrimination, "General Recommendation 23, Rights of Indigenous Peoples (Fifty-First Session, 1997)" U.N. Doc. A/52/18, Annex V at p. 122 (1997), para. 5.

146 *Second Stage of the Proceedings Between Eritrea and Yemen* (Maritime delimitation) (17 December 1999) 22 RIAA 335–410, para. 101.

147 *Philippines v China* (n 110), para. 685.

148 ibid.

149 ibid., para. 686.

150 ibid., para. 688; Ministry of Foreign Affairs of the People's Republic of China, "Position Paper of the Government of the People's Republic of China on the Matter of Jurisdiction in the South China Sea Arbitration Initiated by the Republic of the Philippines" (7 December 2014), para. 8, available at <http://in.chineseembassy.org/eng/xwfb/t1217157.htm> accessed 19 November 2019.

142 Breaches of State territory

otherwise.[151] It held that China did not breach its obligations under the UNCLOS by holding erroneous claims in good faith[152] but by its conduct to assert those claims.[153] The ICJ gave a similar verdict in the *Costa Rica v Nicaragua* case.[154] Invariably, a State could breach the territory of another State unwittingly when it exercises a function that rightfully belongs to a sovereign State within its territory.

5.3.3.1D ENFORCEMENT

Law enforcement in territorial waters is complicated because of competing rights of States. For example, the right of a littoral State to regulate the usage of its waters might conflict with the right of innocent passage of other States. Therefore, law enforcement could be abused or a nursery for conflict. The UNCLOS permits States to respond to a provocative act by a foreign ship[155] or when a foreign ship makes phantom territorial claims.[156] As shall be seen, the lawfulness of enforcement measures adopted by a State depends on whether they are reasonable, necessary and proportionate.[157]

5.3.3.1E THE TRIPOD THRESHOLD TEST IN LAW ENFORCEMENT

(1) Proportionality Other reasons, apart from the rights of exploration and exploitation, might warrant coastal States to take enforcement measures in their territorial waters. It could be for security reasons, to protect the marine environment from pollution or to enforce EEZ-specific provisions.[158] Article 221 permits States "to take and enforce measures beyond the territorial sea proportionate to the actual or threatened damage to protect their coastline or related interests ...."[159] The Security Council uses the word "measure" to authorise coercive and non-coercive interventions in the internal affairs of States. Unfortunately, the UNCLOS does not elucidate the amount of force that might be deployed because it might include the destruction of vessels and its cargo.[160]

---

151 *Philippines v China* (n 110), para. 697.

152 ibid., para. 705.

153 ibid., paras 708–716.

154 *Certain Activities Carried Out by Nicaragua in the Border Area* (Costa Rica v Nicaragua) Judgment ICJ Reports (2009) p. 1, para. 93.

155 For the definition of a ship, see *Convention for the Suppression of Unlawful Acts Against the Safety of Maritime Navigation* (Done at Rome on 10 March 1988, entered into force on 1 March 1992) 1678 UNTS 221, art. 1.

156 Francesco Francioni, "Peacetime Use of Force, Military Activities, and the New Law of the Sea" (1985) 18(2) *Cornell International Law Journal* 203–226, 207.

157 *SAIGA No. 2* (n 106), paras 155–156; *PCA Award on Greenpeace* (n 104), paras 221–224; *M/V "Virginia G"* (Panama v Guinea-Bissau) Judgment ITLOS Reports (2014) p. 1, para. 270.

158 Rob McLaughlin, "Coastal State Use of Force in the EEZ Under the Law of the Sea Convention 1982" (1999) 18(1) *University of Tasmanian Law Review* 11–21, 14.

159 *UNCLOS* (n 92), art. 221.

160 McLaughlin (n 158), 15.

Breaches of State territory   143

Besides, the level of water pollution that might require proportionate intervention by littoral States is unclear. Hence, the law provides that measures taken must be reasonable and subject to the discretion of the intervening State.[161]

The *International Convention Relating to Intervention on High Seas in Cases of Oil Pollution Casualties* provides some guidelines.[162] Proportionality is calculated by (a) the "... probability of imminent damage if those measures are not taken; and (b) the likelihood of those measures being effective; and (c) the extent of the damage which may be caused by such measures."[163] Yet it does not resolve all the problems, especially in connection with the exemption of warships from enforcement measures.

(2) Reasonable and necessary   Hot pursuit[164] is one of the law enforcement measures under the UNCLOS. To be lawful, a hot pursuit must commence when the offending vessel is within the territorial waters of the pursuing State, and the pursuit must be discontinued if it is interrupted.[165] In the *I'm Alone* case, the arbitration commission held that "necessary and reasonable force (might be used) for the purpose of effecting the objects of boarding, searching, seizing and the bringing into port the suspected vessel."[166] The word "necessary" means that the forcible measures can only be applied as a last resort with the intent to end the ongoing violation or to inspect a foreign vessel.[167]

The *United Nations Agreement for the Implementation of the Provisions of the United Nations Convention on the Law of the Sea of 10 December 1982 Relating to the Conservation and Management of Straddling Fish Stocks and Highly Migratory Fish Stocks*[168] urges the inspecting State to deploy forcible measures only when it is reasonable and to the degree, necessary. As McLaughlin put it, "necessary" deals mostly with proportionality[169] and proportionality assesses whether the limitation of a right conforms with the constitution or not.[170] This entails making an informed judgment based on available facts. Reasonableness evaluates whether a

---

161 Albert E. Utton, "Protective Measures and the Torrey Canyon" (1968) 9(3) *Boston College Industrial and Commercial Law Review* 613–632; Archie Hovanesian, "Post Torrey Canyon: Toward a New Solution to the Problem of Traumatic Oil Spillage" (1970) 2(3) *Connecticut Law Review* 632–647.

162 *International Convention Relating to Intervention on the High Seas in Cases of Oil Pollution Casualties* (Concluded at Brussels on 29 November 1969) 970 UNTS 211, art. V(3).

163 ibid.

164 *UNCLOS* (n 92), art. 111.

165 ibid., art. 111(1).

166 *I'm Alone* case (n 107), 1615 -1617.

167 Robin R. Churchill and Alan V. Lowe, *The Law of the Sea*, Third Edition (Manchester, Manchester University Press, 1999) 216; *ICJ Opinion on Nuclear Weapons* (n 81), para. 41; *Nicaragua* case (n 19), para. 176.

168 2167 UNTS 3, art. 22(1)(f).

169 McLaughlin (n 158), 15.

170 Pavel Ondrejek, "Limitations of Fundamental Rights in the Czech Republic and the Role of the Principle of Proportionality" (2014) 20(3) *European Public Law* 451–466, 452.

144 Breaches of State territory

State intending to interdict a foreign vessel has grounds to believe that a foreign ship has breached its obligations.[171]

In the *M/V "SAIGA" (No. 2)*, the International Tribunal for the Law of the Sea (ITLOS) held that a State that enforces its rights must ensure that the measures it takes are lawful. For instance, firing warning shots when a State had not issued repeated leave orders to a trespassing vessel would be disproportionate. On the contrary, a State engulfed in internal armed conflict might be justified to sink a ship attempting to smuggle in ammunitions to dissidents in its country.[172] But to apply such measures on a foreign vessel fishing illegally within a State's territorial waters will be unreasonable and disproportionate.[173] What will be reasonable and proportionate is for the delinquent foreign vessel to be arrested or escorted out of the State's territorial waters.[174]

5.3.3.1F RIGHT TO INTERCEPT, ARREST, SEIZE OR DETAIN A FOREIGN SHIP

The littoral States may intercept, arrest, seize and/or detain crew members of foreign vessels as well as their vessels if they violate their territorial waters.[175] The motive could be for security reasons or self-defence.[176] An example is the covert naval operations with submarines in the Scandinavian internal waters and the Gulf of Taranto.[177]

When North Korea arrested occupants of Pueblo and seized their vessels in 1968, Aldrich questioned the legality of North Korea's action because warships sailing on international waters have immunity[178] in accordance with Article 8 of the 1958 *Convention on the High Seas*. He contends that Pueblo is "a lightly armed vessel" that poses no threat to North Korea.[179] Although Aldrich is correct statutorily, law enforcement is discretionary. *A contrario*, why would warships intend to make innocent passage without notification? In fact, many coastal States

---

171 UNCLOS does not specify what constitutes reasonableness. It uses terminologies that indicate what might be considered the threshold required before a State could enforce its sovereign rights on territorial sea. Phrases such as: "reasonable grounds for believing," see *UNCLOS* (n 92), arts 108, 206 and 211(6); "clear grounds for believing," see *UNCLOS* (n 92), arts 217(3), 220 and 226.
172 I. A. Shearer, "Problems of Jurisdiction and Law Enforcement against Delinquency Vessels" (1986) 35(2) *International and Comparative Law Quarterly* 320–343, 325–330.
173 ibid.
174 ibid.
175 *Guyana v Suriname* (n 109), para. 270.
176 Francioni (n 156), 210–212, 226; *UNCLOS* (n 92), art. 25(1).
177 Francioni (n 156), 212.
178 George H. Aldrich, "Questions of International Law Raised by the Seizure of the U.S. S. Pueblo" (1969) 63 *Proceedings of the American Society of International Law* 2–6.
179 ibid., 3.

Breaches of State territory 145

have revoked the right of innocent passage.[180] Aldrich's argument that "there is neither precedent nor scholarly support for a claim that a warship may be seized in self-defence to prevent it from making a visual or electronic observation of a coastal state"[181] left one to wonder what is left of exclusive sovereignty. It is disturbing because the United States signed an agreement with North Korea and admitted that Pueblo trespassed "the territorial waters of the Democratic People's Republic of Korea on many occasions and conducted espionage activities of spying out important military and state secrets of the Democratic People's Republic of Korea."[182]

5.3.3.1G MISAPPLIED LAW ENFORCEMENT

Misapplied law enforcement could inadvertently violate the territory of the initial offender. In the *Netherlands v Russia*, the Greenpeace movement proposed a demonstration at *Prirazlomnaya* to protest against the harmful effects of Russia's exploratory activities to the Arctic environment. It conflicts with Russia's rights to explore and exploit living and non-living resources in its EEZ.[183] Third parties enjoy the freedom of navigation and overflight if they comply with laws and regulations put in place by a littoral State.[184] Before the proposed date for the protest, Russia declared *Prirazlomnaya* a safety zone and prohibited navigation around it.[185] When Greenpeace defied the orders, Russia arrested, detained and prosecuted those on board the *Arctic Sunrise*. The PCA held not only that Russia breached its international obligations by "boarding, investigating, inspecting, arresting, detaining and seizing the *Arctic Sunrise* without the prior consent of the Netherlands,"[186] but also faulted its enforcement measures for its failure to give visual or auditory signals to the *Arctic Sunrise* RHIBs.[187]

180 Malta's declaration upon ratification states: "Effective and speedy means of communication are easily available and make the prior notification of the exercise of the right of innocent passage of warships reasonable and not incompatible with the convention." See, United Nations, *Law of the Sea Bulletin* Issue No. 25 (New York, United Nations, 1994) 16 (subsequent citations from this bulletin will be as follows: *Law of the Sea Bulletin*, issue no, year of publication and page number).
181 Aldrich (n 178), 4.
182 See Keesing's Record of World Events, "Jan 1969 North Koreans Release Crew of U. S.S. 'Pueblo'" (Volume 15, January 1969) 23120, available at <http://web.stanford. edu/group/tomzgroup/pmwiki/uploads/1379-1969-01-KS-e-EYJ.pdf> accessed 14 November 2019. However, it could be argued that the agreement was a political strategy to secure the release of the US crew because the United States quickly denounced the agreement as soon as the crew members were freed. See United States, "Department of State Telegram of 8 February 1968 – Seizure of USS Pueblo" (1968) 62 *American Journal of International Law* 756–757.
183 *UNCLOS* (n 92), arts 56, 60, 73; *Philippines v China* (n 110), para. 690.
184 *UNCLOS* (n 92), art. 58; *SAIGA No. 2* (n 106), para. 127.
185 *PCA Award on Greenpeace* (n 104), para. 144.
186 ibid., para. 401.
187 ibid.

146   *Breaches of State territory*

Similarly, the arbitrators in the *I'm Alone*[188] and *Red Crusader*[189] cases faulted measures taken by the respective littoral States as disproportionate and in breach of international law.[190] In the *Guyana v Suriname* case, the captain of the Surinamese Patrol Boats ordered Guyanese drilling at the disputed waters to "leave the area in 12 hours" or the "consequences will be yours."[191] The PCA construed this to mean an explicit threat that force might be used if the order were not obeyed.[192]

5.3.3.1H RIGHT OF INNOCENT PASSAGE – ITS LIMITS

Article 17 of the UNCLOS provides as follows: "[s]ubject to this Convention, ships of all States, whether coastal or land-locked, enjoy the right of innocent passage through the territorial sea."[193] The word,

1   Passage means navigation through the territorial sea for the purpose of:

    a   traversing that sea without entering internal waters or calling at a roadstead or port facility outside internal waters; or

    b   proceeding to or from internal waters or a call at such roadstead or port facility.

2   Passage shall be continuous and expeditious. However, passage includes stopping and anchoring, but only in so far as the same are incidental to ordinary navigation or are rendered necessary by *force majeure* or distress or for the purpose of rendering assistance to persons, ships or aircraft in danger or distress.[194]

A passage conducted in a manner that poses no threat to coastal States is "innocent." In the *Corfu Channel* case, the ICJ held that the passage of a warship in a ready-combat-mode could be innocent if the ship had been attacked previously.[195] Otherwise, "a ready-combat-mode" might constitute a threat. The coastal States may intercept a presumed "innocent passage" if they reasonably suspect an intent to commit acts that could be prejudicial to the peace, good order

---

188 *I'm Alone* case (n 107), 1615, 1617.
189 *Red Crusader* case (n 108), 538; Olivier Corten , *The Law Against War: The Prohibition on the Use of Force in Contemporary International Law* (Oxford and Portland, Hart Publishing 2010) 58–59.
190 *SAIGA No. 2* (n 106), para. 159; *Case Concerning Oil Platforms* (Iran v United States of America) Judgment ICJ Reports (2003) p. 161, para. 76.
191 *Guyana v Suriname* (n 109), para. 433. Similarly, the PCA held that China violated Philippines' sovereign rights under Article 77 of the UNCLOS when two of its vessels ordered MV Veritas Voyager to stop the production and leave the area. See *Philippines v China* (n 110), paras 707–708.
192 *Guyana v Suriname* (n 109), para. 439.
193 *UNCLOS* (n 92), art. 17.
194 ibid., art. 18.
195 *Corfu Channel* case (n 80), 30–31.

Breaches of State territory 147

or national security of their State.[196] Although the ICJ held that coastal States could not prevent innocent passage,[197] State practice appears to have departed from that. For instance, the Islamic Republic of Iran clarifies that customary law requires "prior authorisation for warships willing to exercise the right of innocent passage through the territorial sea."[198] Similarly, the *Maritime Zones of Maldives Acts No. 6/96*[199] states: "no foreign vessel shall enter the internal waters of Maldives except with prior authorization from the Government of Maldives in accordance with the laws and regulations of Maldives."[200]

Currently, many States have restricted innocent passage without prior authorisation. Saudi Arabia,[201] Malaysia,[202] Yemen,[203] Iran,[204] Egypt[205] and Seychelles[206] require prior authorisation. Pakistan,[207] Malta,[208] Republic of Korea[209] and the United Arab Emirates[210] require prior notification. Lithuania[211] and Romania[212] prohibit passage for ships carrying nuclear and other weapons of mass destruction. These declarations and reservations show States' determination to exercise full sovereignty in their territorial waters.

5.4 Freedom of the High Seas

The *Convention on the High Seas* defines "High Seas" as "all parts of the seas that are not included in the territorial sea or in the internal waters of a State."[213] Although, *opinio juris* holds that "no state may purport to subject

196 *UNCLOS* (n 92), art. 19; see also United Nations Law of the Sea, "Declaration made by Brazil upon signature of the Convention" in *Law of the Sea Bulletin* (Issue No. 1, September 1983) 21.
197 *Corfu Channel* case (n 80), 29.
198 *Law of the Sea Bulletin* (Issue No. 1, September 1983) 17; see also "Declaration No. 2 on the passage of warships through Omani territorial waters" in *Law of the Sea Bulletin* (Issue No. 25, June 1994) 17.
199 The text of this document is reproduced in the *Law of the Sea Bulletin* (Issue No. 41, 1999) 16–18.
200 *Law of the Sea Bulletin* (Issue No. 41, 1999), para. 11 (for conditions for using Maldives' archipelagic waters, territorial sea, exclusive economic zone, and airspace, see paras 12–15).
201 ibid. (Issue No. 31, 1996) 10, para. 6.
202 ibid. (Issue No. 33, 1997) 8, para. 4.
203 ibid. (Issue No. 25, 1994) 20, para. 1.
204 ibid., 30, para. 2.
205 ibid. (Issue No. 3, 1984) 13.
206 ibid. (Issue No. 48, 2002) 21, para. 16(2).
207 *Territorial Waters and Maritime Zones Act, 1976* (see the section on "Use of territorial waters by foreign ships"), para. 3(4), available at <www.un.org/Depts/los/LEGISLA TIONANDTREATIES/PDFFILES/IND_1976_Act.pdf> accessed 15 November 2019.
208 *Law of the Sea Bulletin* (Issue No. 25, 1994) 16.
209 ibid. (Issue No. 33, 1997) 45–54, art. 5.
210 ibid. (Issue No. 25, 1994) 94–100, art. 5(4).
211 ibid., 75–81, art. 12.
212 ibid. (Issue No. 19, 1991) 9–20, art. 10.
213 *Convention on the High Seas* (n 94), art. 1.

148 *Breaches of State territory*

any part of them to its sovereignty,"[214] the debate is not definitively fore-closed. While some authors classify it as *res nullius,* others describe it as *res communis.*[215] But it could be both. It is *res nullius* insofar as it is subject to the jurisdiction of the flag State. However, since no State could exercise abso-lute authority to the exclusion of every other State, it is *res communis.* Unlike territorial waters, therefore, States do not exercise exclusive sovereignty on the High Seas. Hence, it is beyond the scope of this work. It is mentioned here in passing because States exercise transient sovereignty on the High Seas. This creates the required nexus for a potential violation of State territory. We shall illustrate this with the right to visit and search vessels on the High Seas and closure of the High Seas for weapon testing.

5.4.1 *Right to visit and search – policing*

In peacetime, a State may visit and search a vessel belonging to another nationality on the High Seas if it has "reasonable ground for suspecting that" it is used for commission of a crime.[216] The same applies to territorial waters under the exclu-sive control of States. The right to visit and search has been augmented by the *Convention for the Suppression of Unlawful Acts Against the Safety of Maritime Navigation*[217] (SUA). Policing the High Seas is becoming increasingly important because of the high rate of crimes in international waters.[218] However, it does not imply indiscriminate interception of State's vessels for no just cause. Unilateral enforcement of the right of visit without the consent of the flag State is unac-ceptable. Consequently, the *Protocol of 2005 to the Convention for the Suppression of Unlawful Acts Against the Safety of Maritime Navigation*[219] permits the right to board and search if the flag State has authorised it. A State should not board or search vessels of another State if the consent were declined.[220]

5.4.2 *Closure and weapon testing on the High Seas*

When States close part of the High Seas to test weapons, it could constitute an exercise of jurisdiction to the exclusion of all other States. According to Hugo

---

214 Jennings and Watts (n 73), 726; *Convention on the High Seas* (n 94), art. 2; *UNCLOS* (n 92), art. 89.
215 Efthymios Papastavridis, *The Interception of Vessels on the High Seas: Contemporary Challenges to the Legal Order of the Oceans* (Oxford, Hart Publishing, 2013) 23.
216 *UNCLOS* (n 92), art. 110. In time of war, States may visit and search any vessel on the High Seas irrespective of its nationality or destination, see also Papastavridis (n 215), 42.
217 1678 UNTS 201, art. 6.
218 Tullio Treves, "Piracy, Law of the Sea, and Use of Force: Developments off the Coast of Somalia" (2009) 20(2) *European Journal of International Law* 399–414, 399–400; UNSC Res. S/RES/2018 (31 October 2011), operative para. 1; UNSC Res. S/RES/2039 (24 May 2012), operative para. 1.
219 UN Doc. LEG/CONF.15/21 (1 November 2005), art. 8*bis*(5)(b).
220 ibid., art. 8*bis*(5)(c)(iv).

Breaches of State territory   149

Grotius, the use of the High Seas by a State must not exclude others.[221] The intent was to mitigate the tension that had existed between *mare clausum* and *mare liberum*. When a State closes High Seas, it is contrary to the character of High Seas. For instance, it obstructs the freedom of navigation or freedom of overflight for other States.[222] Jennings and Watts believe that States may not exercise jurisdiction over or police the High Seas[223] which temporal closures presuppose. "Jurisdiction" refers to a State's "ability to regulate the conduct of natural and juridical persons."[224] Regulation here contemplates the activities of the three arms of government which according to the *Lotus* case is restricted to a State's territory but could apply extra-territorially in criminal matters.[225]

Our concern is not whether States exercise jurisdiction on the High Seas since a State's vessel sailing on the High Seas exercises transient sovereignty insofar as other States are prohibited from obstructing it. We are concerned about those actions that have a direct impact on other States. Based on the narrow interpretation of Article 2(4) of the UN Charter, a State is responsible for the action of its military outside its national territory – whether lawful or unlawful.[226] It follows from this that the closure of the High Seas and the consequences of actions that might result from the use of the closed part (say weapon testing) are attributable to the State that did it.

In the *Nuclear Tests* case,[227] New Zealand brought an action against France over a series of nuclear tests it conducted in the South Pacific region. New Zealand pleaded the ICJ to declare that France "violates the right of New Zealand to freedom of the high seas, including freedom of navigation and overflight ... without interference or detriment resulting from nuclear testing."[228] The ICJ restricted its judgment to the environmental hazards from the fallout of the radioactive particles.[229] Judges Onyeama, Dillard, Jimenez de Arechaga and Sir

---

221 Crawford 2012 (n 50) 297; Hugo Grotius, *The Rights of War and Peace: Including the Law of Nature and of Nations* (translated by A. C. Campbell with an Introduction by David J. Hill) (Washington D.C. and London, M. Walter Dunne Publisher, 1901) 104; *Island of Palmas* case (n 74), 838. For a brief discussion on the origin of the right of the freedom of the high seas, see Efthymios Papastavridis, "The Right of Visit on the High Seas in a Theoretical Perspective: Mare Liberum versus Mare Clausum Revisited" (2011) 24(1) *Leiden Journal of International Law* 45–69.
222 Crawford 2012 (n 50), 298.
223 Jennings and Watts (n 73), 727.
224 Crawford 2012 (n 50), 456.
225 *The Case of S.S. Lotus* (France v Turkey) Judgment PCIJ Series A, No. 10 (1927) 20; Sarah Miller, "Revisiting Extraterritorial Jurisdiction: A Territorial Justification for Extraterritorial Jurisdiction under the European Convention" (2009) 20(4) *European Journal of International Law* 1223–1246.
226 *Case of Issa and Others v Turkey* (Application No. 31821/96) Judgment ECtHR (2004), para. 69.
227 *Nuclear Tests* (New Zealand v France) Judgment ICJ Reports (1974) p. 457 [hereinafter *New Zealand v France*].
228 ibid. (Pleadings, Nuclear Tests, Vol. II), para. 28.
229 A. M. Bracegirdle, "Case to the International Court of Justice on Legality of French Nuclear Testing" (1996) 9(2) *Leiden Journal of International Law* 431–443, 441.

150 *Breaches of State territory*

Humphrey Waldock reasoned that the Court should have considered whether the said nuclear tests violated New Zealand's territory based on the character of the High Seas as *res communis*.[230] Unfortunately, the Court failed to strengthen the law on the freedom of the High Seas which would have given force to the *erga omnes* character of treaties that prohibit nuclear weapon tests.[231] This observation is without prejudice to the ICJ's advisory opinion that "there is in neither customary nor conventional international law any comprehensive and universal prohibition of the threat or use of nuclear weapons as such."[232]

Nonetheless, the increase in military activities on the High Seas in times of peace is disturbing. For example, North Korea continues to conduct nuclear tests despite the Security Council's prohibitive resolutions,[233] albeit it is not a State party to the *Comprehensive Nuclear-Test-Ban Treaty*.[234] Such behaviour in the High Seas could strain international relations. The usage of the High Seas requires States to exercise "due regard" for the rights of other States.[235]

5.5 Airspace – trespasses

Hardly a month can pass by without a report of violation of airspace of a State either by civil or State aircraft. In 2014, NATO reported it had intercepted Russian aircraft over 100 times.[236] Amidst heightened tension between NATO and Russia over a civil war in Syria, Turkey shot down a Russian fighter jet in 2015.[237] At the peak of the dispute between China and the Philippines over the South China Sea, it was alleged that China violated the airspaces of some Asian countries.[238] On 21 September 1999, the Islamic Republic of Pakistan filed a complaint before the

---

230 *New Zealand v France* (n 227), para. 7 (Joint Dissenting Opinion of Judges Onyeama, Dillard, Jimenez de Arechaga and Sir Humphrey Waldock).
231 *Treaty Banning Nuclear Weapon Tests in the Atmosphere, in Outer Space and Under Water* (Concluded at Moscow on 5 August 1963, entered into force on 10 October 1963) 480 UNTS 43; *Treaty on the Non-Proliferation of Nuclear Weapons* (Done at London, Moscow and Washington on 1 July 1968, entered into force on 5 March 1970) 729 UNTS 161; *Treaty on the Limitation of Anti-Ballistic Missile Systems* (Signed at Moscow on 26 May 1972, entered into force on 3 October 1972) 944 UNTS 13.
232 *ICJ Opinion on Nuclear Weapons* (n 81), para. 105.
233 UNSC Res. S/RES/2270 (2 March 2016), operative para. 1.
234 For list of state parties at the time of writing, see *Comprehensive Nuclear-Test-Ban Treaty Organisation*, available at <www.ctbto.org/the-treaty/status-of-signature-and-ratification/> accessed 15 November 2019.
235 Jennings and Watts (n 73), 729.
236 *NATO Tracks Large-Scale Russian Air Activity in Europe; Allied Command Operations release, 29th October 2014*, available at <www.nato.int/cps/en/natohq/news_114274.htm> accessed 15 November 2019.
237 See: BBC News, "Turkey shoots down Russian warplane on Syria Border" (24 November 2015), available at <www.bbc.co.uk/news/world-middle-east-34907983> accessed 15 November 2019.
238 Associated Press, "Japan Warns China Over Fighters Challenging Airspace" (Real Clear Defence, 26 September 2016), available at <www.realcleardefense.com/articles/2016/09/26/japan_warns_china_over_fighters_challenging_airspace_110125.html> accessed 15 November 2019.

Breaches of State territory 151

ICJ alleging that India shot down its "unarmed Atlantique aircraft."[239] On 17 May 2016, the Sudanese government warned that it would take decisive action after 20 aircraft belonging to Ilyushin and 76 belonging to international and regional organisations violated its airspace.[240] In July 2019, South Korea made a similar allegation against Russia which the latter denied.[241] In summary, violation of States' airspace is becoming worrisome.

5.5.1 States' rights over their airspace

As discussed in Chapter 2, a State's sovereignty extends to the airspace above its land and territorial waters and beneath the ground to the limits determined by law. "Sovereignty over the airspace is comparable with that exercised over territorial waters."[242] Aircrafts flying over navigable airspace of a State are required to comply with all signals, regulations and directives. The *Chicago Convention* of 1944 permits subjacent States to set up no-fly zones "above which no international flight was lawful."[243]

5.5.2 Causes of aerial conflicts between States

Many factors contribute to aerial conflicts between States; namely, security, surveillance, intelligence gathering, reconnaissance, aerial espionage, enforcement of territorial sovereignty and in rare cases, a show of military strength. Although States protest against every violation, military confrontations in peacetime are rare unlike in wartime. The downing of Russia's fighter jet by Turkey could be a political statement of its disapproval of Russia's support to Assad's regime in Syria. But the situation could have been worse had Russia responded militarily. NATO did not confront Russia militarily when Russian jets trespassed the airspace of its member States but sternly warned Russia to desist from such acts.[244] While a display of air power immediately and directly engages Article 2(4) of the UN

---

239 *Application Instituting Proceedings Filed in the Registry of the Court on 21 September 1999* (Pakistan v India) ICJ 1999 General List No. 119.
240 See: All Africa, "Sudan: Govt Issues Stern Warning on Airspace Violations" (1 June 2016), available at <http://allafrica.com/stories/201606020181.html> accessed 15 November 2019.
241 See ITV Report, "Russia Calls for Investigation Over South Korean Airspace Violation Claims" (24 July 2019), available at <www.itv.com/news/2019-07-24/russia-calls-for-investigation-over-south-korean-airspace-violation-claims/> accessed 15 November 2019.
242 Arthur K. Kuhn, "Aerial Navigation in its Relation to International Law" (1908) 5 *Proceedings of the American Political Science Association* 83–93, 88.
243 Albert I. Moon, "A Look at Airspace Sovereignty" (1963) 29(4) *Journal of Air Law and Commerce* 328–345, 331.
244 Thomas Frear *et al.*, *Dangerous Brinkmanship: Close Military Encounters between Russia and the West in 2014*, available at <www.europeanleadershipnetwork.org/wp-content/uploads/2017/10/Dangerous-Brinkmanship.pdf> accessed 16 November 2019.

152 *Breaches of State territory*

Charter, other subtle causes are never condoned by States. For lack of space, we shall examine conjointly aerial espionage and reconnaissance.

5.5.2.1 *Aerial espionage and reconnaissance*

According to Article 29 of the Hague Regulation, a spy is a person who secretly obtains vital information from an enemy combatant "with the intention of communicating it to the hostile party."[245] The context is wartime and reconnaissance would be the opposite – that is, applies in peacetime. The controversy surrounding the legality of espionage has been discussed in Chapter 4. Sadly, State practice is ambivalent. However, there have been cases of aerial incidents involving civil aircrafts mistaken for intelligence gathering.[246] A question that needs an answer is since international law does not condemn espionage outrightly, why should States attack or intercept an aircraft used for espionage or reconnaissance? It shows that States do not support it.

5.5.2.2 *Lessons learned from past aerial incidents*

Between 1952 and 1978 there were at least five aerial incidents involving civilian aircrafts. On 29 April 1952, the Soviet Union shot down Douglas DC-4 (F-BELI) belonging to France for violating its airspace.[247] China brought down Cathay Pacific on 23 July 1954.[248] Bulgaria shot down an EL AL Airlines flight on 27 July 1955 when it could not properly identify it.[249] The United States, the United Kingdom and Israel petitioned the ICJ but the court declined jurisdiction.[250] However, the UK had argued that civil aircraft is immune from military attack in peacetime.[251] Ironically, Israel shot down the Libyan Airline on 21 February 1973[252] which Egypt described as "a monstrous and savage crime which is full of perfidy and which is not only a violation of international law but of all human values."[253] The international

---

245 *Hague Regulations* (n 83), art. 29.
246 The Soviet Union claims that KAL-007 was used for intelligence gathering. See John T. Phelps, "Aerial intrusions by Civil and Military Aircraft in Time of Peace" (1985) 107 *Military Law Review* 255–304, 264. Israel gave a similar reason when it shot down Libyan Airliner over the Sinai in 1973. See William J. Hughes, "Aerial Intrusions by Civil Airliners and the Use of Force" (1980) 45(3) *Journal of Air Law and Commerce* 595–620, 611–614.
247 Oliver J. Lissitzyn, "The Treatment of Aerial Intruders in Recent Practice and International Law" (1953) 47(4) *American Journal of International Law* 559–589, 574.
248 Hughes (n 246), 602.
249 David B. Green, "This Day in Jewish History 58 Dead After EL AL Plane Shot Down Over Bulgaria" (*Haaretz*, 25August 2016), available at <www.haaretz.com/jewish/this-day-in-jewish-history/.premium-1.607298> accessed 25 November 2019.
250 *Case Concerning the Aerial Incident of July 27th, 1955* (Israel v Bulgaria) Preliminary Objections Judgment ICJ Reports (1959) p. 127, 146.
251 Hughes (n 246), 604.
252 ibid., 611.
253 As quoted by Hughes, ibid.

Breaches of State territory 153

community condemned the excessiveness of the force used because of the fatality involved. Yet the cycle has continued unabated.[254]

It was after the Soviet Su-15 interceptor brought down Flight 007 belonging to South Korea that the debate on how to protect civilian aircraft accelerated. In the Security Council debate, member States never questioned whether the Soviet's airspace was violated but rather the reasonableness of forcible counter-measures taken. Japan, for instance, asks "[h]ow can we live together in this small world if trespassing will immediately result in mortal danger?"[255] Except for the United States that accused the Soviet Union of violating Article 2(4) of the UN Charter,[256] other States based their assessment on other principles. Canada said it was disproportionate[257] and Bill Hayden argued that shooting down a civilian aircraft cannot be justified under any circumstance.[258] The show of solidarity is humane and noble, but the root causes are distrust, mistrust and political dishonesty. At the peak of the Syrian civil war, "the report of the Independent Commission of Inquiry on the Syrian Arab Republic" described the situation in Syria as "a multisided proxy war steered from abroad by an intricate network of alliances."[259] Boris Johnson representing the UK at the Security Council described it as a "barbaric proxy war ... being fed, nourished, armed, abetted, protracted and made more hideous by the actions and inactions of Governments represented in this Chamber."[260]

Although State practice does not treat reconnaissance as illegal,[261] it should be noted that the Korean Airline Flight 007 was mistaken for a US spy plane. During the Cold War era, the Soviet Union shot down an American RB-47 reconnaissance plane off the Soviet coastline. Other incidents of interception of States' reconnaissance aircrafts were as follows: in 2007, Norway intercepted Russian Tupolev-95 over Norwegian EEZ and the UK Royal Air intercepted "eight Russian Tu-95s in the airspace off the northern coast of Great Britain near Scotland."[262] One time United States Secretary of Defence Donald H. Rumsfeld was reported to have said that "between December 2000 and April 2001 there were 44 aerial interceptions of U.S. reconnaissance flights off Chinese coasts by the

---

254 Jin-Tai Choi, *Aviation Terrorism: Historical Survey, Perspectives, and Responses* (New York, St Martin's Press,1994) 199–203.
255 UNSCOR, UN Doc. S/PV.2470 (2 September 1983), para. 65.
256 ibid., para. 39; *Letter Dated 1 September 1983 from the Acting Permanent Representative of the United States of America to the United Nations Addressed to the President of the Security Council*, UN Doc. S/15947 (1 September 1983), paras 9–10; UNSCOR, UN Doc. S/PV.2471 and Corr. 1 (6 September 1983), para. 18.
257 UNSCOR, UN Doc. S/PV.2470 (2 September 1983), para. 82.
258 Phelps (n 246), 257.
259 United Nations Human Rights Council, "Report of the Independent Commission of Inquiry on the Syrian Arab Republic" A/HRC/31/68 (11 February 2016), para. 17; UN Doc. A/HRC/24/46 (16 August 2013), para. 23.
260 UNSCOR, UN Doc. S/PV.7774 (21 September 2016), 23.
261 Peter A. Dutton, "*Caelum Liberam:* Air Defense Identification Zones Outside Sovereign Airspace" (2009) 103(4) *American Journal of International Law* 691–709, 705.
262 ibid., 702.

154 *Breaches of State territory*

People's Liberation Army Airforce."[263] The list seems endless. If reconnaissance is lawful why shoot down an aircraft suspected to have engaged in it?

5.5.2.3 *Pre-emptive self-defence and military necessity*

According to the US's rule of engagement, military necessity[264] allows US armed forces to shoot down any intruding aircraft if an attack is imminent.[265] After the 9/11 terrorist attack on the United States, Germany enacted the Aerial Security Act which authorised armed forces to apply physical force to civil aircraft reasonably suspected to have been hijacked.[266] When challenged, the constitutional court held that such a law would be incompatible with the right to life and therefore void.[267] The doctrine of pre-emptive self-defence developed after 9/11, which in the reasoning of the German court is faulty. Put differently, Article 51 of the UN Charter is invoked when there is an armed attack.

But for Article *3bis* of the *Protocol to Chicago Convention*,[268] neither the *1919 Paris Convention* nor the *1944 Chicago Convention* specifies law enforcement

---

263 ibid., 705.

264 The principle of military necessity states that "force resulting in death and destruction will have to be applied to achieve military objectives, but its goal is to limit suffering and destruction to that which is necessary to achieve a valid military objective." See Joint Departments of Defense and Homeland Security, *Commander's Handbook on the Law of Naval Operations* (July 2007 Edition), para. 5.3.1, available at <www.jag.navy. mil/documents/NWP_1-14M_Commanders_Handbook.pdf> accessed 16 November 2019 [hereinafter *The US Commander's Handbook*]; Yoram Dinstein, *War Aggression and Self-defence*, Fifth Edition (Cambridge, Cambridge University Press, 2011) 262; Yishai Beer, "Humanity Considerations Cannot Reduce War's Hazards Alone: Revitalizing the Concept of Military Necessity" (2015) 26(4) *European Journal of International Law* 801–828, 803; Niaz A. Shah, "The Use of Force under Islamic Law" (2013) 24(1) *European Journal of International Law* 343–365, 359; Janina Dill, "The 21st-Century Belligerent's Trilemma" (2015) 26(1) *European Journal of International Law* 83–108, 91.

265 *Aerial Incident – Israel v Bulgaria* (Memorial submitted by the Government of the United States of America, 2 December 1958) 239–240, available at <www.icj-cij.org/en/case/36> accessed 27 March 2020.

266 Nina Naska and Georg Nolte, "Legislative Authorization to shoot down Aircraft Abducted by Terrorists if Innocent Passengers are on Board Incompatibility with Human Dignity as Guaranteed by Article 1(1) of the German Constitution" (2007) 101(2) *American Journal of International Law* 466–471, 466; *Act on the Reorganisation of Aviation Security Tasks (Luftsicherheitsgesetz, LuftSiG)* (11 January 2005), section 14(3), available at <http://germanlawarchive.iuscomp.org/?p=735> accessed 16 November 2019.

267 *Germany Federal Constitutional Court* Judgment of the First Senate of 15 February 2006–1 BvR 357/05, paras 131–132, available at <www.bundesverfassungsgericht. de/SharedDocs/Entscheidungen/EN/2006/02/rs20060215_1bvr035705en.html> accessed 16 November 2019.

268 *Protocol Relating to an Amendment to the Convention on International Civil Aviation* (Signed at Montreal on 10 May 1984, entered into force on 1 October 1998) 2122 UNTS 337, art. *3bis* (it provides that States should demand intruding aircraft to land at a designated place for proper checks).

Breaches of State territory 155

available to States. Therefore, Article 3*bis* neither exonerates intruding aircraft from a wrongful act nor eliminates the possibility that disproportionate measures might be used against them. It is meant to mitigate civilian casualties. An extreme example is whether a civil aircraft loaded with WMD and flown by suicide bombers should be spared if it heads to a State's military base? States must cultivate the culture of respect as the basis for building a mutual trust.

5.5.2.4 Unmanned aerial vehicles

The invention of Unmanned Aerial Vehicles (drones) changed the dynamics of conventional warfare. It is by far safer in terms of risk involved and drones can be deployed for strikes, surveillance, espionage, reconnaissance and other hazardous operations. In 2010 alone, Barack Obama's administration was said to have used more drones in north-west Pakistan than when George W. Bush was in office.[269] By early 2012, the estimation was that the Pentagon was in control of about 7,500 drones.[270] With the rate of scientific development in drone technology, self-piloted drones will make attribution of responsibility harder than ever.

Drones and cyberspace will determine how warfare is conducted in the future.[271] Already, this has raised some ethical, moral and legal questions;[272] two of which border on accountability and responsibility for civilian deaths.[273] Technically, drones warfare does not fit well into the cross-border movement of armed forces as explained by the ICJ in *Armed Activities on the Territory of the Congo*.[274] But the effect caused by drone warfare could rise to the gravity threshold within the Charter meaning of an armed attack. Also, it has been argued that drones do not meet the criteria of State aircraft.[275] Yet drones serve military purposes and as such qualify.[276] Therefore, the claim by the

---

269 Stuart Casey-Maslen, "Pandora's Box? Drone Strikes Under *Jus ad Bellum, Jus in Bello*, and International Human Rights Law" (2012) 94(886) *International Review of the Red Cross* 597–625, 598.

270 W. J. Hennigan, "New Drone Has No Pilot Anywhere, So Who's Accountable?" (*Los Angeles Times*, 26 January 2012), available at <http://articles.latimes.com/2012/jan/26/business/la-fi-auto-drone-20120126> accessed 16 November 2019.

271 Afsheen John Radsan, "Loftier Standards for the CIA's Remote-Control Killing" (Accepted Paper No. 2010–11, William Mitchell College of Law, St Paul, Minnesota, May 2010) 1–10, available at <http://papers.ssrn.com/sol3/papers.cfm?abstract_id=1604745> accessed 16 November 2019.

272 International Committee of the Red Cross, "Editorial: Science cannot be placed above its Consequences" (2012) 94(886) *International Review of the Red Cross* 457–876; Jelena Pejic, "Extraterritorial Targeting by Means of Armed Drones: Some Legal Implications" (2014) 96(893) *International Review of the Red Cross* 67–106.

273 UNSC Res. S/RES/2286 (3 May 2016), preamble para. 19.

274 *DRC v Uganda* (n 90), paras 35, 47, 110, 114 and 131.

275 Paul W. Khan, "Imagining Warfare" (2013) 24(1) *European Journal of International Law* 199–226, 222–226.

276 Michael N. Schmitt, "Drone Attacks Under the *Jus ad Bellum* and *Jus in Bello*: Clearing the 'Fog of Law'" (2010) 13 *Yearbook of International Humanitarian Law* 311–326, 315; *The US Commander's Handbook* (n 264), para. 2.4.4; *Convention on*

156 Breaches of State territory

Pakistani government that flying drones over its airspace without its approval is a breach of its sovereignty is credible.[277] Moreover, the United Nations General Assembly and regional bodies recommend that the use of armed drones must comply with international law and the UN Charter.[278]

International Civil Aviation (Done at Chicago on 7 December 1944, entered into force on 4 April 1947) 15 UNTS 295, art. 8.

277 Government of Pakistan Press Information Department, "*PR No. 8* Pakistan Demands End to Illegal Drone Strikes" (Islamabad, 2 July 2016), available at <www.pid.gov.pk/?p=22382> accessed 16 November 2019; Peshawar High Court, *Writ Petition No. 1551-P/2012,* Judgment by Justice Dost Muhammad Khan (11 April 2013) 18, available at <www.peshawarhighcourt.gov.pk/app/site/75/c/Mr._Justice_Dost_Muhammad_Khan.html> accessed 16 November 2019; National Assembly of Pakistan, "Resolution: The House Strongly Condemns the Drone Attacks by the Allied Forces on the Territory of Pakistan" (10 December 2013), available at <www.na.gov.pk/en/resolution_detail.php?id=140> accessed 16 November 2019.

278 UNGA Res. A/RES/68/178 (18 December 2014), paras 6(s) and 17; United Nations, "Report of the Special Rapporteur on Extrajudicial, Summary or Arbitrary Executions, Philip Alston" UN Doc. A/HRC/14/24/Add.6 (28 May 2010), paras 79–86; European Parliament, "Resolution on the Use of Armed Drones" (Adopted by European Parliament at Strasbourg on 27 February 2014) P7_TA(2014)0172, preamble para. E.

6 Non-State actors, Article 2(4) and the sanctity of State territory

6.0 Introduction

The Uppsala Conflict Data Program reveals that non-State based violence was higher than State-based violence between 1975 and 2018 thanks to Article 2(4) which has deterred inter-State armed conflict. However, there has been an increase in "internationalised" armed conflicts misconceived as beyond the purview of Article 2(4). Three questions help to steer this chapter. First, do States' covert and overt support of unlawful activities of non-State actors (NSA) fall within the scope of Article 2(4)? Second, if yes, what is the appropriate response for the victim State since the right to self-defence is unavailable? Third, if no, could such conducts jeopardise international peace and security? Based on preceding chapters, it seems that a State would breach Article 2(4) if it initiates, instigates, sponsors or directly gets involved in unlawful activities of non-State actors in another State.

6.1 Working definition of non-State actors

The definition of non-State Actors (NSAs) depends on the body defining – whether national or international. Nationally, it is used broadly to refer to groups which may or may not be independent of a State such as financial institutions, intergovernmental organisations or State-sponsored terrorist groups.[1] Internationally, it relates to "certain territorial or political units other than states and which to a limited extent, may be directly the subject of rights and duties under international law."[2] For our purposes, the NSAs include militia, belligerents, insurgents or terrorist groups. This inclusiveness in thinking is reflective of resolution 2325 adopted by the Security Council (SC) in 2016.[3] It covers groups with political or religious affiliation and which possess the *de facto* economic, financial

---

1 Daphne Josselin and William Wallace, "Non-state Actors in World Politics: A Framework" in Daphne Josselin and William Wallace (eds), *Non-state Actors in World Politics* (New York, Palgrave, 2001) 2.
2 Robert Jennings and Arthur Watts (eds), *Oppenheim's International Law*, Ninth Edition, Volume 1: Peace (London and New York, Longman, 1996) 17 (emphasis added).
3 UNSC Res. S/RES/2325 (15 December 2016), preamble para. 5, operative para. 8.

158 *Article 2(4) and the sanctity of State territory*

and institutional government capable of controlling part of State territory and in opposition to, or running a parallel government. It does not include any State-sponsored insurgent group since such bodies technically constitute an agent of the State such that their activities are attributable to the State. Also, it excludes non-governmental organisations (NGOs)[4] or State-like entities such as Palestine or the Vatican City State.[5]

6.2 Status of non-State actors under international law

The usual practice is that NSAs do not acquire recognisable legal status until they attain the status of belligerent.[6] Recognition means according NSAs rights and obligations under international law. Once recognised, a third State may lawfully train their armed forces, assist them with arms or fund and provide them with other help they might need. But this can only happen if they satisfy some conditions. For instance, a group seeking external validation must have effective control over the territory it occupies, and the armed conflict must have reached a certain degree of intensity and duration.[7] However, not all recognitions confer legal status to the NSA. In some cases, terms used are a mere political ploy,[8] such that a State purporting to recognise such entities may not lawfully treat them as a subject of rights and duties as such.

Unfortunately, the international community has not adopted criteria of eligibility upon which States could make informed assessment partly because international law does not specify when a group of rebels starts to possess international rights and duties.[9] The downside to this floating practice is that States confronted by internal armed struggles quickly outlaw them as terrorists. Even when a case of terrorism is established, there is no universally accepted legal framework for assessment. As the saying goes, a terrorist to one might be a freedom fighter to another.[10] It is, therefore, imperative to evolve a common standard by way of a convention.

---

4 Jennings and Watts (n 2), 18.
5 John R. Morss, "The International Legal Status of the Vatican/Holy See Complex" (2015) 26(4) *European Journal of International Law* 927–946.
6 Andrew Clapham, *Human Rights Obligations of Non-State Actors* (New York, Oxford University Press, 2006) 271.
7 Antonio Cassese, *International Law*, Second Edition (Oxford, Oxford University Press, 2005) 125.
8 For more on recognition see James Crawford, *The Creation of States in International Law*, Second Edition (New York, Oxford University Press, 2006) 17–23.
9 Antonio Cassese, *International Law in a Divided World* (New York, Oxford University Press, 1986) 82.
10 Boaz Ganor, "Defining Terrorism: Is One Man's Terrorist another Man's Freedom Fighter?" (2002) 3(4) *Police Practice and Research* 287–304, 287; Walter Laqueur, *The Age of Terrorism* (Boston and Toronto, Little, Brown and Company, 1987) 7, 302.

Article 2(4) and the sanctity of State territory 159

Nonetheless, other branches of international law such as the international humanitarian law and the international human rights law attribute corporate responsibility to NSAs. For example, Article 3 common to the four Geneva Conventions of 1949 obliges the warring parties to respect the human personality of the *hors de combat*.[11] Article 13 of the 1977 Protocol II to the four Geneva Conventions[12] which protects the civilian population from armed attack equally applies to NSAs. Similarly, Article 19 of the *Convention for the Protection of Cultural Property in the Event of Armed Conflict*[13] obliges warring parties "to respect cultural property."

That international treaties bind NSAs dilute the claim that they have no legal standing, at least technically. Therefore, NSAs are "quasi-States"[14] since they have statutory duties and perhaps enjoy limited rights. They could exercise *de facto* authority over a portion of a State territory. But not being "subjects" of international law, Bekker argues that NSAs cannot be held directly liable under international law.[15] Except for the cases of colonial domination, alien occupation and racist regimes,[16] international law does not recognise NSAs. Israel refused to accord prisoner of war status to captured members of the "Organization of the Popular Front for the Liberation of Palestine"[17] and the South African Court denied Petane the status of a prisoner of war.[18]

6.3 Is Article 2(4) applicable to non-State actors?

Prima facie, Article 2(4) regulates States conducts. Henkin praises the laudable achievements of Article 2(4) in preventing inter-State war as follows: "[e]xpectation

11 *Geneva Convention for the Amelioration of the Condition of the Wounded and Sick in Armed Forces in the Field* (Done at Geneva on 12 August 1949, entered into force on 21 October 1950) 75 UNTS 31, art. 3; *Geneva Convention for the Amelioration of the Condition of Wounded, Sick and Shipwrecked Members of Armed Forces at Sea* (Concluded at Geneva on 12 August 1949, entered into force on 21 October 1950) 75 UNTS 85, art. 3; *Geneva Convention Relative to the Treatment of Prisoners of War* (Done at Geneva on 12 August 1949, entered into force on 21 October 1950) 75 UNTS 135, art. 3; *Geneva Convention Relative to the Protection of Civilian Persons in Time of War* (Done at Geneva on 12 August 1949, entered into force on 21 October 1950) 75 UNTS 287, art. 3.
12 *Protocol Additional to the Geneva Conventions of 12 August 1949, and Relating to the Protection of Victims of Non-international Armed Conflicts (Protocol II)* (Adopted at Geneva on 8 June 1977, entered into force on 7 December 1978) 1125 UNTS 609, art. 13.
13 *Convention for the Protection of Cultural Property in the Event of Armed Conflict* (Done at The Hague on 14 May 1954, entered into force on 7 August 1956) 249 UNTS 240, art. 19.
14 Cassese 1986 (n 9), 84.
15 Pieter H. F. Bekker, "Corporate Aiding and Abetting and Conspiracy Liability Under International Law" in Wybo P. Heere (ed.), *From Government to Governance* (The Hague, T. M. C. Asser Press, 2004) 209–216.
16 UNGA Res. A/RES/3103 (XXVIII) (12 December 1973), operative para. 1.
17 See generally, *Military Prosecutor v Omar Mahmud Kassem and Others* [1971] 42 ILR 470.
18 See generally, *S v Petane* [1988] 3 SALR 51.

160 *Article 2(4) and the sanctity of State territory*

of international violence no longer underlie every political calculation of every nation, and war plans lie buried deep in national files."[19] But the bigger question being contested here is "whether Article 2(4) ... or customary international law prohibit the use of force by non-State actors and, as a result, whether States are allowed under international law to exercise their right to self-defence in response to such forcible measures?"[20] Times have passed, and the call for the expansion of the scope of the addressees has become louder. As shall be seen, *opinio juris* and legal instruments these days use inclusive language. Therefore, this section focuses on not whether NSAs qualify as the subject of international law within the meaning of Article 2(4) but on holding States directly responsible and accountable for the misconducts of NSAs. Also, it shall examine how the right to self-defence applies to NSAs.

6.3.1 The political debate

The 9/11 terrorist attacks on the United States of America made President George W. Bush declare war on the NSAs. In his address to the nation, President Bush says, "[w]e will make no distinction between the terrorists who committed these acts and those who harbor them."[21] This policy which forms part of the US rule of military engagement,[22] changed the political discourse as it relates to the scope of Article 2(4). First, it recognised that self-defence is available against NSAs; implying that Article 2(4) extends to NSAs as well. Second, it acknowledged that States could be held accountable for harbouring terrorists. President Bush's position was a departure from the inter-State character of Article 51 of the UN Charter. The policy statement gives armed forces of the United States an unprecedented right to fight terrorists without the consent of a host State. The US reaction is understood because of the instinct of self-preservation after the 9/11 terrorist attacks. But its reasonableness must be tested against the backdrop of the existing legal framework. Gardner doubts the effectiveness of unilateral approach to fighting terror in our contemporary world, arguing that respect for territorial integrity should still be upheld.[23] The perplexing aspect of Bush's policy is the doctrine of unilateral pre-emptive self-defence which has no solid legal basis. For instance, the SC "strongly condemn[ed]" Israel's attack on Iraq's nuclear reactor in 1981.[24] A high-level panel of experts sanctions unilateral pre-emptive self-

---

19 Louis Henkin, "The Reports of the Death of Article 2(4) are Greatly Exaggerated" (1971) 65(3) *American Journal of International Law* 544–548, 544.
20 Vladyslav Lanovoy, "The Use of Force by Non-State Actors and the Limits of Attribution of Conduct" (2017) 28(2) *European Journal of International Law* 563–585, 564.
21 George W. Bush, "Address to the Nation on Terrorist Attacks" (11 September 2001), available at <www.presidency.ucsb.edu/documents/address-the-nation-the-terrorist-attacks> accessed 17 November 2019.
22 The White House, *The National Security Strategy of the United States of America* (Washington D.C., The White House, 2002) 6, 15, available at <www.state.gov/documents/organization/63562.pdf> accessed 22 April 2016.
23 Richard N. Gardner, "Neither Bush nor the Jurisprudes" (2003) 97(3) *American Journal of International Law* 585–589, 588.
24 UNSC Res. S/RES/487 (19 June 1981), operative para. 1.

Article 2(4) and the sanctity of State territory 161

defence "as long as the threatened attack is *imminent*."[25] Has the report crystallised into law? As Hakimi pointed out, the law in this area "is potentially in flux"[26] but it seems to be gaining currency in the United States and the UK after 9/11.

Again, States are not "responsible for private conduct, the notion of control has become an essential element of the classical conception of attribution."[27] That seemed to have changed with President Bush's policy. However, inaction seems no longer healthy for States because of a dysfunctional SC.[28] But unilateralism is a license to anarchy. Gardner has suggested four conditions under which a State's consent might be discarded. First, when the host State fails to discharge its international obligations to suppress terrorism. Second, when the host State does not prevent the supply of WMD to terrorists. Third, when the victim State wants to rescue its nationals abroad. Fourth, when the intervention is to prevent genocide or crimes against humanity.[29] We do not yet have specific components of the conditions. What, for example, amounts to a failure of a State to discharge its international obligations?[30] Therefore, the recommendation of the high-level panel of experts that matters that require pre-emptive measures should be tabled before the SC is reasonable,[31] notwithstanding the SC's inefficiency.[32]

6.3.2 Argument based on customary law

As mentioned earlier, Article 3 common to the Geneva Conventions applies to NSAs. Other instruments which apply to NSAs include "the 1977 Additional Protocol II to the Geneva Conventions, the Hague Regulations, the Convention for Protection of Cultural Property in the Event of Armed Conflict, and Customary International Law."[33] Outside the context of armed conflict, NSAs are bound by the *Terrorism Suppression Conventions* and the *Genocide Convention*.[34] Besides, SC's resolutions addressed to "all parties" to the conflict apply to States as

---

25 See, *A More Secure World: Our Shared Responsibility – Report of the High-level Panel on Threats, Challenges and Change*, UN Doc. A/59/565 (2 December 2004), para. 188 [hereinafter *A More Secure World*].

26 Monica Hakimi, "North Korea and the Law on Anticipatory Self-Defence" (EJIL: *Talk!*, 28 March 2017), available at <www.ejiltalk.org/north-korea-and-the-law-on-anticipatory-self-defense/#more-15104> accessed 17 November 2019.

27 Lanovoy (n 20), 566.

28 Arthur L. Goodhart, "Some Legal Aspects of the Suez Situation" in Philip W. Thayer (ed.), *Tensions in the Middle East* (Baltimore, Johns Hopkins Press, 1958) 243ff.

29 Gardner (n 23), 590.

30 Would the Afghan government deemed to have failed to discharge its international obligations when it was not in total control of the Al-Qaeda? See Nico Schrijver *et al.* (eds), *Counterterrorism Strategies in a Fragmented International Legal Order* (Chatham House, the Royal Institute of International Affairs, 10 March, 2014) 4.

31 *A More Secure World* (n 25), para. 190.

32 ibid., para. 186.

33 Lanovoy (n 20), 564 (see footnote 6 for relevant instrument).

34 *International Convention for the Suppression of the Financing of Terrorism* (Concluded in New York on 9 December 1999, entered into force on 10 April 2002) 2178 UNTS 197, art. 2; *Convention on the Prevention and Punishment of the Crime of Genocide*

162   *Article 2(4) and the sanctity of State territory*

well as NSAs.[35] Some SC resolutions, such as Resolution 1474 "stresses the obligation of all States and other actors to comply fully with resolution 733 (1992), and *reaffirms* that non-compliance constitutes a violation of the provisions of the Charter of the United Nations."[36] These developments would suggest that the legal status of NSAs has appreciated over time significantly or that State parties now regard NSAs as "quasi-States."

Andrew Clapham gives four reasons to justify direct application of international laws to NSAs. "First, private individuals and groups are bound as nationals of the state that has made the international commitment."[37] Yet, there is no evidence to suggest, let alone prove, that international commitments can be enforced upon individuals or groups without express approval or consent of their States. "Second, where a group is exercising government-like functions it should be held accountable as far as it is exercising the *de facto* governmental functions of the state. Third, the treaty itself directly grants rights and imposes obligations on individuals and groups. Fourth, obligations such as those in Common Article 3 are aimed at rebel groups ..."[38]

The fact remains that until a group is recognised as a State, it would be unlawful to treat it as such. Most States domesticate international conventions. Accountability of a *de facto* group mostly applies in criminal jurisdiction and through a judicial process. One would expect the involvement or at least the co-operation of the host State.

Again, reflecting on self-defence in relation to Article 2(4), the exact meaning of the phrase "inherent right of individual or collective self-defence" in Article 51 has not been resolved. Daniel Bethlehem has published principles under which it extends to imminent and actual attack by the NSAs.[39] Brownlie is of the view that it does not without the express consent of the host State.[40] Gray and Dinstein answer in the affirmative because of the phrase "inherent right" which they say is an indication that it is a customary law.[41] According to Bowett, the ICJ's *obiter* that the right to self-defence is fundamental[42] means that it allows States to protect their "legitimate interests."[43]

(Concluded at Paris on 9 December 1948, entered into force on 12 January 1951) 78 UNTS 277, art. 4.

35 UNSC Resolutions: S/RES/1304 (16 June 2000), operative para. 1; S/RES/1371 (26 September 2001), operative para. 6.
36 UNSC Res. S/RES/1474 (8 April 2003), operative para. 1.
37 Andrew Clapham, "Human Rights Obligations of Non-state actors in Conflict Situations" (2006) 88(863) *International Review of the Red Cross* 491–523, 498.
38 ibid., 498–499.
39 Daniel Bethlehem, "Self-Defense Against an Imminent or Actual Armed Attack by Nonstate Actors" (2012) 106 *American Journal of International Law* 770–777.
40 Ian Brownlie, *International Law and the Use of Force by States* (New York, Oxford University Press, 1963) 112–113.
41 Christine Gray, *International Law and the Use of Force*, Third Edition (New York, Oxford University Press, 2008) 117; Yoram Dinstein, *War Aggression and Self-defence*, Fifth Edition (Cambridge, Cambridge University Press, 2011) 191.
42 *Legality of the Threat or Use of Nuclear Weapons*, Advisory Opinion ICJ Reports (1996) pp. 226, 263.
43 Derek W. Bowett, *Self-defence in International Law* (Manchester, Manchester University Press, 1958) 186.

Article 2(4) and the sanctity of State territory   163

The pressure of inclusiveness is building up towards a flexible construction of Article 51 to include the use of force against NSAs irrespective of whether or not the host State gives its consent.[44] Such a move is a direct consequence of the 9/11 terrorist attacks on the United States.[45] Before that incident, terror orchestrated by NSAs against a State was governed by national criminal code.[46] Although a teleological interpretation of Article 51 could justify the expansion, it does not furnish the legal basis for violating the territory of the host State.[47] Hence, State practice,[48] *opinio juris*[49] and the jurisprudence of the ICJ[50] do not favour broadening the scope of Article 51.

6.3.3 Universal jurisdiction and NSAs

One might, however, asks: what role does universal jurisdiction play in holding NSAs accountable for their actions? Here we intend to focus on the incapacity of the host State to discharge its international obligation. Lanovoy summarises States' responsibilities under customary and treaty law to include the duty "to prevent the activities of non-state actors from breaching the rights of third states."[51] He elaborates: "[t]hese obligations, particularly in the domain of human rights and environmental law, comprise taking all means reasonably available to the state in order to prevent unlawful non-state actors' conduct on their territory and, in certain circumstances, even extraterritorially."[52] We shall examine these obligations a

---

44 Christian J. Tams, "The Use of Force against Terrorism" (2009) 20(2) *European Journal of International Law* 359–397, 367; Olivier Corten, *The Law Against War: The Prohibition on the Use of Force in Contemporary International Law* (Oxford and Portland, Oregon, Hart Publishing, 2010) 126.
45 For analysis, see Sean D. Murphy, "Contemporary Practice of the United States Relating to International Law" (2002a) 96(1) American Journal of International Law 237–263.
46 Antonio Cassese, "Terrorism is Also Disrupting some Crucial Legal Categories of International Law" (2001) 12(5) *European Journal of International Law* 993–1001; Gareth D. Williams, "Piercing the Shield of Sovereignty: An Assessment of the Legal Status of the Unwilling or Unable Test" (2013) 36(2) *University of New South Wales Law Journal* 619–641, 622. For a traditional view, see: Oscar Schachter, "The Lawful Use of Force by a State against Terrorists in another Country" (1989) 19 *Israel Yearbook on Human Rights* 209–232, 216.
47 Constantine Antonopoulos, "Force by Armed Groups as Armed Attack and the Broadening of Self-Defence" (2008) 55(2) *Netherlands International Law Review* 159–180, 168.
48 Gray (n 41), 136–140; UNSC Res. S/RES/573 (4 October 1985), operative paras 1 and 3; UNSC Res. S/RES/527 (15 December 1982), operative para. 1; UNSC Res. S/RES/546 (6 January 1984), operative para. 1; UNGA Res. A/RES/41/38 (20 November 1986), operative para. 1.
49 Patrick Thornberry, "International Law and its Discontents: The U.S. Raid on Libya" (1986) 8(1) *Liverpool Law Review* 53–64, 57.
50 *Legal Consequences of the Construction of a Wall in the Occupied Palestinian Territory*, Advisory Opinion ICJ Reports (2004) p. 136, para. 139 [hereinafter *ICJ Opinion on the Palestinian Wall*].
51 Lanovoy (n 20), 565.
52 ibid.

164 *Article 2(4) and the sanctity of State territory*

bit later but it is pertinent to underline that every State is required to use "all means reasonably available to" it. State "A's" capacity may not be the same as State "B's." If it varies, would State "A" be judged incompetent based on the ability of State "B"? If State "A" has optimised its capacity, would it be compelled by State "B" to adopt State "B's" criteria if none exists internationally? This comparison touches on the idea of the sovereign equality of States in an unequal society. This kind of argument resonates when intervention is premised on the doctrine of "unwilling or unable" to take the necessary steps to protect other States' interests.

After the *Lockerbie Incident*, two Libyan nationals were charged with 193 felony counts by the United States.[53] The request for their extradition to stand trial in the United States was made informally through Belgium by the United States and the United Kingdom.[54] The Libyan government declined the request but opted to exercise jurisdiction in accordance with the provision of Article 5(2) of the *Montreal Convention*.[55] Libya solicited the cooperation of the US and the UK and requested that they provide Libya with intelligence so that the accused could be prosecuted in Libya.[56] Both countries rejected the offer and threatened Libya with the use of armed force if it failed to extradite the suspects.[57] Libya argued that the US' refusal to cooperate was a breach of Article 11(1) of the *Montreal Convention*.[58]

This dispute raises the question of how far a State could go in addressing a wrongful act from NSAs when the host State is "unwilling or unable" to prevent the crime. Apparently, Libya manifested the "willingness" to prosecute the suspects based on the treaty law to which the affected countries were a party. Since *nemo judex in causa sua*, the US and its allies doubted the fairness (ability) of Libya's judicial system in prosecuting the crime. But the basis for extradition was questionable because Libya's domestic law at the material time did not permit that.[59] The Security Council prevailed on Libya to provide full and efficient response to the requests[60] and imposed economic sanctions on Libya when it defaulted.[61] In this case, not only that the Security Council's resolution prevailed against the treaty law (1971 *Montreal Convention*) but also it showed how the legal maxim

---

53 UN Doc. S/23317 (23 December 1991) 9, para. (v).
54 Michael Plachta, "The Lockerbie Case: The Role of the Security Council in Enforcing the Principle *Aut Dedere aut Judicare*" (2001) 12(1) *European Journal of International Law* 125–140, 126; UN Doc. S/23308 (31 December 1991), Annex, para. 4; UN Doc. S/23306 (31 December 1991), Annex, para. 4; UN Doc. S/23309 (31 December 1991), Annex, para. 3.
55 *Convention for the Suppression of Unlawful Acts Against the Safety of Civil Aviation* (Signed at Montreal on 23 September 1971, entered into force on 26 January 1973) 974 UNTS 177, art. 5(2) [hereinafter *1971 Montreal Convention*].
56 Plachta (n 54), 127.
57 ibid., 127–128.
58 *1971 Montreal Convention* (n 55), art. 11.
59 Christopher C. Joyner and Wayne P. Rothbaum, "Libya and the Aerial Incident at Lockerbie: What Lessons for International Extradition Law?" (1993) 14(2) *Michigan Journal of International Law* 222–261, 223.
60 UNSC Res. S/RES/731 (21 January 1992), operative paras 1 and 3; UNSC Res. S/RES/748 (31 March 1992), operative para. 1.
61 UNSC Res. S/RES/883 (11 November 1993), operative para. 3.

Article 2(4) and the sanctity of State territory 165

nemo iudex in causa sua disengaged the *Lotus Principle*.[62] For instance, Libya petitioned the ICJ and applied for a provisional order to stop the US from taking any forcible measures that could undermine its territorial sovereignty.[63] The ICJ declined,[64] thereby validating the SC resolution 748.[65]

In the past, States have applied "lawful" lethal force against insurgents occupying territory of a host State when a host State is adjudged "unwilling or unable" to tackle the problem.[66] But for the 2005 World Summit that established collective enforcement of the R2P,[67] State practice condemns unilateral invasions of the territory of the host State.[68] After it was confirmed that chemical weapon were used in Syria, the Obama administration attributed culpability to Assad's government and wanted to enforce the R2P.[69] We agree with *opinio juris* that such measures would have been unlawful without express authorisation from the SC.[70] However, the Committee on the use of force differentiates "force against the non-state actor as opposed to force against the host state."[71] Hence, the "… non-consensual force would not be a violation of Article 2(4) as it would be a lawful exercise of an exception to the

---

62 *Case of S.S Lotus* (France v Turkey) Collection of Judgments, PCIJ Series A, No. 10 (1927) 19.

63 *Questions of Interpretation and Application of the 1971 Montreal Convention arising from the Aerial Incident at Lockerbie* (Libyan Arab Jamahiriya v United States of America) Order of 14 April 1992 ICJ Reports (1992) p. 114, para. 3.

64 ibid., para. 43.

65 ibid., para. 40 (the court declared it was not called upon to determine the legal effect of the said resolution).

66 Ian Brownlie, "International Law and the Activities of Armed Bands" (1958) 7(4) *International and Comparative Law Quarterly* 712–735, 732–733.

67 UNGA Res. A/RES/60/1 (24 October 2005), para. 139.

68 Jorg Kammerhofer, "The Armed Activities Case and Non-State Actors in Self-Defence Law" (2007) 20(1) *Leiden Journal of International Law* 89–113, 105.

69 White House Office of the Press Secretary, "Statement by the President on Syria" (31 August 2013), available at <www.whitehouse.gov/the-press-office/2013/08/31/statement-president-syria> accessed 27 November 2019; Prime Minister's Office Guidance, "Chemical Weapon Use by Syrian Regime: UK Government Legal Position" (29 August 2013), available at <www.gov.uk/government/publications/chemical-weapon-use-by-syrianregime-uk-government-legal-position/chemical-weapon-use-by-syrian-regime-uk-government-legal-positionhtml-version> accessed 27 November 2019; White House Office of the Press Secretary, "Joint Statement on Syria" (6 September 2013), available at <www.whitehouse.gov/the-press-office/2013/09/06/joint-statementsyria> accessed 27 November 2019.

70 Carsten Stahn, "Syria and the Semantics of Intervention, Aggression and Punishment; On 'Red Lines and Blurred Lines'" (2013) 11(5) *Journal of International Criminal Justice* 955–978, 958–963; Marcelo Kohen, "The Principle of Non-Intervention 25 Years after the *Nicaragua* Judgment" (2012) 25(1) *Leiden Journal of International Law* 157–164, 162.

71 Michael Wood *et al.*, *Report on Aggression and the Use of Force* (International Law Association, Committee on the Use of Force), section B.2.c, available at <www.ila-hq.org/images/ILA/DraftReports/DraftReport_UseOfForce.pdf> accessed 17 November 2019 [hereinafter *ILA Report on the Use of Force*].

166 *Article 2(4) and the sanctity of State territory*

prohibition."[72] This view, we think, is at variance with the finding of a high-level panel of experts.[73]

6.4 States' responsibility towards third States

A State's exclusive right to its territory creates rights and obligations. The International Law Commission adopted the *Draft Articles on Responsibility of States for Internationally Wrongful Acts*[74] in 2001 (Draft Articles). The UN General Assembly resolution 56/83[75] recommends the Draft Articles as a means to promote inter-State relations. The Draft Article was further studied in the General Assembly subsequent sessions[76] in which comments and observations made by States[77] were considered in connection with the decisions of the judicial institutions.[78] There is no consensus on its normative value. The United States recognises it as a non-binding document that provides "a guide to States and other international actors on either what the law is or how the law might be progressively developed."[79] Portugal has proposed a draft[80] that will examine critical issues raised in it. For instance, concerns were raised about the nature of countermeasures in Articles 49 through 54 as well as Article 48 which permits the invocation of responsibility "by other States other than the injured State."[81] Other issues noted were the character of Articles 40 and 41 which deal with "serious breaches" of norms *jus cogens*. The Russian Federation recommended the establishment of a working group to study the Draft Articles while El Salvador called for its codification.[82]

The legal status of the Draft Articles is uncertain. *Opinio juris,* especially within academia, favours the view that States have inherent obligations to protect,

---

72 ibid.
73 *A More Secure World* (n 25), para. 190.
74 International Law Commission, *Draft Articles on Responsibility of States for Internationally Wrongful Acts* (adopted by the International Law Commission at its Fifty-Third Session in 2001) (Volume II, Part II, *Yearbook of the International Law Commission,* 2001) 31 [hereinafter *Articles on States Responsibility*].
75 UNGA Res. A/RES/56/83 (12 December 2001), preamble para. 3; UNGA Res. A/RES/59/35 (2 December 2004), preamble para. 3, operative paras 1 and 4.
76 UNGA Res. A/RES/59/35 (2 December 2004), operative para. 4; UNGA Res. A/RES/62/61 (6 December 2007), operative para. 4; UNGA Res. A/RES/65/19 (6 December 2010), operative para. 4; UNGA Res. A/RES/68/104 (16 December 2013), operative para. 5.
77 For summary of the statements made by 32 States that deliberated on the matter, see generally, UNGAOR, UN Doc. A/C.6/59/SR.15 (28 October 2004); UNGAOR, UN Doc. A/C.6/59/SR.16 (29 October 2004).
78 For a compiled decision by the United Nations Secretary-General, see generally, UN Doc. A/62/62 and Corr.1 and Add.1 (17 April 2007); UN Doc. A/65/76 (8 December 2010); UN Doc. A/68/72 (30 April 2013).
79 UN Doc. A/62/63/Add.1 (12 June 2007), para. 4.
80 UN Doc. A/68/69/Add.1 (28 June 2013), para. 3.
81 James Crawford and Simon Olleson, "The Continuing Debate on a UN Convention on State Responsibility" (2005) 54(4) *International and Comparative Law Quarterly* 959–972, 961.
82 ibid., 961; UN Doc. A/65/96/Add.1 (30 September 2010), para. 2.

Article 2(4) and the sanctity of State territory 167

prevent, prosecute and punish NSAs for their nefarious activities.[83] While these obligations prohibit States from allowing their territory to be used as safe haven, it does not presuppose that the failure to discharge those duties creates a nexus for imputation of liability.

6.4.1 Basic principle

Articles 1 through 3 of the Draft Articles set out basic principles of States' responsibility to Third States. Article 1 states: "[e]very internationally wrongful act of a State entails the international responsibility of that State."[84] A commentary on this article as proffered by the International Law Commission (ILC) explains that "an internationally wrongful act of a State may consist in one or more actions or omissions or a combination of both."[85] This has two elements to it – actions and omissions. The first element which is doing "something" finds expression in the jurisprudence of the International Judicial Bodies. In "the *Phosphates in Morocco* case, PCIJ affirmed that when a State commits an internationally wrongful act against another State international responsibility is established 'immediately as between the two States.'"[86] It went on to enumerate a few of other cases in which the ICJ has applied the principle such as, "in the *Corfu Channel* case, in the *Military and Paramilitary Activities in and Against Nicaragua* case, and in the *Gabcíkovo-Nagymaros Project* case"[87] The second element which is "refusal to fulfil a treaty obligation" is found in the ICJ's "advisory opinions on *Reparation for Injuries*, and on the *Interpretation of Peace Treaties (Second Phase)*,"[88] among others. Article 2 of the Draft Articles further explains the two elements, stressing that "the conduct in question" and "omissions" (negligence) must be attributed to a State and "must constitute a breach of an international legal obligation."[89]

6.4.2 Attribution of conduct of NSAs to a State

The United Nations General Assembly on receipt of the Draft Articles requested the ILC to compile "decisions of international courts, tribunals and other bodies referring to the articles, to invite Governments to submit information on their practice in that regard …"[90] "The compilation reproduces the extracts of decisions under each of the articles referred to by international courts, tribunals and bodies, following the structure and numerical order of the State responsibility articles finally adopted in 2001."[91] In all, there are 59 articles and "there have been 129

---

83 Robert P. Barnidge, *Non-State Actors and Terrorism* (The Hague, T. M. C. Asser Press, 2008) 68–78.
84 *Articles on States Responsibility* (n 74), art. 1.
85 ibid., 32.
86 ibid.
87 ibid.
88 ibid.
89 ibid., 34
90 UN Doc. A/62/62 (1 February 2007), para. 1.
91 ibid., para. 4.

168 *Article 2(4) and the sanctity of State territory*

instances in which international courts, tribunals and other bodies have referred in their decisions" to them.[92] Indispensable conditions for attribution of conduct to a State were set out by the ICJ in the *United States Diplomatic and Consular Staff in Tehran* case as follows:

> First, it must determine how far, legally, the acts in question may be regarded as imputable to the Iranian State. Secondly, it must consider their compatibility or incompatibility with the obligations of Iran under treaties in force or under any other rules of international law that may be applicable.[93]

The two *ad hoc* Criminal Tribunals articulated other conditions.[94] In the *Application of the Convention on the Prevention and Punishment of the Crime of Genocide*,[95] the ICJ reiterates that the act in question must be a conduct of a State organ. Article 8 of the Draft Articles explains that attribution is allowed when a State exercises control over such groups or persons.[96] In summary, the conduct in question or omission (as the case may be) must be either executed by a State or its organ or a person or group of persons under the control of a State. We shall not review the entire Draft Articles here. Instead, we shall illustrate how States assume responsibility for conducts of NSAs by examining three levels, namely: (1) NSA as an organ of a State, (2) effective control by a State and (3) aiding a wrongful act.

6.4.2.1 NSA as an organ of a State

The threshold to establish that this condition has been met is laid out well in the *Military and Paramilitary Activities In and Against Nicaragua* case as follows:

> What the Court has to determine at this point is whether or not the relationship of the *contras* to the United States Government was so much one of dependence on the one side and control on the other that it would be right to equate the *contras*, for legal purposes, with an organ of the United States Government, or as acting on behalf of that Government.[97]

---

92 ibid., para. 5; see also UN Doc. A/62/62/Add.1 (17 April 2007), 1–9.

93 *United States Diplomatic and Consular Staff in Tehran*, Judgment ICJ Reports (1980) p. 3, para. 56 [hereinafter *Consular Staff in Tehran*].

94 *The Prosecutor v Tadić (Duško)* (Case No. IT-94-1-A, ICL 93) Appeal Judgment ICTY (1999), paras 120, 122, 123 and 128, 131; *The Prosecutor v Du [Ko Tadi]* (Case No. IT-94-1-T) Judgment Trial Chamber ICTY (1997), para. 584; *The Prosecutor v Akayesu* (Case No. ICTR-96-4-T) Trial Chamber I ICTR (1998), paras 704–705; *The Prosecutor v Alfred Musema* (Case No. ICTR-96-13-A) Trial Chamber I ICTR (2000), paras 125–126.

95 *Application of the Convention on the Prevention and Punishment of the Crime of Genocide* (Bosnia and Herzegovina v Serbia and Montenegro) Judgment ICJ Reports (2007) p. 43, para. 385 [hereinafter *Genocide* case].

96 *Articles on States Responsibility* (n 74), art. 8.

97 *Military and Paramilitary Activities In and Against Nicaragua*, Judgment ICJ Reports (1986) p. 14, para. 109 [hereinafter *Nicaragua* case].

Article 2(4) and the sanctity of State territory 169

The analysis of the financial assistance given to the *contras*[98] made the ICJ to declare that the United States government had control over the *contras*.[99] But the aid was not overwhelming to justify treating the *contras* as acting on behalf of the United States.[100] Therefore, the assistance was "insufficient to demonstrate their complete dependence on United States aid."[101] This doctrine of "complete dependence" implies that NSA in question has no independence and constitutes a *de facto* "organ" of the controlling power.[102] Thus, a victim State must prove that the host State has, not only the capacity to, but equally controls the NSAs "in all fields" of their nefarious activities.[103] This threshold is too high and places victim States in a disadvantaged position. It makes attribution harder to prove and is oblivious of how financial assistance dismembers States' territory.[104]

As a general rule, conducts attributed to States are those of "its organs of government, or of others who have acted under the direction, instigation or control of those organs, i.e. as agents of the State."[105] After the "assassination" of "the Chairman and several members of an international commission entrusted with the task of delimiting the Greek-Albanian border" on Greek territory, the commission of inquiry set up by the League of Nations held that NSA's conduct can be attributed to a State "if the State has neglected to take all reasonable measures for the prevention of the crime and the pursuit, arrest and bringing to justice of the criminal."[106] Automatic attribution applies to public institutions constituted as such in law like the police force even when they act *ultra vires* or *motu proprio* but in their official capacity. This doctrine is articulated in Article 7 of the Draft Articles. However, the conduct of private persons or a group of persons may be adopted by a State under the provision of Article 11 "if and to the extent that the State acknowledges and adopts the conduct in question as its own."[107] This was the situation when the agent of Iran's government initiated policies that sustained the occupation of the United States' Embassy and detention of its officials.[108] However, "in order to attribute an act to the State, it is necessary to identify with reasonable certainty the actors and their association with the State."[109]

98 ibid., paras 95–99.
99 ibid., para. 109.
100 ibid.
101 ibid., para. 110.
102 Stefan Talmon, "The Responsibility of Outside Powers for Acts of Secessionist Entities" (2009) 58(3) *International and Comparative Law Quarterly* 493–518, 499.
103 ibid., 498.
104 Daniel Byman *et al.*, *Trends in Outside Support for Insurgent Movements* (Pittsburgh, RAND, 2001) 83–100.
105 *Articles on States Responsibility* (n 74), 38.
106 Quoted in *Articles on States Responsibility* (n 74), 38.
107 ibid., 52.
108 *Consular Staff in Tehran* (n 93), para. 74.
109 Quoted in *Articles on States Responsibility* (n 74), 39.

170 Article 2(4) and the sanctity of State territory

6.4.2.2 Effective control by a State

Article 8 of the Draft Articles provides that:

> [t]he conduct of a person or group of persons shall be considered an act of a State under international law if the person or group of persons is in fact acting on the instructions of, or under the direction or control of, that State in carrying out the conduct.[110]

In the *Nicaragua* case, the ICJ identifies two crucial elements in attributing responsibility as "dependence" and "control."[111] Being "effective" means exercising authority in "such a degree of control in all fields …"[112] Again, control is leveraged upon dependence such that it must be shown that the host State has the potential for control based on NSAs' dependence. Even when dependence is established, the ICJ maintains that "general control" is not sufficient to attribute responsibility to a State "without further evidence" that the accused State has "directed or enforced the perpetration of the acts …"[113] The ICJ concludes that:

> despite the heavy subsidies and other support provided to them by the United States, there is no clear evidence of the United States having actually exercised such a degree of control in all fields as to justify treating the contras as acting on its behalf.[114]

This high threshold ignores many subtle and covert ways States use to scuttle sovereignty of other States. In 1997, for example, Burundi invaded Tanzania because the latter provided military training and weapons to the rebels fighting the government forces.[115]

The high threshold requires an applicant to substantiate the link between accused State and delict conduct of NSAs up to the level of policy and operations.[116] An attempt to establish this link failed in the *DRC v Uganda* case.[117] Yet States victimised by such attacks vigorously resist it. The Appeal Chamber of the International Tribunal for the Former Yugoslavia has shown disapproval of this high threshold when it says, "[t]he Appeals Chamber fails to see why in each and every circumstance international law should require a high threshold for the test of

---

110 ibid., art. 8.
111 *Nicaragua* case (n 97), para. 109.
112 ibid.
113 ibid., para 115; Talmon 2009 (n 102) 499.
114 ibid., para. 109.
115 Tom Ruys and Sten Verhoeven, "Attacks by Private Actors and the Right of Self-Defence" (2005) 10(3) *Journal of Conflict and Security Law* 289–320, 314.
116 Talmon (n 102), 502.
117 *Armed Activities on the Territory of the Congo* (Democratic Republic of the Congo v Uganda) Judgment ICJ Reports (2005) p. 168, paras 130–135, 145, 160 [hereinafter *DRC v Uganda*].

Article 2(4) and the sanctity of State territory 171

control."[118] In the *Lockerbie Incident*, for instance, one would expect attribution to succeed if the Libyan government knows of the attack and fails to take reasonable steps to prevent it. It may not succeed with the Nicaraguan threshold. The Appeals Chamber in the *Prosecutor v Duško Tadić* case held that "it is sufficient to require that the group as a whole be under the overall control of the State."[119] We acknowledge the difference in the legal question being addressed: Nicaragua addresses States' responsibility and the Appeals Chamber addresses criminal liability. Yet the common element is attribution of responsibility to a State for illegal activities of NSAs. Therefore, the position taken by the Appeals Chamber is a good step forward because a broad interpretation of Article 2(4) might include financing, instigating and supporting NSAs in a way that could impair territorial sovereignty of another State. A commentary on Article 8 of the Draft Articles observes that "instructions, direction, and control are disjunctive; it is sufficient to establish any one of them."[120]

6.4.2.3 Aiding a wrongful act

Article 16 of the Draft Articles is crucially important because it prohibits States from aiding or assisting the commission of an internationally wrongful act. The two *Ad hoc Criminal Tribunals* classify aiding and abetting an illegal act as a form of accessory liability.[121] In the *Duško Tadić* case, the Appeals Chamber held that "no proof is required of the existence of a common concerted plan, let alone of the pre-existence of such a plan"[122] and according to the ICTR "aiding and abetting include all acts of assistance in the form of either physical or moral support."[123] Antonio Cassese is of the view that what is required to prove complicity is that the aider and/or abettor has constructive knowledge of the crime.[124] Invariably, supplying of weapons, training of militia, and financing of NSAs to carry out nefarious acts against other States will qualify. Therefore, a pre-emptive self-defence against NSAs without consent of a host State could either mean a presumption of guilt of the host State or a breach of the territory of the host State. Unfortunately, the high threshold established in Nicaragua does not help much.

---

118 *Prosecutor v Duško Tadić*, International Tribunal for the Former Yugoslavia, Case IT-94-1-A (1999) 38(6) *ILM* 1518–1623, para. 117 [hereinafter *Duško Tadić* case].
119 ibid., para. 120.
120 *Articles on States Responsibility* (n 74), 48.
121 *Duško Tadić* case (n 118), para. 229; *Prosecutor v Kunarac et al.* (Case No. IT-96–23-T) Trial Chamber, Judgment ICTY (2001), paras 391–399; *Prosecutor v Akayesu* (Case No. ICTR-96–4-T) Trial Chamber I ICTR (1998), paras 525–548, 704–717; *Prosecutor v Alfred Musema* (Case No. ICTR-96–13-A) Trial Chamber I ICTR (2000), paras 125–126 [hereinafter *Alfred Musema* case].
122 *Duško Tadić* case (n 118), para. 229.
123 *Alfred Musema* case (n 121), para. 126.
124 Antonio Cassese, *Cassese's International Criminal Law*, Third Edition (Oxford, Oxford University Press, 2013) 193–205.

172 *Article 2(4) and the sanctity of State territory*

Customarily, States may invoke the doctrine of necessity when there is an armed attack provided the measures taken are reasonable and proportionate.[125] However, a State that is a victim of an international tort may not invoke the right of self-defense unless it is proven that the host State aided the act.[126] In such a scenario, the maxim *nemo judex in causa sua* takes precedence. The grey area might be how to classify States who, though "willing" are "unable" to prevent NSAs from using their territory as safe haven. In such matters, we think Chapter VII of the UN Charter should be activated. This is because non-compliance with the demands of a victim State and/or its allies does not necessarily mean complicity but could be an exercise of sovereignty.[127] Therefore, a thorough investigation by an independent body from the UN is required to establish whether passivity translates into complicity.

6.5 Matters arising – State-sponsored NSA

In what appears unprecedented in the history of diplomatic relations between States, some Gulf States closed all their borders with Qatar in 2017. They accused Qatar of "destabilising the region by backing extremist groups."[128] Qatar denies the charges as baseless but "a pre-arranged campaign of incitement against it."[129] The diplomatic tie has not been restored as at the time of writing. Qatar has refused to comply with the 13 demands made of it.[130] The veracity of these claims against Qatar have not been tested in the court of law. However, Qatar was asked, among others, to "sever (its) ties to all terrorist, sectarian and ideological groups ..." and to "stop all funding of individuals, groups and organisations designated terrorists by the blockading countries ..."[131] It is suicidal to underrate the negative impact of State-sponsorship of NSAs on international peace and security. Hence, President Donald J. Trump describes the isolation of Qatar by some Gulf States as "perhaps ... the beginning of the end to the horror of terrorism."[132] Are we witnessing an inauguration of a new custom on how to deal with covert State-sponsorship of NSAs?

---

125 Kimberley N. Trapp, "Back to Basics: Necessity, Proportionality and the Right of Self-Defence against Non-State Terrorist Actors" (2007) 56(1) *International and Comparative Law Quarterly* 141–156, 145–156.

126 Kimberley N. Trapp, "The Use of Force Against Terrorists: A Reply to Christian J. Tams" (2009) 20(4) *European Journal of International Law* 1049–1055, 1053.

127 ibid., 1054–1055 (Trapp thinks it might be a sign of complicity)

128 Aubrey Allegretti, "Qatar Isolated as Gulf States Cut Links Over Terror Claims" (*Sky News*, 5 June 2017), available at <http://news.sky.com/story/qatar-isolated-as-gulf-states-cut-links-over-terror-claims-10904788> accessed 24 November 2019.

129 UNGAOR, UN Doc. A/73/PV.6 (25 September 2018), 40.

130 Alia Chughtai, "Understanding the Blockade Against Qatar" (*Aljazeera News*, 5 June 2018), available at <www.aljazeera.com/indepth/interactive/2018/05/understanding-blockade-qatar-180530122209237.html> accessed 24 November 2019.

131 Ibid. (bracketed word not in the original).

132 Roberta Rampton, "Trump Takes Sides in Arab Rift, Suggests Support for Isolation of Qatar" (*Reuters*, 7 June 2017), available at <www.reuters.com/article/us-gulf-qatar-idUSKBN18X0KF> accessed 24 November 2019.

6.5.1 Resolution 1373 (2001)

After the 9/11 terrorist attacks on the United States, the SC unanimously adopted Resolution 1373, which condemned the act in the strongest terms possible.[133] Operative paragraph 1 "[*d*]*ecides* that all States shall prevent and suppress the financing of terrorist acts ..." Operative paragraph 2 obliges States to "refrain from providing any form of support, active or passive, to entities or persons involved in terrorist acts ..."[134] Equally, States must prevent terrorists from using their territory as safe haven for exporting terrorism abroad and should not be complicit in such acts.[135]

Apparently, resolution 1373 revolutionised thinking about the unhealthy practice of States financing criminal activities against other States. Hence, it is a watershed in the fight against terrorism in many respects. For instance, it declares that "acts, methods, and practices of terrorism" are against "the purposes and principles of the United Nations ..." It establishes a UN's supervised Counter-Terrorism Committee (CTC) to monitor States' compliance with the UN's counter-terrorism strategy.[136] Consequently, member States are encouraged to sign up to and ratify international conventions and protocols[137] prohibiting terrorism.[138] However, resolution 1373 and other instruments prohibiting terrorism encourage member States to work together[139] to defeat terrorism. They do not authorise unilateral actions against host States.

---

133 UNSC Res. S/RES/1373 (28 September 2001), operative paras 1–9; see also UNSC Res. S/RES/1368 (12 September 2001), operative para. 1; UNSC Res. S/RES/1267 (15 October 1999), operative para. 1.

134 UNSC Res. S/RES/1373 (28 September 2001), operative paras 1–2.

135 ibid., operative para. 2(c).

136 ibid., operative paras 5–6.

137 See generally, *Convention on Offences and Certain Other Acts Committed on Board Aircraft* (Signed at Tokyo on 14 September 1963, entered into force on 4 December 1969) 704 UNTS 220; *Convention for the Suppression of Unlawful Seizure of Aircraft* (Signed at The Hague on 16 December 1970, entered into force on 14 October 1971) 860 UNTS 105; *Protocol for the Suppression of Unlawful Acts of Violence at Airports Serving International Civil Aviation, Supplementary to the Convention for the Suppression of Unlawful Acts against the Safety of Civil Aviation* (Signed at Montreal on 24 February 1988, entered into force on 9 August 1989) 1589 UNTS 474; *Convention on the Prevention and Punishment of Crimes Against Internationally Protected Persons*, including Diplomatic Agents (Opened for signature at New York on 14 December 1973, entered into force on 20 February 1977) 1035 UNTS 167; *International Convention against the Taking of Hostages* (Signed at New York on 18 December 1979, entered into force on 3 June 1983) 1316 UNTS 205; *Convention on the Physical Protection of Nuclear Material* (Signed at New York and Vienna on 3 March 1980, entered into force on 8 February 1987) 1456 UNTS 124; *Safety of Maritime Navigation* (n 34); *Protocol for the Suppression of Unlawful Acts Against the Safety of Fixed Platforms Located on the Continental Shelf* (Signed at Rome on 10 March 1988, entered into force on 1 March 1992) 1678 UNTS 304.

138 UNSC Res. S/RES/1373 (28 September 2001), operative para. 3(d).

139 ibid., operative para. 3(c); UN Doc. A/60/825 (27 April 2006); UNGA Res. A/RES/56/1 (12 September 2001), operative para. 4.

174 *Article 2(4) and the sanctity of State territory*

According to Murphy, the UN General Assembly neither classified 9/11 as an "attack" "nor recognised a right to respond in self-defense"[140] On this basis, Murphy argues that reliance on the right to self-defence is misplaced because of the difficulty in establishing that the hijackers (Al Qaeda) were an "organ" of or controlled by the Taliban government.[141] The ICJ in the *Oil Platforms* case reiterates that an armed attack is a condition that triggers the right to self-defence to the point that the court wanted the United States to prove that the mines were laid not only by Iran but also with the intent of attacking vessels belonging to the United States.[142] This fails to recognise the clandestine manner in which such attacks are financed or facilitated by States. Since State practice has not caught up with the trend, instruments relating to terrorism, such as the *Convention for the Suppression of Unlawful Seizure of Aircraft*[143] should facilitate the extradition and prosecution of suspects of terrorist attacks.

6.5.2 *Resolution 1441 (2002) – subsisting authorisation*

The United States and its allies intervened militarily in Iraq in 2003 because Iraq was "in material breach" of its international obligations.[144] Resolution 678 passed by the SC in 1990 sets the deadline on which Iraq was to fully comply with the demands of the SC, failure of which led to member States being requested to co-operate with the Government of Kuwait and "to use all necessary means … to restore international peace and security in the area."[145] Since the SC resolution 1441 does not authorise the use of force, the legal basis for a retroactive enforcement is puzzling.[146] It is ambiguous because resolution 1441 expressly states that the SC has seized of the matter and will decide on further measures to be taken should Iraq persists in the material breach.[147] It is assumed that the most recent resolution on a particular issue overrules the previous decisions unless expressly upheld. The UN member States that implied force into resolution 1441 did so in the belief that other member States have constructive knowledge that force might be used.[148] But this interpretation was

140 Sean D. Murphy, "Terrorism and the Concept of Armed Attack in Article 51 of the U.N. Charter" (2002) 43(1) *Harvard International Law Journal* 41–52, 46; UNGA Res. A/RES/56/1 (18 September 2001), operative para. 1.
141 Murphy 2002 (n 140), 46.
142 *Case Concerning Oil Platforms* (Iran v United States of America) Judgment ICJ Reports (2003) p. 161, paras 61–64 [hereinafter *Oil Platforms* case].
143 As enumerated in footnote n 137 above.
144 UNSC Res. S/RES/1441 (8 November 2002), operative paras 1 and 4; Mahmoud Hmoud, "The Use of Force Against Iraq: Occupation and Security Council Resolution 1483" (2004) 36(3) *Cornell International Law Journal* 435–453, 436.
145 UNSC Res. S/RES/678 (29 November 1990), operative para. 2.
146 Michael Byers, "Agreeing to Disagree: Security Council Resolution 1441 and Intentional Ambiguity" (2004) 10(2) *Global Governance* 165–186, 172.
147 UNSC Res. S/RES/1441 (8 November 2002), operative paras 1–14.
148 To prove that the Security Council members had constructive knowledge that the continued material breach could trigger the use of force, see Maria Luisa B. Bunggo, "Legal Authority for the Possible Use of Force Against Iraq" (1998) 92 *American Society of International Law Proceedings* 136–150, 141; Ruth Wedgwood, "The Enforcement of Security

Article 2(4) and the sanctity of State territory   175

rejected by States who described the invasion as a breach of international law.[149] It follows from this that inconsistent interpretation of legal instruments might lead to a violation of States' territory.[150] In some instances, coercive measures permitted for the protection of civilians[151] were enforced in a manner that ousts a legitimate government. This calls into question whether the SC should interpret its resolutions[152] before its execution by concerned States. The Permanent Court of International Justice observes "that the right of giving an authoritative interpretation of a legal rule belongs solely to the person or body who has power to modify or suppress it."[153]

6.6 Addressees of the right to self-defence

The analysis made thus far is that Article 2(4) of the UN Charter is not directly applicable to NSAs. States cannot lawfully invoke the right of self-defence against NSAs without authorisation by the host State or if the conditions for attribution as stated above, were not met. The ICJ's judgment in the *Nicaragua* case limits the beneficiary of the right to self-defence to States for an armed attack from another State or its agents.[154] Of concern to us, though, is that conducts (such as financing terrorist groups), traditionally classified as *de minimis*, equally breaches the territory of victim States. Stahn has suggested that the right to self-defence applies to NSAs.[155] However, ICJ is clear that

> Article 51 of the Charter recognizes the existence of an inherent right of self-defence in the case of armed attack by one State against another State. However, Israel does not claim that the attacks against it are imputable to a foreign State.[156]

Any attempt to apply Article 51 to NSAs against the consent of a host State may inadvertently violate its territorial sovereignty unless authorised by the SC. In fact,

Council Resolution 687: The Threat of Force against Iraq's Weapons of Mass Destruction" (1998) 92(4) *American Journal of International Law* 724–728, 727; UN Doc. S/25091 (11 January 1993), para. 9 (the president of the Security Council warned "Iraq of the serious consequences that will flow from such continued defiance").

149 UNSCOR, UN Doc. S/PV.4726 (26 March 2003) (the position taken by Malaysia at page 8, the League of Arab States at page 8, Algeria at page 10, Yemen at page 13 *et cetera*).

150 Louis Henkin, "Kosovo and the Law of 'Humanitarian Intervention'" (1999) 93(4) *American Journal of International Law* 824–828.

151 UNSC Res. S/RES/1973 (17 March 2011), operative para. 4.

152 For further discussion, see Michael C. Wood, "The Interpretation of the Security Council Resolutions" (1998) 2(1) *Max Planck Yearbook of United Nations Law* 73–95, 82–86; Efthymios Papastavridis, "Interpretation of Security Council Resolutions under Chapter VII in the Aftermath of the Iraqi Crisis" (2007) 56(1) *The International and Comparative Law Quarterly* 83–118, 90–91.

153 *Question of Jaworzina* (Polish-Czechoslovakian Frontier) Advisory Opinion PCIJ Series B, No. 8 (1923) 37.

154 *Nicaragua* case (n 97), paras 195, 199, 232–236.

155 Carsten Stahn, "Terrorist Acts as Armed Attack: The Right to Self-Defense, Article 51 (1/2) of the UN Charter, and International Terrorism" (2003) 27(2) *Fletcher Forum of World Affairs* 35–54, 36.

156 *ICJ Opinion on the Palestinian Wall* (n 50), para. 139.

176 *Article 2(4) and the sanctity of State territory*

robust suggestions[157] on how to adapt the right to self-defence to the actions of NSAs have encountered stiff oppositions.[158] What appears to be missing is consent. Insofar as self-defence is an exception to the *jus cogens* character of Article 2 (4), Article 51 should be interpreted strictly.[159]

6.6.1 NSAs – jus ad bellum *and* jus in bello

To further strengthen our arguments on possible dangers that might result from an undue expansion of the scope of self-defence, we defer to *jus ad bellum* and *jus in bello* as two limbs of the laws of war under modern international law. The *jus ad bellum* provides the grounds that could justify a breach of a State territory while *jus in bello* moderates how it may proceed within the ambit of the law.[160]

Traditionally, *jus ad bellum* allows a State to wage war against an offending State to seek redress for an injury suffered.[161] In its Roman Law origin, such a war is considered "just." The word "just" is not tied to morality, albeit that *fetiales* (priests in Ancient Rome) must legitimise wars implies that just wars are morally justifiable.[162] A war is *justum* (legally correct) if it complies with the rules of the *fetial* proceedings,[163] and *pium* if sanctioned by a religious authority.[164]

---

157 The Chatham House, "Principles of International Law on the Use of Force in Self-Defence" (2006) 55(4) *International and Comparative Law Quarterly* 963–972; Bethlehem (n 39), 775; Nico Schrijver and Larissa van den Herik, "Leiden Policy Recommendations on Counter-terrorism and International Law" (2010) 57(3) *Netherlands International Law Review* 531–550.

158 Mary Ellen O'Connell, "Dangerous Departures" (2013) 107(2) *The American Journal of International Law* 380-386, 381; Gabor Rona and Raha Wala, "No Thank You to a Radical Rewrite of the *Jus ad Bellum*" (2013) 107(2) American Journal of International Law 386–390.

159 Mary Ellen O'Connell, "The Choice of Law Against Terrorism" (2010) 4(2) *Journal of National Security Law & Policy* 343–368, 359; *Oil Platforms* case (n 142), paras 61–64; *DRC v Uganda* (n 117), paras 146, 301; *Genocide* case (n 95), para. 391.

160 Carsten Stahn, "'*Jus ad bellum*', '*jus in bello*' ... '*jus post bellum*'? – Rethinking the Conception of the Law of Armed Force" (2007) 17(5) European Journal of International Law 921–943, 926; Steven R. Ratner, "*Jus Ad Bellum* and *Jus in Bello* after September 11" (2002) 96(4) *American Journal of International Law* 905–921, 905–906.

161 John F. Coverdale, "An Introduction to the Just War Tradition" (2004) 16(2) *Pace International Law Review* 221–277, 229; Jean Bethke Elshtain, "The Just War Tradition and Natural Law" (2005) 28(3) *Fordham International Law Journal* 742–755, 750.

162 Coleman Phillipson, *The International Law and Custom of Ancient Greece and Rome*, Volume I (London, Macmillan, 1911) 327; Arthur Nussbaum, "Just War – A Legal Concept" (1943) 42(3) *Michigan Law Review* 453–479.

163 Note that the member States' opinion is divided on whether compliance with the fetial proceedings is enough for waging a war. The minority opinion seems to suggest that there must be a primordial justifiable cause while the majority opinion maintains that fetial proceedings confer the required legitimacy. See Joachim von Elbe, "The Evolution of the Concept of the Just War in International Law" (1939) 33(4) *American Journal of International Law* 665–688, 666.

164 ibid., 667; Phillipson (n 162), 180.

It could be said that the two limbs have survived mutations over centuries. The current regime on *jus ad bellum* permits war based on self-defence (whether individual or collective) or when authorised by the SC. Therefore, the legality of the US's invasion of Afghanistan in 2001 could have been a matter for concern if the SC did not expressly authorise it. Yet its justification could be disputed if the 9/11 terrorist attacks were not attributable to Afghanistan or that the Afghan government had objected to the said invasion. The work of Hugo Grotius, *De Jure Belli ac Pacis* deals with the concept of law and war in general as well as justness in the conduct of war.[165] His main legacy is his ability to evolve the law of nations from the law of nature,[166] particularly his argument that public war is a conduct of sovereign power.[167] As already noted, NSAs are not subjects of rights and obligations in the strict sense but States are.

The jurisprudence of the ICJ has not departed from the ideal of the classical era. But modern "just war theorists" such as Walzer and Coverdale endorse a unilateral military action to protect a State's national interest or for humanitarian purposes.[168] This kind of consideration is based on the assumption of the inevitability of war when the interests of a State are compromised.[169] It means that "justness" of war no longer depends on two limbs of *jus ad bellum* but on other variables[170] insofar as no harm is redressed or authorisation granted. This development could short-circuit the maintenance of international peace and security.[171] As Corten rightly observed, this is a worrisome adaptation of the UN Charter to the changing times[172] which may crack the foundations of world peace.

6.6.2 Jurying jus ad bellum's threshold established in Nicaragua

The jurisprudence of the ICJ maintains that a State's territory could be breached either for reasons of self-defence or when authorised by the Security Council. In the *Nicaragua* case, the ICJ was requested to declare that the United States violated its customary international law by "recruiting, training, arming, equipping and financing, supplying and otherwise encouraging, supporting, aiding, and

---

165 See generally, Hugo Grotius, *The Rights of War and Peace: Including the Law of Nature and of Nations,* translated by A. C. Campbell with an Introduction by David J. Hill (Washington D.C. and London, M. Walter Dunne, 1901).
166 ibid., 36.
167 ibid., 55.
168 Coverdale (n 161) 238.
169 ibid., 226.
170 Such as to uphold human rights, see ibid., 238–242.
171 For pacific means of settling disputes see J. L. Brierly, *The Law of Nations: An Introduction to the International Law of Peace,* Sixth Edition (Oxford, Clarendon Press, 1963) 346.
172 Corten (n 44), 15.

178   *Article 2(4) and the sanctity of State territory*

directing military and paramilitary actions in and against Nicaragua."[173] These factors, though not armed attack, could destabilise regional order.

6.6.3 Armed attack threshold

For self-defence to be available, the ICJ has established that a State must prove it is a victim of an armed attack from the accused State or its agents.[174] Nicaragua pleaded the ICJ to declare that the United States violated its territory by sponsoring the *contras*.[175] The US justified its financial support to the *contras* as a measure to prevent the unelected Sandinista junta from undermining democracy in Nicaragua.[176] It further argued that the assistance was meant to stop Nicaragua from supplying arms to El Salvadoran guerrilla forces.[177] In other words, to prevent Nicaragua from exporting terrorism abroad. The ICJ rejected the US's arguments on two grounds. First, the right to self-defence is exercised by a State that is a victim of an armed attack.[178] Second, the US cannot rely on the right to collective self-defence since El Salvador did not substantiate it had suffered an armed attack perpetrated by the State of Nicaragua.[179] However, the ICJ clarified that an armed attack includes

> not merely action by regular armed forces across an international border, but also "the sending by or on behalf of a State of armed bands, groups, irregulars or mercenaries, which carry out acts of armed force against another State of such gravity as to amount to" (*inter alia*) an actual armed attack conducted by regular forces, "or its substantial involvement therein."[180]

This judgment provides a definition of an armed attack lacking in the UN Charter. It also extends the right to self-defence to the actions of NSAs acting as agents of the State. However, it failed to address the procedural and substantive issues as to whether a State may rely on Article 51 of the UN Charter against NSAs.

Procedurally, there is no mechanism for establishing when an armed attack has occurred.[181] This has been a thorny issue for the UN member States[182] and has

---

173 *Nicaragua* case (n 97), para. 15.
174 ibid., para. 195.
175 ibid., para. 20.
176 ibid., paras 94–100.
177 ibid. Counter memorial of the United States, Pleadings, Vol. II, 17 August 1984 (Annex 53, Press Conference with President Duarte – San Salvador, 7 July 1984) 298.
178 *Nicaragua* case (n 97), para. 195.
179 ibid., para. 211.
180 Ibid., para. 195.
181 Thomas M. Franck, "Who Killed Article 2(4) or: Changing Norms Governing the Use of Force by States" (1970) 64(4) American Journal of International Law 809–837, 816.
182 Judge Addulqawi A. Yusuf, "The Notion of 'Armed Attack' in the Nicaragua Judgment and Its Influence on Subsequent Case Law" (2012) 25(2) *Leiden Journal of International Law* 461–470, 462.

Article 2(4) and the sanctity of State territory   179

resulted in ambivalent State practice, which undermines Article 2(4).[183] For example, the Swedish government faulted the United States for meddling in the 1958 crisis in Lebanon on the basis that there was no armed attack, since the United Nations had seized of the matter.[184] A State seeking to rely on the right to self-defence must report the interim measures it has taken to the SC. However, the SC can uphold or overrule such measures in its subsequent decisions.

Substantively, the definition of an armed attack as established by the ICJ in the *Nicaragua* case does not allow that support be given to NSAs. To establish that an armed attack has occurred, there should be a cross-border sending of armed bands capable of carrying out an armed attack to a degree of armed forces.[185] Arguably, this threshold[186] tacitly supports *de minimis* incursions, inadvertently diluting the efficacy of States' obligation to respect the inviolability of State territory.[187] Such supports build up over time and undermines State territory.[188] Moreover, State practice does not condone mere frontier incidents.[189] Turkey shot down the Russian warplane for violating its air space for 17 seconds.[190] It demonstrates Turkey's unwillingness to condone *de minimis* overflight, which cannot be justified under Nicaragua's threshold because an armed attack has not occurred. Yet the United States and NATO argue that "Turkey ... has a right to defend its territory and its airspace."[191]

183 Franck (n 181), 816.
184 UNSCOR, UN Doc. S/PV.830 (16 July 1958), paras 44–49; see also "Letter dated 22 May 1958 from the Representative of Lebanon addressed to the President of the Security Council" UN Doc. S/4007 (23 May 1958) 1; UNSC Res. S/RES/128 (11 June 1958), operative para. 1.
185 *Nicaragua* case (n 97), para. 195.
186 ibid., para. 191; *Oil Platforms* case (n 142), para. 191.
187 Martin A. Harry, "The Right of Self-Defense and the Use of Armed Force against States Aiding Insurgency" (1986–1987) 11(4) *Southern Illinois University Law Journal* 1289–1304, 1302–1303.
188 *Protocol Additional to the Geneva Conventions of 12 August 1949, and relating to the Protection of Victims of International Armed Conflicts* (Protocol I) (Concluded at Geneva on 8 June 1977, entered into force on 7 December 1978) 1125 UNTS 3, art. 51(4); *Protocol [II] on Prohibitions or Restrictions on the Use of Mines, Booby Traps and Other Devices as Amended on 3 May 1996 (Protocol II as Amended on 3 May 1996) Annexed to the Convention on Prohibitions or Restrictions on the Use of Certain Conventional Weapons which may be Deemed to be Excessively Injurious or to have Indiscriminate Effects* (Done at Geneva on 3 May 1996, entered into force on 3 December 1998) 2048 UNTS 93, art. 3(8); *Corfu Channel* (United Kingdom v Albania) (Merits) Judgment ICJ Reports (1949) pp. 4, 22.
189 *ILA Report on the Use of Force* (n 71), 4.
190 See BBC News, "Turkey's Downing of Russian Warplane – What We Know" (1 December 2015), available at <www.bbc.co.uk/news/world-middle-east-34912581> accessed 28 September 2019.
191 Barack Obama, "The President's News Conference with President Francois Hollande of France" (24 November 2015), available at <www.presidency.ucsb.edu/node/311533> accessed 28 September 2019; North Atlantic Treaty Organisation, "Statement by the NATO Secretary General after the extraordinary NAC meeting" (24 November 2015), available at <www.nato.int/cps/en/natohq/news_125052.htm> accessed 28 September 2019.

180 *Article 2(4) and the sanctity of State territory*

This conforms with the separate opinion of Judge Simma in the *Oil Platforms* case.[192]

Therefore, Nicaragua's threshold is informed by a narrow construction of Article 2(4). It may have been intended to prevent inter-State war at the slightest provocation. However, it has inadvertently encouraged "mere frontier incidents" through direct and indirect material and financial support of NSAs. Although the ICJ held that such assistance could breach the territory of the affected State,[193] it rejected the submission made by the US that it acted on the ground of collective self-defence at the request of El Salvador.[194] The distinction which the court made between "grave" and "lesser" form of the use of force makes the latter more attractive. Invariably, the "armed attack threshold" departs from the customary law that permits States that suffer material breach to redress the wrong through the right of self-defence.[195] Besides, the ICJ refrained from deciding whether the United States acted under military necessity and failed to adequately analyse whether collective self-defence is an inherent right of States.[196]

Judge Jennings questions why the court assumes jurisdiction of the dispute on the basis of the customary international law.[197] Having accepted jurisdiction, the court should have adjudicated whether States that support NSAs in other States could by so doing breach the territory of those States. Therefore, the ICJ should have declared that Article 2(4) was violated, if on the facts, the US or Nicaragua had supported NSAs fighting legitimate governments in Nicaragua or El Salvador respectively. Again, the ICJ in the *Oil Platforms* case[198] examined whether a single attack constitutes an armed attack for the purposes of self-defence[199] or whether there must be an accumulation of events. The ICJ held, and rightly too, that other factors should be considered such as whether there is a specific intent to commit an international tort.[200] It follows that what might appear mere frontier incidents could, in fact, meet the gravity threshold if the tortfeasor had malicious intent.

Accordingly, Higgins argues that the "gravity threshold" undermines the right to self-defence[201] and Judge Jennings advocates for a liberal interpretation of an

---

192 *Oil Platforms* case (n 142), para. 12 (Separate Opinion of Judge Simma).

193 *Nicaragua* case (n 97), paras 195, 240.

194 ibid., paras 48, 238, 247.

195 Harry (n 187), 1302–1303; Dinstein (n 41), 209; Rosalyn Higgins, *Problems and Process: International Law and How We Use It* (Oxford, Clarendon Press, 1994) 250.

196 *Nicaragua* case (n 97), para. 96 (Dissenting Opinion of Judge Oda).

197 ibid., 534 (Dissenting Opinion of Judge Sir Robert Jennings).

198 *Oil Platforms* case (n 142), para. 64; *Nicaragua* case (n 97), para. 231; *DRC v Uganda* (n 117), para. 146.

199 *Oil Platforms* case (n 142) (written Proceedings, Iran *Reply and Defence to Counter-claim* 10 March 1999), para. 7.32; ibid. (US *Rejoinder* 23 March 2001), paras 5.16, 5.19.

200 *Oil Platforms* case (n 142), para. 64.

201 Higgins (n 195), 250–251; Judge Fitzmaurice argues that such a differentiation is uncalled for. See G. G. Fitzmaurice, "The Definition of Aggression" (1952) 1(1) *International and Comparative Law Quarterly* 137–144, 139. For discussions on small-scale incursions, see Corten (n 44), 403.

armed attack to include substantial assistance given to NSAs.[202] A question might be asked, what constitutes a substantial assistance? The failure to respect the inviolability of State territory leaves States' territory vulnerable to violation by opportunist States. Libya and Syria are examples of how supporting NSAs endanger international peace and security.

---

202 *Nicaragua* case (n 97), 543–44 (Dissenting Opinion of Judge Sir Robert Jennings); Malcolm N. Shaw, *International Law*, Seventh Edition (Cambridge, Cambridge University Press, 2014) 823.

7 An attempt to formulate a theory of respect for the inviolability of State territory

7.0 Introduction

A multicultural world with diverse political ideologies and ways of life must pursue a peace agenda on mutual respect. Antithetical values and conflicting national interests precipitated the formation of the UN which is a melting pot for conflicting and sometimes opposing ideologies. Therefore, the UN must be translucent and objective while discharging its obligations. Research conducted in "philosophy of law, social theory, ethical theory and political philosophy" shows that a stable and crisis-free society is realisable when individuals' rights are respected.[1] That could be said about international peace and security. The findings made in the preceding chapters lead to the conclusion that an evolutive interpretation of Article 2(4) as respect for the inviolability of State territory is the way to proceed. On the balance of probabilities, the chances that international peace and security will be enhanced are higher if respect becomes the bedrock of international relations.

7.1 Clarification of terminologies

First and foremost, we shall clarify two concepts that formed the thrust of this work, namely: respect and inviolability. Later on, an attempt will be made to situate the work within the context of natural law. Although States are artificial legal persons, this chapter borrows a lot from deductive reasoning when it transposes certain human attributes to States. The logic is simply that States are composed of human beings such that States' policies regarding war or peace are determined mainly or influenced by citizens' self-perception in the comity of nations.

7.1.1 Making sense of the word "respect"

The word respect comes to mind when four variables coalesce. They are, "a person who respects (a respector), a respected object, some characteristic in virtue of which the object is respected (the basis of respect), and some evaluative point of

---

1 Giovanni Giorgini and Elena Irrera, "Introduction" in Giovanni Giorgini and Elena Irrera (eds), *Roots of Respect – A Historic-Philosophical Itinerary* (Berlin, Walter de Gruyter, 2017) 1.

Theorising respect for State territory 183

view from which the object is respected."[2] *Prima facie,* one could argue that to anchor respect on certain extrinsic variables is not altruistic. But a closer evaluation suggests that the conditions could be inherent when one conceives, for instance, that the dignity of the human person is not calculated by external qualities. Otherwise, an evaluation of "the characteristics in virtue of which the object is respected" might encourage discriminatory tendencies which negate the inherent nature of the object. The application of discriminatory conditions to States will be deadlocked because of the principle of sovereign equality of States. However, one cannot wholly bracket out the effects of *prolepsis* on the moral judgment of the respector who may likely assess an object based on certain internalised assumptions. In such circumstances, the yardstick for determining what the characteristics are could be questionable as well as the objectivity of the assessor. Where a minimum threshold is required, the goal must be collectively set by parties concerned. Thus, making a value judgment of legal or moral nature in such matters is better left for competent bodies established through the consent of the parties.

To draw from Kant's model, respect as a right due to persons as such is not based on extraneous attributes.[3] According to Kant, the right that is innate in all human beings is freedom; that is, the "independence from being constrained by another's choice, insofar as it can coexist with the freedom of every other in accordance with a universal law."[4] Freedom for Kant is "a pure rational concept" without experiential validation upon which are based "unconditional practical laws, which are called *moral* ... moral laws are *imperatives* (commands or prohibitions) and indeed categorical (unconditional) imperatives."[5] "An imperative is a practical rule by which an action in itself contingent is *made* necessary." Categorical imperatives "refer to no other property of choice ... than simply to its *freedom*."[6] An "*obligation* is the necessity of a free action under a categorical imperative of reason" and "that action is *permitted* (*licitum*) which is not contrary to obligation ..." and freedom "is not limited by any opposing imperative."[7]

Although Hart warns against the fusion of law and morality,[8] it seems that laws are informed by morality – that is, the reasoning behind the codification. Besides, as subjects capable of making moral decisions either as individual or groups, human beings have freedom of action. Such actions are measured by balancing the subjective benefits with the universal acceptability if objectified. The test is simple: given the intended benefit, should other persons in a similar situation act in the same manner to achieve the same goal? Conducts that tick all the boxes in the

---

2 Carl Cranor, "Toward a Theory of Respect for Persons" (1975) 12(4) *American Philosophical Quarterly* 309–319, 310.

3 Colin Bird, "Status, Identity, and Respect" (2004) 32(2) *Political Theory* 207–232, 209.

4 Immanuel Kant, *The Metaphysics of Morals,* translated by M. Gregor (Cambridge, Cambridge University Press, 1991) 63, para 238.

5 ibid., 48, para. 221.

6 ibid., 49, para. 222.

7 ibid., 48, para. 222.

8 H. L. A. Hart, "Positivism and the Separation of Law and Morals" in R. M. Dworkin (ed.), *The Philosophy of Law* (New York, Oxford University Press, 1977) 18.

184 *Theorising respect for State territory*

affirmative qualify as a universal law.[9] Kant's morality approach upturns the hierarchical social model of respect based on the pyramidal structure of performance in favour of egalitarianism. In principle, what counts is common humanity and the guideline is "... *act that you use humanity, whether in your own person or in the person of any other, always at the same time as an end, never merely as a means.*"[10]

According to Steiner, Kant's Categorical Imperatives can be summarised as "requiring one to respect the agency of others by performing no action that subordinates their sets of purposes to one's own."[11] Therefore, "To treat someone as a mere means is to regard his purposes as if they did not count – as if he were just an object that entered one's calculations as an instrument to be used or an obstacle to be pushed aside."[12]

Peace will remain an ideal unless States and individuals key into this basic principle. Often States quote "national interest" as if it were an article of faith that would be pursued at all cost and sometimes at the expense of humanity. Kant points out the difference between "doing the right thing from duty and doing it to promote some other end."[13] The former is akin to respecting things in their natural order while the latter has some ulterior motives attached. Today, the world is witnessing climate change because of the exploitative mindset of human beings.

Although Kant talks about respect between persons, States can imbibe that culture if we accept the view that States come into existence through the consent of the people. Thus, territory as the heartbeat of States provides not only a scope within which States exercise their legitimate functions but also provides a template within which a person's freedom is realised. In the *Island of Palmas* case, Judge Huber endorsed respect of the *de facto* State authority over "an inchoate title derived from discovery" because it safeguards the fundamental rights of the inhabitants.[14] The discussions had in Chapter 3, especially the position held by the weaker States when the UN Charter was drafted, support this finding. According to Hall:

> The ultimate foundation of international law is an assumption that states possess rights and are subject to duties corresponding to the facts of their postulated nature. In virtue of this assumption it is held that since states exist, and are independent beings, possessing property, they have the right to do whatever is necessary for the purpose of continuing and developing their existence, of giving effect to and preserving their independence, and of holding and acquiring property, subject to the qualification that they are bound

9 Kant 1991 (n 4), 51, para. 225.
10 Immanuel Kant, *Groundwork of the Metaphysics of Morals*, translated and edited by M. Gregor (Cambridge, Cambridge University Press, 1997) 37, para. 4: 429.
11 Hillel Steiner, *An Essay on Rights* (Oxford, Blackwell, 1994) 221.
12 ibid.
13 Kant 1997 (n 10), xiii.
14 *Island of Palmas* case (The Netherlands v USA) (The Hague, 1928) II RIAA 829–871, 870.

Theorising respect for State territory   185

correlatively to respect these rights in others. It is also considered that their moral nature imposes upon them the duties of good faith, of concession of redress for wrongs, of regard for the personal dignity of their fellows, and to a certain extent of sociability.[15]

Therefore, respect enhances the chances of achieving the spirit of the law,[16] which ordinarily may be lacking if legal norms were interpreted in a binary mode. In territorial disputes brought before it, the ICJ pays attention to "the conduct of the Parties"[17] either in establishing territorial sovereignty or finding a breach of international law. Conduct might be by way of "the display of sovereignty," "acquiescence" to wrongful acts,[18] a "reasonable mistake"[19] or an act of aggression. A recent incident has shown States manifesting dissatisfaction over unfair treatments meted out to their nationals abroad.[20]

7.1.2 What do we mean by respect?

As one would expect, no single definition of respect will be comprehensive or satisfy curious minds. Cranor has reviewed a couple of them – highlighting their weak and strong points.[21] In Ancient Greece, two words (*aidôs* and *timê*) were translated as respect. *Aidôs* means "modesty and propriety in one's attitude and due respect for gods and men" and *timê* refers to "honor, value, reverence."[22] Here we focus on the definition offered by Kant according to which respect "is the acknowledgement of the dignity (*dignitas*) of another man, i.e., a worth which has no price, no equivalent for which the object of valuation (*aestimii*) could be exchanged."[23]

For a start, Cranor endorses this definition as containing essential elements of respect, namely: acknowledging the inherent dignity, value or worth of a person at no cost attached. However, Cranor faulted the definition for its failure to outline

---

15 William Edward Hall, *A Treatise on International Law*, Third Edition (Oxford, Clarendon Press, 1890) 45.
16 *The Case of the S.S. "Lotus"* (France v Turkey) Judgment PCIJ Series A, No. 10 (1927) 34 (Dissenting opinion of M. Loder).
17 *Sovereignty Over Pedra Branca/Pulau Batu Puteh, Middle Rocks and South Ledge* (Malaysia v Singapore) Judgment ICJ Reports (2008) p. 12, para. 122.
18 ibid., para. 121; *Case Concerning Delimitation of the Maritime Boundary in the Gulf of Maine Area* (Canada v United States of America) Judgment ICJ Reports (1984) p. 305, paras 130, 167.
19 *Land and Maritime Boundary Between Cameroon and Nigeria* (Cameroon v Nigeria: Equatorial Guinea Intervening) Judgment ICJ Reports (2002) p. 303, para. 311.
20 *Avena and Other Mexican Nationals* (Mexico v United States of America) Judgment ICJ Reports (2004) p. 12, para. 30.
21 Cranor (n 2), 309–319.
22 Giovanni Giorgini, "The Notion of Respect in Ancient Greek Poetry" in Giorgini and Irrera (eds) (n 1), 44–45.
23 Immanuel Kant, *The Metaphysical Principles of Virtue*, translated by J. Ellington (Indianapolis, Indiana, The Bobbs-Merrill Company, 1964) 127, para. 462.

186 *Theorising respect for State territory*

the "constraints ... placed on the object of respect."[24] We should like to point out that "man" as used should be understood in a generic sense.

Cranor defines respect as a "complex relationship" whereby "a respector, *R, E*-respects some person, *P*, in virtue of some characteristic, *F*, or alternatively, *R E*-respects *P* in virtue of *F*, or *R E*-respects *P*'s having *F*."[25] The permutations of this thesis are as follows:

R E-respects *P*'s having *F* (where *F* refers to some ability or character-trait of *P* and *E* refers to some evaluative point of view), if and only if,

(1) *R* believes *P* has *F* and that *P*'s having *F* is an *E*-good thing,
(2) R appreciates (has knowledge and understanding of) why *P*'s having *F* is an *E*-good thing,
(3) *R* is disposed to rely upon and have confidence in *P*'s having *F* and *P*'s doing what is appropriate to his having *F*, and
(4) *R* is disposed to acknowledge and recognize the value of *P*'s having *F* in ways appropriate to the *F* in question.[26]

To put this definition in a context, State "A" ought to respect State "B" where "A" believes that "B" has some ability or character-trait and vice versa. Possessing a "good character-trait" forms the basis for respect. This idea of "belongingness" traverses Plato's philosophy as *oikeion*.[27] The crux of respect is that which "belongs to" the other.

The need to identify a character-trait addresses the why question but does not explain how to identify character-traits or the parameters for assessing goodness. Yet it does not undermine our entire edifice since respectful behaviours that promote international peace and security are good in themselves. In a sense, this is not altruistic since the common good is the motivating factor.[28] Nonetheless, the interpretation of character-trait should be egalitarian in a way that globalises what Cranor calls the "characteristic about the person respected."[29] One might synonymise Cranor's notion of characteristic with the criteria for Statehood enunciated in Article 1 of the *Montevideo Convention*. The type of respect that is altruistic does not preclude status and performance-based respect only that the latter is secondary and cannot override the sovereign equality of States. Cranor argues that the reason to respect a person is based on a "property" "and not the attitude of respect"[30] However, State practice shows that States command respect through attitude as well. States that flagrantly violate international law do not command respect

24 Cranor (n 2), 310.
25 ibid., 310.
26 ibid., 310–311.
27 Christopher J. Rowe, "Plato on Respect, and What 'Belongs to' Oneself" in Giorgini and Irrera (eds) (n 1), 67–68.
28 Cranor (n 2), 311 (Cranor argues that respect should have no utilitarian benefit attached whatsoever).
29 ibid., 311.
30 ibid.

Theorising respect for State territory 187

in the comity of nations. The notion of "performance-based respect" could be deduced from the legal instruments that authorise States to interdict vessels of other States if they "believe" that such vessels would be used to commit a crime.[31]

7.1.3 Kinds of respect

Darwall's publication titled "Two Kinds of Respect" identifies two kinds of respect. The first kind is very broad and includes topics such as "law, someone's feeling and social institutions ..."[32] This category falls within what he calls *recognition respect*. The mention of "recognition" resonates with a mode of creation of State under international law.[33] A German philosopher, Fichte, introduced "recognition" into the legal dictionary when he advocated for constitutional protection of the rights of *peregrini*. Rousseau expanded its scope "to include the street as well as the court, mutual acknowledgement a matter of social behaviour as much as of legal right."[34] According to John Rawls, recognition "means respecting the needs of those who are unequal" while for Jurgen Habermas it connotes "respecting the views of those whose interests lead them to disagree."[35]

Interestingly, Darwall designates social institutions as deserving of recognition respect. The second kind of respect is based on specific positive attributes of individuals. This category Darwall calls *appraisal respect*.[36] Although he argues that appraisal respect applies to persons alone, it could equally apply to States since appraisal respect could be earned by compliance with the "code of ethics."[37] States command respect when they distance themselves from the internal affairs of others or uphold human rights. Moreover, law-abiding States and States which excel in certain arts earn respect among the comity of nations. Hence, the permanent members of the Security Council enjoy veto powers due to their military and financial capabilities. This kind of respect is not anchored on sovereign equality. Having said that, we do not intend to investigate appraisal respect further.

Whatever the form it takes, respect means to reckon with a person or a fact of deserving unhindered freedom and to act accordingly. In the law of nations, respect prohibits interference in internal affairs of sovereign States. This implies "to regard the fact that something is the law as restricting the class of actions that would be morally permissible."[38] A distinction should be made between been

---

31 United Nations, *Convention on the Law of the Sea* (Concluded at Montego Bay on 10 December 1982, entered into force on 16 November 1994) 1833 UNTS 397, arts 108, 206, 211(6), 217(3).

32 Stephen L. Darwall, "Two Kinds of Respect" (1977) 88(1) *Ethics* 36–49, 38.

33 James Crawford, *The Creation of States in International Law*, Second Edition (New York, Oxford University Press, 2006) 17–23.

34 Richard Sennett, *Respect in a World of Inequality* (New York, W. W. Norton & Company, 2003) 54.

35 ibid., 54.

36 Darwall (n 32), 38–39.

37 ibid., 41.

38 ibid., 40.

188 *Theorising respect for State territory*

respectful of and having respect for a person or a fact. Take the instance of a person who follows through legal proceedings without having any respect for judges. Compliance could be to avoid the contempt of court, yet that minimum threshold is required for a smooth legal process. In such circumstances, the rule of law provides "the ground of an entitlement *and* determines its nature."[39] Even respect tainted with mental reservations may further the common good. This does not in any way encourage stratification of respect in a manner that produces various degrees of freedom.[40] It does mean, however, that respect should not be coloured by prejudices or subjective assessment of the other.

As a condition for peaceful coexistence, the UN Charter adopts respect of equal rights as a fundamental principle in Article 1(2). The same principle is repeated in Article 55 which deals with economic matters. Chapter XII of the Charter establishes the "International Trusteeship System," yet, Article 78 provides that "[t]he trusteeship system shall not apply to territories which have become Members of the United Nations, relationship among which shall be based on respect for the principle of sovereign equality."[41] In other words, States as subject of international law enjoy sovereign equality before the law. The idea of sovereign equality has a political consequence. It implies that States should not interfere with the political independence of other States.

Article 1(2) of the Dumbarton Oaks Proposals did not contain "respect for the principle of equal rights ..." but it was added as an amendment later.[42] Article 55 of the Dumbarton Oaks Proposals uses "respect" in relation to "human rights and fundamental freedoms."[43] The phrase, "respect for the principle of equal rights ..." was adopted following a motion moved to that effect by a delegation from the United States who supported its inclusion "to make it perfectly clear that there would be no interference by the Economic and Social Council in the domestic affairs of any country."[44] Article 78 was not originally in the Dumbarton Oaks Proposals. However, Article 38(f) of the amendment to Chapter IX as submitted by Mexico provides that mandate territories should be granted sovereign status whenever they become eligible and Article 38(g) provides as follows: "no one of the sovereign States which exist at the time of the signing of this Pact may be entrusted to a mandate."[45] The defunct League of Nations adopted the mandate system. The Mexican proposal featured in the working paper for Commission II,

---

39 Joseph Raz, *The Morality of Freedom* (New York, Oxford University Press, 1986) 223 (emphasis added).

40 Ian Carter, "Respect for Persons and the Interest in Freedom" in Stephen de Wijze *et al.* (eds), *Hillel Steiner and the Anatomy of Justice: Themes and Challenges* (New York, Routledge, 2009) 176–177.

41 United Nations, *Charter of the United Nations* (Signed on 26 June 1945, entered into force on 24 October 1945) 1 UNTS XVI, art. 78 [hereinafter *UN Charter*].

42 United Nations, *Documents of the United Nations Conference on International Organization San Francisco, 1945*, Volume 3 (New York, United Nations, 1955) 622 [hereinafter *UNCIO*].

43 ibid., 19.

44 *UNCIO*, Vol. 10, 57.

45 *UNCIO*, Vol. 3, 142.

Committee 4 which studied the "trusteeship system."[46] A constructive application of relevant Charter provisions leaves no doubt that disrespectful conducts should equally be prohibited.

7.1.4 Respect and Article 2(4) of the UN Charter

Chapter 3 has shown how efforts to broaden Article 2(4) to include other forms of coercion were frustrated. A question that remains unanswered is why was it so? Research shows that *intangible* issues are major causes of inter-State conflicts and war.[47] Intangible refers to "objectives such as influence, prestige, or ideology."[48] Currently, the United States' House Intelligence Committee is investigating President Donald Trump over a whistleblower's complaint that the President is "using the power of his office to solicit interference from a foreign country in the 2020 U.S. election."[49] The veracity of this claim is beyond our scope. But suppose Ukraine undertook to execute the alleged request in a manner that will influence the outcome of the 2020 presidential elections, will that further international peace and security or enhance relationships between both States? Or would making such a request be considered disrespectful to Ukraine? One cannot quickly forget the strained relationship between Russia and the US following the alleged Russian interference in the US general elections.[50] One could only imagine what the response of the US would have been had the said interference been perpetrated by a weaker State – whether militarily or financially.

According to Dzurek, third-party involvement in the internal affairs of a State is an intangible factor which aggravates internal crisis.[51] It is a catalyst to internal crisis as shown by "the dispute over the status of the Caspian Sea ..."[52] Unfortunately, foreign policy decisions are measured by national interest. Hence, Dzurek remarks:

> In terms of U.S. national interest, the top 10 territorial disputes were China–Japan–Taiwan (Senkaku Islands), Canada–United States (Beaufort Sea), Japan–Russia (Kuril Islands), South Korea–Japan (Liancourt Rocks), Iran–Iraq–Turkey

46 *UNCIO*, Vol. 10, 677–678.
47 Paul R. Hensel and Sara McLaughlin Mitchell, "Issue Indivisibility and Territorial Claims" (2005) 64(4) *GeoJournal* 275–285; Paul F. Diehl, "What Are They Fighting For? The Importance of Issues in International Conflict Research" (1992) 29(3) *Journal of Peace Research* 333–344, 333–334.
48 Hensel and Mitchell 2005 (n 47), 275–276.
49 U.S. House of Representatives Permanent Select Committee on Intelligence, "Press Releases – House Intelligence Committee Releases Whistleblower Complaint" (Washington D.C., 26 September 2019), available at <https://intelligence.house.gov/> accessed 28 September 2019.
50 U.S. House of Representatives Permanent Select Committee on Intelligence, "Congress of the United States – Status of the Russia Investigation" (Washington D.C., 13 March 2018), available at <https://intelligence.house.gov/> accessed 28 September 2019.
51 Daniel J. Dzurek, "What Makes Territory Important: Tangible and Intangible Dimensions" (2005) 64(4) *GeoJournal* 263–274, 268.
52 ibid., 268.

190 *Theorising respect for State territory*

(Kurds), Syria–Turkey (Hatay and associated maritime area), Spratly Islands, United Kingdom (Northern Ireland), Spain–United Kingdom (Gibraltar), and China–India. Although the national interest hierarchy did not give any particular weight to being party to a territorial dispute, that over maritime jurisdiction in the Beaufort Sea loomed large in terms of U.S. interest, because it scored highly in most of the hierarchy's components. For purposes of scoring, the U.S. was counted as a U.S. "ally," as was Canada. Gibraltar, though a peaceful dispute over a tiny area, was assessed as important to the U.S., because the two claimants were U.S. allies, major trading partners and significant military powers, and the location was strategic. The fact that one or more of the claimants in the other top disputes was a U.S. ally, major trading partner, or both, accounted for the high scores of the other disputes …[53]

While this observation is no proof that the United States meddles in the affairs of other States, it buttresses how national interests dictate foreign policy. Dzurek argues that "[t]he foregoing discussion of national interest ignores the intrinsic prominence of territorial disputes."[54] Sadly, "territorial issues that have high values of either tangible or intangible salience are more likely to generate militarised conflict."[55] Why not take the bold step to nip the problem militating against international peace and security in the bud through evolutive interpretation? Franck and Henkin have spotted a hiatus which has resulted in inconsistent state practice.[56] The political will may not be universal, but the benefits of obeying the law outweigh the risks. Respect of internationally recognised boundaries bridges this gap.

Today more than ever, the conventional mode of conducting warfare is less fashionable. Therefore, Burghardt's description of territorial integrity as consisting of "all claims based on relative location of an area"[57] has become obsolete. The time has come to broaden the scope of Article 2(4) as suggested by some States at the earliest stage. As Dworkin observes, positivism permits rules to be ascertained not by their textual content but "with their *pedigree* or the manner in which they were adopted or developed."[58] As argued in Chapter 4, any interpretation that includes non-kinetic cyber-attacks within the scope of Article 2(4) seems unduly

---

53 ibid., 272.
54 ibid.
55 Shannon O'Lear, Paul F. Diehl, Derrick V. Frazier and Todd L. Allee, "Dimensions of Territorial Conflict and Resolution: Tangible and Intangible Values of Territory" (2005) 64(4) *GeoJournal* 259–261, 260; John A. Vasquez, "The Tangibility of Issues and Global Conflict: A Test of Rosenau's Issue Area Typology" (1983) 20(2) *Journal of Peace Research* 179–192, 181.
56 Louis Henkin, *How Nations Behave: Law and Foreign Policy*, Second Edition (New York, Columbia University Press, 1968) 69; Thomas M. Franck, *The Power of Legitimacy Among Nations* (New York, Oxford University Press, 1990) 52.
57 Andrew F. Burghardt, "The Bases of Territorial Claims" (1973) 63(2) *Geographical Review* 225–245, 235.
58 R. M. Dworkin, "Is Law a System of Rules?" in R. M. Dworkin (ed.), *The Philosophy of Law* (New York, Oxford University Press, 1977) 38.

Theorising respect for State territory 191

stretched. But the development of law that includes cyberspace within the territory of a State has become necessary.

7.1.5 *Respect as a duty owed* erga omnes

To say that a legal person has rights implies that "others have actual or hypothetical legal obligations to act or not to act in certain ways …"[59] Implicit in Article 2(4) is that such an obligation obliges *erga omnes*. This was the view of the ICJ in *Military and Paramilitary Activities In and Against Nicaragua* as follows:

> Principles such as those of the non-use of force, non-intervention, respect for the independence and territorial integrity of States, and the freedom of navigation, continue to be binding as part of customary international law, despite the operation of provisions of conventional law in which they have been incorporated.[60]

From paragraph 187 of the judgment, the ICJ weighed into various interpretations of the content of Article 2(4) as presented by the parties. At paragraph 188, it resolved to ascertain from *opinio juris* whether States could abstain from "the binding character" of the norm. It evaluated "the attitude of States towards certain General Assembly resolutions, and particularly resolution 2625 (XXV)" and at paragraphs 191 and 192 quoted in verbatim the said resolution. The said resolution imposes upon States the duty not only "to refrain from the threat or use of force" but also "the duty to refrain from organising or encouraging the organisation of irregular forces" in addition to "organising, instigating, assisting or participating in acts of civil strife …"[61] *et cetera*. There is a sense that these prohibitions are indirectly implicated considering the court's designation of them as a "less grave forms of the use of force."[62]

According to Joseph Raz, respect consists of the "duty to give due weight to the interests of persons."[63] Selective application of legal norms could crumble the entire legal system. As Raz noted, "due weight" implies a critical evaluation of the consequences of one's actions on the recipient or a targeted object. Hence, Darwall observes that *recognition respect* obliges respector "to give appropriate weight to the fact that he or she is a person by being willing to constrain one's behaviour in ways required by that fact."[64] As shall be seen, the fact is that States are sovereign irrespective of glaring inequalities. While inequalities are superficial and deal more with appraisal respect, a duty to

---

59 ibid.
60 ICJ Reports (1986) p. 14, para. 174 [hereinafter *Nicaragua* case]; ICJ Reports (1984) p. 392, para. 73.
61 *Nicaragua* case (n 60), paras 191–192.
62 ibid., para. 191.
63 Raz (n 39), 190.
64 Darwall (n 32), 45.

192 *Theorising respect for State territory*

respect might be criticised if respectee lacks self-respect. This sort of argument is often made against States that grossly violate the human rights of their citizens. According to Rawls, mutual respect is a duty owed to "a being with a sense of justice and a conception of the good."[65] Without overstretching Rawls' concept of "a moral being," it is unlikely that the court will endorse unauthorised interventions unless for self-defence. In the *Corfu Channel* case, the ICJ held that "[b]etween independent States, respect for territorial sovereignty is an essential foundation of international relations."[66] Consequently, the ICJ declares that the conduct of either party breached the opponent's territory in some respects

7.2 Areas of emphasis – the contemporary disrespectful conducts

A couple of issues need to be underlined for the sake of emphasis. The issues in question point to how restrictive construction has inadvertently undermined peace and security. We shall narrow it down to three factors: dysfunctional Security Council, humanitarian interventions and *de minimis* territorial incursions.

7.2.1 Dysfunctional Security Council

Russia annexed Crimea in 2014 while the international community watched in horror because of a dysfunctional Security Council (SC). It could be recalled that part of the reason why the permanent members of the SC have veto powers is for swift and prompt response to threats to international peace and security. It seems that national interests sometimes obscure this function in a way that undermines the legitimacy of the SC. Many factors are to blame but we do not intend to go into details here. However, a pathology conducted on the SC's legitimacy has returned a negative verdict.[67] The areas studied include the effects of its powers on States' territory, the procedural matters and how it has performed over the years. Franck defines legitimacy as "*the perception of those addressed by a rule or a rule-making institution that the rule or institution has come into being and operates in accordance with generally accepted principles of right process.*"[68] How some permanent members use veto powers put "the credibility and legitimacy of the United Nations"[69] at risk. Thus, about 73% of

---

65 John Rawls, *A Theory of Justice* (Oxford, Oxford University Press, 1971) 337.
66 ICJ Reports (1949) pp. 4, 35.
67 Martin Binder and Monika Heupel, "The Legitimacy of the UN Security Council: Evidence from Recent General Assembly Debates" (2015) 59(2) *International Studies Quarterly* 238–250, 239.
68 Franck 1990 (n 56), 19.
69 UNSCOR, UN Doc. S/PV.7564 (20 November 2015), 12 (statement of Mr. Pressman of the United States of America).

Theorising respect for State territory 193

States interviewed concerning the activities of the SC complained about its inefficiency.[70] This has resulted in a call for its reform.[71]

7.2.2 Humanitarian interventions

Arguments on whether or not humanitarian intervention is permissible have been on for decades now. The acclaimed founder of modern international law, Hugo Grotius, permitted it when a State grossly violated the rights of its citizens.[72] It is unlikely Hegel would agree with Grotius because a "people" devoid of a government "is a formless mass."[73] A State is brought into being when the formless mass transforms into an "organic totality."[74] Ideally, disorderliness is not of the essence of a State and cannot be attributed to it. The Social Contract Theory implies this. Even in the real world, a distinction should be made between a State's officials and the State they represent. The Rwandan genocide was committed by some State officials and not by the Republic of Rwanda. It is wrong to attribute the said genocide to the State as such. *Argumentum a contrario,* the advancement of Platonic idealism renders the doctrine of States' responsibility null and void.[75] The International Law Commission adopted draft legislation on the attribution of responsibility to State[76] and judiciary has identified factors which determine attribution.[77]

---

70 Binder and Heupel (n 67), 244; Daniel Bodansky, "The Legitimacy of International Governance: A Coming Challenge for International Environmental Law" (1999) 93 (3) *American Journal of International Law* 596–624, 605, 608.
71 Yehuda Z. Blum, "Proposals for UN Security Council Reform" (2005) 99(3) *The American Journal of International Law* 632–649; UNSCOR, UN Doc. S/PV.7505 (18 August 2015), 24–25.
72 Hugo Grotius, *On the Law of War and Peace (1625),* translated by A. C. Campbell (Kitchener, Batoche Books, 2001) Book 2, Chapter 20, part vii; Hugo Grotius, *The Rights of War and Peace: Including the Law of Nature and of Nations,* translated by A. C. Campbell with an introduction by David J. Hill (London, Walter Dunne, 1901) 227.
73 G. W. F. Hegel, *Philosophy of Right,* translated by S. W. Dyde (Kitchener, Batoche Books, 2001) 227.
74 ibid., 227; Joachim Ritter, "Person and Property in Hegel's Philosophy of Right" in Robert B. Pippin and Otfried Hoffe (eds), *Hegel on Ethics and Politics* (New York, Cambridge University Press, 2004) 116.
75 Hegel 2001 (n 73), 96; G.W.F. Hegel, *Elements of the Philosophy of Right,* edited by Allen W. Wood and translated by H. B. Nisbet (Cambridge, Cambridge University Press, 1991) xiv.
76 International Law Commission, *Draft Articles on Responsibility of States for Internationally Wrongful Acts, with Commentary* (Volume II, Part II, *Yearbook of the International Law Commission,* 2001), art. 4.
77 *Rome Statute of the International Criminal Court* (Done at Rome on 17 July 1998, entered into force on 1 July 2002) 2187 UNTS 90, arts 5–9; *Application of the Convention on the Prevention and Punishment of the Crime of Genocide* (Bosnia & Herzegovina v Serbia & Montenegro) Judgment ICJ Reports (2007) p. 43, para. 169; *The Prosecutor v Radislav Krstic* (Case No. IT-98–33-T) Judgment ICTY (2 August 2001), para. 599.

194 *Theorising respect for State territory*

Nonetheless, protagonists of humanitarian intervention ignore the fact that the two world wars resulted in humanitarian crises. Yet, all the instruments examined so far prohibit unauthorised intervention in the internal affairs of States. While the UN Charter protects human rights and the rights of peoples to self-determination, there is no indication that States can facilitate that without violating international law. Otherwise, the supervisory role of the UN General Assembly and collective enforcement mechanism will be sacrificed on the altar of unilateralism. The law prohibits unilateral intervention unless a State is a victim of an armed attack. Therefore, the collective enforcement mechanism remains an acceptable means to prevent or remove the threat of peace.[78]

Chesterman has put on notice how the incremental interpretation of Article 39 of the UN Charter augmented humanitarian interventions since the post-Cold War era.[79] The international community must weigh carefully the dangers associated with opening the floodgate. Besides, questions have been asked regarding the necessity and proportionality[80] of the so-called humanitarian interventions when the human rights condition of victims to be rescued are worsened by the said intervention.[81] Libya remains a sad example. While the need to intervene might be just,[82] if the evolving concept of the Responsibility to Protect is premised on unilateralism, then the collapse of the UN is imminent.

7.2.3 De minimis *territorial incursions*

Part of the reasons Franck mourns the death of Article 2(4) is because of "the effect of small-scale warfare …"[83] on State territorial sovereignty. It could take the form of State-sponsored "hit-and-run operations by small bands of fighters, sometimes not in uniform and often lightly armed."[84] Visionary States had wanted a broad scope of Article 2(4). Three years after the Charter went into force, the inadequacy of armed attack threshold started manifesting. First, the regime of

---

78 *UN Charter* (n 41), art. 1(1).

79 Simon Chesterman, *Just War or Just Peace? Humanitarian Intervention and International Law* (Oxford, Oxford University Press, 2001) 113; Nicholas J. Wheeler, *Saving Strangers: Humanitarian Intervention in International Society* (Oxford, Oxford University Press, 2000) 172–241.

80 Christine Gray, *International Law and the Use of Force*, Third Edition (New York, Oxford University Press, 2008) 241–252.

81 Ben Chigara, "Humanitarian Intervention Missions: Elementary Considerations, Humanity and the Good Samaritans" (2001) *Australian International Law Journal* 66–89.

82 See generally, Michael Walzer, *Just and Unjust Wars: A Moral Argument with Historical Illustrations*, Fourth Edition (New York, Basic Books, 1977); Michael Walzer, "The Argument about Humanitarian Intervention" (2002) 49(1) *Dissent* 29–36; Michael Walzer, *Thinking Politically: Essays in Political Theory* (New Haven and London, Yale University Press, 2007).

83 Thomas M. Franck, "Who Killed Article 2(4) or: Changing Norms Governing the Use of Force by States" (1970) 64(4) *American Journal of International Law* 809–837, 812.

84 ibid., 812.

Theorising respect for State territory 195

Benes-Masaryk of Czechoslovakia was "overthrown by the internal Communist minority" through the "participation of representatives of the Union of Soviet Socialist Republics."[85] Second, Greece was overrun by the "indigenous Communist insurgents" through the assistance of Yugoslavia.[86] None of the conduct meets Article 2(4)'s threshold because the "support ranges from military supplies and the training of recruits to money and radio propaganda."[87] The pattern has remained the same in the twenty-first century, and in fact, State-sponsored terrorism[88] and State-sponsored cybercrimes are the newest arrivals. It is difficult to identify all the forms and shapes of wrongful conducts or to proscribe and prescribe appropriate punishment for every offence from a broad range of related but dissimilar conducts. In some cases, technicalities in determining the "factual question of who attacked whom" or "of defining the level of foreign intervention which should suffice to permit counter-intervention by way of collective self-defense"[89] render the legal norm impotent. It engenders mistrust which could snowball to a full-blown diplomatic row or inter-State conflicts. Franck could not have put it better when he says "… one has only to have experienced a revolution in Africa or the Middle East to know that an effective, powerful radio transmitter may be worth more than its weight in grenades and pistols."[90] While it might be utopic to envisage a world free of rancour and distrust, legal norms should aim at ideals to guarantee the basic minimum threshold.

7.2.4 A distress call

Another area to comment on is how to interpret a distress call from a State fighting insurgents. The assistance which Russia gave to Ukraine in the wake of the political crisis that erupted in 2013 and Russia's assistance to Assad's regime in Syria are two recent incidents.[91] Concerning Ukraine, Russia responded to a distress call from a colleague in line with a treaty regime.[92] But the question of timing and the eventual reunification of Crimea with the Russian Federation questions whether the assistance was altruistic *ab initio*. Russia seems to have

---

85 ibid., 812–813.
86 ibid., 813.
87 ibid.
88 U.S. Department of State, "State Sponsors of Terrorism," available at <www.state.gov/state-sponsors-of-terrorism/> accessed 1 October 2019; UNSCOR UN Doc. S/PV.7351 (19 December 2014), 38 (statement of the Syrian Arab Republic, Mr. Ja'afari in the Security Council).
89 Franck 1970 (n 83), 814.
90 ibid.
91 For further analysis, see Tom Ruys, "Of Arms, Funding and 'Non-lethal Assistance' – Issues surrounding Third-State Intervention in the Syrian Civil War" (2014) 13 *Chinese Journal of International Law* 15–53.
92 Partition Treaty on the Status and Conditions of the Black Sea Fleet signed between Russia and Ukraine on 28 May 1997 permits Russia to lawfully maintain up to 25,000 troops, 24 artillery systems, 132 armoured vehicles and 22 military planes on the Crimean Peninsula.

196 *Theorising respect for State territory*

benefited from the dismemberment of Ukraine. Whether a State territory could be modified other than through an agreement remains unanswered. Besides, it leaves one wondering whether international law allows States to facilitate self-determination of peoples without that of itself constituting intervention in the internal affairs of another State. Probably not, although Russia cited Kosovo as a precedent.

When Syria's crisis of 2011 escalated, about 12 draft resolutions that could have allowed the SC to take collective measures in Syria did not pass because they were either vetoed by Russia, sometimes with China.[93] Moreover, Mr Churkin indicts "some influential members of the international community" for undermining "any possibility of a political settlement, calling for regime change, encouraging the opposition towards power, indulging in provocation and nurturing the armed struggle."[94] About a year later, President Vladimir Putin of Russia warned against any military intervention in Syria without the SC's authorisation. He alleged that internal conflict was "fuelled by foreign weapons supplied to the opposition."[95] He sternly warned against the possible collapse of the UN because of States' hypocritical attitude towards international law.[96]

Under modern international law, every assistance can be given only to States and not non-State actors, unless they have attained the status of belligerent.[97] Additionally, the non-State actors should have effective control over the territory they occupy and the conflict must have reached a certain degree of intensity and duration.[98] Unfortunately, State practice is unclear when these conditions are met.[99] Consequently, assessments as to when non-State actors are entitled to receive assistance are made by States. One cannot rule out that national interests might influence the decision-making process. The asymmetrical support witnessed in Syria calls for a rethink of where lies the balance between the law and State practice. One wonders whether the internal crisis in Syria would not have been resolved long ago but for the assistance received from various quarters by parties to the conflict. To maintain that States are sole beneficiaries of

---

93 They are: UN Docs. S/2012/538 (19 July 2012); S/2016/846 (8 October 2016); S/2016/1026 (5 December 2016); S/2017/172 (28 February 2017); S/2017/315 (12 April 2017); S/2017/962 (16 November 2017); S/2017/970 (17 November 2017); S/2018/321 (10 April 2018); S/2019/756 (19 September 2019).

94 UN Doc. S/PV.6711 (4 February 2012) 9.

95 Vladimir V. Putin, "A Plea for Caution from Russia: What Putin Has to Say to Americans About Syria" (*The New York Times*, 11 September 2013) available at <www.nytimes.com/2013/09/12/opinion/putin-plea-for-caution-from-russia-on-syria.html> accessed 10 May 2020.

96 *Address by President of the Russian Federation* (The Kremlin Moscow, 18 March 2014), available at: <http://eng.kremlin.ru/news/6889> accessed 5 October 2019.

97 Andrew Clapham, *Human Rights Obligations of Non-State Actors* (New York, Oxford University Press, 2006) 271.

98 Antonio Cassese, *International Law in a Divided World* (New York, Oxford University Press, 1986) 81.

99 ibid., 82. For the list of the conditions, see Rosalyn Higgins, "International Law and Civil Conflict" in Evan Luard (ed.), *The International Regulation of Civil Wars* (London, Thames and Hudson, 1972) 170–171.

external assistance could open a Pandora's box. For instance, it could trigger a debate concerning legitimacy of a government engulfed in political crisis or the question of justice and fairness[100] if agitators pursue the right to self-determination or other fundamental human rights. While Russia claims it enhanced its military presence in Ukraine at the request of the ousted President Yanukovych, the opposition questions the legitimacy of the said government at the material time. It seems that respect of State territory would require unbiased objective assessment and authorisation by the SC. The formation of camps based on political and economic affiliations will not enhance international peace and security.[101]

7.3 Respect as the foundation of world peace

An attempt to construe Article 2(4) broadly finds expression in the *Universal Declaration of Human Rights*. Paragraph 1 of the preamble provides as follows: "whereas recognition of the inherent dignity and of the equal and inalienable rights of all members of the human family is the foundation of freedom, justice and peace in the world."[102] The concept of "family" has an exciting history from antiquity and in the history of private law in Europe. Initially, it refers to persons related by blood (*consanguinity*) but later a social institution. In the latter, the *paterfamilias* was the head of a family which comprised himself, his wife, their children and in some cases, their children's families and their slaves. Thus, the idea of household (*haus, huis*) developed in the late Middle Ages. According to Aristotle, States come into existence "when several villages are united in a single complete community..., originating in the bare needs of life; and continuing in the existence for the sake of a good life."[103] Therefore, the expression "all members of the human family" points to States' obligation of custodianship. This principle was domesticated in the 1949 *Basic Law for the Federal Republic of Germany* (*Grundgesetz für die Bundesrepublik Deutschland*). Article 1 imposes upon States the duty "to respect and protect" human dignity.[104] This narrative is changing in lieu of the contemporary debates surrounding human rights protection, crime against humanity, responsibility to protect, universal jurisdiction and the vague concept of globalisation. The UN is not aiming at a global system of democratic governance since territorial States remain the fulcrum of State relations.

100 Fairness requires everyone in the social chain to do his or her part. See Rawls (n 65), 342.
101 UNSCOR, UN Doc. S/PV.7915 (5 April 2017), 6 (the representative of the Plurinational State of Bolivia calls for unity so that the council chamber is not used as a sounding board for war propaganda); see generally, UNSCOR, UN Doc. S/PV.7922 (12 April 2017).
102 UNGA Res. A/RES/217A (III) (10 December 1948), preamble para. 1.
103 B. Jowett, "Politics" in Jonathan Barnes (ed.), *The Complete Works of Aristotle – The Revised Oxford Translation* (Princeton, Princeton University Press, 1984) Book I, para. 1252^{b}1.
104 Deutscher Bundestag, *Grundgesetz für die Bundesrepublik Deutschland* (23 May 1949), art. 1(1), it states: "*Die Würde des Menschen ist unantastbar. Sie zu achten und zu schützen ist Verpflichtung aller staatlichen Gewalt*," available at <www.bundestag.de/gg> accessed 4 October 2019.

198 *Theorising respect for State territory*

7.3.1 Respect, question of indeterminacy and the limit to respect

Respect, when viewed as *timé*, creates a problem of indeterminacy because of its uncountable nature. For instance, the degree of approximation of words like honour, value and reverence vary according to the receiver's perception. This kind of analysis relates to *"appraisal-respect"* that measures quality or functionality instead of the quiddity of the object.[105] In such circumstances, persons (in our case States) are reckoned as objects of respect if they possess distinguishable quality. This means that respect is earned and not an innate right attributable to all. It seems *appraisal respect* is a second category of respect and can be lost or restricted. For instance, no State is obliged to enter into diplomatic relations with its neighbour if it chooses otherwise. Yet, *recognition respect* does not diminish *appraisal respect* since the latter is premised on value earned through capacity building. The fluctuation associated with earned respect does not go to the heart of sovereign equality of States. Even when a case of dissolution is established, the constitutive parts attain sovereign equality status through a process. So, respect earned through obedience to the law can be lost through disobedience. Recognition respect applies even to failed States. Separate opinions of some judges of the ICJ in *Armed Activities (DRC v Uganda)* affirm, although hesitantly, that an inherent right of self-defence is permissible for a State that is a victim of an armed attack from a failed State.[106]

7.4 The concept of inviolability

Leonid Brezhnev, a former General Secretary of the Communist Party of the Soviet Union, was first to say that inviolability of frontiers is a condition for lasting peace in Europe.[107] In 2012, the Organisation for Security and Co-operation in Europe's Ministerial Council held a meeting in Dublin. Part of its agenda was to review the growing concerns regarding State parties' commitment to full implementation of the principles enunciated in the Helsinki Final Act.[108] The principles that relate to State territory include the following: "(I) Sovereign equality, respect for the rights inherent in sovereignty; (II) Refraining from the threat or use of force; (III) Inviolability of Frontiers; (IV) Territorial integrity of States and (VIII) Equal rights and Self-determination of Peoples."[109] Sadigbayli's article provides a link that connects all the principles that relate to State territory together. For instance, while some writers X-ray the

---

105 Bird (n 3), 219.
106 ICJ Reports (2005) p. 168, 314 (Judge Kooijmans), 337 (Judge Simma).
107 A. Movchan, "Problems of Boundaries and Security in the Helsinki Declaration" in *Recueil Des Cours: Collected Courses of the Hague Academy of International Law*, Volume I (Alphen aan den Rijn, Sijthoff & Noordhoff, 1978) 14.
108 OSCE, "Decision on the OSCE Helsinki+40 Process" (Dublin, 7 December 2012), preamble para. 1, available at <www.osce.org/mc/97974> accessed 6 October 2019.
109 Rovshan Sadigbayli, "Codification of the Inviolability of Frontiers Principle in the Helsinki Final Act: Its Purpose and Implications for Conflict Resolution" (2013) 24 *Security and Human Rights* 392–417, 393 (footnote number 6).

theoretical contradiction within the Final Act, specifically between the principles of territorial integrity and self-determination … others argue that territorial integrity does not mean the inviolability of borders, thus juxtaposing the foundational legal norm of territorial integrity and the consequential principle designed to protect this very norm.[110]

We shall not engage in this perennial debate but shall attempt to decode what the drafters meant when they penned down inviolability of frontiers. In doing this, we heed Sadigbayli's advice that the Helsinki Final Act must not be interpreted in a manner that contradicts the "existing doctrine of international law" or defeats "the logic and purpose of the Final Act" itself.[111]

7.4.1 The origins – Helsinki Final Act

A proper interpretation of any legal document should begin with the context accessible through *travaux préparatoires*, diplomatic correspondence and other relevant acts of government on the subject matter. The Helsinki Final Act was conceived against the backdrop of antagonism between the Western European countries and the Socialist countries after two centuries of wars.[112] The purpose was to prevent "future conflicts emanating from violent attempts to redraw borders. They recognized the stability of frontiers without exceptions and reservations as a basic prerequisite for the lasting peace in Europe."[113] Nonetheless, political considerations influenced the legal status of the Helsinki Final Act in two aspects. First, it was a non-binding document[114] and second, it "recognized the Soviet annexation of Estonia, Latvia, and Lithuania and acquiesced to Soviet domination of Eastern Europe."[115] *Prima facie*, this defeats any supposition that it immortalizes the principle of respect of the inviolability of frontiers. Yet, none of the State parties questioned the implied obligations under international law. Instead, they avoided committing themselves to accept that borders could not be altered under any circumstances.[116] It must be noted that the first draft sets out ten principles (what was later known as the Decalogue). Sovereign equality, refraining from the threat or use of force and inviolability of frontiers were the top three.[117] The Soviet negotiators had wanted the Final Act to be legally binding and to prioritise the principles in a way that "would place the inviolability of frontiers and

110 ibid., 394.
111 ibid.
112 ibid., 396.
113 ibid., 396–397; Sarah B. Snyder, *Human Rights Activism and the End of the Cold War: A Transnational History of the Helsinki Network* (Cambridge, Cambridge University Press, 2011) 15–37.
114 Sadigbayli (n 109), 397.
115 Sarah B. Snyder, "'Jerry, Don't Go': Domestic Opposition to the 1975 Helsinki Final Act" (2010) 44(1) *Journal of American Studies* 67–81, 68.
116 Sadigbayli (n 109), 398.
117 Angela Romano, *From Détente in Europe to European Détente: How the West Shaped the Helsinki CSCE* (Brussels, P.I.E Peter Lang, 2009) 37–38.

200 *Theorising respect for State territory*

territorial integrity at the top."[118] The West wanted to explore "the human dimension in the international relations" as well as "the delegitimization of the Brezhnev doctrine."[119] Therefore, the Helsinki Final Act must be construed in light of those interests.

7.4.2 Making sense of the principle of inviolability of frontiers

While the principles were debated, one of the issues that arose was the question of legal legitimacy. The question concerning historical antecedent was raised and in response to which it was said that the UN Charter was the source.[120] Therefore, those principles which were not explicit in the Charter must be legitimised through legal adoption. This is the fate of the inviolability of frontiers. Neither the phrase "inviolability of frontiers" nor the word "inviolability" appeared in the UN Charter. It may have been derived either from a norm codified in the Charter or from an Article that serves the same or similar objectives. One cannot but believe that principles I–IV of the Helsinki Final Act cover a broad range of State conducts. A syllogism might be put up as follows: since States are sovereign equals, they must refrain from the threat or use of force and must respect the inviolability of their frontiers for peaceful coexistence. The text of principle II, particularly the first paragraph is substantially the same as Article 2(4) of the UN Charter.

Additionally, the "Final Recommendations of the Helsinki Consultations" mandated the drafting committee to "take into account in particular the Declaration on Principles of International Law concerning Friendly Relations and Cooperation among States in accordance with the Charter of the United Nations."[121] Opposing views notwithstanding, "the Final Act reaffirms the obligations of States under international law through reaffirming these principles and referencing the purposes and principles of the U.N. Charter."[122] Moreover, it drew States' attention to "… those obligations arising from the generally recognised principles and rules of international law and those obligations arising from treaties or other agreements, in conformity with international law, to which they are parties."[123] The European States understood other agreements as referring to vast peace agreements concluded before the Helsinki Final Act. For instance, "the

---

118 ibid., 38.
119 ibid.
120 Sadigbayli (n 109), 398.
121 OSCE, "Stage I of the CSCE – Final Recommendations of the Helsinki Consultations Adopted" (3 July – 7 July 1973), Title 2 (1)(20), available at <www.osce.org/event/mc_1973> accessed 7 October 2019.
122 Sadigbayli observes that the Declaration on Principles of International Law concerning Friendly Relations and Co-operation among States in accordance with the Charter of the United Nations was not referred to in the preamble because of the opposition against it as a source. See Sadigbayli (n 109), 399.
123 *Conference on Security and Co-operation in Europe Final Act* (Signed at Helsinki on 1 August 1975) (1975) 73(1888) *Department of State Bulletin* 323–350, principle 10, [hereinafter *Helsinki Final Act 1975*].

1972 Prague Declaration on Peace, Security, and Co-operation in Europe" defined the inviolability of frontiers as follows:

> The borders now existing between the European States, including those which have taken shape as a result of the Second World War, are inviolable. Any attempts to violate them would jeopardise European peace. That is why the inviolability of the existing borders, the territorial integrity of the States of Europe must continue to be strictly observed, and territorial claims of one State against another must be completely ruled out.[124]

Although this definition is vague in terms of content, it does show that States accept to be bound by the principle of inviolability of frontiers.

7.5 The nexus between inviolability of frontiers and Article 2(4) of the UN Charter

When the principle of inviolability of frontiers was adopted, the general feeling in Europe was, and still is, that it is "an indispensable condition (*conditio sine qua non*) for peace, security and co-operation in Europe."[125] This understanding was anchored on the intent to build a postwar world where inviolability of State territory must be respected "irrespective of the legal status."[126] The goal is laudable since any attempt to redress a wrong might jeopardise international peace and security. Lauri Hannikainen makes a connection between the principles we find in the Helsinki Final Act and those on the *Declaration on Principles of International Law Concerning Friendly Relations and Co-operation Among States in Accordance with the Charter of the United Nations*. The latter contains seven principles. The three missing principles are "respect for human rights ... inviolably of borders and territorial integrity of States."[127] Hannikainen further argues that the omission of respect for human rights is based on the fact that it is well established in international law like the UDHR. The last two principles were "included into the principle of prohibition of the threat or use of force."[128]

This argument seems plausible, although strong critiques will object since the Declaration on Friendly Relations was mentioned in the preamble of the Helsinki Final Act. As earlier noted, the "Final Recommendations of the Helsinki Consultations" mandated the drafting committee to take that into account. We had argued in previous chapters that States that participated in the drafting of the UN Charter and the Declaration on Friendly Relations had seriously objected to any form of intervention in the internal affairs of States. For the first time, the Helsinki

124 Movchan (n 107), 14.
125 ibid., 18.
126 Sadigbayli (n 109), 400.
127 Lauri Hannikainen, "The Declaration of Principles Guiding Relations Between States of the European Security Conference from the Viewpoint of International Law" (1976) 6(3) *Instant Research on Peace and Violence* 93–101, 94.
128 ibid.

202 *Theorising respect for State territory*

Final Act disentangles various limbs of Article 2(4) to stand independently as substantive rights.[129] Although hard critics would argue that the word "assaulting" implies force, a broad interpretation is persuasive insofar as the threat or use of force is treated separately. The Russian text reads "*posegat* which is the equivalent of refraining from encroaching on frontiers."[130]

7.5.1 The content

Principle III of the Helsinki Final Act provides as follows:

> The participating States regard as inviolable all one another's frontiers as well as the frontiers of all States in Europe and therefore they will refrain now and in the future from assaulting these frontiers.
>
> Accordingly, they will also refrain from any demand for, or act of, seizure and usurpation of part or all of the territory of any participating State.[131]

According to Movchan, this principle encapsulates the determination of the European States to prevent another world war.[132] Although the Helsinki Final Act is a regional instrument, we find similar construction in legal documents from other regions,[133] some of which are either contemporaneous with the UN Charter or predate the Helsinki Final Act. Therefore, the Helsinki Final Act is used for a pilot analysis in the belief that the reasoning could have universal appeal. It is noteworthy that principle III decrees that States territories are inviolable. The participating States are not limited to Europe, but include the United States of America and Canada. In simple terms, it prohibits both direct and indirect use of military force and non-military coercion in a manner that undermines the territorial integrity of a State.[134] As Movchan put it, the participating States undertake to "scrupulously" respect others' frontiers "irrespective of their political, economic or social systems as well as of their size, geographical location or level of economic development."[135]

---

129 Movchan (n 107), 15.
130 Harold S. Russell, "The Helsinki Declaration: Brobdingnag or Lilliput?" (1976) 70(2) *The American Journal of International Law* 242–272, 251.
131 *Helsinki Final Act 1975* (n 123), principle III.
132 Movchan (n 107), 18.
133 Inter-American Conference on War and Peace, *Act of Chapultepec* (Concluded at Mexico on 3 March 1945) (1945) 12(297) *Department of State Bulletin* 339–340, 340, part 1, third declaration; *Charter of the Organization of American States* (Signed at Bogotá on 30 April 1948, entered into force on 13 December 1951) 119 UNTS 3, arts 17, 24 and 25; *Charter of the Organisation of African Unity* (Done at Addis Ababa on 25 May 1963, entered into force on 13 September 1963) 479 UNTS 39, art. 3; Organisation of African Unity, *Constitutive Act of the African Union* (Adopted on 11 July 2000, entered into force on 26 May 2001) 2158 UNTS 3, art. 4(b); League of Arab States, *Charter of Arab League* (Done at Cairo on 22 March 1945, entered into force on 10 May 1945) 70 UNTS 248, art. 5 (although not expressed).
134 Sadigbayli (n 109), 402–403.
135 Movchan (n 107), 20.

Theorising respect for State territory 203

7.5.2 Some deductions from status of diplomatic missions

Another area to point out very briefly is extraterritorial sovereignty. Unsurprisingly, inviolability is a language adopted in the *Vienna Convention on Diplomatic and Consular Relations* in connection with the status of diplomats, diplomatic premises, properties, documents, bags and communications.[136] These documents are designed to prevent host States from interfering in the activities of a foreign State domiciled within their geographical territory. The inviolability status accorded to diplomatic missions and consulates is granted to States they represent based on sovereign equality and in accordance with recognition respect. This principle has been effective because of the political will on the part of State parties to enforce it. But most importantly because of the mutual benefit and mutual respect. Otherwise, nothing stops States that are militarily and economically strong from violating the diplomatic mission of other States within their land. Instead, States provide adequate security for diplomatic missions within their territory. Hence, it is immaterial that a State is strong or weak, rich or poor, developed or undeveloped and so forth. The failure to respect State sovereignty affects diplomatic relations. States recall their diplomats, or they may be expelled as witnessed in 2016 when the US expelled some Russian diplomats from its soil over the alleged Russian interference in the United States' elections.

In the *United States Diplomatic and Consular Staff in Tehran*,[137] the ICJ held that "the obligation of a receiving State to protect the inviolability of the archives and documents of a diplomatic mission ..." applies "at any time and whenever they may be." Receiving States are obliged to "accord full facilities for the performance of the functions of the mission" and "to ensure to all members of the mission freedom of movement and travel in its territory."[138] The ICJ found that Iran defaulted in its "obligations under general international law" for not taking "appropriate steps to protect the premises, staff and archives of the United States' mission against attack by the militants, and to take any steps either to prevent this attack or to stop it before it reached its completion."[139]

The inviolability of diplomatic missions provides a legal template for State relations that should be explored for mutual respect based on the principle of sovereign equality of States. According to Crawford, diplomacy "relates to communication friendly or hostile, rather than the material forms of economic or military conflict."[140] One might add, truthful communication enhances diplomacy. The need to respect diplomatic mission is borne out "long-established state

---

136 *Vienna Convention on Diplomatic Relations* (Done at Vienna on 18 April 1961, entered into force on 24 April 1964) 500 UNTS 95, arts 22, 24, 27, 29, 30, 31(3), 38 and 40; *Vienna Convention on Consular Relations* (Done at Vienna on 24 April 1963, entered into force on 19 March 1967) 596 UNTS 261, arts 31–36, 41, 54(3), 61, 71.

137 Judgment ICJ Reports (1980) p. 3, para. 62.

138 ibid.

139 ibid., para. 63.

140 James Crawford, *Brownlie's Principles of Public International Law*, Eighth Edition (Oxford, Oxford University Press, 2012) 395.

204 *Theorising respect for State territory*

practice reflected in treaties, national legislation, and judicial decisions."[141] Crawford hinted that the theory supporting extraterritorial sovereignty is unsustainable but its "functional model" is premised on mutual recognition of "sovereign and independent status"[142] of States. Even when "a defence of necessity or *force majeure*" is invoked, host States may call for a reinforcement.[143] Unfortunately, the backlash to inviolability of diplomatic missions and consular area is that States could take advantage of it to commit crimes against other States. This lacuna could be addressed through diplomatic channels.[144]

7.6 Sovereign equality of States – applied natural law

At this stage, it is proper to examine what sovereign equality meant for States in 1945 when the UN Charter was adopted. Chapter 2 reviewed some theories of territory to justify why States exercise sovereignty over a definite portion of the earth designated as territory. In Chapter 3, we saw by studying the *travaux préparatoires* that weaker States were reassured that the UN Charter was founded on the principle of sovereign equality of States. This section seeks to analyse what that means through the prism of natural law. The aim is to show that respect for formal equality will enhance international peace and security.

7.6.1 Natural law reasoning method

The development of natural law theory and how it relates to international law is beyond the scope of this work.[145] We shall rather abstract and apply natural law reasoning to the principle of sovereign equality of States. Worthy of note, at the outset, is that natural law is not confined to antiquity as some thinkers would believe, it is equally the foundation on which Grotius built his thoughts. Its legacies are found in the works of modern authors. A contemporary natural law theorist, John Finnis refers to it as "natural law tradition."[146] The reasoning method is the seal uniting the various strands of this tradition. In the philosophy of law, natural law tradition grapples with, *inter alia*, "how an understanding of law presupposes a practical understanding ... of community, justice and rights, and authority – as reasons for choice and action."[147] Equally, it studies "how positive laws are derived from natural law (moral principles) in at least two radically different ways."[148] For

---

141 ibid., 395.
142 ibid., 397.
143 ibid., 403.
144 Adaoye A. Akinsanya, "Reflections on the Inviolability of Diplomatic Premises and Diplomatic Bags" (1989) 42(3/4) *Pakistan Horizon* 98–120, 112–113.
145 For a discussion on four contemporary natural law theories see Whang Shang Ying, "Four Contemporary Natural Law Theories" (1990) 32(2) *Malaya Law Review* 254–270.
146 John Finnis, "The 'Natural Law Tradition'" (1986) 36(4) *Journal of Legal Education* 492–495, 492.
147 ibid.
148 ibid.

Theorising respect for State territory 205

instance, there is a view that international law is not a positive law as conceived by Austin but "is founded on the common consent as well as the common sense of the world."[149] Therefore, its benchmark is a reasonable value judgment. Faced with the absurdity of wars, Grotius had backed up his arguments by allegiance to the law of nature. At one instance, he wrote:

> I have used in favour of this law, the testimony of philosophers, historians, poets, and even of orators: not that they are indiscriminately to be relied on as impartial authority; ... but because where many minds of different ages and countries concur in the same sentiment, it must be referred to some general cause ... this cause must be either a just deduction from the principle of natural justice, or universal consent.[150]

We cannot, therefore, dismiss as mere hallucination the debate that went on during the drafting of the UN Charter in which States upheld sovereign equality of States. The same argument applies to the haggle that went on during the drafting of the General Assembly Resolution 2625 (XXV). Besides, the inviolability of State territory as expressly codified in various regional documents and the *Vienna Conventions on Diplomatic and Consular Relations* is premised on the notion of sovereign equality of States. When the opening statement of the UN Charter starts with "we the peoples of the United Nations determined to save succeeding generations from the scourge of war ...," it is a statement of fact based on a "universally valid legal and moral principles *that* can be inferred from nature."[151] Legal jurisprudence does not shy away from tackling questions concerning human nature[152] and Gottmann argues that territorial sovereignty is inseparable "from a definite human will and purpose."[153] We must think outside the box to realise this noble objective.

7.6.2 Natural law or natural right?[154]

A distinction needs to be made between natural law and natural rights before we link them up with States. Both concepts have something in common because they

149 Philip Marshall Brown, "The Theory of the Independence and Equality of States" (1915) 9(2) *The American Journal of International Law* 305–335, 307. Cf Ying (n 145), 260 (holding a contrary view).
150 As quoted in Henry Wheaton, *Elements of International Law: With a Sketch of the History of the Science* (Philadelphia, Carey, Lea & Blanchard, 1836) 37.
151 R. D. Schwarz, "Natural Law" in Neil J. Smelser and Paul B. Baltes (ed.), *International Encyclopedia of the Social & Behavioral Sciences* (New York, Elsevier, 2001) 10388–10392 (emphasis mine).
152 Jeffrey A. Pojanowski, "Redrawing the Dividing Lines Between Natural Law and Positivism(s)" (2015) 101(4) *Virginia Law Review* 1023–1027, 1024.
153 Jean Gottmann, *The Significance of Territory* (Charlottesville, University Press of Virginia, 1973) 5.
154 This title is derived from John Finnis book, *Natural Law and Natural Rights* published by Oxford University Press in 1980. The book has been described as the "the

206 *Theorising respect for State territory*

refer to some innate qualities, values or potentialities accessible through reason. Yet, they differ significantly in that both are not the same thing. The concept of "natural" means that "these laws and rights could be known by human reason independently of revelation."[155] There is some moral imperatives. Derivatively, positivists subscribe to sanction as a factor inducing compliance. Yet within the natural law family, the belief is that there is an internal inducing agent which Murphy calls "a positive internal claim between law and decisive reasons for action."[156] The positivists' assumption that morality and law never meet even when there is no external sovereign law-giver is unsustainable. Moral imperative implies that an inducing element is innate in all human beings. Hence, Thomas Aquinas defines natural law as "... *praeceptum legis naturae* ..."[157] The suffix "law" connotes "what ought to be done and what ought not to be done through freely chosen human actions."[158] The "oughtness" manifests what Hart describes as the belief that things follow a certain pattern.[159] States exhibit similar behaviour when they invoke the principle of self-preservation. Therefore, natural law identifies "the characteristic *reasons* people have for acting in the ways which go to constitute distinctive social phenomena (such as law)."[160] A State that responds aggressively to external breach of its territory might do so because of the internalised notion that sovereign equality imposes a certain pattern of behaviour upon States; hence, the idea of natural right.

The Gratian work, *Tractatus de legibus* uses *ius* and *lex* as synonyms to show that "rights" can be derived from natural law; "*ius naturae est, quod in lege et euangelio continetur.*"[161] The debate on whether "law" and "right" are synonymous is beyond our scope.[162] Gratian could also mean that *ius naturale* is part of what canon lawyers later classified as "*jus positivum.*" But since the idea of positive law came much later, Gratian had argued that natural law imposed obligations upon all to treat others fairly and justly. To that end, it is a right which nature bequeaths to all human beings. Vattel equates natural rights of human beings with sovereign rights of States as follows:

> most significant and influential book on natural law ever written in English," see Santiago Legarre, "HLA Hart and the Making of the New Natural Law Theory" (2017) 8(1) *Jurisprudence* 82–98, 92.

155 Thomas Mautner, "Natural Law and Natural Rights" in Peter R. Anstey (ed.), *The Oxford Handbook of British Philosophy in the Seventeenth Century* (Oxford, Oxford University Press, 2018) 472–497, 472.

156 Mark C. Murphy, *Natural Law in Jurisprudence and Politics* (Cambridge, Cambridge University Press, 2006) 1.

157 Quoted in Denis J. M. Bradley, *Aquinas on the Twofold Human Good* (Washington D.C., The Catholic University of America, 1997) 259.

158 ibid.

159 H. L. A. Hart, *The Concept of Law* (Oxford, Oxford University Press, 1961) 187.

160 Finnis (n 146), 493.

161 Kenneth Pennington, "*Lex Naturalis* and *Ius Naturale*" (2008) 68(2) *The Jurist* 569–591, 570 (see footnote number 2).

162 For an analysis see Peter Westen, "The Empty Idea of Equality" (1982) 95(3) *Harvard Law Review* 537–596.

Since men are naturally equal, and a perfect equality prevails in their individual rights and obligations, as equally proceeding from nature – Nations composed of men, and considered as so many free persons living together in a state of nature, are naturally equal, and inherit from nature the same obligations and rights. Power or weakness does not in this respect produce any difference. A dwarf is as much a man as a giant; a small republic is no less a sovereign State than the most powerful kingdom.[163]

To connect this with Kantian categorical imperative, actions initiated by a State against another State that it would not accept if done to it cannot be universally acceptable. Such actions are opposed to reason and unjustifiable. Perhaps, this explains why States detest any infringement on their sovereign personality. Otherwise, why would the United States of America invest time and resources to investigate Russia's interference in its political process since no part of its territory was invaded militarily?

7.6.3 Equality as a fundamental right of States

A thought-provoking article on the questions of right and equality with the title "the empty idea of equality" was published by *Harvard Law Review* in 1982 by Peter Westen.[164] The author's revolutionary approach to equality has been adequately responded to.[165] However, we must not gloss over his views that any effort to analyse equality distinctly is "unnecessary" but also "engenders profound conceptual confusion."[166] His conclusion derives from the battle for supremacy between right and equality over a period of time. Thus, Westen recommends that equality "be banished from moral and legal discourse ..."[167] However, we find Chemerinsky's rejoinder to Westen's criticisms persuasive.[168] Aristotle offers a working definition of equality according to which "things that are alike should be treated alike, while things that are unalike should be treated unalike in proportion to their unalikeness."[169] Although "alike" is not "sameness" such that equality accommodates dissimilarities in treatment,[170] equality is often articulated in terms

---

163 Emer de Vattel, *The Law of Nations, or the Principles of Natural Law Applied to the Conduct and Affairs of Nations and Sovereigns*, Sixth American Edition from a new edition by Joseph Chitty (T. Philadelphia & J. W. Johnson, Law Booksellers, 1844) 59, preliminaries § 18.
164 Westen (n 162) 537–596.
165 Christopher J. Peters, "Equality Revisited" (2010) 110(6) *Harvard Law Review* 1210–1264; Erwin Chemerinsky, "In Defense of Equality: A Reply to Professor Westen" (1983) 81(3) *Michigan Law Review* 575–599; Anthony D'Amato, "Is Equality a Totally Empty Idea?" (1983) 81(3) *Michigan Law Review* 600–603; Sheila Foster, "Difference and Equality: A Critical Assessment of the Concept of 'Diversity'" (1993) 1993(1) *Wisconsin Law Review* 105–162.
166 Westen (n 162), 542.
167 ibid.
168 Chemerinsky (n 165), 575–599.
169 Quoted by Westen. See Westen (n 162), 543.
170 Peters (n 165), 1211.

208   *Theorising respect for State territory*

of "moral standard of treatment."[171] If a class is determined, rights and duties apply to those within that category "in regard to the sort of treatment they should receive."[172] Hence, formal equality in the UN Charter's framework requires first the identification of the protected characteristics.

Article 2, paragraph 1, establishes the United Nations on the "principle of the sovereign equality of all its Members."[173] Article 76 safeguards "equal treatment in social, economic, and commercial matters for all Members of the United Nations …"[174] Under the provision of Article 78, the trusteeship system is prohibited for sovereign States. The Dumbarton Oaks Proposals contain as follows: "The Organization is based on the principle of the sovereign equality of all peace-loving states."[175] Committee I/1 underlined "equal rights" of "nations large and small."[176] According to Bolivia, the principle of sovereign equality of States requires that "the inviolability of their territories shall be respected …"[177] It was suggested that "sovereign equality" in the Dumbarton Oaks Proposals be deleted[178] or replaced with juridical equality.[179] The Belgian delegate found it untenable amidst apparent inequalities and moved a motion to have it removed. Uruguay supported the motion and proposed that "juridical equality"[180] be adopted instead. The proposals were rejected.

The representative of Peru, Mr Belaunde at the Opera House on 15 June 1945 during a second meeting of Commission I had argued that the UN should be "constituted in its essence by respect for the personality of the states, with its attributes of sovereignty, political independence, juridical equality, and territorial integrity."[181] Further, Mr Belaunde argued:

> States ought to be respected, not only because they are sovereign and have territory. The elements that ought to be respected in states are not only the political elements embodied in the physical state, and the material element, that is the territory … and the elements of the state most worthy of respect are its cultural values, which are the essence of personality.[182]

To this end, Turkey observes that the consequence of the principle of sovereign equality is that any lawful infringement upon a State territory must be authorised by the General Assembly or the Security Council.[183]

---

171 Kent Greenawalt, "How Empty is the Idea of Equality?" (1983) 83(5) *Columbia Law Review* 1167–1185, 1167.
172 ibid., 1170.
173 *UN Charter* (n 41), art. 2(1).
174 ibid., art. 76.
175 UNCIO, Vol. 3, 3.
176 UNCIO, Vol. 6, 366.
177 UNCIO, Vol. 3, 582.
178 UNCIO, Vol. 6, 304.
179 ibid., 310.
180 ibid., 332.
181 ibid., 66–70.
182 ibid., 67.
183 UNCIO, Vol. 9, 274.

7.6.4 *Moscow Declaration on the sovereign equality model*

The Moscow Declaration conceived a peace model based on sovereign equality of States. Vague as both concepts might appear, they are "two generally recognized characteristics of the States as subjects of international law."[184] Both concepts are intimately linked in that "equality of states is explained as a consequence of or as implied by their sovereignty."[185] As explained earlier, "sovereignty" in the Moscow Declaration means "supreme authority."[186] The legislative history of the UN Charter presumed this knowledge. In fact, delegations at San Francisco Conferences clarified that States' sovereignty could be limited only by international law. Therefore, the UN inaugurated a world order guided by international law based on a system of general security. To the extent that States are "figuratively" subjects of international law, they have relative "supreme authority" and as such are not absolute.[187]

Prima facie, equality means that "States as subjects of international law ... have the same duties and the same rights."[188] This formal interpretation is subject to treaty regime or customary law that could create different rights and duties. For example, "a littoral State ... has other duties and rights than an inland."[189] However, we are concerned with formal equality and not particularities that differentiate States. Hence, no objection is made to a consensual arrangement that gives some States an added advantage in matters relating to the maintenance of peace and security. Moreover, we had earlier commented on *appraisal respect* which acknowledges inequality in functionality and capabilities. In line with international law, equality means that "under the same conditions States have the same duties and the same rights."[190]

As Oppenheim articulated, sovereign equality of States implies four things. First, each State has a right to participate in and vote in political discussions brought before the UN. Second, all votes cast have equal weight. Third, no State can claim jurisdiction over another in criminal or civil matters. Fourth, national laws are enforced within a State territory and no domestic court can question the validity of such laws insofar as such laws are territorially circumscribed.[191] According to Brierly, the doctrine of sovereign equality refers to rights protected by law and

---

184 Hans Kelsen, "The Principle of Sovereign Equality of States as a Basis for International Organization" (1944) 53(2) *The Yale Law Journal* 207–220, 207.
185 ibid., 207.
186 ibid.
187 ibid., 208.
188 ibid.
189 ibid., 209.
190 ibid.
191 Robert Jennings and Arthur Watts (eds), *Oppenheim's International Law*, Ninth Edition (London and New York, Longman, 1996) 339; Herbert Weinschel, "The Doctrine of the Equality of States and Its Recent Modifications" (1951) 45(3) *American Journal of International Law* 417–442, 419; *Nicaragua* case (n 60), paras 59, 70, 202 and 284; *Chae Chan Ping v United States*, Supreme Court of the United States (1888) 130 U.S. 581, 604.

210 *Theorising respect for State territory*

does not mean that all States have equal rights.[192] Lucy approaches the discourse from three perspectives. First, the "presumptive identity" which means that States consent to be bound by the same bundle of formal and legal rights and abilities. Second, the "uniformity identity" under which the judicial interpretation of positive laws must be subject to objective legal standard equally applicable to all. Third, the "limited avoidable element" which admits inequalities that exist in law as admissible exceptions to the general rule.[193] Nevertheless, a lack of uniformity in the application of the principle makes it controversial although Kelsen prefers to call it "equality of capacity for duties and rights."[194]

7.7 Way forward – an agenda for peace

This chapter argues that respect for territory will enhance international peace and security. Perhaps puzzling is that 74 years after the United Nations entered into force, the question of whether its purposes have been achieved remains uncertain. Instead, international peace and security are further threatened by other forms of overt and covert breaches short of the threat or use of force by States. Consequently, the arms race has doubled since the UN Charter entered into force. The political terrain that gave birth to the UN responded to "the realities of power" at play, partly to pacify the "victors of World War II."[195] This affected systematisation required in handling some pertinent issues such as "breaches of the peace; principles of justice and international law; humanitarian concerns; human rights; self-determination of states and peoples …"[196] One area of conflict is that which exists between territorial sovereignty and humanitarian intervention.

A problem of this nature is foreseeable given the multi-worldviews of sovereign States that make up the United Nations. The bigger picture is captured by Higgins' assertion that "excessive 'flexibility' is a recipe for operational uncertainty and non-compliance by the protagonists."[197] Higgins is critical of the use of unauthorised force against a State by regional bodies and other security outfits. It appears that "*pragmatic flexibility*" emboldens narrow construction of Article 2(4) to the detriment of peace and security. As the former UN Secretary-General, Boutros Boutros-Ghali observed, the world is witnessing a "global transition marked by uniquely contradictory trends."[198] Some of the new trends are the liquification of "national boundaries … by

192 J. L. Brierly, *The Law of Nations: An Introduction to the International Law of Peace*, Sixth Edition (Oxford, Clarendon Press, 1963) 131–132.
193 William Lucy, "Equality Under and Before the Law" (2011) 61(3) *The University of Toronto Law Journal* 411–466, 413–414.
194 Kelsen (n 184), 209.
195 John N. Petrie, "Myths and Misconceptions About the United Nations" (1996) 49(1) *Naval War College Review* 74–89, 75–76.
196 ibid., 77.
197 Rosalyn Higgins, "Peace and Security – Achievements and Failures" (1995) 6 *European Journal of International Law* 445–460, 459.
198 Boutros Boutros-Ghali, *An Agenda for Peace: Preventive Diplomacy, Peacemaking and Peace-Keeping* (New York, United Nations, 1992) 5.

Theorising respect for State territory 211

blurred advanced communications and global commerce" as well as "fierce new assertions of nationalism" threatening territorial sovereignty.[199] We live in an era confronted by a storm of terrorism sponsored by States. Thus, physical force has become an irrelevant concept amidst soft forms of intervention that endanger international peace and security. In sum, conventional warfare has become obsolete with the advancement in technology and new methods of warfare – some of which are non-kinetic.

Additionally, international peace and security have degenerated due to changes in demography caused by migration crisis as a result of wars and conflicts or due to natural causes. As of 1992, reported fatalities stood at 20 million with a crippled SC.[200] Boutros-Ghali concludes that "the foundation-stone of this work (peace agenda) is and must remain the State. Respect for its fundamental sovereignty and integrity are crucial to any common international progress."[201]

7.7.1 Merits of respect for the inviolability of State territory

Pertinent reasons abound why respect for the inviolability of State territory is a way forward. Apart from the fact that Article 2(4) does not apply to cyberspace, three other reasons can be adduced. They are conceptual, teleological and practical.

7.7.1.1 Conceptual reason

In the words of Albert Einstein, "peace is not merely the absence of war but the presence of justice, of law, of order – in short, of government."[202] This opinion is credible to the extent that peace for him is not the absence of war. It goes deeper to capture the internal mindset of States and how States' mental processes evaluate self-awareness in relation to other States. History has debunked the myth that peace is achieved through war. The world has witnessed many wars and peace treaties have been concluded, yet international peace and security have not been achieved. Civil unrest, conflicts and wars which in the past calibrated European history are the current experience in Africa and Asia. The mindset needs to change.

However, Einstein campaigned for the UN to be constituted as the world seat of government, which invariably defeats territorial sovereignty. While territorial sovereignty could be retained, peace is achievable if States respect one another. Conceptually, peace promotes the national interest of every State since it is the primary responsibility of any reasonable government. States will likely accept a peace model that enhances that objective. It will be absurd to suggest, even remotely, that States abhor peace. International peace and security must be seen as

---

199 ibid., 6.
200 ibid., 7.
201 ibid., 9 (peace agenda not in the original).
202 Joseph Preston Baratta, *The Politics of World Federation: United Nations, UN Reform, Atomic Control* (Westport and London, Praeger, 2004) 157.

212 *Theorising respect for State territory*

processes that must be built on mutual trust. Since genuine dialogue obtains among equals, States might be prepared to genuinely engage one another if they believe and trust that others will respect their sovereign personality. Otherwise, the pursuit of national interest will continue to undermine the peace agenda. Hence, the language of the Helsinki Declaration considers "inviolability of frontiers" as a "*conditio sine qua non* for peace, security, and co-operation in Europe."[203] Peace is feasible through a proper reorientation of the minds of States, based on mutual trust that others will respect their territorial sovereignty.

7.7.1.2 Teleological reason

The teleological reason is deduced from the purposes for which the United Nations is established. To prevent wars that could bring untold hardships to the human race, conducts capable of breeding distrust must be avoided. Hence, it requires States to rise above minimalistic interpretation of Article 2(4) which often rears its ugly head when States engage in *de minimis* incursions that strain diplomatic channels. A peace agenda must be approached holistically. Therefore, States must accept that most armed conflicts do not start abruptly but develop over time after a series of unpleasant experiences. Diplomatic protest whenever a State territory is breached might result in tension between the parties. It is preferable to initiate a process of reorientation by broadening the scope of Article 2(4). Resistance by States allergic to change is anticipated but it is in the interest of peace that the element of dogmatism in the interpretation of law should be progressively adjusted in a manner that stand the test of time.

7.7.1.3 Practical reason

The third reason to flag up is the practical value of respect. While it is wrong to assume that individuals are naturally prone to respect other people, respect is somehow contagious. If the international community is committed to stopping human rights abuses and humanitarian crises, unilateral covert or overt support of internal armed conflicts by individual States or groups of States cannot be the way forward. It is irrelevant that armed attack threshold is not met to indict a State. The wisdom in adhering to collective measures as provided for in the UN Charter is that it makes for checks and balances in the polity. Unless a case of collusion or complicity is established, adherence to collective measures enhances transparency and objectivity in the process. One wonders whether the civil war in Syria would have dragged on for years if not for the financial and military supports which States give to Assad's government in Syria or to the moderate opposition. Although the ICJ in the *Nicaragua* case holds that financial assistance does not meet the armed attack threshold, it equally never ratifies it as an acceptable conduct.[204] Therefore, States should adopt the principle of neutrality unless the SC has explicitly authorised intervention in the internal affairs of a State.

---

203 Movchan (n 107), 18.
204 *Nicaragua* case (n 60), para. 195.

Bibliography

Books

Andress, Jason and Winterfeld, Steve, *Cyber Warfare: Techniques, Tactics and Tools for Security Practitioners*, Second Edition (Amsterdam, Elsevier, 2014).

Anghie, Antony, *Imperialism, Sovereignty and the Making of International Law* (Cambridge, Cambridge University Press, 2004).

Anstey, Peter R. (ed.), *The Oxford Handbook of British Philosophy in the Seventeenth Century* (Oxford, Oxford University Press, 2018).

Asch, Ronald G., *The Thirty Years War: The Holy Roman Empire and Europe 1618–1648* (London, Macmillan Press, 1997).

Austin, John, *The Province of Jurisprudence Determined*, edited by Wilfred E. Rumble (Cambridge, Cambridge University Press, 1999).

Barlow, John Perry, *A Declaration of the Independence of Cyberspace* (San Francisco, Electronic Frontier Foundation, 1996).

Barnes, Jonathan (ed.), *The Complete Works of Aristotle – The Revised Oxford Translation*, Volumes One and Two (Princeton, Princeton University Press, 1984).

Barnidge, Robert P., *Non-State Actors and Terrorism* (The Hague, T. M. C. Asser Press, 2008).

Baron de Montesquieu, *Reflections on the Causes of the Rise and Fall of the Roman Empire*, Fourth Edition (Glasgow, Robert Urie, 1758).

Baynes, Norman H., *The Political Ideas of St. Augustine's De Civitate Dei* (London, G. Bell and Sons, 1936).

Beiner, Ronald (ed.), *Theorizing Nationalism* (Albany, State University of New York Press, 1999).

Beissinger, Mark R., *Nationalist Mobilization and the Collapse of the Soviet State* (Cambridge, Cambridge University Press, 2002).

Bell, Philip M. H., *The Origins of the Second World War in Europe*, Second Edition (New York, Longman, 1997).

Beneyto, Jose Maria and Corti Varela, Justo (eds), *At the Origins of Modernity: Francisco de Vitoria and the Discovery of International Law* (Cham, Springer, 2017).

Benvenisti, Eyal, *The International Law of Occupation* (Princeton, Princeton University Press, 1993).

Biersteker, Thomas J. and Weber, Cynthia (eds), *State Sovereignty as Social Construct* (Cambridge, Cambridge University Press, 1996).

Bittencourt Neto, Olavo de Oliveira, *Defining the Limits of Outer Space for Regulatory Purposes* (Cham, Springer, 2015).

214 Bibliography

Boutros-Ghali, Boutros, *An Agenda for Peace: Preventive Diplomacy, Peacemaking and Peace-Keeping* (New York, United Nations, 1992).

Bowett, Derek W., *Self-defence in International Law* (Manchester, Manchester University Press, 1958).

Bradley, Denis J. M., *Aquinas on the Twofold Human Good* (Washington D.C., The Catholic University of America, 1997).

Brierly, J. L., *The Law of Nations: An Introduction to the International Law of Peace*, Sixth Edition (Oxford, Clarendon Press, 1963).

Brownlie, Ian, *International Law and the Use of Force by States* (New York, Oxford University Press, 1963).

Brownlie, Ian, *Principles of Public International Law*, Seventh Edition (Oxford, Oxford University Press, 2008).

Bryce, James, *The Holy Roman Empire* (London, Macmillan, 1901).

Bull, Hedley, *The Anarchical Society: A Study of Order in World Politics*, Fourth Edition (New York, Palgrave Macmillan, 2012).

Byman, Daniel *et al.*, *Trends in Outside Support for Insurgent Movements* (Pittsburgh, RAND, 2001) 83–100.

Byman, Daniel, Waxman, Matthew C. and Larson, Eric, *Air Power as a Coercive Instrument* (Washington D.C., Rand Corporation, 1999).

Cassese, Antonio, *Cassese's International Criminal Law*, Third Edition (Oxford, Oxford University Press, 2013).

Cassese, Antonio, *International Law in a Divided World* (New York, Oxford University Press, 1986).

Cassese, Antonio, *International Law*, Second Edition (Oxford, Oxford University Press, 2005).

Cassese, Antonio, *Self-determination of Peoples: A Legal Reappraisal* (Cambridge, Cambridge University Press, 1995).

Cavelty, Myriam D. *et al.* (eds), *Power and Security in the Information Age: Investigating the Role of the State in Cyberspace* (Farnham, Ashgate Publishing, 2007).

Charlesworth, Hilary and Coicaud, Jean-Marc (eds), *Fault Lines of International Legitimacy* (New York, Cambridge University Press, 2010).

Chesterman, Simon, *Just War or Just Peace? Humanitarian Intervention and International Law* (Oxford, Oxford University Press, 2001).

Chigara, Ben, *Legitimacy Deficit in Custom: A Deconstructionist Critique* (Farnham, Ashgate Publishing, 2001).

Choi, Jin-Tai, *Aviation Terrorism: Historical Survey, Perspectives, and Responses* (New York, St Martin's Press, 1994).

Churchill, R. and Lowe, A.V., *The Law of the Sea*, Third Edition (Manchester, Manchester University Press, 1999).

Clapham, Andrew, *Human Rights Obligations of Non-State Actors* (New York, Oxford University Press, 2006).

Clark, Sir George, *The Seventeenth Century*, Second Edition (London, Oxford University Press, 1947)

Cook, Chris and Paxton, John, *European Political Facts of the Twentieth Century*, Fifth Edition (New York, Palgrave, 2001).

Cornell, Svante E., Starr, S. Frederic and Tsereteli, Mamuka, *A Western Strategy for the South Caucasus* (Washington D.C., The Central Asia-Caucasus Institute and Silk Road Studies Program, 2015).

Bibliography 215

Corten, Olivier, *The Law Against War: The Prohibition on the Use of Force in Contemporary International Law* (Oxford and Portland, Hart Publishing, 2010).

Cownie, Fiona, *Legal Academics: Culture and Identities* (Oxford, Hart Publishing, 2004).

Cox, Kevin, *Political Geography: Territory, State and Society* (Oxford, Blackwell, 2002).

Crawford, James, *Brownlie's Principles of Public International Law*, Eighth Edition (Oxford, Oxford University Press, 2012).

Crawford, James, *The Creation of International Law*, Second Edition (New York, Oxford University Press, 2006).

Croxton, Derek, *Westphalia: The Last Christian Peace* (New York, Palgrave Macmillan, 2013).

D'Amato, Anthony, *International Law: Process and Prospect*, Second Edition (New York, Transnational Publishers, 1995).

de Bracton, Henry, *De Legibus et Consuetudinibus Angliae*, Volume II (Londini, Typis Milonis Flesher & Roberti Young, 1640).

de Vattel, Emer, *The Law of Nations, or the Principles of Natural Law Applied to the Conduct and Affairs of Nations and Sovereigns*, Sixth American Edition from a new edition by Joseph Chitty (T. Philadelphia & J. W. Johnson, Law Booksellers, 1844).

de Wet, Erika, *The Chapter VII Powers of the United Nations Security Council* (Oxford, Hart Publishing, 2004).

de Wijze, Stephen *et al.* (eds), *Hillel Steiner and the Anatomy of Justice: Themes and Challenges* (New York, Routledge, 2009).

Derks, Ton and Roymans, Nico (eds), *Ethnic Constructs in Antiquity* (Amsterdam, Amsterdam University Press, 2009).

Dicey, A. V., *Introduction to the Study of the Law of the Constitution* (London, Macmillan, 1959).

Dickinson, Edwin D., *The Equality of States in International Law* (Cambridge, Harvard University Press, 1920).

Dinstein, Yoram, *The International Law of Belligerent Occupation* (Cambridge, Cambridge University Press, 2009).

Dinstein, Yoram, *War Aggression and Self-defence*, Fifth Edition (Cambridge, Cambridge University Press, 2011).

Djeffal, Christian, *Static and Evolutive Treaty Interpretation: A Functional Reconstruction* (Cambridge, Cambridge University Press, 2016).

Dworkin, R. M. (ed.), *The Philosophy of Law* (New York, Oxford University Press, 1977).

Elden, Stuart, *Terror and Territory: The Spatial Extent of Sovereignty* (Minneapolis, University of Minnesota Press, 2009).

Elden, Stuart, *The Birth of Territory* (Chicago and London, The University of Chicago Press, 2013).

Finnemore, Martha, *The Purpose of Intervention: Changing Beliefs About the Use of Force* (Ithaca, Cornell University Press, 2003).

Foucault, Michel, *Sécurité, Territoire, Population: Cours au Collège de France (1977–1978)* (Paris, Gallimard/Seuil, 2004).

Franck, Thomas M., *Recourse to Force: State Action Against Threats and Armed Attack* (Cambridge, Cambridge University Press, 2002).

Franck, Thomas M., *The Power of Legitimacy Among Nations* (New York, Oxford University Press, 1990).

216   Bibliography

Friedman, Wolfgang, *The Changing Structure of International Law* (London, Stevens & Sons, 1964).

Furstenerii, Caesarini, *De Jure Suprematus Ac Legationis Principum Germaniae* (Londini, Passau, 1678).

Gilbert, Felix, *The End of the European Era, 1890 to the Present*, Second Edition (New York and London, Norton, 1984).

Giorgini, Giovanni and Irrera, Elena (eds), *Roots of Respect – A Historic-Philosophical Itinerary* (Berlin, Walter de Gruyter, 2017).

Gold, Andrew S. and Miller, Paul B. (eds), *Philosophical Foundations of Fiduciary Law* (Oxford, Oxford University Press, 2014).

Goodman, Martin, *The Roman World 44 BC – AD 180* (London, Routledge, 1997)

Goodrich, Leland M. and Hambro, Edvard, *Charter of the United Nations: Commentary and Documents* (Boston, World Peace Foundation, 1946).

Goodrich, Leland M., Hambro, Edvard and Simons, Patricia Anne, *Charter of the United Nations: Commentary and Documents*, Third and Revised Edition (New York, Columbia University Press, 1969).

Gottmann, Jean, *The Significance of Territory* (Charlottesville, University Press of Virginia, 1973).

Gray, Christine, *International Law and the Use of Force by State*, Third Edition (Oxford, Oxford University Press, 2008).

Grosby, Steven, *Biblical Ideas of Nationality: Ancient and Modern* (Winona Lake, Eisenbranus, 2002).

Grotius, Hugo, *On the Law of War and Peace (1625)*, translated by A. C. Campbell (Kitchener, Batoche Books, 2001).

Grotius, Hugo, *The Rights of War and Peace: Including the Law of Nature and of Nations*, translated by A. C. Campbell with an Introduction by David J. Hill (Washington D.C. and London, M. Walter Dunne, 1901).

Hall, William Edward, *A Treatise on International Law*, Third Edition (Oxford, Clarendon Press, 1890).

Hannikainen, Lauri, *Peremptory Norms (Jus Cogens) in International Law: Historical Development, Criteria, Present Status* (Helsinki, Finnish Lawyers Publication Co., 1988).

Hansen, Mogens Herman, *Polis and City-State: An Ancient Concept and its Modern Equivalent* (Copenhagen, Munksgaard, 1998).

Hart, H. L. A, *The Concept of Law* (Oxford, Oxford University Press, 1961).

Hart, H. L. A., *The Concept of Law*, Second Edition (Oxford, Oxford University Press, 1994).

Heere, Wybo P. (ed.), *From Government to Governance* (The Hague, T. M. C. Asser Press, 2004) 209–216.

Hegel, G. W. F., *Elements of the Philosophy of Right*, edited by Allen W. Wood and translated by H. B. Nisbet (Cambridge, Cambridge University Press, 1991).

Hegel, G. W. F., *Philosophy of Right*, translated by S. W. Dyde (Kitchener, Batoche Books, 2001).

Heickero, Roland, *Emerging Cyber Threats and Russian Views on Information Warfare and Information Operations* (Stockholm, Swedish Defence Research Agency, 2010).

Henkin, Louis, *How Nations Behave: Law and Foreign Policy*, Second Edition (New York, Columbia University Press, 1968).

Henkin, Louis *et al.* (eds), *Right v. Might: International Law and the Use of Force* (New York and London, Council on Foreign Relations Press, 1989).

Hertslet, Edward, *The Map of Europe by Treaty: Showing the Various Political and Territorial Changes Which Have Taken Place since the General Peace of 1814; With Numerous Maps and Notes*, Volumes 1 & 2 (London, Butterworths, 1875).

Higgins, Rosalyn, *Problems and Process: International Law and How We Use It* (Oxford, Oxford University Press, 1994).

Hinsley, F. H., *Sovereignty*, Second Edition (London, Cambridge University Press, 1986).

Hobbes, Thomas, *Leviathan*, edited by Richard Tuck (Cambridge, Cambridge University Press, 1991).

Hohmann, Jessie and Weller, Marc (eds), *The UN Declaration on the Rights of Indigenous Peoples: A Commentary* (Oxford, Oxford University Press, 2018).

Hollis, Duncan B., *The Oxford Guide to Treaties* (Oxford, Oxford University Press, 2012).

Holsti, Kalevi J., *Peace and War: Armed Conflicts and International Order, 1648–1989* (Cambridge, Cambridge University Press, 1991).

Hudson, John, *Land, Law and Lordship in Anglo-Norman England* (Oxford, Clarendon Press, 1997).

Hurd, Ian, *After Anarchy: Legitimacy and Power in the United Nations Security Council* (Princeton, Princeton University Press, 2007).

International Humanitarian Law Research Initiative, *Commentary on the HPCR Manual on International Law Applicable to Air and Missile Warfare* (Cambridge, Cambridge University Press, 2013).

International Law Commission, *Draft Articles on Responsibility of States for Internationally Wrongful Acts, with Commentary* (Volume II, Part II, *Yearbook of the International Law Commission*, 2001).

Jackson, Nicola, Stevens, John and Pearce, Robert, *Land Law*, Fourth Edition (London, Sweet and Maxwell, 2008).

Janczewski, Lech J. and Colarik, Andrew M. (eds), *Cyber Warfare and Cyber Terrorism* (Hershey and New York, Information Science Reference, 2008).

Jennings, Robert and Watts, Arthur (eds), *Oppenheim's International Law*, Ninth Edition, Volume 1: Peace (London and New York, Longman, 1996).

Jonsson, Christer, Tagil, Sven and Tornqvist, Gunnar, *Organizing European Space* (London, Sage, 2000).

Josselin, Daphne and Wallace, William (eds), *Non-state Actors in World Politics* (New York, Palgrave, 2001).

Kant, Immanuel, *The Metaphysical Principles of Virtue*, translated by James Ellington (Indianapolis, The Bobbs-Merrill, 1964).

Kant, Immanuel, *The Metaphysics of Morals*, translated by M. Gregor (Cambridge, Cambridge University Press, 1991).

Kant, Immanuel, *Groundwork of the Metaphysics of Morals*, translated and edited by Mary Gregor (Cambridge, Cambridge University Press, 1997).

Karoubi, Mohammad Taghi, *Just or Unjust War? International Law and Unilateral Use of Armed Force by States at the Turn of the 20th Century* (Burlington, Ashgate Publishing, 2004).

Klimburg, Alexander (ed.), *National Cyber Security Framework Manual* (Tallinn, NATO CCD COE Publication, 2012).

Klimburg, Alexander and Tirmaa-Klaar, Heli, *Cybersecurity and Cyberpower: Concepts, Conditions and Capabilities for Cooperation for Action within the EU* (Brussels, European Parliament, 2011).

218 Bibliography

Kohen, Marcelo G. (ed.), *Secession: International Law Perspectives* (Cambridge, Cambridge University Press, 2006).

Kolb, Robert, *Peremptory International Law – Jus Cogens: A General Inventory* (Oxford, Hart Publishing, 2015).

Kolers, Avery, *Land, Conflict, and Justice* (Cambridge, Cambridge University Press, 2009).

Korman, Sharon, *The Right of Conquest: The Acquisition of Territory by Force in International Law and Practice* (Oxford, Clarendon Press, 1996).

Krasner, Stephen D., *Sovereignty: Organized Hypocrisy* (Princeton, Princeton University Press, 1999).

Kuijer, Martin, and Wouter, Werner (eds), *Netherlands Yearbook of International Law 2016: The Changing Nature of Territoriality in International Law* (The Hague, Asser Press, 2017).

Langstrom, Tarja, *Transformation in Russia and International Law* (Leiden and Boston, Martinus Nijhoff Publishers, 2003).

Laqueur, Walter, *The Age of Terrorism* (Boston and Toronto, Little, Brown and Company, 1987).

Leese, Matthias and Wittendorp, Stef (eds), *Security/Mobility* (Manchester, Manchester United Press, 2017).

Lehning, Percy B. (ed.), *Theories of Secession* (London, Routledge, 1998).

Leibniz, Gottfried Wilhelm, *Leibniz: Political Writings*, Second Edition (Cambridge, Cambridge University Press, 1988).

Libicki, Martin C., *Conquest in Cyberspace: Natural Security and Information Warfare* (New York, Cambridge University Press, 2007).

Locke, John, *Two Treatises of Government*, edited by P. Laslett (Cambridge, Cambridge University Press, 1988).

Luard, Evan (ed.), *The International Regulation of Civil Wars* (London, Thames and Hudson, 1972).

Malanczuk, Peter, *Akehurst's Modern Introduction to International Law*, Seventh Revised Edition (London and New York, Routledge, 1997).

Maresca, John J., *To Helsinki: The Conference on Security and Cooperation in Europe, 1973–1975* (Durham, Duke University Press, 1985).

McFarlane, Ben *et al.*, *Land Law: Text, Cases and Materials*, Second Edition (Oxford, Oxford University Press, 2012).

Mestrovic, Stjepan G., *The Balkanization of the West* (London, Routledge, 1994).

Millar, Fergus, *Rome, the Greek World and the East*, Volume 2 (Chapel Hill and London, The University of North Carolina Press, 2004).

Miller, David Hunter, *The Drafting of the Covenant* (New York, G. P. Putnams' Sons, 1928).

Moir, Lindsay, *Reappraising the Resort to Force: International Law, Jus Ad Bellum and the War on Terror* (Oxford, Hart Publishing, 2010).

Murray, Williamson and Lacey, Jim (eds), *The Making of Peace: Rulers, States, and the Aftermath of War* (Cambridge, Cambridge University Press, 2009).

O'Connell, Daniel P., *The International Law of the Sea*, Volume 2 (Oxford, Clarendon Press, 1984).

O'Sullivan, Aisling, *Universal Jurisdiction in International Criminal Law: The Debate and the battle for Hegemony* (Abingdon and New York, Routledge, 2017).

Ohmae, Kenichi, *The End of the Nation State: The Rise of Regional Economies* (London, Harper Collins, 1995).

Bibliography   219

Oliver, Roland and Sanderson, G. N. (eds), *The Cambridge History of Africa from 1870 to 1905*, Volume 6 (Cambridge, Cambridge University Press, 1985).

Oppenheim, L., *The League of Nations and its Problems: Three Lectures* (London, Longmans, Green and Co Ltd, 1919).

Oppenheim, L., *International Law: A Treatise*, Seventh Edition (London, Longmans, Green and Co Ltd, 1963).

Orakhelashvili, Alexander, *Peremptory Norms in International Law* (Oxford, Oxford University Press, 2006).

Papastavridis, Efthymios, *The Interception of Vessels on the High Seas: Contemporary Challenges to the Legal Order of the Oceans* (Oxford, Hart Publishing, 2013).

Parry, Clive (ed.), *A British Digest of International Law: Compiled Principally from the Archives of the Foreign Office*, Volume 2b (London, Stevens and Sons, 1967).

Phillipson, Coleman, *The International Law and Custom of Ancient Greece and Rome*, Volume I (London, Macmillan, 1911).

Pippin, Robert B. and Otfried, Hoffe (eds), *Hegel on Ethics and Politics* (New York, Cambridge University Press, 2004).

Plato, *Complete Works*, edited by John M. Cooper (Indianapolis and Cambridge, Hackett Publishing Company, 1997).

Pope Innocent III, *Nobili Viro, Willelmo, Domino Montispessulani. De Legitimatione Liberorum in Patrologia Latina Database*, Volume 214 (Alexandria, Chadwyck-Healey Inc., 1996).

Rawls, John, *A Theory of Justice* (Oxford, Oxford University Press, 1971).

Raz, Joseph, *The Morality of Freedom* (New York, Oxford University Press, 1986).

Reus-Smit, Christian (ed.), *The Politics of International Law* (Cambridge, Cambridge University Press, 2004).

Renehan, Edward J., *The Monroe Doctrine: The Cornerstone of American Foreign Policy* (New York, Infobase Publishing, 2007).

Reveron, Derek S. (ed.), *Cyberspace and National Security: Threats, Opportunity, and Power in a Virtual World* (Washington D.C., Georgetown University Press, 2012).

Romano, Angela, *From Détente in Europe to European Détente: How the West Shaped the Helsinki CSCE* (Brussels, P.I.E Peter Lang, 2009).

Rosenzweig, Paul, *Cyber Warfare: How Conflicts in Cyberspace are Challenging America and Changing the World* (Santa Barbara, Praeger, 2013).

Russett, Bruce, Starr, Harvey and Kinsella, David, *World Politics: The Menu for Choice*, Ninth Edition (Boston, Wadsworth, 2010).

Ryngaert, Cedric, *Jurisdiction in International Law*, Second Edition (Oxford, Oxford University Press, 2015).

Sage, Michael M., *Warfare in Ancient Greece* (London, Routledge, 1996)

Schjolberg, Stein and Ghernaouti-Helie, Solange, *A Global Treaty on Cybersecurity and Cybercrime*, Second Edition (Oslo, AiTOslo, 2011).

Schmitt, Michael N. (ed.), *Tallinn Manual on the International Law Applicable to Cyber Warfare* (New York, Cambridge University Press, 2013).

Schmitt, Michael N. and Liis, Vihul (eds), *Tallinn Manual 2.0 on the International Law Applicable to Cyber Operations* (Cambridge, Cambridge University Press, 2017).

Schmitt, Michael N. and O'Donnell, Brian T. (eds), *Computer Network Attack and International Law* (Newport, US Naval War College, 2002).

Schrijver, Nico, *Sovereignty over Natural Resources* (Cambridge, Cambridge University Press, 1997).

Schrijver, Nico *et al.* (eds), *Counterterrorism Strategies in a Fragmented International Legal Order* (Chatham House, The Royal Institute of International Affairs, 2014).

220 Bibliography

Schwarzenberger, Georg, *International Law*, Volume 1 (London, Stevens and Sons, 1957).

Seiderman, Ian D., *Hierarchy in International Law: The Human Rights Dimension* (Antwerp, Intersentia, 2001).

Sennett, Richard, *Respect in a World of Inequality* (New York, W. W. Norton & Company, 2003).

Sexton, Jay, *The Monroe Doctrine: Empire and Nation in Nineteenth-Century America* (Basingstoke, Macmillan, 2011).

Sharp, Walter Gary, *Cyberspace and the Use of Force* (Fall Church, Aegis Research Corporation, 1999).

Shaw, Malcolm N., *International Law*, Fifth Edition (Cambridge, Cambridge University Press, 2003).

Shaw, Michael N., *International Law*, Sixth Edition (Cambridge, Cambridge University Press, 2008).

Shaw, Malcolm N., *International Law*, Seventh Edition (Cambridge, Cambridge University Press, 2014).

Sidgwick, Henry, *The Elements of Politics*, Second Edition (London, Macmillan, 1897).

Simma, Bruno *et al.* (eds), *The Charter of the United Nations: A Commentary*, Second Edition (New York, Oxford University Press, 2002).

Sinclair, Ian, *The Vienna Convention on the Law of Treaties*, Second Edition (Manchester, Manchester University Press, 1984).

Smelser, Neil J. and Baltes, Paul B. (eds), *International Encyclopedia of the Social & Behavioral Sciences* (New York, Elsevier, 2001).

Snyder, Sarah B., *Human Rights Activism and the End of the Cold War: A Transnational History of the Helsinki Network* (Cambridge, Cambridge University Press, 2011).

Stankiewicz, W. J. (ed.), *In Defense of Sovereignty* (New York, Oxford University Press, 1969).

Steiner, Hillel, *An Essay on Rights* (Oxford, Blackwell, 1994).

Stevenson, David, *The First World War and International Politics* (Oxford, Clarendon Press, 1991).

Stiglitz, Joseph E. and Charlton, Andrew, *Fair Trade for All: How Trade can Promote Development* (Oxford, Oxford University Press, 2005).

Strauss, Leo, *The Arguments and Actions of Plato's Laws* (Chicago, University of Chicago Press, 1975).

Tarling, Nicholas (ed.), *The Cambridge History of Southeast Asia: The Nineteenth and Twentieth Centuries*, Volume 2 (Cambridge, Cambridge University Press, 1992).

Teschke, Benno, *The Myth of 1648: Class, Geopolitics and the Making of Modern International Relations* (London, Verso, 2003).

Thayer, Philip W. (ed.), *Tensions in the Middle East* (Baltimore, Johns Hopkins Press, 1958).

The White House, The National Security Strategy of the United States of America (Washington D.C., 2002).

The White House, International Strategy for Cyberspace: Prosperity, Security, and Openness in a Networked World (Washington D.C., May 2011) 9.

Tilly, Charles (ed.), *The Formation of National States in Western Europe* (Princeton, Princeton University Press, 1975).

Tunkin, G. I., *Curso de Derecho Internacional: Manual* (Moscow, Progresso, 1979).

Twining, William and Miers, David, *How to Do Things with Rules*, Fifth Edition (Cambridge, Cambridge University Press, 2014).

United Nations, *Documents of the United Nations Conference on International Organization San Francisco, 1945*, Volumes 1–21 (New York, United Nations, 1955).

Bibliography 221

United States Department of Homeland Security, *The Commander's Handbook on the Law of Naval Operations* (July 2007 Edition), available at <www.jag.navy.mil/documents/NWP_1-14M_Commanders_Handbook.pdf> accessed 29 September 2019.

United States Department of State, *The International Court of Justice: Selected Documents Relating to the Drafting of the Statute* (Washington D.C., Government Printing Office, 1946).

Vasquez, John A., *The War Puzzle* (Cambridge, Cambridge University Press, 2009).

Verzijl, Jan H. W., *International Law in Historical Perspective*, Volume 3 (Leyden, A.W. Sijthoff, 1970).

Walter, Christian *et al.* (ed.), *Self-determination and Secession in International Law* (Oxford, Oxford University Press, 2014).

Walzer, Michael, *Just and Unjust Wars: A Moral Argument with Historical Illustrations*, Fourth Edition (New York, Basic Books, 1977).

Walzer, Michael, *Thinking Politically: Essays in Political Theory* (New Haven and London, Yale University Press, 2007).

Weiss, Thomas G. and Daws, Sam (eds), *The Oxford Handbook on the United Nations*, Second Edition (Oxford, Oxford University Press, 2018).

Wheaton, Henry, *Elements of International Law: With a Sketch of the History of the Science* (Philadelphia, Carey, Lea & Blanchard, 1836).

Wheeler, Nicholas J., *Saving Strangers: Humanitarian Intervention in International Society* (Oxford, Oxford University Press, 2000).

Wingfield, Thomas C., *The Law of Information Conflict: National Security Law in Cyberspace* (Falls Church, Aegis Research Corporation, 2000).

Woodruff, William, *A Concise History of the Modern World*, Fourth Edition (New York, Palgrave Macmillan, 2002).

World Trade Organisation, *Dispute Settlement Reports 2017*: Volume VIII Papers 3767 to 4372 (Cambridge, Cambridge University Press, 2018).

Zacher, Mark W., *International Conflicts and Collective Security, 1946–77: The United Nations, Organization of American States, Organization of African Unity and Arab League* (New York, Praeger, 1979).

Articles/other materials

Agnew, John, "Sovereignty Regimes: Territoriality and State Authority in Contemporary World Politics" (2005) 95(2) *Annals of the Association of American Geographers* 437–461.

Agnew, John, "The Territorial Trap: The Geographical Assumptions of International Relations Theory" (1994) 1 *Review of International Political Economy* 53–80.

Akinsanya, Adaoye A., "Reflections on the Inviolability of Diplomatic Premises and Diplomatic Bags" (1989) 42(3/4) *Pakistan Horizon* 98–120.

Akweenda, S., "Territorial Integrity: A Brief Analysis of a Complex Concept" (1989) 1(3) *African Journal of International and Comparative Law* 500–506.

Aldrich, George H., "Questions of International Law raised by the Seizure of the U.S.S. Pueblo" (1969) 63 *Proceedings of the American Society of International Law* 2–6.

Ali, Yasmin, "Who Owns Outer Space?" (BBC News, 25 September 2015), available at <www.bbc.co.uk/news/science-environment-34324443> accessed 1 November 2019.

All Africa, "Sudan: Govt Issues Stern Warning on Airspace Violations" (1 June 2016), available at <http://allafrica.com/stories/201606020181.html> accessed 15 November 2019.

222 Bibliography

Allegretti, Aubrey, "Qatar Isolated as Gulf States Cut Links Over Terror Claims" (*Sky News*, 5 June 2017), available at <http://news.sky.com/story/qatar-isolated-as-gulf-states-cut-links-over-terror-claims-10904788> accessed 24 November 2019.

Alvarez, Jose E., "Hegemonic International Law Revisited" (2003) 97(4) *American Journal of International Law* 873–887

Alvarez, Jose E., "The UN's War on Terrorism" (2003) 31(2) *International Journal of Legal Information* 238–250.

Amnesty International, "Oil and Injustice in Nigeria: Ken Saro-Wiwa" (2005) 32(106) *Review of African Political Economy* 636–637.

Andersen, Niels *et al.*, "International Boundary Disputes: An Unfinished Tale of Geology, Technology, Money, Law, History, Politics and Diplomacy" (Offshore Technology Conference,, Texas, USA, 5–8 May 2014).

Anonymous, "United States and China Reach Agreement Regarding Economic Espionage and International Cybersecurity Norms" (2015) 109(4) *American Journal of International Law* 878–882.

Antonopoulos, Constantine, "Force by Armed Groups as Armed Attack and the Broadening of Self-Defence" (2008) 55(2) *Netherlands International Law Review* 159–180.

Asirvatham, Eddy, "The United Nations and World Peace" (1958) 19 *Indian Journal of Political Science* 45–52.

Associated Press, "Japan Warns China Over Fighters Challenging Airspace" (*Real Clear Defence*, 26 September 2016), available at <www.realcleardefense.com/articles/2016/09/26/japan_warns_china_over_fighters_challenging_airspace_110125.html> accessed 15 November 2019.

Baade, Hans W., "The Eichmann Trial: Some Legal Aspects" (1961) 10(3) *Duke Law Journal* 400–420.

Badinter, Robert, "Conference on Yugoslavia Arbitration Committee – Opinions" (1991) 31(6) *International Legal Materials* 1494–1526.

Baine, Kevin T., "The Use of Nonviolent Coercion: A Study in Legality Under Article 2(4) of the Charter of the United Nations" (1974) 122(4) *University of Pennsylvania Law Review* 983–1011.

Bakker, Edwin, "The Recognition of Kosovo: Violating Territorial Integrity is a Recipe for Trouble" (2008) 19(3) *Security and Human Rights* 183–186.

Banai, Ayelet and Moore, Margaret, "Introduction: Theories of Territory Beyond Westphalia" (2014) 6(1) *International Theory* 98–104.

Bariagaber, Assefaw, "United Nations Peace Mission in Africa: Transformation and Determinants" (2008) 38 *Journal of Black Studies* 830–849.

Barrett, Malcolm, "Illegal Fishing in Zones Subject to National Jurisdiction" (1998) 5 *James Cook University Law Review* 1–26.

BBC News, "Libya Removing Gaddafi Not Allowed, Says David Cameron" (21 March 2011), available at <www.bbc.co.uk/news/uk-politics-12802749> accessed 9 November 2019.

BBC News, "Turkey shoots down Russian warplane on Syria Border" (24 November 2015), available at <www.bbc.co.uk/news/world-middle-east-34907983> accessed 15 November 2019.

BBC News, "Turkey's Downing of Russian Warplane – What We Know" (1 December 2015), available at <www.bbc.co.uk/news/world-middle-east-34912581> accessed 28 September 2019.

BBC News, "African Union Backs Mass Withdrawal from ICC" (1 February 2017), available at <www.bbc.co.uk/news/world-africa-38826073> accessed 9 April 2017.

Bibliography   223

Beer, Yishai, "Humanity Considerations Cannot Reduce War's Hazards Alone: Revitalizing the Concept of Military Necessity" (2015) 26(4) *European Journal of International Law* 801–828.

Benvenisti, Eyal, "Sovereigns as Trustees of Humanity: On the Accountability of States to Foreign Stakeholders" (2013) 107(2) *American Journal of International Law* 295–333.

Bethlehem, Daniel, "Self-Defense Against an Imminent or Actual Armed Attack by Non-state Actors" (2012) 106 *American Journal of International Law* 770–777.

Binder, Martin and Heupel, Monika, "The Legitimacy of the UN Security Council: Evidence from Recent General Assembly Debates" (2015) 59(2) *International Studies Quarterly* 238–250.

Bird, Colin, "Status, Identity, and Respect" (2004) 32(2) *Political Theory* 207–232.

Bishku, Michael B., "The South Caucasus Republics: Relations with the U.S. and the EU" (2015) 22(2) *Middle East Policy* 40–57.

Blum, Yehuda Z., "Proposals for UN Security Council Reform" (2005) 99(3) *The American Journal of International Law* 632–649.

Bodansky, Daniel, "The Legitimacy of International Governance: A Coming Challenge for International Environmental Law" (1999) 93(3) *American Journal of International Law* 596–624.

Bork, Robert H., "Comments on the Articles on the Legality of the United States Action in Cambodia" (1971) 65(1) *American Journal of International Law* 79–81.

Bouve, Clement L., "Private Ownership of Airspace" (1930) 1(2) *Air Law Review* 232–258.

Bracegirdle, A. M., "Case to the International Court of Justice on Legality of French Nuclear Testing" (1996) 9(2) *Leiden Journal of International Law* 431–443.

Brewer, Thomas L., "Collective Legitimization in International Organizations Concept and Practice" (1972) 2(1) *Denver Journal of International Law and Policy* 73–88.

Briggs, Herbert W., "Rebus Sic Stantibus Before the Security Council: The Anglo-Egyptian Question" (1949) 43(4) *American Journal of International Law* 762–769.

Brown, Gary and Poellet, Keira, "The Customary International Law of Cyberspace" (2012) 6(3) *Strategic Studies Quarterly* 126–145.

Brown, Philip Marshall, "The Theory of the Independence and Equality of States" (1915) 9(2) *The American Journal of International Law* 305–335.

Brown, Philip Marshall, "Self-Determination in Central Europe" (1920) 14(1) *American Journal of International Law* 235–239.

Brownlie, Ian, "International Law and the Activities of Armed Bands" (1958) 7(4) *International and Comparative Law Quarterly* 712–735.

Bull, Millie, "US-IRAN tensions erupt as Tehran accuses Washington Think Tank of 'Economic Terrorism'" (UK, *Express Newspapers*, 26 August 2019).

Bunggo, Maria Luise B., "Legal Authority for the Possible Use of Force Against Iraq" (1998) 92 *American Society of International Law Proceedings* 136–150.

Burghardt, Andrew F., "The Bases of Territorial Claims" (1973) 63(2) *Geographical Review* 225–245.

Bush, George W., "Address to the Nation on Terrorist Attacks" (11 September 2001), available at <www.presidency.ucsb.edu/documents/address-the-nation-the-terrorist-attacks> accessed 17 November 2019.

Byers, Michael, "Agreeing to Disagree: Security Council Resolution 1441 and Intentional Ambiguity" (2004) 10(2) *Global Governance* 165–186.

Caflisch, Lucius C., "The Recent Judgment of the International Court of Justice in the Case Concerning the Aerial Incident of July 27, 1955, and the Interpretation of Article

224 Bibliography

36 (5) of the Statute of the Court" (1960) 54(4) *American Journal of International Law* 855–868.

Carino, Joji, "Indigenous Peoples' Right to Free, Prior, Informed Consent: Reflections on Concepts and Practice" (2005) 22(1) *Arizona Journal of International and Comparative Law* 19–40.

Casey-Maslen, Stuart, "Pandora's Box? Drone Strikes Under Jus ad Bellum, Jus in Bello, and International Human Rights Law" (2012) 94(886) *International Review of the Red Cross* 597–625.

Cassese, Antonio, "Terrorism is Also Disrupting some Crucial Legal Categories of International Law" (2001) 12(5) *European Journal of International Law* 993–1001.

Charney, Jonathan I., "Anticipatory Humanitarian Intervention in Kosovo" (1999) 93(4) *American Journal of International Law* 834–841.

Chemerinsky, Erwin, "In Defense of Equality: A Reply to Professor Westen" (1983) 81(3) *Michigan Law Review* 575–599.

Cheng, Bin, "The Legal Status of Outer Space and Relevant Issues: Delimitation of Outer Space and Definition of Peaceful Use" (1983) 11(1&2) *Journal of Space Law* 89–105.

Chigara, Ben, "Humanitarian Intervention Missions: Elementary Considerations, Humanity and the Good Samaritans" (2001) *Australian International Law Journal* 66–89.

Chughtai, Alia, "Understanding the Blockade Against Qatar" (*Aljazeera News*, 5 June 2018), available at <www.aljazeera.com/indepth/interactive/2018/05/understanding-blockade-qatar-180530122209237.html> accessed 24 November 2019.

Clapham, Andrew, "Human Rights Obligations of Non-state actors in Conflict Situations" (2006) 88(863) *International Review of the Red Cross* 491–523.

Claude, Inis L., "Collective Legitimization as a Political Function of the United Nations" (1966) 20(3) *International Organization* 367–379.

CNN, "Staged Cyber Attack Reveals Vulnerability in Power Grid" (26 September 2007), available at <https://edition.cnn.com/2007/US/09/26/power.at.risk/index.html> accessed 7 November 2019.

Cobb Cooper, John, "The International Air Navigation Conference, Paris 1910" (1952) 19(2) *Journal of Air Law and Commerce* 127–143.

Colangelo, Anthony J., "De Facto Sovereignty: Boumediene and Beyond" (2009) 77(3) *The George Washington Law Review* 632–676.

Commission of the European Communities, "Joint Statement on Yugoslavia – 28 August 1991" (1991) 24(7/8) *Bulletin of the European Communities* 107–108..

Coppel, Jason, "A Hard Look at the Effects Doctrine of Jurisdiction in Public International Law" (1993) 6(1) *Leiden Journal of International Law* 73–90.

Costello, John, "The Strategic Support Force: Update and Overview" (2016) 16(19) *China Brief*, available at <https://jamestown.org/program/strategic-support-force-update-overview/> accessed 26 October 2019.

Coverdale, John F., "An Introduction to the Just War Tradition" (2004) 16(2) *Pace International Law Review* 221–277.

Cranor, Carl, "Toward a Theory of Respect for Persons" (1975) 12(4) *American Philosophical Quarterly* 309–319.

Craven, Matthew C. R., "The European Community Arbitration Commission on Yugoslavia" (1996) 66(1) *British Yearbook of International Law* 333–413.

Crawford, James and Olleson, Simon, "The Continuing Debate on a UN Convention on State Responsibility" (2005) 54(4) *International and Comparative Law Quarterly* 959–972.

Criddle, Evan J., "Proportionality in Counterinsurgency: A Relational Theory" (2012) 87 (3) *Notre Dame Law Review* 1073–1112.

Criddle, Evan J., "Standing for Human Rights Abroad" (2015) 100(2) *Cornell Law Review* 269–334.

Criddle, Evan J. and Fox-Decent, Evan, "A Fiduciary Theory of Jus Cogens" (2009) 34(1) *Yale Journal of International Law* 331–388.

Croxton, Derek, "The Peace of Westphalia of 1648 and the Origins of Sovereignty" (1999) 21(3) *International History Review* 569–591.

D'Amato, Anthony, "Is Equality a Totally Empty Idea?" (1983) 81(3) *Michigan Law Review* 600–603.

D'Amato, Anthony, "The Invasion of Panama was a Lawful Response to Tyranny" (1990) 84(2) *American Journal of International Law* 516–524.

Darwall, Stephen L., "Two Kinds of Respect" (1977) 88(1) *Ethics* 36–49.

Delupis, Ingrid, "Foreign Warships and Immunity for Espionage" (1984) 78(1) *American Journal of International Law* 53–75.

Dembling, Paul G. and Arons, Daniel M., "The Evolution of the Outer Space Treaty" (1967) 33(3) *Journal of Air Law and Commerce* 419–446.

Demchak, Chris C. and Dombrowski, Peter, "Rise of a Cybered Westphalian Age" (2011) 5(1) *Strategic Studies Quarterly* 32–61.

Dickinson, Edwin D, "Jurisdiction Following Seizure or Arrest in Violation of International Law" (1934) 28(2) *American Journal of International Law* 231–245.

Diehl, Paul F., "What Are They Fighting For? The Importance of Issues in International Conflict Research" (1992) 29(3) *Journal of Peace Research* 333–344.

Dietrich, Frank, "Territorial Rights and Demographic Change" (2014) 6(1) *International Theory* 174–190.

Dill, Janina, "The 21st-Century Belligerent's Trilemma" (2015) 26(1) *European Journal of International Law* 83–108.

Dutton, Peter A., "Caelum Liberam: Air Defense Identification Zones Outside Sovereign Airspace" (2009) 103(4) *American Journal of International Law* 691–709.

Dzurek, Daniel J., "What Makes Territory Important: Tangible and Intangible Dimensions" (2005) 64(4) *GeoJournal* 263–274.

Eichensehr, Kristen E., "The Cyber-Law of Nations" (2015) 103(2) *Georgetown Law Journal* 317–380.

Elden, Stuart, "How Should We do the History of Territory?" (2013) 1(1) *Territory, Politics, Governance* 5–20.

Elden, Stuart, "Thinking Territory Historically" (2010) 15 *Geopolitics* 757–761.

Elden, Stuart, "The Significance of Territory" (2013) 68(1) *Geographica Helvetica* 65–68.

El-Masri, Samar, "The Legality of the International Criminal Court's Decision Against Omar Al-Bashir of Sudan" (2011) 66(2) *International Journal* 371–390.

Elshtain, Jean Bethke, "The Just War Tradition and Natural Law" (2005) 28(3) *Fordham International Law Journal* 742–755.

Erickson, Norman N., "A Dispute Between a Priest and a Knight" (1967) 111(5) *Proceedings of the American Philosophical Society* 288–309.

Etherington, John, "Nationalism, Nation and Territory: Jacint Verdaguer and the Catalan Renaixenca" (2010) 33(10) *Ethic and Racial Studies* 1814–1832.

Ezenwajiaku, Josephat Chukwuemeka, Respect for the Inviolability of State Territory (Unpublished Doctoral Thesis submitted to Brunel University, London, 2017).

Falk, Richard A., "The Cambodian Operation and International Law" (1971) 65(1) *American Journal of International Law* 1–25.

Fenwick, C. G., "The 'Failure' of the League of Nations" (1936) 30(3) *American Journal of International Law* 506–509.

226   *Bibliography*

Ferrari, Leo, "The Origin of the State According to Plato" (1956) 12(2) *Laval theologique et philosophique* 145–151.

Finnis, John, "The 'Natural Law Tradition'" (1986) 36(4) *Journal of Legal Education* 492–495.

Fitzmaurice, G.G., "The Definition of Aggression" (1952) 1(1) *International and Comparative Law Quarterly* 137–144.

Foster, Sheila, "Difference and Equality: A Critical Assessment of the Concept of 'Diversity'" (1993) 1993(1) *Wisconsin Law Review* 105–162.

Fox-Decent, Evan and Criddle, Evan J., "The Fiduciary Constitution of Human Rights" (2009) 15(4) *Legal Theory* 301–336.

Francioni, Francesco, "Peacetime Use of Force, Military Activities, and the New Law of the Sea" (1985) 18(2) *Cornell International Law Journal* 203–226.

Franck, Thomas M., "Who Killed Article 2(4) or: Changing Norms Governing the Use of Force by States" (1970) 64(4) *American Journal of International Law* 809–837.

Frear, Thomas *et al.*, "Dangerous Brinkmanship: Close Military Encounters between Russia and the West in 2014," available at <www.europeanleadershipnetwork.org/wp-content/uploads/2017/10/Dangerous-Brinkmanship.pdf> accessed 16 November 2019.

Friedmann, Wolfgang, "Comments on the Articles on the Legality of the United States Action in Cambodia" (1971) 65(1) *American Journal of International Law* 77–79.

Ganor, Boaz, "Defining Terrorism: Is One Man's Terrorist another Man's Freedom Fighter?" (2002) 3(4) *Police Practice and Research* 287–304.

Gao, Zhiguo and Jia, Bing Bing, "The Nine-Dash Line in the South China Sea: History, Status, and Implications" (2013) 107(1) *American Journal of International Law* 98–124.

Garner, J. W., "The Doctrine of Rebus Sic Stantibus and the Termination of Treaties" (2009) *American Journal of International Law* 509–516.

Garner, J.W., "The Doctrine of Rebus Sic Stantibus and the Termination of Treaties" (1927) 21(3) *American Journal of International Law* 509–516.

Gilmour, D. R., "The Meaning of 'Intervene' Within Article 2(7) of the United Nations Charter – An Historical Perspective" (1967) 16(2) *International and Comparative Law Quarterly* 330–351.

Gioia, Andrea, "Tunisia's Claims Over Adjacent Seas and the Doctrine of 'Historic Rights'" (1984) 11(2) *Syracuse Journal of International Law and Commerce* 327–376.

Goedhuis, D., "Reflections on the Evolution of Space Law" (1966) 13(2) *Netherlands International Law Review* 109–114.

Gold, Dore, "Legal Acrobatics: The Palestinian Claim that Gaza is Still 'Occupied' Even After Israel Withdraws" (2005) 5(3) *Jerusalem Issue Brief*, available at <http://jcpa.org/brief/brief005-3.htm> accessed 9 December 2019.

Goodrich, Leland M., "The United Nations and Domestic Jurisdiction" (1949) *International Organization* 14–28.

Gordon, Edward, "Article 2(4) and Permissive Pragmatism" (1984) 78 *Proceedings of the Annual Meeting (American Society of International Law)* 87–99.

Gosnell, Cullen Bryant, "The Compulsory Jurisdiction of the World Court" (1927–1928) 14(8) *Virginia Law Review* 618–643.

Gottmann, Jean, "The Evolution of the Concept of Territory" (1975) 14(3) *Social Science Information* 29–47.

Grant, Thomas D., "Current Developments: Annexation of Crimea" (2015) 109 *American Journal of International Law* 68–95.

Grant, Thomas D., "Defining Statehood: The Montevideo Convention and its Discontents" (1999) 37(2) *Columbia Journal of Transnational Law* 403.

Green, David B., "This Day in Jewish History 58 Dead After EL AL Plane Shot Down Over Bulgaria" (*Haaretz*, 25 August 2016), available at <www.haaretz.com/jewish/this-day-in-jewish-history/.premium-1.607298> accessed 25 November 2019.

Green, James A. and Grimal, Francis, "The Threat of Force as an Action in Self-Defense under International Law" (2011) 44(2) *Vanderbilt Journal of Transnational Law* 285–329.

Green, James Frederick, "The Dumbarton Oaks Conversations" (1944) 11(278) *The Department of State Bulletin* 462–643.

Greenawalt, Kent, "How Empty is the Idea of Equality?" (1983) 83(5) *Columbia Law Review* 1167–1185.

Griffiths, Ryan, "The Future of Self-Determination and Territorial Integrity in the Asian Century" (2014) 27(3) *The Pacific Review* 457–478.

Gross, Leo, "The Peace of Westphalia, 1648–1948" (1948) 42(1) *American Journal of International Law* 20–41.

Hackett, John H., "State of the Church: A Concept of the Medieval Canonists" (1963) 23 (3) *The Jurist* 259–290.

Hakimi, Monica, "State Bystander Responsibility" (2010) 21(2) *European Journal of International Law* 341–385.

Hakimi, Monica, "North Korea and the Law on Anticipatory Self-Defence" (EJIL: Talk!, 28 March 2017), available at <www.ejiltalk.org/north-korea-and-the-law-on-anticipatory-self-defense/#more-15104> accessed 17 November 2019.

Hannikainen, Lauri, "The Declaration of Principles Guiding Relations Between States of the European Security Conference from the Viewpoint of International Law" (1976) 6 (3) *Instant Research on Peace and Violence* 93–101.

Happold, Matthew, "Security Council Resolution 1373 and the Constitution of the United Nations" (2003) 16(3) *Leiden Journal of International Law* 593–610.

Harry, Martin A., "The Right of Self-Defense and the Use of Armed Force against States Aiding Insurgency" (1986–1987) 11(4) *Southern Illinois University Law Journal* 1289–1304.

Hathaway, Oona A. *et al.* "The Law of Cyber-Attack" (2012) 100(4) *California Law Review* 817–886.

Hazard, John N., "The Sixth Committee and New Law" (1963) 57(3) *American Journal of International Law* 604–613.

Henkin, Louis, "Force, Intervention, and Neutrality in Contemporary International Law" (1963) 57 *Proceedings of the American Society of International Law at Its Annual Meeting* 147–173.

Henkin, Louis, "The Reports of the Death of Article 2(4) are Greatly Exaggerated" (1971) 65 *American Journal of International Law* 544–548.

Henkin, Louis, "Kosovo and the Law of Humanitarian Intervention" (1999) 93(4) *American Journal of International Law* 824–828.

Hennigan, W.J., "New Drone Has No Pilot Anywhere, So Who's Accountable?" (*Los Angeles Times*, 26 January 2012), available at <http://articles.latimes.com/2012/jan/26/business/la-fi-auto-drone-20120126> accessed 16 November 2019.

Hensel, Paul R., Allison, Michael E. and Khanani, Ahmed, "Territorial Integrity Treaties and Armed Conflict over Territory" (2009) 26(2) *Conflict Management and Peace Science* 120–143.

Hensel, Paul R. and McLaughlin Mitchell, Sara, "Issue Indivisibility and Territorial Claims" (2005) 64(4) *GeoJournal* 275–285.

228 Bibliography

Herbst, Jeffrey, "The Creation and Maintenance of National Boundaries in Africa" (1989) 43(4) *International Organization* 673–692.

Herz, John H., "Rise and Demise of the Territorial State" (1957) 9(4) *World Politics* 473–493.

Herzog, Stephen, "Revisiting the Estonian Cyber Attacks: Digital Threats and Multinational Responses" (2001) 4(2) *Journal of Strategic Security* 49–60.

Higgins, Rosalyn, "Peace and Security – Achievements and Failures" (1995) 6 *European Journal of International Law* 445–460.

Hmoud, Mahmoud, "The Use of Force Against Iraq: Occupation and Security Council Resolution 1483" (2004) 36(3) *Cornell International Law Journal* 435–453.

Hojnik, Janja, "De Minimis Rule within the EU Internal Market Freedoms: Towards a More Mature and Legitimate Market?" (2013) 6(1) *European Journal of Legal Studies* 25–45.

Hovanesian, Archie, "Post Torrey Canyon: Toward a New Solution to the Problem of Traumatic Oil Spillage" (1970) 2(3) *Connecticut Law Review* 632–647.

Hudry, Jean Louis, "Aristotle on Deduction and Inferential Necessity" (2013) 67(1) *The Review of Metaphysics* 29–54.

Hudson, Manley O., "Permanent Court of International Justice" (1921–1922) 35(3) *Harvard Law Review* 245–275.

Hudson, Manley O., "Obligatory Jurisdiction Under Article 36 of the Statute of the Permanent Court of International Justice" (1933–1934) 19(2) *Iowa Law Review* 190–217.

Hughes, William J., "Aerial Intrusions by Civil Airliners and the Use of Force" (1980) 45 (3) *Journal of Air Law and Commerce* 595–620.

Hulsroj, Peter, "The Legal Function of the Security Council" (2002) 1(1) *Chinese Journal of International Law* 59–93.

Hurd, Ian, "Legitimacy, Power, and the Symbolic Life of the UN Security Council" (2002) 8(1) *Global Governance* 35–52.

International Civil Aviation Organisation, "Rules of the Air" (1983) 22 *International Legal Materials* 1154–1189.

International Committee of the Red Cross, "Articles and Interviews in New Technologies and Warfare" (2012) 94(886) *International Review of the Red Cross* 457–876.

ITV Report, "Russia Calls for Investigation Over South Korean Airspace Violation Claims" (24 July 2019), available at <www.itv.com/news/2019-07-24/russia-calls-for-investigation-over-south-korean-airspace-violation-claims/> accessed 15 November 2019.

Jaafar, Abdul Aziz "The Majority of Potential Maritime Boundaries Worldwide and the South China Sea Remain Undelimited: Does it Matter?" (2013) 4(1) *The Journal of Defence and Security* 1–10.

James, Alan, "Comment on J. D. B. Miller" (1986) 12(2) *Review of International Studies* 91–93.

Jenkins, Ryan, "Is Stuxnet Physical? Does it Matter?" (2013) 12(1) *Journal of Military Ethics* 68–79.

Jessup, Phillip C., "'The Law of Territorial Waters and Maritime Jurisdiction' in Harvard Law School's Draft Convention on Territorial Waters" (1929) 23 *American Journal of International Law (Special Supplement)* 243–380.

Jova, Joseph John, "A Review of the Progress and Problems of the Organization of American States" (1971) 65 *Department of State Bulletin* 284–294.

Joyner, Christopher C. and Rothbaum, Wayne P., "Libya and the Aerial Incident at Lockerbie: What Lessons for International Extradition Law?" (1993) 14(2) *Michigan Journal of International Law* 222–261.

Bibliography 229

Juda, Lawrence, "Innocent Passage by Warships in the Territorial Seas of the Soviet Union: Changing Doctrine" (1990) 21(1) *Ocean Development & International Law* 111–116.

Judge Addulqawi A. Yusuf, "The Notion of 'Armed Attack' in the Nicaragua Judgment and Its Influence on Subsequent Case Law" (2012) 25(2) *Leiden Journal of International Law* 461–470.

Justin, Tito, "South Sudan Rejects Regional Troop Deployment by UN" (*Voice of America News*, 10 August 2016).

Kahgan, Carin, "Jus Cogens and the Inherent Right to Self- Defense" (1997) 3(3) *ILSA Journal of International & Comparative Law* 767–828.

Kammerhofer, Jorg, "The Armed Activities Case and Non-State Actors in Self-Defence Law" (2007) 20(1) *Leiden Journal of International Law* 89–113.

Kania, Elsa, "PLA Strategy Support Force: The Information Umbrella for China's Military" (*The Diplomat*, 1 April 2017), available at <https://thediplomat.com/2017/04/pla-strategic-support-force-the-information-umbrella-for-chinas-military/> accessed 26 October 2019.

Kassan, Shalom, "Extraterritorial Jurisdiction in the Ancient World" (1935) 29 *American Journal of International Law* 237–247.

Kelsen, Hans, "Collective Security under General International Law" (1954) 49 *International Law Studies Series. US Naval War College* 34–52.

Kelsen, Hans, "Organization and Procedure of the Security Council of the United Nations" (1946) 59(7) *Harvard Law Review* 1087–1121.

Kelsen, Hans, "Recognition in International Law: Theoretical Observations" (1941) 35(4) *American Journal of International Law* 605–617.

Kelsen, Hans, "The Principle of Sovereign Equality of States as a Basis for International Organisation" (1944) 53(2) *Yale Law Journal* 207–220.

Kelsen, Hans, "The Pure Theory of Law and Analytical Jurisprudence" (1941) 55(1) *Harvard Law Review* 44–70.

Keyuan, Zou, "Historic Rights in International Law and in China's Practice" (2001) 32(2) *Ocean Development and International Law* 149–168.

Khan, Paul W., "Imagining Warfare" (2013) 24(1) *European Journal of International Law* 199–226.

Khan, Riaz Mohammad, "Vienna Convention on Law of Treaties — Article 62 (Fundamental Change of Circumstances)" (1973) 26(1) *Pakistan Horizon* 16–28.

Kohen, Marcelo, "The Principle of Non-Intervention 25 Years after the Nicaragua Judgment" (2012) 25(1) *Leiden Journal of International Law* 157–164.

Kolb, Robert, "The Eternal Problem of Collective Security: From the League of Nations to the United Nations" (2007) 26(4) *Refugee Survey Quarterly* 220–226.

Koskenniemi, Martti, "Occupied Zone – A Zone of Reasonableness" (2008) 41(1&2) *Israel Law Review* 13–40.

Koskenniemi, Martti, "The Police in the Temple Order, Justice and the UN: A Dialectical View" (1995) 6(3) *European Journal of International Law* 325–348.

Koskenmaki, Riikka, "Legal Implications Resulting from State Failure in Light of the Case of Somalia" (2004) 73(1) *Nordic Journal of International Law* 1–36.

Krasner, Stephen D., "Rethinking the Sovereign State Model" (2001) 27(5) *Review of International Studies* 17–42.

Kritsiotis, Dino, "Reappraising Policy Objections to Humanitarian Intervention" (1998) 19 (4) *Michigan Journal of International Law* 1005–1050.

Kuhn, Arthur K., "Aerial Navigation in its Relation to International Law" (1908) 5 *Proceedings of the American Political Science Association* 83–93.

230   Bibliography

Kunz, Josef L., "Bellum justum and bellum legale" (1951) 45(3) *American Journal of International Law* 528–534.

Kyriazis, Nicholas, and Paparrigopoulos, Xenophon, "War and Democracy in Ancient Greece" (2014) 38(1) *European Journal of Law and Economics* 163–183.

Lanovoy, Vladyslav, "The Use of Force by Non-State Actors and the Limits of Attribution of Conduct" (2017) 28(2) *European Journal of International Law* 563–585.

Lanza, Nicholas, "The Thirty Years War" (2014) 1(1) *Histories* 43–51.

Laruelle, Marlene, "The Paradigm of Nationalism in Kyrgyzstan. Evolving Narrative, the Sovereignty Issue, and Political Agenda" (2012) 45 *Communist and Post-Communist Studies* 39–49.

Latchford, Stephen, "Freedom of the Air – Early Theories, Freedom, Zone, Sovereignty" (1948) 1(5) *Documents & State Papers* 303–322.

Lauterpacht, Hersch, "Sovereignty over Submarine Areas" (1950) 27 *British Yearbook of International Law* 376–433.

Lawson, Sean, "The Law That Could Allow Trump to Shut Down the US Internet" (*Forbes*, 2 December 2016), available at <www.forbes.com/sites/seanlawson/2016/12/02/the-law-that-could-allow-trump-to-shut-down-the-u-s-internet/> accessed 27 October 2019.

League of Nations, "Report of the International Committee of Jurists Entrusted by the Council of the League of Nations With the Task of Giving an Advisory Opinion Upon the Legal Aspects of the Aaland Islands Question" (1920) 3 *League of Nations Official Journal Supplement* 3–19.

Lee, Luke T., "The Mexico City Conference of the United Nations Special Committee on Principles of International Law Concerning Friendly Relations and Co-Operation among States" (1965) 14(4) *International and Comparative Law Quarterly* 1296–1313.

Legarre, Santiago, "HLA Hart and the Making of the New Natural Law Theory" (2017) 8 (1) *Jurisprudence* 82–98.

Leib, Ethan J. and Galoob, Stephen R., "Fiduciary Political Theory: A Critique" (2016) 125(7) *Yale Law Journal* 1820–1878.

Lissitzyn, Oliver J., "The Treatment of Aerial Intruders in Recent Practice and International Law" (1953) 47(4) *American Journal of International Law* 559–589.

Lissitzyn, Oliver J., "Treaties and Changed Circumstances (Rebus Sic Stantibus)" (1967) 61(4) *American Journal of International Law* 895–922.

Lo, Margaret, "IBM v Commissioner: The Effects Test in the EEC" (1987) 10(1) *Boston College of International and Comparative Law Review* 125–133.

Loridas, Kara, "United States-China Trade War: Signs of Protectionism in a Globalised Economy" (2011) 34(2) *Suffolk Transnational Law Review* 403–427.

Luban, David, "Just War and Human Rights" (1980) 9(2) *Philosophy & Public Affairs* 160–181.

Lucy, William, "Equality Under and Before the Law" (2011) 61(3) *The University of Toronto Law Journal* 411–466.

MacChesney, Brunson, "Some Comments on the 'Quarantine' of Cuba" (1963) 57(3) *American Journal of International Law* 592–597.

MacMullen, Ramsay, "Ancient Rome" in *Encyclopaedia Britannica*, available at <https://academic-eb-com.kuleuven.ezproxy.kuleuven.be/levels/collegiate/article/ancient-Rome/106272> accessed 5 August 2019.

Mann, Michael, "Has Globalization Ended the Rise and Rise of the Nation-State?" (1997) 4(3) *Review of International Political Economy* 472–496.

Bibliography 231

Marceau, Gabrielle, "Evolutive Interpretation by the WTO Adjudicator" (2018) 21(4) *Journal of International Economic Law* 791–813.

Matthews , Robert O., "Interstate Conflicts in Africa: A Review" (1970) 24(2) *International Organisation* 335–360.

McDougal, Myres S. and Burke, William T., "Claims to Authority over the Territorial Sea" (1962) 1(1) *Philippines International Law Journal* 29–138.

McLaughlin, Rob, "Coastal State Use of Force in the EEZ Under the Law of the Sea Convention 1982" (1999) 18(1) *University of Tasmanian Law Review* 11–21.

McNair, Arnold D., "The Stimson Doctrine of Non-Recognition" (1933) 14 *British Yearbook of International Law* 65–75.

McWhinney, Edward, "The New Countries and the New International Law: The United Nations' Special Conference on Friendly Relations and Co-Operation among States" (1966) 60(1) *American Journal of International Law* 1–33.

Meester, Daniel H., "The International Court of Justice's Kosovo Case: Assessing the Current State of International Legal Opinion on Remedial Secession" (2010) 48 *Canadian Yearbook of International Law* 215–254.

Merkouris, Panos, "(Inter)Temporal Considerations in the Interpretive Process of the VCLT: Do Treaties Endure, Perdure or Exdure?" (2014) 45 *Netherlands Yearbook of International Law* 121–156.

Miller Maguire, T., "The War Policy of the United States" (1917) 62 *Journal of the Royal United Service Institution* 260–268.

Miller, D. B., "Sovereignty as a Source of Vitality for the State" (1986) 12(2) *Review of International Studies* 79–89.

Miller, David, "Territorial Rights: Concept and Justification" (2012) 60(2) *Political Studies* 252–268.

Miller, Sarah, "Revisiting Extraterritorial Jurisdiction: A Territorial Justification for Extraterritorial Jurisdiction under the European Convention" (2009) 20(4) *European Journal of International Law* 1223–1246.

Miquelson-Weismann, Miriam F., "The Convention on Cybercrime: A Harmonized Implementation of International Penal Law: What Prospects for Procedural Due Process" (2005) 23(2) *John Marshall Journal of Computer and Information Law* 329–362.

Moon, Albert I., "A Look at Airspace Sovereignty" (1963) 29(4) *Journal of Air Law and Commerce* 328–345.

Moore, John N. "Legal Dimensions of the Decision to Intercede in Cambodia" (1971) 65 (1) *American Journal of International Law* 38–75.

Moraw, Peter, "Cities and Citizenry as Factors of State Formation in the Roman-German Empire of the Late Middle Ages" (1989) 18(5) *Theory and Society* (Special Issue on Cities and States in Europe, 1000–1800) 631–662.

Morgenstern, Felice, "Jurisdiction in Seizures Effected in Violation of International Law" (1952) 29 *British Yearbook of International Law* 265–282.

Morss, John R., "The International Legal Status of the Vatican/Holy See Complex" (2015) 26(4) *European Journal of International Law* 927–946.

Mrazek, Josef, "Prohibition of the Use and Threat of Force: Self-Defence and Self-Help in International Law" (1989) 27 *Canadian Yearbook of International Law* 81–112.

Murphy, Sean D., "Contemporary Practice of the United States Relating to International Law" (2002) 96(1) *American Journal of International Law* 237–263.

Murphy, Sean D., "Terrorism and the Concept of Armed Attack in Article 51 of the U.N. Charter" (2002) 43(1) *Harvard International Law Journal* 41–52.

232   Bibliography

Murray, J., "Art. V.-1. The Mycenaean Age" (1898) 188(375) *The Quarterly Review* 90–112.

Naska, Nina and Nolte, Georg, "Legislative Authorization to shoot down Aircraft Abducted by Terrorists if Innocent Passengers are on Board Incompatibility with Human Dignity as Guaranteed by Article 1(1) of the German Constitution" (2007) 101(2) *American Journal of International Law* 466–471.

Nussbaum, Arthur, "Just War – A Legal Concept" (1943) 42(3) *Michigan Law Review* 453–479.

O'Connell, Mary Ellen, "The Choice of Law Against Terrorism" (2010) 4(2) *Journal of National Security Law & Policy* 343–368.

O'Connell, Mary Ellen, "Dangerous Departures" (2013) 107(2) *The American Journal of International Law* 380–386.

O'Connell, Mary Ellen, "The True Meaning of Force" (2014) 108 *American Journal of International Law Unbound* 141–144.

O'Lear, Shannon, Diehl, Paul F., Frazier, Derrick V. and Allee, Todd L., "Dimensions of Territorial Conflict and Resolution: Tangible and Intangible Values of Territory" (2005) 64(4) *GeoJournal* 259–261.

Obama, Barack, "The President's News Conference with President Francois Hollande of France" (24 November 2015), available at <www.presidency.ucsb.edu/node/311533> accessed 28 September 2019.

Oda, Shigeru, "The Compulsory Jurisdiction of the International Court of Justice: A Myth? A Statistical Analysis of Contentious Cases" (2000) 49(2) *International and Comparative Law Quarterly* 251–277.

Ohlin, Jen David, "The Bounds of Necessity" (2008) 6(2) *Journal of International Criminal Justice* 289–308.

Ondrejek, Pavel, "Limitations of Fundamental Rights in the Czech Republic and the Role of the Principle of Proportionality" (2014) 20(3) *European Public Law* 451–466.

Osiander, Andreas, "Sovereignty, International Relations, and the Westphalian Myth" (2001) 55(2) *International Organisation* 251–287.

Ouali, Abdelhamid El, "Territorial Integrity: Rethinking the Territorial Sovereign Right of the Existence of the States" (2006) 11(4) *Geopolitics* 630–650.

Oxman, Bernard H., "The Regime of Warships Under the United Nations Convention on the Law of the Sea" (1984) 24(4) *Virginia Journal of International Law* 809–864.

Papastavridis, Efthymios, "Interpretation of Security Council Resolutions under Chapter VII in the Aftermath of the Iraqi Crisis" (2007) 56(1) *The International and Comparative Law Quarterly* 83–118.

Papastavridis, Efthymios, "The Right of Visit on the High Seas in a Theoretical Perspective: Mare Liberum versus Mare Clausum Revisited" (2011) 24(1) *Leiden Journal of International Law* 45–69.

Paquette, Jeremy, "A History of Viruses" (*Symantec Corporation*, 16 July 2000), available at <www.symantec.com/connect/articles/history-viruses> accessed 29 October 2019.

Pejic, Jelena, "Extraterritorial Targeting by Means of Armed Drones: Some Legal Implications" (2014) 96(893) *International Review of the Red Cross* 67–106.

Pellet, Alain, "The Opinions of the Badinter Arbitration Committee: A Second Breath for the Self-determination of Peoples" (1992) 3(1) *European Journal of International Law* 178–185.

Pellet, Alain, "Can a State Commit a Crime? Definitely, Yes!" (1999) 10(2) *European Journal of International Law* 425–434.

Pennington, Kenneth, "Lex Naturalis and Ius Naturale" (2008) 68(2) *The Jurist* 569–591.

Bibliography 233

Percy, Lord Eustace, "The League of Nations" (1919) 64 *Journal of the Royal United Service Institution* 682–703.

Peters, Christopher J., "Equality Revisited" (2010) 110(6) *Harvard Law Review* 1210–1264.

Petras, James F. and LaPorte, Robert, "Can We Do Business with Radical Nationalists? Chile: No" (1972) 7 *Foreign Policy* 132–158.

Petrie, John N., "Myths and Misconceptions About the United Nations" (1996) 49(1) *Naval War College Review* 74–89.

Phelps, John T., "Aerial Intrusions by Civil and Military Aircraft in time of Peace" (1985) 107 *Military Law Review* 255–304.

Plachta, Michael, "The Lockerbie Case: The Role of the Security Council in Enforcing the Principle Aut Dedere aut Judicare" (2001) 12(1) *European Journal of International Law* 125–140.

Pojanowski, Jeffrey A., "Redrawing the Dividing Lines Between Natural Law and Positivism(s)" (2015) 101(4) *Virginia Law Review* 1023–1027.

Polišenský, J.V., "The Thirty Years War" (1954) 6 *Past and Present* 31–43.

Pollock, John, "70 Years of Successful Security and Fatal Failures at the UNSC" (*International Policy Digest*, 1 November 2016), available at <https://intpolicydigest.org/2016/01/11/70-years-of-successful-security-and-fatal-failures-at-the-unsc/> accessed 5 April 2020.

Preuss, Lawrence, "Kidnaping of Fugitives from Justice on Foreign Territory" (1935) 29 (3) *American Journal of International Law* 502–507.

Pritchard, David M., "Public Finance and War in Ancient Greece" (2015) 62(1) *Greece & Rome* 48–59.

Putin, Vladimir V., "A Plea for Caution from Russia: What Putin Has to Say to Americans About Syria" (*The New York Times*, 11 September 2013).

Qizhi, He, "The Problem of Definition and Delimitation of Outer Space" (1982) 10(2) *Journal of Space Law* 157–164.

Radsan, Afsheen John, "Loftier Standards for the CIA's Remote-Control Killing" (Accepted Paper No. 2010–11, William Mitchell College of Law, St Paul, Minnesota, May 2010).

Ragazzi, Maurizo, "Conference on Yugoslavia Arbitration Commission: Opinions on Questions Arising from the Dissolution of Yugoslavia" (1992) 31(6) *International Legal Materials* 1488–1493.

Rampton, Roberta, "Trump Takes Sides in Arab Rift, Suggests Support for Isolation of Qatar" (*Reuters*, 7 June 2017), available at <www.reuters.com/article/us-gulf-qatar-idUSKBN18X0KF> accessed 24 November 2019.

Ratner, Steven R., "Drawing a Better Line: UTI Possidetis and the Borders of New States" (1996) *American Journal of International Law* 590–624.

Ratner, Steven R., "Jus Ad Bellum and Jus in Bello after September 11" (2002) 96(4) *American Journal of International Law* 905–921.

Rees, W.J., "The Theory of Sovereignty Restated" (1950) 59(236) *Mind* 495–521.

Reisman, W. Michael, "Article 2(4): The Use of Force in Contemporary International Law" (1984) 78 *Proceedings of the Annual Meeting (American Society of International Law)* 74–87.

Reisman, W. Michael, "Coercion and Self-determination: Construing Charter Article 2(4)" (1984) 78(3) *American Journal of International Law* 642–645.

Richemond, Daphne, "Normativity in International Law: The Case of Unilateral Humanitarian Intervention" (2003) 6 *Yale Human Rights & Development Law Journal* 45–80.

234 Bibliography

Roelf, Wendell, "Spike Seen in African Offshore Disputes, Oil Companies Watching" (*Reuters*, 6 November 2014), available at <http://uk.reuters.com/article/uk-africa-oil-disputes-idUKKBN0IQ1OL20141106> accessed 12 November 2019.

Rona, Gabor and Wala, Raha, "No Thank You to a Radical Rewrite of the Jus ad Bellum" (2013) 107(2) *American Journal of International Law* 386–390.

Roscini, Marco, "Threats of Armed Force and Contemporary International Law" (2007) 54(2) *Netherlands International Law Review* 229–277.

Rosenberg, Justin, "A Non-Realist Theory of Sovereignty?: Giddens' the Nation-State and Violence" (1990) 19(2) *Journal of International Studies* 249–259.

Russell, Harold S., "The Helsinki Declaration: Brobdingnag or Lilliput?" (1976) 70(2) *The American Journal of International Law* 242–272.

Ruys, Tom, "Of Arms, Funding and 'Non-lethal Assistance' – Issues surrounding Third-State Intervention in the Syrian Civil War" (2014) 13 *Chinese Journal of International Law* 15–53.

Ruys, Tom, "The Meaning of 'Force' and the Boundaries of the Jus ad Bellum: Are 'Minimal' Uses of Force Excluded from UN Charter Article 2(4)" (2014) 108(2) *American Journal of International Law* 159–210.

Ruys, Tom and Verhoeven, Sten, "Attacks by Private Actors and the Right of Self-Defence" (2005) 10(3) *Journal of Conflict and Security Law* 289–320.

Sadigbayli, Rovshan, "Codification of the Inviolability of Frontiers Principle in the Helsinki Final Act: Its Purpose and Implications for Conflict Resolution" (2013) 24 *Security and Human Rights* 392–417.

Sadurska, Romana, "Threats of Force" (1988) 82(2) *American Journal of International Law* 239–268.

Samaras, Athanasios, "Aristotle's Best City in the Context of His Concept of *Aretē*" (2019) 36 (1) *Polis, The Journal for Ancient Greek and Roman Political Thought* 139–152.

Samson, Elizabeth, "Is Gaza Occupied: Redefining the Status of Gaza Under International Law" (2010) 25(5) *American University International Law Review* 915–968.

Schachter, Oscar, "In Defense of International Rules on the Use of Force" (1986) 53(1) *University of Chicago Law Review* 113–146.

Schachter, Oscar, "The Lawful Use of Force by a State Against Terrorists in another Country" (1989) 19 *Israel Yearbook on Human Rights* 209–232.

Schmehl, Paul, "Malware Infection Vectors: Past, Present and Future" (*Symantec Corporation*, 5 August 2002), available at <www.symantec.com/connect/articles/malware-infection-vectors-past-present-and-future> accessed 29 October 2019.

Schmitt, Michael N., "Computer Network Attack and the Use of Force in International Law: Thoughts on a Normative Framework" (1999) 37(3) *Columbia Journal of Transnational Law* 885–938.

Schmitt, Michael N., "Drone Attacks Under the Jus ad Bellum and Jus in Bello: Clearing the 'Fog of Law'" (2010) 13 *Yearbook of International Humanitarian Law* 311–326

Schmitt, Michael N., "The Law of Cyber Targeting" (2015) 68(2) *Naval War College Review* 10–29.

Schrijver, Nico and van den Herik, Larissa, "Leiden Policy Recommendations on Counter-Terrorism and International Law" (2010) 57(3) *Netherlands International Law Review* 531–550.

Schuchhardt, C., "Art. V.- 1. Schliemann's Excavations: An Archaeological and Historical Study" (1892) 175(360) *The Edinburgh Review* 399–434.

Schwelb, Egon, "Some Aspects of International Jus Cogens as Formulated by the International Law Commission" (1967) 61(4) *American Journal of International Law* 946–975.

Bibliography   235

Scott, Gary L. and Csajko, Karen D., "Compulsory Jurisdiction and Defiance in the World Court: A Comparison of the PCIJ and the ICJ" (1988) 16(2&3) *Denver Journal of International Law and Policy* 377–392.

Shah, Niaz A., "The Use of Force Under Islamic Law" (2013) 24(1) *European Journal of International Law* 343–365.

Shearer, I. A., "Problems of Jurisdiction and Law Enforcement Against Delinquency Vessels" (1986) 35(2) *International and Comparative Law Quarterly* 320–343.

Shen, Jianming, "China's Sovereignty Over the South China Sea: A Historical Perspective" (2002) 1(1) *Chinese Journal of International Law* 94–157.

SHI, Jiuyong</string-name>, "Maritime Delimitation in the Jurisprudence of the International Court of Justice" (2010) 9(2) *Chinese Journal of International Law* 271–291.

Shultz, George P., "U.S. Terminates Acceptance of ICJ Compulsory Jurisdiction" (1986) 86(2106) *Department of State Bulletin* 67–71.

Simma, Bruno, "NATO, the UN and the Use of Force: Legal Aspects" (1999) 10(1) *European Journal of International Law* 1–22.

Simmons, A. John, "On the Territorial Rights of States" (2001) 11 *Philosophical Issues* 300–326.

Smith, Michael J., "Humanitarian Intervention: An Overview of the Ethical Issues" (1998) 12(1) *Ethics and International Affairs* 63–79.

Snyder, Sarah B., "'Jerry, Don't Go': Domestic Opposition to the 1975 Helsinki Final Act" (2010) 44(1) *Journal of American Studies* 67–81.

Soldatov, Andrei and Borogan, Irina, "The Mutation of the Russian Secret Services," available at <www.agentura.ru/english/dosie/mutation/> accessed 27 October 2019.

Ssenyonjo, Manisuli, "The International Criminal Court Arrest Warrant Decision for President Al Bashir of Sudan" (2010) 59(1) *International and Comparative Law Quarterly* 205–225.

Stahn, Carsten, "Terrorist Acts as Armed Attack: The Right to Self-Defense, Article 51(1/2) of the UN Charter, and International Terrorism" (2003) 27(2) *Fletcher Forum of World Affairs* 35–54.

Stahn, Carsten, "'Jus ad bellum', 'jus in bello' … 'jus post bellum'? – Rethinking the Conception of the Law of Armed Force" (2007) 17(5) *European Journal of International Law* 921–943.

Stahn, Carsten, "Syria and the Semantics of Intervention, Aggression and Punishment; On 'Red Lines and Blurred Lines'" (2013) 11(5) *Journal of International Criminal Justice* 955–978.

Stephens, Pamela J., "A Categorical Approach to Human Rights Claims: Jus Cogens as a Limitation on Enforcement?" (2004) 22(2) *Wisconsin International Law Journal* 245–272.

Stettinius, Edward, "What the Dumbarton Oaks Peace Plan means" (1945) 12(292) *The Department of State Bulletin* 115–119.

Stilz, Anna, "Nations, States, and Territory" (2011) 121(3) *Ethics* 572–601.

Sumner, Brian Taylor, "Territorial Disputes at the International Court of Justice" (2004) 53(6) *Duke Law Journal* 1779–1812.

Swaine, Jon, "Georgia: Russia 'Conducting Cyber War'" (*The Telegraph*, 11 August 2008), available at <www.telegraph.co.uk/news/worldnews/europe/georgia/2539157/Georgia-Russia-conducting-cyber-war.html> accessed 27 October 2019.

Talmon, Stefan, "The Responsibility of Outside Powers for Acts of Secessionist Entities" (2009) 58(3) *International and Comparative Law Quarterly* 493–518.

Tams, Christian J., "The Use of Force Against Terrorism" (2009) 20(2) *European Journal of International Law* 359–397.

236 Bibliography

The Chatham House, "Principles of International Law on the Use of Force in Self-Defence" (2006) 55(4) *International and Comparative Law Quarterly* 963–972.

The European Community, "Declaration on Yugoslavia and on the Guidelines on the Recognition of New States" (1992) 31(6) *International Legal Materials* 1485–1487.

Thornberry, Patrick, "International Law and its Discontents: The U.S. Raid on Libya" (1986) 8(1) *Liverpool Law Review* 53–64.

Thurer, Daniel, "The 'Failed State' and International Law" (1999) 81(836) *International Review of the Red Cross* 731–761.

Tierney, Brian, "'Tria Quippe Distinguit Iudicia …' A Note on Innocent III's Decretal Per Venerabilem" (1962) 37(1) *Speculum* 48–59.

Tladi, Dire, "The Duty on South Africa to Arrest and Surrender President Al-Bashir under South African and International Law" (2015) 13(5) *Journal of International Criminal Justice* 1027–1047.

Trapp, Kimberley N., "Back to Basics: Necessity, Proportionality and the Right of Self-Defence against Non-State Terrorist Actors" (2007) 56(1) *International and Comparative Law Quarterly* 141–156.

Trapp, Kimberley N., "The Use of Force Against Terrorists: A Reply to Christian J. Tams" (2009) 20(4) *European Journal of International Law* 1049–1055.

Treves, Tullio, "Piracy, Law of the Sea, and Use of Force: Developments off the Coast of Somalia" (2009) 20(2) *European Journal of International Law* 399–414.

Tsagourias, Nicholas, "Security Council Legislation, Article 2(7) of the UN Charter, and the Principle of Subsidiarity" (2011) 24 *Leiden Journal of International Law* 539–559.

Tsagourias, Nicholas, "The Tallinn Manual on the International Law Applicable to Cyber Warfare: A Commentary on Chapter II – The Use of Force" (2012) 15 *Yearbook of International Humanitarian Law* 19–43.

U.S. House of Representatives Permanent Select Committee on Intelligence, "Congress of the United States – Status of the Russia Investigation" (Washington D.C., 13 March 2018), available at <https://intelligence.house.gov/> accessed 28 September 2019.

U.S. House of Representatives Permanent Select Committee on Intelligence, "Press Releases – House Intelligence Committee Releases Whistleblower Complaint" (Washington D.C., 26 September 2019), available at <https://intelligence.house.gov/> accessed 28 September 2019.

United States Department of State, "State Sponsors of Terrorism," available at <www.state.gov/state-sponsors-of-terrorism/> accessed 1 October 2019.

United States Department of State, "Washington Conversations on International Organization" (1944) 11(276) *The Department of State Bulletin* 365.

United States Department of State, "What the Dumbarton Oaks Peace Means" (1945) 12 (292) *The Department of State Bulletin* 115–148.

United States, "Department of State Telegram of 8 February 1968 – Seizure of USS Pueblo" (1968) 62 *American Journal of International Law* 756–757.

Utton, Albert E., "Protective Measures and the Torrey Canyon" (1968) 9(3) *Boston College Industrial and Commercial Law Review* 613–632.

Vasquez, John A., "The Tangibility of Issues and Global Conflict: A Test of Rosenau's Issue Area Typology" (1983) 20(2) *Journal of Peace Research* 179–192.

Vasquez, John A., "The Causes of the Second War in Europe: A New Scientific Explanation" (1996) 17(2) *International Political Science Review* 161–178.

Verdross, Alfred, "Jus Dispositivum and Jus Cogens in International Law" 60(1) *American Journal of International Law* 55–63.

Bibliography 237

Vidmar, Jure, "Territorial Integrity and the Law of Statehood" (2013) 44(4) *The George Washington International Law Review* 697–747.

von Elbe, Joachim, "The Evolution of the Concept of the Just War in International Law" (1939) 33(4) *American Journal of International Law* 665–688.

von Heinegg, Wolff Heintschel, "Territorial Sovereignty and Neutrality in Cyberspace" (2013) 89 *International Law Studies* 123–156.

Walker, Tim and Morris, Nigel, "Barack Obama Says David Cameron Allowed Libya to Become a Shit Show" (*Independent*, 10 March 2016), available at <www.independent.co.uk/news/uk/politics/barack-obama-says-david-cameron-allowed-libya-to-become-a-s-show-a6923976.html> accessed 22 October 2019.

Walzer, Michael, "The Argument About Humanitarian Intervention" (2002) 49(1) *Dissent* 29–36.

Wedgwood, Ruth, "The Enforcement of Security Council Resolution 687: The Threat of Force Against Iraq's Weapons of Mass Destruction" (1998) 92(4) *American Journal of International Law* 724–728.

Weinschel, Herbert, "The Doctrine of the Equality of States and Its Recent Modifications" (1951) 45(3) *American Journal of International Law* 417–442.

Weller, Marc, "The International Response to the Dissolution of the Socialist Federal Republic of Yugoslavia" (1992) 86(3) *American Journal of International Law* 569–607.

Westen, Peter, "The Empty Idea of Equality" (1982) 95(3) *Harvard Law Review* 537–596.

Williams, Gareth D., "Piercing the Shield of Sovereignty: An Assessment of the Legal Status of the Unwilling or Unable Test" (2013) 36(2) *University of New South Wales Law Journal* 619–641.

Williams, Robert A., "Encounters on the Frontiers of International Human Rights Law: Redefining the Terms of Indigenous Peoples' Survival in the World" (1990) 39(4) *Duke Law Journal* 660–704.

Wilske, Stephen and Schiller, Teresa, "International Jurisdiction in Cyberspace: Which States May Regulate the Internet" (1997) 50(1) *Federal Communications Law Journal* 117–178.

Wippman, David, "Treaty-Based Intervention: Who Can Say No" (1995) 62(2) *University of Chicago Law Review* 607–688.

Wolter, Detlev, "The UN Takes a Big Step Forward on Cybersecurity" (*Arms Control Association*, 4 September 2013), available at <www.armscontrol.org/act/2013-09/un-takes-big-step-forward-cybersecurity> accessed 30 October 2019.

Wood, Michael C., "The Interpretation of the Security Council Resolutions" (1998) 2(1) *Max Planck Yearbook of United Nations Law* 73–95.

Woolsey, L. H., "China's Termination of Unequal Treaties" (1927) 21(2) *American Journal of International Law* 289–294.

Wright, Quincy, "Legal Aspect of the U-2 Incident" (1960) 54(4) *American Journal of International Law* 836–854.

Wright, Quincy, "The Cuban Quarantine" (1963) 57(3) *American Journal of International Law* 546–565.

Ying, Whang Shang, "Four Contemporary Natural Law Theories" (1990) 32(2) *Malaya Law Review* 254–270.

Zacher, Mark W., "The Territorial Integrity Norm: International Boundaries and the Use of Force" (2001) 55(2) *International Organization* 215–250.

Zekos, Georgios I., "Cyber-territory and Jurisdiction of Nations" (2012) 15(12) *Journal of Internet Law* 3–23.

238 Bibliography

Zimmermann, Andreas and Stahn, Carsten, "Yugoslav Territory, United Nations Trusteeship or Sovereign State? Reflection on the Current and Future Legal Status of Kosovo" (2001) 70(4) *Nordic Journal of International Law* 423–460.

Ziolkowski, Katharina, "Stuxnet – Legal Considerations" 19, available at <https://ccdcoe.org/library/publications/stuxnet-legal-considerations/> accessed 25 October 2019.

Index

Aland Islands Dispute 43, 126
abductions 79, 80
Abkhazia 126
Abyei Arbitration 139
aerial conflicts: causes of 151–152; drone
  warfare 155–156; involving civilian
  aircraft 152–153; lessons from past
  incidents 152–153; pre-emptive
  self-defence and military necessity
  154–155
aerial espionage 152,
  153–154
Afghanistan 68, 177
African Union 69, 106, 127
Ahtisaari, Martti 70–71
airspace: reconnaissance and aerial
  espionage 152, 153–154; State
  sovereignty over 30–33, 151; trespasses
  of 150–156; *see also* aerial conflicts
al-Bashir, Omar 27
Aldrich, George H. 144, 145
Algeria 68
Ancient Greece: conquest and delimitation
  of territory 33–35; state territory in
  16–17
Ancient Rome: conquest and delimitation
  of territory 35–36; jurisdiction 24; state
  territory in 17–19
Anderson, Niels 137
Andress, Jason 103
Anghie, Antony 42
appraisal respect 187, 198, 209
Aquinas, Thomas 206
Arab League Charter (1945) 69
Argentina 80
Aristotle 16, 17, 35, 51, 197, 207
Arnett, C. W. 41
asylum seekers, detention of 25
Australia 53, 58, 118

Badinter, Robert 72
Baine, Kevin T. 73
Bakker, Edwin 71
Bandung *communique* 75
Barry, Brian 15
Bekker, Pieter 159
Belgium 124, 127
Belgium v China 88
Belgrade Declaration 75–76
belligerents *see* non-State
  actors (NSAs)
Bethlehem, Daniel 162
Binder, Martin 124
Bolivia 53
border control 25–27
Bosnian genocide case 46
Botswana 116
Boutros-Ghali, Boutros 210, 211
Bowett, Derek 162
"Brain" virus 104
Brazil 53, 56, 58
breaches of State territory: airspace
  trespasses 150–166; frontier incidents
  125; illegal occupation 133–134;
  interventions to aid self-determination
  126–127; on land 129–134; misapplica-
  tion of Security Council resolution
  127–128; new forms of attack 125;
  regional enforcements 128–129;
  territorial waters 134–147; UN Security
  Council responses to 124–125;
  unauthorised intervention for
  humanitarian reasons 127
Brezhnev, Leonid 198
Brierly, James L. 66, 84, 209–210
Brown, Gary 118
Brownlie, Ian 56, 135, 162
Bulgaria 152
Burghardt, Andrew 190

240   *Index*

Burkina Faso v Mali 43–44, 46, 65, 107
Bush, George W. 105, 155, 160, 161

Cambodia 64, 68
Cameron, David 128
Cameroon 68, 138–139
Canada 68
Carolin incident 74
categorical imperatives 183,
    184, 207
Central African Republic 68
Ceylon 68
Charter of Paris for a New Europe
    (1990) 70
Charter of the Commonwealth of
    Independent States 72
Charter of the Organization of African
    Unity (1963) 69
Charter of the Organization of American
    States (1948) 69, 72, 75
Charter of the United Nations: applicability
    in cyberspace 112; on collective
    self-defence 128–129; drafting of 44,
    45, 51, 56, 57; purposes of United
    Nations 73; references to "armed force"
    57; respect for equal rights 188; on
    self-defence 73, 78, 128; and sovereign
    equality of States 188
Charter of the United Nations—Article 2
    (4): applicability to non-State actors
    159–166; broad interpretation 78–80;
    connection with Article 2(7) 60, 69;
    contraventions 58–59; as cornerstone of
    Charter 1; and cyberspace 92–96, 102,
    118–121; *de minimis* breaches 2–3, 51,
    74, 82; distinguished from previous
    peace treaties 52–53; drafting of 2,
    56–57, 73; dual meaning 77–82;
    essential components 54–59; expanded
    reading of 57; expansion of scope
    190–191; interpretive approach to 2, 48;
    and inviolability of frontiers 201–204;
    jus cogens character of 59, 81–82; narrow
    interpretation 77–78; omission of
    "respect" 2, 48, 52–54, 58; "or in any
    other manner" 56, 58–59; positivist
    reading of 51; push for expansion of
    scope 67–68; restrictive reading of
    56–57; retrospective exegesis 73–77;
    scope of 53–59, 67–68, 75–77; and
    sovereign equality of States 54, 58;
    States' submissions on draft 53–59;
    "territorial integrity and political inde-
    pendence" 53, 54, 58; threat of force 1,
55–56; and unconventional warfare 1, 3;
    use of force 1, 56–57, 73–75
Charter of the United Nations—Article 2
    (7): and adjudication of humanitarian
    intervention 63–64; as clawback article
    62–63; connection with Article 2(4) 60,
    69; principle of non-intervention 59–61
Chemerinsky, Erwin 207
Chicago Convention 31, 32–33, 154
Chigara, Ben 126
Chile 54, 68
China 188; cyberlaw 110; cyberwarfare
    model 99–100, 101; dispute over
    territorial waters 93, 136, 137–138,
    139, 140, 141–142, 150; shooting
    down of civilian aircraft 152; trade war
    with US 77; violation of airspace of
    Asian countries 150
Christianity 36, 39
Clapham, Andrew 162
Coastal Fisheries Protection Act 1985 (Can)
    29
Colangelo, Anthony 107
Colombia 68
Comprehensive Nuclear-Test-Ban
    Treaty 150
concurrent sovereignty 107
Conference on Security and Co-operation
    in Europe 70, 71
Congo (Leopoldville) 68
Congress of Paris (1815) 42
Congress of Vienna (1815) 42
conquest and delimitation of territory: in
    Ancient Greece 33–35; in Roman anti-
    quity 35–36
Constitutive Act of the African Union 69
Contiguous Zone 28–29
Continental Shelf 28–29
Convention (II) Respecting the Limitation
    of the Employment of Force for the
    Recovery of Contract Debts (1908) 74
Convention Abolishing International
    Servitudes 86
Convention for the Protection of Cultural
    Property in the Event of Armed
    Conflict 159
Convention for the Suppression of Unlawful
    Seizure of Aircraft 174
Convention for the Suppression of Unlawful
    Acts Against the Safety of Maritime
    Navigation 148
Convention on Cyber Security and Personal
    Data Protection 106
Convention on Cybercrime 102, 114–115

Index 241

Convention on International Civil Aviation 31, 32–33, 154
Convention on the High Seas 135, 147
Convention on the Law of the Sea 32
conventional war 3, 190
Corfu Channel case 56, 122, 133, 146, 167, 192
Corten, Olivier 79, 177
Costa Rica 86
Costa Rica v Nicaragua 142
Council of Europe 114
counterterrorist operations 79
Covenant of the League of Nations 43–44, 49, 52, 60, 88
Coverdale, John 177
Cranor, Carl 185–186
Crawford, James 24, 46, 203–204
Crema, Luigi 49–50
Crimea 130, 131–132, 133, 134, 192
Croxton, Derek 22–23, 40
Cuba 58, 76, 107
cultural property 159
customary cyberlaw 118–119
customary international law 30, 52, 59, 68, 180
cyber espionage 103
cyberattacks: *de minimis* attacks 95, 96; distinguishing between State and civilian targets 120–121; impact of 3; and law of armed conflict 120–121; perpetrators 104; self-defence against 98, 117, 119; targets 98–99, 104–105; *see also* cyberwarfare
cybercrime: Council of Europe convention on 114–115; definition 101–102; illegal acquisition of computer data 116; illegal interception of computer data 116–117; legislation covering 113; State-sponsored 195; unlawful access or hacking 115–116, 118
cyberlaw 114: customary cyber law 118–119; domestication of 115–117; enforcement 117–118; substantive cyberlaw 113–117
cybersecurity, political discourse 104–106
cyberspace 58; applicability of United Nations Charter 112; application of international law to 92, 103, 106, 110, 112, 118–119; areas of concern for States 96–101; Article 2(4) of UN Charter and 92–96, 102, 118–121; attempts to delimit 103–104; definition 91–92; impact of invention of Internet 96–97; inclusion in State territory 2, 3,

49, 91; jurisdiction in 94–95; policing of 104; as *res communis omnium* 92, 108, 118; sovereignty in 93–94; State sovereignty and 3, 33; States' obligations in 121–122; territorialising 104–108; use of force in 95–96
cyberspace governance 110
cyberspace infrastructure 93, 94; State jurisdiction over 109
cyber-territory 3, 33; *de facto* cyber-sovereignty 106–108; *de jure* cyber-sovereignty 107, 108–113; *de minimis* attacks in 95, 96; definition 91n2; elements of sovereignty 106–108; impact of cyberattacks 78; jurisdiction over ICT infrastructure 109; regulation of 95, 102
cyberwarfare: Chinese model 99–100; defensive cyberwarfare 98; definition 97–98; distinguishing between military and civilian targets 98–99, 120–121; and law of armed conflict 120–121; military strategies 99–101; offensive cyberwarfare 98; Russian model 100; scale and effects threshold 98, 119–120, 122; US model 100–101
Czechoslovakia 53, 56, 62, 67, 75, 80, 125, 195

Dahomey 68
Darfur 124
Darwell, Stephen 187, 191
de facto secession 127
de minimis territorial incursions 2–3, 51, 74, 82, 95, 96, 125, 179, 194–195
de minimis rule 78–80
debt recovery 74
Declaration on Friendly Relations 58, 67, 201
Declaration on the Granting of Independence to Colonial Countries and Peoples 64–65
decolonisation 20, 38, 64–65
deductive reasoning 50–51
Democratic Republic of Congo v Uganda 3, 8, 82, 134, 155, 170, 198
Denmark 68
Diggs v Richardson case 119
digital violence *see* cyberattacks; cyberwarfare
Dinstein, Yoram 162
diplomatic missions, status of 203–204
domestic sovereignty 21

242   *Index*

Draft Articles on Responsibility of States for Internationally Wrongful Acts 166–188, 169, 171
drone warfare 155–156
Dzurek, Daniel 189–190

East Timor case 82
economic coercion 56, 68, 76–77
Economic Community of West African States 127
economic espionage 76–77, 101, 103
economic jurisdiction 24–25
Ecuador 76
Eekelen, Willem van 72
egalitarianism 184
Egypt 54, 76, 147, 152
Eichensehr, Kirsten 97
Eichmann, Adolf 80
Einstein, Albert 211
El Salvador 138, 166, 178, 180
Elden, Stuart 16–17, 20, 23, 38
equality, as fundamental right of States 207–208
Eritrea 139
Eritrea/Ethiopia Claims Commission Award 78–79
espionage: aerial espionage 152, 153–154; cyber espionage 103; economic espionage 76–77, 101, 103; industrial espionage 103; status under international law 103; by US against North Korea 145
Ethiopia 54, 68, 78–79
European Community 71, 72
European Council 71, 102
European Court of Human Rights 100
European Union 134
evolutive interpretation, doctrine of 49–50
Exclusive Economic Zones (EEZ) 28–29, 62, 145
exempt jurisdiction 107
Extended Continental Shelf 137
extraterritoriality 26–27, 62, 95, 118, 203–204

Falkland Islands 129
Fauchille, Paul 30
Finnis, John 204
First World War 43
Fisheries Jurisdiction case 29
foreign policy, national interest and 189–190
Foucault, Michel 39
France 149–150, 152

Franck, Thomas 2, 43, 79, 123, 124, 125, 128, 190, 192, 194, 195
freedom 183
Friedman, Wolfgang 7
Frontier Dispute case 43–44, 46, 65, 107

Gabčíkovo-Nagymaros Project case 167
Gardner, Richard 160, 161
General Framework for Peace in Bosnia and Herzegovina 70
Geneva Conventions 161
Geneva Conventions (1949) 121, 159, 161
genocide 63, 124, 193
Genocide case 168
George 126
Georgia 98, 100, 117, 119
Germany 116, 124, 127
Ghana 62, 67
globalisation: border control and 25–26; and cyberspace activities 3
Google 102
Gottman, Jean 16, 38, 205
Grant, Thomas 131
Gratian 206
Gray, Christine 162
Greece 195
Greenpeace 145
Gregory VII, Pope 36
Grotius, Hugo 10, 37, 148–149, 177, 193, 204, 205
Group of Seven (G7) Industrialised Democracies, on cyberspace 111–112
Guantanamo Bay 107–108
Guyana v Suriname case 146

Habermas, Jurgen 187
Hague Regulations IV (1907) 65–66, 121
Hague Regulations IV (1949) 66, 121–122
Hakimi, Monica 161
Hall, William Edward 184–185
Hannikainen, Lauri 201
Hart, H. L. A. 183, 206
Havana Convention (1928) 32
Hayden, Bill 153
Hegel, G. W. F. 193
Heinegg, Wolff Heintschel von 122
Helsinki Final Act (1975) 69, 70, 72, 131, 198–200, 201–202
Henkin, Louis 2, 123, 159–160, 190
Heupel, Monika 124
Higgins, Rosalyn 210
High Seas: closure and weapons testing on 148–150; definition 147–148; policing

Index 243

of 148; right to visit and search vessels
148; transient sovereignty of States on
148
Hobbes, Thomas 10
Homer 35
Honduras 54, 138
hot pursuit 143–144
Huber, Max 45, 132
human rights, military occupation and
65–66
humanitarian interventions 63–64, 127,
193–194
Hurd, Douglas 71

ideological coercion 74
Ilyushin 151
I'm Alone case 136, 143, 146
India 62, 67, 151
indirect aggression 74
individualist theory of territory
11–13
Indonesia 68
industrial espionage 103
information warfare 97
Innocent III, Pope 19
insurgencies, State calls for assistance
against 195–197
insurgents *see* non-State actors (NSAs)
interdependence sovereignty 21
International Code of Conduct for
Information Security 110
International Commission of Jurists 126
International Court of Justice: aerial
incidents involving civilian aircraft 152;
balancing of conflicting elements 138;
elements of territorial claims 129–130;
interpretation of treaties 49, 50; on
intervention to aid self-determination
127; jurisdiction 46, 87–90; on *jus
cogens* 81; on minimal incursions 78; on
right of self-determination 82; and
territorial sovereignty 87–88
International Criminal Court 89
International Human Rights Law 64
international human rights law 159
international humanitarian law 159
international law, rights and obligations 47
international legal sovereignty 21
International Telecommunications Union
112–113
International Tribunal for the Former
Yugoslavia 170–171
International Tribunal for the Law of the
Sea 136, 144

Internet: impact of invention 96–97;
national routing of traffic 112–113; *see
also* cyberspace
inter-state conflicts, intangible issues as
major cause of 189–190
intertemporality, doctrine of 49
inviolability: concept of 198–201; of
diplomatic missions 203–204
inviolability of frontiers: making sense of
principle 200–201; nexus with Article 2
(4) of UN Charter 201–204
inviolability of State territory, respect for: as
general principle of law 72; historic
rights to territorial waters 139–140;
need for codification 62; and prohibition
on threat or use of force 2, 52–53, 61;
recognition of new States 72; in regional
instruments 69–72; self-determination
and 70–71; States' desire for 2, 53–54;
as way forward 211–212
Iran 94, 98, 101, 104, 117, 147, 174
Iraq 127, 128, 160, 174–175, 177
Island of Palmas case 9, 24, 45, 93,
132, 184
Israel 76, 98, 124, 152, 159, 160

Jacob-Salomon, Berthold 80
Japan 68, 153
Jennings, Robert 149
Jessup, Phillip 135
Johnson, Boris 153
Jordan 128
jurisdiction: economic jurisdiction 24–25;
territorial jurisdiction 24–27; universal
jurisdiction 26–27
jus ad bellum 176–178
jus in bello 176–177

Kant, Immanuel 12, 183, 184, 185
Kassan, Shalom 16
Kazakhstan 116, 124
Kellogg-Briand Pact 52
Kelsen, Hans 74, 89–90, 209–210
Kierkegaard, Sylvia 102
*Kingdom of the Netherlands v the Russian
Federation* 136
Klimburg, Alexander 121
Kolb, Robert 79
Kolers, Avery 10
Korean War 124
Koskenniemi, Martti 86
Kosovo 70–71, 126, 196
Krasner, Stephen 20, 21
Kuwait 124, 127, 174

244 *Index*

LaGrand case 47
Lakhdar Boumediene et al. v George W. Bush 107
Lampersberger, Josef 80
land, legal definition 27–28
Latvia 199
Lauterpacht, Hersch 30, 132
law and morality 183–184, 206
Laws (Plato) 16, 17
League of Nations 41–44, 126, 188
Lebanon 127–128, 179
Legal Status of Eastern Greenland 106, 129
Legality of the Threat or Use of Nuclear Weapons 55, 85
Leibniz, Gottfried 23
Liberia 68, 127
Libya 64, 124, 128, 139, 164–165, 171, 194
Lissitzyn, Oliver 31
Lithuania 147, 199
Locarno Pact 53
Locke, John 11, 12
Lockerbie incident 117, 119, 164, 171
Lotus case 94, 102, 108, 149
Lotus Principle 164

Madrid Convention (1926) 32
Malaysia 147
Maldives 147
Mali 68
Malta 147
maritime boundary disputes *see* territorial waters
Maritime Zones of Maldives Acts No. 6/96 147
McLaughlin, Rob 143
Medieval period: conquest and delimitation of territory 36–37; state territory in 18
Mexico 54, 188
military occupation, territorial integrity and human rights 65–66
militia *see* non-State actors (NSAs)
Millar, Fergus 18
Miller, David 10, 12–13, 14
minimal incursions 78–80
Monroe, James 38, 41
Monroe Doctrine 20, 38, 72
Montevideo Convention (1933) 73
Montreal Convention 164
moral laws 183
morality and law 183–184, 206
Morocco 68
"Morris" worm 104
Moscow Declaration 209–210

Movchan, A. 202
Murphy, Mark 206
M/V "SAIGA" No. 2 136, 144

Namibia Advisory Opinion 49
nation-bullying 73
national interest 184, 189–190
nationalism 37
nationalist theory of territory 13–14
nations, definition 13
NATO 150; cybersecurity 105; intervention in Iraq 127; intervention in Serbia 126, 127; violations of airspace by Russia 150, 151, 179
natural law: distinguished from natural right 205–207; reasoning method 204–205; sovereign equality of States and 204–210
Netherland v Russia 145
Netherlands 54
New Zealand 54, 149–150
Nicaragua case 3, 26, 61, 74, 89, 92, 125, 167, 168–169, 170, 175, 177–178, 179, 180, 191
Nicomachean Ethics (Aristotle) 16
Nigeria 68, 138–139
Nine, Cara 10 9/11 terrorist attacks 86, 160, 161, 163, 173–174, 177
non-intervention, principle of 59–61, 73
non-State actors (NSAs): aiding of a wrongful act by host State 171–172; applicability of Article 2(4) of UN Charter 159–166; attribution of conduct to a State 167–172; customary law and 161–163; definition 157–158; effective control by a State 170–171; as organ of a State 168–169; as quasi-States 159; State-sponsored NSA 172–175; status under international law 158–159; universal jurisdiction and 163–166
North Korea 101, 144–145, 150
North Sea Continental Shelf cases 9, 46, 130
Norway 54, 153
Nuclear Tests case 149–150
nuclear weapons 55, 85, 95
nuclear weapons testing 149–150
Nuremberg Charter 74–75

Obama, Barak 92, 105–106, 155
occupation, illegal occupation 133–134
occupying powers, obligations of 65–66
O'Connell, Mary Ellen 79
Oil Platforms case 174, 180

Index 245

oil pollution 143
Olney-Pauncefote Arbitration Treaty of 1897 60
Operation Cast Lead 98
Operation Orchard 98
Organisation of African Unity 69
Osiander, Andreas 22, 23
Outer Space Treaty 108

Pakistan 68, 147, 150–151, 156
Palau 66, 130
Palestine 124, 158
Paris Convention (1919) 32, 154
peace, as absence of war 8
peace, agenda for 210–212
Peace of Augsburg 37, 40
Per Venerabilem 19
Percy, Eustace 41
Permanent Court of Arbitration 93, 136, 139, 140
Permanent Court of International Justice 60, 66, 87, 88, 122
permanent sovereignty 25
Peru 54, 58, 208
Philip II, King of France 19
Philippines v China 136, 137–138, 139, 140, 141–142, 150
Phosphates in Morocco case 167
Pinochet, Augusto 26
Plato 16–17, 186
Playboy Enterprises, Inc., v Chuckleberry Publishing Inc. 119–120
Poellet, Keira 118
polis 16–17, 35
political coercion 56–57, 67, 68, 74, 76, 77
political theories of territory 9–11, 15; individualist theory 11–13; nationalist theory 13–14; statist theory 14–15
Politics (Aristotle) 16, 17
Pollock, John 124–125
Prague Declaration on Peace, Security, and Cooperation in Europe 201
pre-emptive self-defence 160–161
pre-emptive self-defence, doctrine of 154
Project of an International Declaration Concerning the Laws and Customs of War 133
Prosecutor v Duško Tadić case 171
Protocol to Chicago Convention 154
Public International Law 64
Putin, Vladimir 131, 196

Qatar 172

ratione loci, doctrine of 93, 109
Rawls, John 192
Raz, Joseph 191
rebus sic stantibus 66
recognition respect 187, 191, 198
Red Crusader case 136, 146
Reference re Secession of Quebec 126
regional enforcement 128–129
regional instruments 69–72
religious tolerance 39
Republic (Plato) 16, 17
res communis 11, 31, 148, 150
res communis omnium 92, 108, 118
res nullius 148
rescue operations 79, 80
residual sovereignty 25, 26, 46–47
respect: appraisal respect 187, 198, 209; and Article 2(4) of UN Charter 189–191; definition 185–187; as duty owed *erga omnes* 191–192; as foundation of world peace 197–198; indeterminacy question 198; kinds of 187–189; limits to 198; making sense of the word 182–185; recognition respect 187, 191, 198
Responsibility to Protect (R2P) 127, 164, 194
Roman Empire: conquest and delimitation of territory 35–36; jurisdiction 24; state territory in 17–19
Romania 147
Roosevelt, Franklin D. 44
Roosevelt, Theodore 20
Rousseau, Jean-Jacques 187
Rumsfeld, Donald 153
Russia 100, 101, 102, 110, 127, 166; airspace violations of other countries 150, 151; annexation of Crimea 130, 131–132, 133, 134, 192; assistance to Assad regime 151, 195, 196; fighter jet shot down by Turkey 150, 151, 179; interference in US elections 189; intervention in Ukraine 126, 132–133, 195–196, 197
Ruys, Tom 79
Rwanda 63, 86, 193
Rwandan Genocide 63, 86, 124, 193

Sadigbayli, Rovshan 198–199
Saudi Arabia 147
Schmitt, Michael 99
Second World War 44
self-defence: addressees of the right to 175–181; armed attack threshold 73,

246 *Index*

179–181; against cyberattacks 98, 117, 119; against *de minimis* incursions 125, 179; expansion of the scope of 175; against non-State actors 175–176; pre-emptive self-defence 154; right to 79; against terrorism 174; unilateral pre-emptive self-defence 160–161

self-determination 63; in Covenant of League of Nations 43; decolonisation and 65; interventions to aid 126–127; inviolability of State territory and 70–71

Serbia 126

Seychelles 147

Sharp, Walter Gary 79–80

Sidgwick, Henry 15

Sierra Leone 68

Simmons, John 10, 11, 14–15

Snowden, Edward 112

Social Contract Theory 10, 14, 193

soft law, and State territory 67–69

Somalia 68

South Africa 159

South China Sea dispute 93, 136, 137–138, 139, 140, 141–142, 150

South Korea 147, 151, 153

South Ossetia 126

South Sudan 124, 127

sovereign equality of States: application of natural law 204–210; equality as fundamental right 207–208; Moscow Declaration peace model 209–210; UN Charter and 54, 58, 84–85, 86–87, 188, 205

sovereignty: categories 21; concurrent sovereignty 107; convergence with territory 20, 22–24; in cyberspace 93–94; definition 93; as legal concept 22; permanent sovereignty 25; as political concept 21; residual sovereignty 25, 26, 46–47; territorial sovereignty; *see also* territorial sovereignty

Soviet Union: 1977 Constitution 14; cyberwarfare 104; and Helsinki Final Act 199; and Korean War 124; shooting down of civilian aircraft 152, 153; *see also* Russia

Spain 129, 132

Stahn, Carsten 175

State sovereignty: economic and political coercion and 77; protection under Article 2(7) of UN *Charter* 61; and States' responsibility towards third states

166–172; territory as heartbeat of 45–46; *see also* sovereign equality of States

State territory: airspace 30–33; in Ancient Greece 16–17; boundary disputes 130–134, 189–190; cession of a territory 132; conceptual derivation of 15–19; impact of conquest in evolution of 33–38; land 27–28; in Middle Ages 18–19; as political construct in the twentieth century 19–20; in Roman antiquity 17–18; scope of 27–33; soft law and 67–69; Territorial Sea 28–30; treaty regime and 66; *see also* breaches of State territory; cyber-territory; inviolability of State territory

statist theory of territory 14–15

Steiner, Hillel 10, 12, 184

Stettinius, Edward, Jr. 54

Stilz, Anna 10, 14

Stimson, Henry 44

Stuxnet worm 94, 98

Sudan 151

Sumner, Brian Taylor 129–130

supranational bodies, effects on territorial sovereignty 83–90

Supreme Court of Canada 126

Suriname 146

Sweden 68, 179

Switzerland 80

Syria 68, 98, 127

Syrian Civil War 124, 150, 151, 153, 195, 212

Tadić case 86

Tajikistan 110

Tanganyika 68

terra nullius 11, 12, 38

territorial jurisdiction: border control 25–27; economic jurisdiction 24–25; over cyberspace 94–5

Territorial Sea 28–30

territorial sovereignty 65–66; and accountability of officeholders 64; birth of 22–23; distinguished from territorial integrity 94; effects of supranational bodies 83–90; and extraterritoriality 26–27, 62; non-intervention and 62; treaty regime and 46–47

territorial waters: applicable law 134–136; causes of conflicts in 137; claims to title based on historic right 137–147; definition 134; exploration and exploitation 140–142; historic rights 137–139;

inviolability of State territory and historic rights 139–140; limitations of right of innocent passage 146–147

territorial waters law enforcement 142; hot pursuit 143–144; interception, arrest, seizure and detention 144–145; mis-application of 145–146; tripod threshold test 142–144; water pollution 142–143

territory: categories 11; correlation with sovereignty 20–24; definition 8–9, 45; as heartbeat of State sovereignty 45–46, 184; modes of acquisition 129; political theories of 9–15; *see also* State territory

terrorism 173–174, 195

terrorist groups *see* non-State actors (NSAs)

Teschke, Benno 15–16

Thirty Years' War 38, 41

Tirmaa-Klaa, Heli 121

treaties: binding of non-State actors 159; interpretation of 49–50; territorial boundaries established by 130–134; *see also* treaty regime

Treaties of Nuremberg 40

Treaty for the Renunciation of War (1928) 74

Treaty of Munster 38, 40

Treaty of Osnabruck 38, 39, 40

Treaty of Paris (1856) 28

Treaty of Peace with Germany (1919) 46

Treaty on Non-proliferation of Nuclear Weapons 85

treaty regime: and effect of *lex specialis* 132–133; and State territory 66; and territorial sovereignty 46–47

Trump, Donald 172, 189

Tsagourias, Nicholas 60, 98

Tunisia 139

Turkey 150, 151, 179, 208

Uganda 3, 8, 82, 127, 134, 155, 170, 198

Ukraine 124, 126, 131, 132–133, 195–196, 197

UN General Assembly: and cybersecurity 105–106, 112; decolonisation instruments 64–65; functions and powers 83–84; non-intervention in internal affairs of States 61–62; structure 44, 83; and territorial sovereignty 83–85; voting system 47

UN Security Council: collective enforcement provisions 85, 123–125, 194; dysfunction 192–193; failure to stop genocide 63; legitimacy deficit 124–125; misapplication of resolutions

127–128; need for reform 193; powers 85–86; response to 9/11 terrorist attacks 86, 173; on shooting down of civilian aircraft 153; and sovereign equality of States 86–87; structure 44; and territorial sovereignty 85–87; tribunals 86; and US invasion of Iraq 174–175; veto arrangement 124, 192; voting arrangements 85, 86; on Yugoslavia 45

unconventional warfare 1, 3

unfair business practices 77

unilateralism 63, 161, 194

United Arab Emirates 147

United Arab Republic 68, 127

United Kingdom 63, 129, 153

United Nations: Bill of Rights 14; counter-terrorism strategy 173; and cyberspace threats 110; Dumbarton Oaks Proposals 44, 45, 53–54, 55, 83, 128, 188, 208; formation 44–45, 83 as mechanism for States' accountability 84; peace agenda 1, 2, 7–8, 38, 45, 51; peacekeeping missions 65–66; and sovereign equality of States 84–85; trusteeship system 188–189; *see also* UN General Assembly; UN Security Council

United Nations Charter *see* Charter of the United Nations

United Nations Convention on the Law of the Sea 134–136

United Nations Convention on the Law of the Sea 28, 140, 142, 146

United States 127, 152, 153, 179; breach of airspace by military aircraft 55; cyberlaw 116, 118; cybersecurity 105; cyberspace governance 110; cyberwarfare model 100–101; invasion of Iraq 174–175, 177; jurisdiction over Guantanamo Bay detainees 107–108; and *Lockerbie* incident 164–165; quarantine of Cuba 58, 76; reconnaissance flights off Chinese coast 153–154; Russian interference in elections 189; spying on North Korea 144–145; trade war with China 77; "war on terror" 160; *see also Nicaragua* case

United States Diplomatic and Consular Staff in Tehran case 168, 203

United States v Drew 118

United States v Ivanov 118

United States v Robert Thomas 119–120

Universal Declaration of Human Rights 197–198

248 *Index*

universal jurisdiction 26–27
unmanned aerial vehicles 155–156
Uppsala Conflict Data Program 123, 125, 157
USSR *see* Soviet Union
uti possidetis, doctrine of 69
Uzbekistan 110

Vatican City State 158
Vattel, Emer de 206–207
Vereschaguin, A. 30
Vienna Convention on Diplomatic and Consular Relations 203, 205
Vienna Convention on the Law of the Treaties 49, 81
Vienna Convention on Succession of States in Respect of Treaties 66, 81–82
violence, non-State based violence 157
Von Liszt, Franz 45

Walzer, Michael 177
water pollution 142–143
Watts, Arthur 149
Westen, Peter 207
Westphalian sovereign state model 20–21
Westphalian sovereignty 21
William of Montpellier 19
Wilson, Woodrow 43, 72
Winterfield, Steve 103
World Summits on Information Society 111
World Trade Organisation 77

Yemen 139, 147
Yugoslavia 45–46, 56, 62, 67, 68, 70–72, 75, 86, 195

Zeineddine, Farid 58